LIFE

AFTER

GRIEF

An Astrological Guide to Dealing with Loss

by

Darrelyn Gunzburg

The Wessex Astrologer

Published in 2004 by
The Wessex Astrologer Ltd
PO Box 2751
Bournemouth
BH5 2XZ
England

www.wessexastrologer.com

ISBN 1902405145

A catalogue record of this book is available at The British Library

All charts used and astrological calculations generated using Solar Fire v.5.

All Time Maps designed and laid out by Darrelyn Gunzburg.

ACKNOWLEDGEMENTS

Mal McKissock set me sailing on my voyage to the land of conscious grief in 1982. For this gift I give thanks. I am deeply appreciative of the work of John W. James and Russell Friedman who extended my knowledge and allowed me to find a pathway through unresolved grief. Many courageous and willing astrology students, personal clients, friends and people who attended my lectures participated in my research and allowed me to nudge and tap at the well of their grief. I express my gratitude to all of them, especially those who, with infinite grace, allowed me to reproduce their precious and personal journeys in this book. Some are happy to let me publish their real names and I have done so including their surnames. I have respected the wishes of those who prefer to remain anonymous. One of the latter was 'Ewan' who gave generously of his experience and for which I thank him deeply. His reaction when he heard I was writing this book was: "I'd like a book about grief that, when you open it up, it just says: 'My God, that's dreadful, how on earth can you cope?' and then listens to you cry for four hours." I pay tribute to Isaac Gunzburg who began it all, Michael Gunzburg who continued it and Milton Gunzburg who completed it. They provided the clay on the wheel and I owe much to them. Professor Michael York helped shape my thinking with his insights. Michael Lutin suggested the final title and the manuscript is the better for it. Ysha de Donna was the first-run editor of the manuscript and supported it with the gift of her wisdom and her friendship. Margaret Cahill heard me lecture on this subject in Reading, September 2000, saw its potential as a book and was patient enough to midwife it through all its permutations, including long sentences. My love and respect for her as a publisher remain unbounded. To all these individuals I am profoundly grateful. I owe more than it is possible to note to my partner of the heart, Bernadette Brady, the first friend of this work, who insisted that writing a book was different to writing a play and then supported me all the way through doing it. She has truly taught me, in more ways than she can imagine, "that in black inck my love may still shine bright."

PERMISSIONS

To Bernadette

Contents

INTRODUCTION

HOW TO HOLD ON TO IT.

Hold on to it like you hold a day old chicken

Hold on to it like you hold a live fish.

Hold on to it like you hold a horse.

Hold on to it like you hold a bowl of soup.

Hold on to it like you hold a door open for the Queen Mother.

Letting go of it is just as difficult and shall be dealt with at some later stage.

Leunig

This book is about letting go. Specifically it is about letting go of life as you knew it when death comes to call. It is about letting go of the master plan so carefully mapped about length of life and the attainment of things worthwhile and which segues to another gig where the musicians are unknown and the music riffs in a language you have never heard before. This book is also about walking forwards into your future when that future seems over, a space without time, a time without end, when there is no fire in the grate and the pilot light is out. If you have walked that journey and you are a professional astrologer, then you can guide others across the sullen earth to sorrows' end. You just don't know it yet. If you have ever huddled in the rain and darkness of an inconsolable transit, bent over the personal guide map that the cosmos has provided for us so we can manage our lives better, seen the options that have lain ahead of you and wondered how on earth you will have the strength to put one step ahead of the other, then you are well-equipped to understand the sweep and tract of grief and be a lodestar for others as they encounter loss.

The experience of grief is among the most fundamental and inescapable aspects of the human and animal condition. Western society acknowledges it as a profound truth in literature, film, theatre, art and music, for the poet, the writer and the artist are the touchstones of society who express this heightened awareness of intense emotion for the rest of society. Who could fail to be affected by writer Isabel Allende's heart-rending lament for her daughter Paula? Who could remain untouched by Julie's pain when a fatal car crash kills her husband and young daughter in *Blue*, Part One of Krzysztof Kieslowski's *Three Colours* trilogy? In the film *Four Weddings and A Funeral*, the funeral belongs to Gareth, the rather large, flamboyant homosexual who wore the rather colourful and extravagant waistcoats. Screenwriter Richard Curtis has Gareth's lover, Matthew, open the eulogy in this way: "Gareth used to prefer funerals to weddings. He said it was easier to get enthusiastic about a ceremony one at least had an outside chance of eventually being involved in." [1] Artists are the seers of society. They allow us to feel by proxy. They encourage us to encounter the intensity of loss through death by the situations they construct in ink, pigment, light, music, shape and form, flagging this most intense of experiences as one we, too, will have to face one day in our unique way, for human emotion has not changed in quality throughout recorded history. Poets, writers, dancers, artists and musicians have never allowed death to become a taboo subject. Why has it become so for the rest of us?

For as long as I can remember my parents were part of the Chevra Kadisha, a voluntarily organisation of men and women within the Jewish community whose sole function was the care of the dead from the time of death until burial. This guardianship, known as "Chesed Shel Emes", represents an act of genuine kindness, since it can never be repaid by the recipient. Women attending women and men attending men would undertake Tahara, the preparation of the body in accordance with Jewish tradition through ritual purification and the dressing of it in traditional shrouds. Since death did not have a timetable, my parents could be called out at a moment's notice. This care of the dead, this act of kindness, was part of what my parents did, yet somehow it was different when it came to grief. When I was twelve, my ninety-one year old grandfather died at home in the early hours of the morning. My mother was in hospital and so it was his son, my father, who woke me up. "Grandpa's dead," he told me. "Do you want to see his body?" I hesitated. The house we lived in was the one he'd built. I had lived with him all my life. I heard my voice as from a distance, cracked and strained, "I don't ...know...." A man of few words, my father squeezed my hand. "You don't have to," he whispered and then he was gone. I dressed and made my way downstairs to my grandfather's room, then froze in the doorway. The bed was made, the white coverlet drawn over a bed neatened too soon for the time of day. My stomach knotted. My grandfather was gone and I hadn't said goodbye. Too late I realised my father had heard me say "know" and translated that as "no". My father was a gentle man and felt the loss deeply but there were other burdens on him at the time. It wasn't until twenty-three years later as a published playwright that I finally realised how unresolved was that childhood grief and how it had remained an unconscious time warp of sorrow, permeating my life with its own colour of guilt and remorse. I did not know then what I know now, that I had to make grief my friend in the turmoil of life.

Recently I received an email from a client who wanted a consultation and as always I asked him what he wanted from the reading. He wrote back: "I would like to know if my book will be published? If so, will it be successful? Will I find the love of my life? Will I be healthy and die a natural death?" This last is a good question to ask and one of the essential tools in every medieval astrologer's toolkit was to be able to answer queries about length of life. On the other hand, what is a natural death? We would like to think that it is one where, after a life of fulfilment at a ripe old age, we lie down to sleep and "go gently into that good night", in stark opposition to Dylan Thomas. We would like to think that there is wisdom and order to how life is lived but all around us we see that this is not the case. For example, in the *Radio Times* magazine of 4th-10th October, 2003, [2] singer Robin Gibb of The Bee Gees speaks of the pain of the loss of his twin brother Maurice, aged just fifty-three. Maurice was admitted to a Miami hospital with stomach pains on 12th January, 2003. Doctors did not detect he had a twisted bowel which caused his intestine to burst and he died unexpectedly from brain damage following cardiac arrest. Still unable to talk freely of the death, Gibb remembers the funeral as traumatic: "Looking at the coffin, knowing Maurice was lying in that box, was the most cruel and grotesque ritual on the face of the planet." He deals with the loss by not thinking about it, yet it has inspired him to do everything he wants to do now and not wait for the mists of an unknowable future. As another illustration, a man rings a talk-back radio station, agitated and distressed. He has just broken a terracotta pot and feelings of rage and guilt flood his body. He can't understand what is happening to him, yet twelve months earlier his wife had died and the terracotta pot was the last item they had bought together. As a consulting astrologer how would you handle these people with their illogical fear that their known world was fragmenting before their very eyes? In our contemporary western society, it is the bereavement counsellor, the funeral director and the medical practitioner who are asked to help people in positions of extreme loss and to make predictions for a light in the night, yet the simple truth is it is only the astrologer in the consulting room who has the tools to read that predictive work accurately. While people grieve many things, the principal aim of this book is to look at grief specifically as it relates to death and present ways for an astrologer in the consulting room to effectively work with clients grieving from the death of someone close to them.

✳   ✳   ✳

Endnotes
1. Curtis, Richard. (screenplay dated 18/1/1993). *Four Weddings and a Funeral,* © Working Title Films, London, UK, pp 94-96.
2. Duncan, Andrew. *Jibe Talking.* The Radio Times Interview. Radio Times, London: BBC Worldwide Limited, pp. 30-30.

THE MYTH OF GRIEF:
Lying Down With the Seals

Death is the uninvited guest in our lives, the unexpected visitor, and it has to be that way otherwise we couldn't live fully and functionally. However, Death walks towards us carrying Grief in her arms and Grief has to be honoured immediately Death arrives. The difficulty is that we are not taught how to honour grief. Indeed astrology, like every other body of knowledge in the West, has denied the grief we will all have to encounter at some stage in our lives. Astrologers avoid acknowledging a death in the chart and see grief as a "one-off" event - "My mother died, I was having transiting Saturn conjunct my Pluto". Yet there is a myth of grief which has been quite neglected and it is the myth of Proteus, the son of Tethys and Oceanus, and Menelaus, the husband of Helen, who fought for ten long years in the Trojan War.

We are told in Homer's *The Odyssey* [1] that, after the ten-year Trojan War, Menelaus and his men wandered a further eight years in the Mediterranean. Finally, on the verge of returning home, their ships were kept idle for twenty days on the isle of Pharos on the Egyptian coast,

> "in the rolling seas off the mouth of the Nile, a day's sail
> out for a well-found vessel with a roaring wind astern."

Now this island was the home of the immortal seer Proteus, the "Old Man Of The Sea" who owed allegiance to Poseidon and kept guard over Poseidon's herd of seals. Each day at noon he emerged from the waves and counted the herd and then moved to the shelter of a cave and lay down amongst them,

> "those children of the brine, the flippered seals."

It was Proteus' daughter, Eidothee, who took pity on the starving Menelaus and gave him the solution. "Disguise yourself in sealskin," she told him, "and wait for my father to lie down with the seals. Then grasp his hands and ask him why this has happened and how you can make amends. But," she warned, "my father never speaks oracularly unless forced to do so and he can change shape at will. Do not be intimidated by these changes. Hold onto him tightly and when he realises you will not be shaken, then he will admit defeat and answer your questions faithfully."

Becalmed by the weather and unable to proceed home, Menelaus had little choice. He covered himself in sealskins and gently he lay down with the seals; and as Eidothee had said it would happen, so it happened. At noon, Proteus emerged from the waves and one by one he counted the herd. Satisfied he moved to the shelter of the cave and with the protective gesture of a loving shepherd and the sigh of a job well done, he lowered his aged body and he, too, lay down amongst his seals.

Immediately Menelaus sprang up and seized Proteus with both hands. Proteus gave a shout of alarm. Instantly he changed into a bearded lion whose roar echoed across the recesses of the land. His rapier-sharp teeth slashed without warning and Menelaus trembled in his shoes but he remembered Eidothee's words and he held on tight. The lion cavorted, desperate to shake him off but Menelaus hung on. Then a mighty dragon stood in his place, his scales glinting in the sun, breathing fire as hot as a furnace. Menelaus' body shrieked from the heat but he remembered Eidothee's words and he tightened his grip. The dragon paced and bellowed, smoke rose and choked Menelaus, yet still he did not loosen his hold. Then the dragon disappeared and a powerful panther paced the forest floor. Menelaus' skin grazed and shredded as the panther ran through the undergrowth but he remembered Eidothee's words and he held on tenaciously. Then he found himself gripping the tough hide of a giant boar whose long tusks thrust menacingly at Menelaus. He could smell the fear in his own sweat but he heard Eidothee's words, "Stay with the process, don't be intimated by the changes." Then the boar was gone and he was drifting out to sea, carried deep, deep to the ocean floor ⁓ ... Now, now I can let go ⁓ ... He came to with a jolt! He had not let go his grip but he had come perilously close to doing so. He struggled to the surface, knuckles clenched, lungs bursting and greedily gasped in lungfuls of salt air, kicking valiantly to stay above the slapping waves. Then the sea disappeared and his legs were no longer pushing against the weight of the ocean but against the trunk of a great tree in leaf. The cover of leaves reached far above him and cool air licked at his face. The invigorating smell of forest air was intoxicating. He felt life surge back through his body, rejuvenated and as strong as this great tree whose roots reached far into the earth for sustenance and whose canopy embraced the sky. And a voice said to him: "Who are you who has maintained your grip on me, despite where I have taken you? Who are you who has endured suffering and misery, desolation and despair that you may see my true face?" Then Menelaus looked around him and he saw an old man whose eyes told of a pained and wounded life and whose aged face was writ with the lines of anguish and torment; and he realised he was looking into the face of Life itself and that behind the pain there was the light of understanding and wisdom, love and courage. Gently

Proteus released Menelaus' grip from his shoulders and he massaged the hands that had refused to give in.

And Menelaus spoke, saying, "Show me the way home. Tell me what I must do to start the winds playing amidst the sails of my ship?" and Proteus answered: "You omitted to make due sacrifice to Zeus before the journey began. Now you must return to the heaven-fed waters of the Nile once more and make ceremonial offerings to the gods who live in the broad sky. When that is done, you may return home." Menelaus did as Proteus said and he returned home, home to his mundane life in Sparta with Helen and a changed world; and the cycle and process of grief was completed.

Myths are not simply stories told to please children. They were the way the ancients made sense of the world. They contained inherent behaviour patterns that explained the human mindset and made it possible to choose responses that were ethically and morally viable. They answered the basic questions: Who am I? Where have I come from? Where am I going? How do I live during the journey? Myths externalised the psychology of the ancient world, for divinity was seen in everything and it was thought that all life contained answers. Today myths continue to illustrate human qualities and behavioural attitudes that remain unchanging over time, begging us to understand them, develop the themes offered and rise above the plot to reinterpret or even change the endings through our own wisdom. However, while most myths describe an unfolding journey, the myth of grief is made of a totally different texture, for grief always enters our lives without notice and so this myth only comes alive once the person's context and history has empowered it: "... and Proteus turned into ... (you add your ferocious animal in here)". What is it that you fear? What is it that you have been taught about loss and letting go that makes this such a dreaded process?

In this encounter of Menelaus with Proteus after the ravages of the Trojan War and the loss of friends dear to him, Homer illustrates the process of grief. Like Menelaus, we think we are on a journey but grief comes unexpectedly and keeps us idle, in an immobile state in a sheltered cove, laid off-course and uncertain of how to proceed. The island is the home of the immortal seer Proteus who can only use his gift of prophecy to answer questions about the future if he is captured. Proteus' daughter, Eidothee, gives Menelaus the solution, suggesting he hide himself amongst the seals until Proteus is asleep. One can interpret seals as representing our instincts. However, we are so often socialised not to talk about our grief that we can't hear that inner voice and the grief becomes stuck. We call this repressed or unresolved grief, articulated through Menelaus being caught in the bay, unable to move forward. Only by going inward into the process of grief to face this dramatically changeable, emotional energy that floods, erupts and shatters our mundane lives can we gain any answers. However, answers don't come directly: we have to stay with the process through all its varying disguises - pain, bodily distress, panic, sadness, isolation and confusion. Finally Proteus turns into a great tree in leaf, telling us that at the end of the process we emerge stronger for the journey and embracing the Tree of Life from which new growth can occur. The last leg of the journey is to return to the Nile, the waters of life, for Menelaus "omitted to make due sacrifice ... before the journey began," the recognition that we who are born will someday die. How long does grief last? When does Proteus turn into this Tree of Life? Each person's grief is unique and depends both on the nature of the relationship we had with the person who has died and our willingness to complete our relationship to the pain of grief. However, Grief also carries people in her arms, the twins of Love and Compassion. At the end of the journey we are gifted with a love for the one who has died at a deeper level and we are more open to compassion for others who find themselves in similar situations. With such knowledge to inform and invigorate us, we can move forward once more into the realm of living beings. Then and only then have we learned the truth of grief: only after we have lain down with the seals can we understand that loss is a fundamental and necessary part of human life in order to live fully in this present moment and that there is life to be lived after grief has come to call.

Endnotes

1. Homer. *The* Odyssey, trans. E.V.Rieu. (1946) Middlesex, England: Penguin Books, pp. 73-77.

Leunig

Dear God,

Let us prepare for winter. The sun

has turned away from us and the nest of

summer hangs broken in a tree. Life slips

through our fingers and, as darkness gathers,

our hands grow cold. It is time to go inside.

It is time for reflection and resonance. It is

time for contemplation. Let us go inside.

Amen.

1
What is Grief?

Time engraves our faces with all the tears we have not shed.
- Natalie Clifford Barney, author (1876-1972)

In the eighteenth century Benjamin Franklin stated that there were only two certainties in life: Death and Taxes. In truth, the two things that are most certain in life are Death and Time. Death and Time are the two great immutables we encounter in the turmoil of human life: we live with time, we will die in time and somewhere along the path, we will experience a person intimately involved with our life ebbing, declining and finally vanishing physically from time.

Time is the most precious commodity we have. We spend it passing the rooks and knights of life; we climb the ladders of reason and ambition and gnash our teeth when we are forced to slide with the snakes. However, since time moves us inexorably towards death, death is the ally we must make in order to understand that time is limited. It is only by letting go of acute pain and making the transition from despair to wholeness that we learn how to live in present time and thus to make the most of this blessing of existence. The way the cosmos makes this clear to us is through the emotion of grief, since grief awakens us to Death.

The fear of death and the experience of grief are two sides of the coin called loss. Homer, one of the great bards of the ancient world and the father of Western literature, writing as far back as the 8th century BCE, was one of the first to encapsulate this overwhelming and primal response. In Chapter XVIII of *The Iliad* [1] entitled "Armour for Achilles", Homer writes:

> "...King Nestor's son halted before him with the hot tears pouring down his cheeks and gave him the lamentable news: 'Alas, my royal lord Achilles! I have a dreadful thing to tell you - I would to God it were not true. Patroclus has been killed. They are fighting round his naked corpse and Hector of the flashing helmet has your arms.'
>
> When Achilles heard this he sank into the black depths of despair. He picked up the dark dust in both hands and poured it on his head. He soiled his comely face with it, and filthy ashes

settled on his scented tunic. He cast himself down on the earth
and lay there like a fallen giant, fouling his hair and tearing it out
with his own hands. The maidservants whom he and Patroclus
had captured caught the alarm and all ran screaming out of doors.
They beat their breasts with their hands and sank to the ground
beside their royal master.

On the other side, Antilochus shedding tears of misery held
the hands of Achilles as he sobbed out his noble heart for fear that
he might take a knife and cut his throat."

Grief can be defined as the emotional response to loss and the process of
adjustment to a new situation. Grief occurs when familiar patterns of behaviour
end or change and in so doing, cause conflicting emotions. [2] If someone you
love has been ill and in physical pain for a long time, there may be a sense of
relief at their death. There will also be sorrow at not being able to continue
that relationship and, possibly, fear of the future. A woman in her seventies
who has been married for forty or fifty years may, during her husband's
protracted illness, secretly yearn for the time when her spouse dies in order to
gain her freedom, only to find upon his death that she is overwhelmed by the
distress of the loss and immobilized with fear at stepping out alone into her
own life.

Mal McKissock, one of Australia's best known and respected
bereavement counsellors and educators, defines the difference between
bereavement and grief in this way:

"Linguistically, bereavement is the condition, and grief is the
emotional experience of it... grief therefore would be a response
to almost any sort of loss, whereas bereavement defines one sort of
loss. So how you react in your bereavement will be your grief. So
that's why people grieve, but they don't bereave." [3]

Grief belongs to all of us and, whether we like it or not, it is the universal
signal that life's beat will never again be the same, that the solid rock upon
which we once stood is now a passage to an uncertain future. In our lifetime
any one of us will experience a variety of losses: the death of a relative, divorce,
moving home, job loss, loss of limb, and so on. Whilst responses to these
losses share similar form, it is generally agreed that loss through death is the
most significant, perhaps because its finality forces us to confront our own
mortality.

Statistics tell us that once every nine-to-thirteen years we will lose
someone close to us through death and, given that we come from a family
where we know both parents, that at least twice in our life we will make
funeral arrangements for someone we love. In the USA, approximately 8

million people out of a population of 293 million[4] have first-time encounters with loss and bereavement from death each year. In the UK, over 600,000 people die every year, leaving an estimated 1.5 million out of a population of 58 million facing a major bereavement. [5] Grief is exhausting, complex and confusing. Faced with the end of an intimate relationship built on connection and togetherness, how we live in the world as a single entity can seem alien and difficult to comprehend and as we attempt to integrate this experience into our life and sort out a new relationship with the person who has died, we will often feel swamped with child-like reactions and vulnerable in a way that is bewildering. As a result, this process of adjustment takes time; indeed it is not uncommon for it to last up to five years, not as a linear ongoing state but tidal and cyclic in its cast. This tells us a significant fact, that whilst loss through death may be an uncommon occurrence in our personal lives, if every thirteen years or so we encounter a major loss and the grief process takes around five years to unravel, then thirty percent of our life may be spent dealing with some degree of loss. Hence it is likely that, as consulting astrologers, thirty percent of all adult clients we see will be going through this process also; in some manner, shape or form, they will be lying down with the seals.

Grief makes us wiser, less innocent and develops our inherent resilience. It is a part of life, an experience we will all encounter. In Shakespeare's *Troilus and Cressida* (3.3.163-169; *The Norton Shakespeare*, p.1877), Ulysses recognizes that death brings us all to equality when he cries:

> "O let not virtue seek
> Remuneration for the thing it was;
> For beauty, wit,
> High birth, vigour of bone, desert in service,
> Love, friendship, charity, are subjects all
> To envious and calumniating time.
> One touch of nature makes the whole world kin…"

Yet few people plan for it and at least two thirds of the population do not even make a will. [6] Instead we live as a death-denying society which prefers to believe in the weakness of scientific thought which is the tendency to separate ourselves from the natural processes of life. Couple that with a medical profession which views the loss of life as a failure, the demands of advertising with its mandate to look and stay young and the fast-disappearing rituals of life and we end up with a society unconsciously believing that aging and death are to be feared. The current spate of young women taking anabolic steroids in order to lose weight fast as part of their gym training programme is as much alarming for their physical side effects (edginess and irritability, panic attacks and palpitations, hair loss, acne, deepening of the voice, growth of body hair and shrinking of the breasts) as for the underlying reasons for taking them. Nancy, a twenty-five-year old woman from New York, has been taking steroids for six months. She says she will continue to take them for her athletic femininity and improved sex life and because "this summer will be my best yet because I am twenty-five and I don't look a day over eighteen." [7] Is it any wonder that when we come to face loss through death, we have few tools to handle the separation and isolation and believe that within a week, two weeks or three weeks after the funeral we should start to feel better?

Once, death was an integral part of extended family life and bereaved people were supported by family and friends. The Romans thought death should be kept in mind at all times, especially when life at its peak might make one forget the other, equally necessary part of the cycle. When a military hero entered Rome in triumphal procession, riding in a golden chariot, hailed as a god, a person wearing the mask and costume of Death stood at his shoulder, preserving him from the sin of hubris by saying each moment in his ear: "Man, remember you will die." Today our experience of death is lonelier for, as a society, we tend to live as couples or on our own and put our parents into residential care when they grow old in order for them to receive appropriate nursing and medical attention. The price we pay for this is the loss of intimacy and the opportunity to share in their last moments of life. Our society is one where the living have become isolated from the dying. Several years ago the Grief Recovery Institute, USA, conducted a survey that asked: "What is the best way to act around someone who has just experienced the death of a loved one?" From the multiple choice answers, ninety-eight percent of the respondents chose: "Act as if nothing had happened." Of those who had experienced such a loss in the past five years they asked: "In the weeks and months immediately following the death of your loved one, what did you most want and need to do?" Ninety-four percent responded: "Talk about what happened and my relationship with the person who died." If we are not allowed to verbalise or handle these issues as they arise, if the immediate need to understand the excruciating pain by talking about it does not have a clear channel in which to run, how can we find ways to make sense of what is happening to us? If we block what is most urgent inside us, it develops into a spur, silently, invisibly, endlessly pulling on our energy, forcing us to dodge from life. How can we stop this? The truth is always simple: all relationships exist on the assumption that we have endless time. When death cuts a swathe through that belief, we have nowhere to go with the unfinished plans of the relationship, the conversations we still want to have, the hours of love-making that now will never be, the actions and intentions that have no room to flower. If we can discover the nature of these truncated concerns - the actions we still want to take, the things we wished we'd said and the things we regretted saying - then the grief will be whole. By discovering what is incomplete in the relationship, we are able to say goodbye to the shock and the pain of the separation and remember instead the love and warmth, the joy and exhilaration that existed between us. In this way we can begin to build a new emotional and spiritual relationship with our beloved for the rest of our lives.

Death is an 8th house issue. Grief is its response.

The 8th house in the natal chart is the house of irrevocable change. It is where we encounter birth, sex, other people's money and death, issues western society finds difficult to handle, for they force us into situations from which we emerge forever changed. This is learned knowledge, acquired through interaction. Women do not automatically know how to give birth, nor men how to support their partner in so doing and it is now common practice in the west for both partners in an expectant birth situation to attend ante-natal classes. Initially we fumble with sexual technique and if we are lucky to have a partner who takes the time to explore this domain with us, we gain sexually-fulfilling lives. We do not, as a matter of course, know how to handle money and many a person in low-income conditions who wins the lottery has, within a short period of time, lost that money. We are, however, forced to invest time explaining the monies we have earned each year so we can pay taxes. Why do we not, as a society, do the same annual inventory for emotional change? Instead we are forced to pretend that death does not exist and that grief will never touch us. If we treated our taxes in the same way as we treated loss, we would be thrown into prison and the financial economy of the country would grind to a halt.

Until recently no-one had seriously considered that there was such a thing as the emotional economy of a country, nor that it could, in any way, be connected with loss and grief. In November, 2002, The Grief Recovery Institute, USA, published the results of the 25,000 interviews it had conducted with people in grief in North America in its twenty-five years of operation. Almost all people interviewed said their job performance was affected by grief. Using conservative estimates and assuming that the death of a loved one produces just one primary mourner who, over the next two years, loses a total of thirty days of productivity, the Grief Index, the term used by the Institute for measuring the hidden annual costs of grief in America's workplace, indicated that the minimum annual effect for U.S. businesses in lost productivity and on-the-job errors was $37.6 billion. [8] Given that workplace grief includes not only the death of a loved one but also divorce/marital problems, family crisis, death of an acquaintance, money issues at home and pet loss, the study estimates that hidden grief costs U.S. companies more than $75 billion annually in reduced productivity, increased errors and accidents. As a statement of how little consideration is given to grief and workplace behaviour, no other industry groups, including those representing funeral directors, hospices and others that monitor and study grief, had any comparable statistics. Three days used to be the typical amount of time given for "bereavement leave" throughout corporate America. A recent survey by The Society for Human Resource Management [9], an organization for human-resource executives, showed that ninety-two percent of companies offer paid bereavement leave for four days or fewer and sixty-eight percent of businesses said they have employee-assistance programs for people in grief, up from sixty-four percent in 1999. The Grief Recovery Institute, USA, advocates ten days bereavement leave and encourages "grief breaks" for employees, such as a walk outside or a talk with a co-worker, to allow them to be more productive the rest of the day. The aims of The Grief Recovery Institute are admirable and designed to help businesses gain greater awareness of the needs of people in grief, yet it is also a reflection of society that they have had to use the only model the business world understands: the mechanistic, reductionist model which equates a human being to an automaton whose productivity is diminished by loss. Needing to convert the human emotion of grief into dollars and cents is a statement of how little business understands how to deal with grief in the workplace.

For all that, let us not be too harsh on the commercial world. Since major emotional losses are not regular occurrences in our lives, few people have any preparation for handling grief or are equipped to support family and friends at times of personal loss. We are only given relevant information about how to deal with funerals in the days following the death and, more often than not, it is left to the funeral director and the medical practitioner to help people deal with the cascade of emotions. Here is a recent example. In *The Eye* magazine of 10th-16th January, 2004, [10] television screenwriter Paul Abbott describes his impoverished childhood. Born second last of ten children, his mother left without explanation when he was nine. His father became an alcoholic and abandoned the family to the care of the eldest sibling, a pregnant seventeen year old, when Abbott was eleven. At the age of fifteen Abbott attempted suicide. He became "a ward niner", the term used for the local psychiatric facility and in this black hole of destitution, he determined he would turn his life around. He was fostered and then went to Manchester

University to study psychology, leaving after two years when a play he'd written was performed on Radio 4. Now happily married, he has a much better relationship with his father whom he describes as "a reformed character, adored by his grandchildren". It was a different story with his mother who died eighteen months ago. "I felt nothing," he says, "We went to the funeral but it ended up with a brawl between two of my brothers. I think everyone was confused about what they were meant to feel." We prefer to bypass trying to grapple with these feelings until it is necessary, yet our lives are full of loss experiences that produce the same feelings of grief: the death of a pet, moving house and home, starting school, changes to one's health, graduating from high school, university or a place of extended learning, divorce, retirement and the absence of children when they leave home. Since they are not identified as circumstances which produce grief in the same way as death, we pay little attention to how they can teach us to deal with major losses when they occur. Furthermore, if any of these losses are emotionally significant to us and are not dealt with appropriately at the time, then, like mineral salts in hard water, they build up as unresolved issues that accumulate over time and which influence how one will respond to the death of a loved one in the future. How has this come to be?

Acquisition versus letting go

Any capitalistic society is an acquisitive society. From an early age we are taught to look outwards and to acquire things, emotionally as well as physically: our parents' love and respect, a good education, a job, a house, car and family of our own. No-one teaches us what to do when things pass out of our lives or when the goals we set are not achieved. No-one teaches us the true meaning of feelings of failure and despair. In his introduction to *The Prayer Tree*, Australian cartoonist and philosopher Michael Leunig writes:

> "Nature requires that we form a relationship between our joy and our despair, that they not remain divided or hidden from one another. For these are the feelings which must cross-pollinate and inform each other in order that the soul be enlivened and strong. It is the soul, after all, which bears the burden of our experience. It is the soul through which we love and it is the soul which senses most faithfully our function within the integrity of the natural world."[11]

Every loss, every death we encounter, throws us into winter, into that shapeless void in which poet John Keats so elegantly states, no birds sing and the sedge is withered from the lake. "I knew that I had moved inexplicably and without return from the white squares of the tiles on my kitchen floor onto the black squares when my mother died," remarked one client. This is the old season which dies before spring arrives, "the night that lies between two days".[12] This is the balsamic phase of any cycle, offering release without replacement. You can see the balsamic Moon each month in the sky, the thin sliver of the dying moon once full and glorious with luminous sun, now dark against the growing pre-dawn light, outlining the shape and the shadow of what has been, a transcript of the vital processes of the previous month now concluded. The balsamic phase is the phase of letting go, when life clears a space for us to reprioritise our life without immediately filling it with people and events. Often such action is accompanied by panic, since from an early age, we are taught Replacement Theory:

Breakdown = Substitute or Replace

We learn this by observing how our parents reacted to change in the material world: when the washing machine which laboured for years in the sweaty drudge of cleaning our clothes, stopped working, they called in someone to repair it or bought another; when the car broke down, they called for road service or traded it in for a new one. Nowadays obsolescence is often deliberately built into motor-driven items such as electric toothbrushes and vacuum cleaners. We are encouraged to see household goods as short-term and to replace them when they burn out. This made sense with domestic appliances but Replacement Theory also cascaded into emotional territory when our parents encouraged us to eat something when we were upset, rather than deal with the excruciating pain of being shunned or excluded in some way and to solve that first before substituting those emotions. The same applies to our audio environment. In our daily lives it is rare to walk into a shop that does not bombard us with raucous music or talkback radio, drowning the opportunity to hear our own thoughts and to make considered judgments, relying instead on advertising to unconsciously drive us. It is a potent combination: we refuse to allow the mechanics of our life to stop us from moving forward and we learn to replace silence and space with noise. So when personal relationships and intimate connections "break down", we have a ready-made template built from years of Replacement Theory to apply to the situation. It takes many years to understand our own motivations and it can take just as many to appreciate another in relationship.

Relationship dynamics change as people change; there is no blame in this. Sometimes we simply outgrow the other and different pathways beckon us across a growing gulf. However, we are not taught how to deal with the often-enormous emotional cost of the end of a living relationship, let alone one that is severed by death, for any separation, no matter how amicable, will cause a Moon-Saturn reaction - feelings of rejection, isolation and emotional pain - whether or not the person has a Moon-Saturn configuration in their natal chart. Coupled with the balsamic phase, this is an extremely painful place in which to exist. "Our species brings to it the capacity for self-reflexive awareness and responsible acts," writes social critic and ecofeminist Charlene Spretnak.[13] Yet apart from the first few days after a loved one dies, the extended family is usually no longer physically around to support and help a person in grief and in the precious few days when they are, our culture has determined what sort of behaviour is acceptable, behaviour which does not necessarily relate to the needs of the bereaved. Achilles' reaction would neither be tolerated nor condoned if he received Patroclus' news today and yet that response in the moment was the healthiest thing he could have done.

There are two ways to avoid grief in human life: the first is to die young before anyone you love precedes you. In 1989 I had the privilege of working with young people from the depressed western suburbs of Adelaide, South Australia. I was their playwright-in-residence, working with them to create a play about youth and alcohol. The catch cry amongst their difficult and straitened lives was: "Die young, stay pretty". The second way to prevent grief is to avoid ever really loving or caring for someone. That way you never have to be emotionally involved with death or its consequences. Grief is the price we pay for living a full life. If we think of a life as a complete picture, when we lose a loved one it is as if that picture crazes, like a jigsaw puzzle, and some of the pieces fall out. Most people do not take steps to recover those pieces, so unconsciously we carry that fragmentary image around inside us, believing we are still whole. These empty spaces accumulate over time and when we next encounter loss, without realising it more pieces of the puzzle fall out. Unless we pay attention to these lost fragments, we walk around as incomplete puzzles our whole life. These buried or forgotten losses extend the pain and frustration of how to deal with letting go. This is unresolved grief and it becomes our learned response to the world. Honouring Replacement Theory, unconsciously we look for people to fill those spaces for us. Such unconscious projections can create explosive situations when we encounter loss as an adult.

Bereavement counselling versus astrological consultation

There are two things that astrology does extraordinarily well: it describes the shape and nature of the personality; and it describes the shape and nature of the future. Both are intimately connected. What astrology, as a profession, does best is to give a client a clear understanding of their future based on what is contained in the natal chart. No other profession can do this in the same way or as accurately. Whilst acknowledging a person's free will, astrology is the last area of expertise that uses Fate as its raw material. The concept of Fate becomes understandable once one realises that everyone's life contains difficulties, turmoil and strife, as well as happiness and pleasure, and that no life is a smooth plane of existence. Given that awareness, it is important to recognise that, as Bernadette Brady tells our students when teaching them predictive astrology, as astrologers we read a person's Fate, we don't write it. [14] Therefore a good predictive astrologer with an understanding of the grief process can do a great deal for a client in the consulting room. In an astrological consultation, the astrologer is not aiming to alleviate suffering but rather to facilitate the healing process by acknowledging what has occurred, including any past patterns, and shifting it into a bigger picture for the client. This is similar to what occurs in a bereavement counselling session only in this last regard. A bereavement counsellor is facilitating memories, enabling the past relationship to become part of the person's present, validating it, making the memories normal and putting them into the context of the storyline of the person's life. Bereavement counselling by its very nature takes many short sessions over an extended period of time. The astrologer, on the other hand, may see the client once only or once a year for a few consecutive years. In such circumstances the astrologer reads a client's predictive work utilising the understanding of grief and recognising that the needs of the client will be modified accordingly. Therefore, as astrologers we need to know the process of grief, that this process fits into the predictive work for the client and how to read that predictive work for a client who is still grieving.

There is an added responsibility for an astrologer dealing with a grieving client. Someone profoundly affected by grief can't distinguish between "want" and "able". They feel a raw "wanting" for someone to fill the yawning gap carved out by the death and in that state are highly vulnerable. However, a client in grief needs someone who can provide an able and capable supportive framework in which to feel safe. Accepting the client's need to express their pain may well trigger grief that is still unresolved within us. Therefore, in order to do the clearest work possible, the astrologer must first confront his or her own unique and intensely personal issues around loss and grief. Otherwise what we pass on to the client simply reiterates the inaccuracies we have been taught around loss. As well, in the eighteen years that I have been working with clients in this area, I have found it is best to let at least six months pass before taking on a client who is experiencing grief. This is to enable the client's body to adjust to the extreme physical, mental, emotional and spiritual circumstances of grief and, more importantly, for the work of grief, the completion of what is left unfinished emotionally as a result of the death, to commence.

Is grief a terminal illness?

Any discussion about loss and grief must inevitably bring up the name of Dr Elisabeth Kubler-Ross, the brilliant pioneer working in the field of death and dying. Her contribution has been invaluable and has, in many ways, profoundly affected the manner in which the medical profession deals with terminally ill patients. Through her decisive and shaping work begun in 1965 and outlined in her book, *On Death and Dying*, Kubler-Ross identified five emotional stages that a person experiences when they have been diagnosed with a terminal illness, namely:

> Stage 1: denial by the person and isolation from other people
> Stage 2: anger, rage, envy and resentment of those who are still able to live and function
> Stage 3: bargaining to postpone the inevitable event and extend the person's life
> Stage 4: depression, both reactive to the loss of lifestyle and preparatory for the death

These stages then become the stepping stones towards…

> Stage 5: acceptance

These stages do not replace each other but rather exist next to each other and at times overlap. However, no matter what the stage of the illness or the mechanisms used to handle it, all terminally ill patients maintain hope right until the last moment. Kubler-Ross developed these stages at a time when modern thinking had reached its peak with its emphasis on rationalism and functionality. She developed the system as a psychiatrist and thanatologist for thantaological purposes to help the terminally ill die with grace and dignity whilst having their needs met. Later on she applied her work to large groups of terminally ill people outside the hospital environment, as well as to members of the family connected with the dying and published her work under titles which underlined the work she did: *Death, The Final Stage of Growth*; *On Children and Death*; and *Working It Through*. In *To Live Until We Say Goodbye* she writes:

> "With her favourite music playing, with candlelight on the table, with her children near, and with flowers next to her picked by her own children, she died a very different kind of death than had she stayed in the hospital. Those children will never associate death with loneliness, isolation, playing games and deceit. They will remember it as a time of togetherness with their parents and grandparents, and friends who cared and were able to acknowledge their own anxieties and their own fears, and together were able to overcome them." [15]

Counsellors and therapists, the clergy and the medical profession working in the field of bereavement, influenced by the revelations of Kubler-Ross's investigations and the lack of work done in this taboo area, chose to apply the concept of these stages of dying to the grief that follows death. This occurred because it fitted into a medical model which treats grief as an illness and bereavement as a disease. This linear way of seeing the world moves from diagnosis to prognosis, treatment and, finally, to intervention. "Stages" meant that people could predict moments in time and, as a result, tell grieving people whether they were moving through them as quickly as they should, inferring that the stages are sequential and predictable. However, people are complicated, irrational and emotional and their responses to grief are neither sequential nor predictable. Practitioners forgot that Kubler-Ross's work was carried out in the field of the dying and that her overlapping, co-existent "stages" apply to someone who knows that the end point of their present life is death. The process of grief is the antithesis of this. The word "grief" comes from Old French "grever" meaning burden or encumber, in turn based on the Latin "gravare", from "gravis" heavy, grave. In Middle English the word also means to harm or oppress. The process of moving through grief is the process of unburdening or unencumbering oneself. The end point of grief is life, to live again when one has been awakened to death and grief can do no more harm.

In the same way as architecture changed its tone from modern to post-modern, railing against functionality and demanding respect for the structures of social relationships that make homes and communities flow better, so the perception of grief has undergone a sea change. People working in the field of bereavement now recognise that human beings grieve according to unpredictable dependent variables which include age, gender, day of the week, how close a person was emotionally to the one who died and the nature of the death. They also recognise that the quality, strength, passion and the force of feelings that overwhelm us after a death reflect the quality, strength, passion and the force of feelings of the relationship. McKissock likens grief to Chaos Theory which, he says, reflects his experience of counselling people in grief in clinical practice over the past twenty years or so. In brief, one can think of Chaos Theory as the mechanics of studying nonlinear, dynamic systems which are mathematically deterministic but nearly impossible to predict. McKissock is suggesting that the effect grief has on people and how they deal with it cannot be described by logical, linear systems or pathways and that a person in grief is better off responding to what is happening to them in the "now", rather than in the "what should be". A better model might be the still-evolving Complexity Theory, a refinement of Chaos Theory. Complexity is the observed tendency of seemingly random agents to arrange themselves into patterns.

This zone, known as the Edge of Chaos, lies between stasis and chaos and is thought to be the place where evolution is most likely to occur. Mitchell Waldrop defines complexity as "a class of behaviours in which the components of the system never quite lock into place, yet never quite dissolve into turbulence, either." [16] We can postulate that we, as human beings, respond in the same way, that when confronted with disruption or complex systems, we try to create ordered patterns or, if life is gridlocked over a period of time, then there is an abundantly high probability that it will suddenly erupt with the ferocity of an earthquake and cascade into chaos.

Applying this framework to grief, then, the initial pain, distress and agony catapults a person into chaos. In such a state a person will focus all their energy to fight, scrabble, heave, tug and claw their way back to the regular matrix of ordered life. However, what they encounter on their return is not the world they knew. Grief is a passage which leads to a changed future. If a person can surrender to the grief, then life initially seems chaotic but eventually settles back to the resilient patterns we call equilibrium. If grief is repressed, it pushes a person into stasis, an immobilised state where they can remain for years. Then, Complexity Theory suggests, eventually the person's life will erupt into chaos before they can return to a state of equilibrium. The longer a system stays in stasis, the more the movement out of it is through extreme turmoil. Grief spontaneously throws a person into a period of chaos before harmony returns. We can delay it through repression but we can't avoid it. In order to reach the structure of a changed future, we have to go through chaos. Waldrop describes it in this way:

> "... we are made of the same elemental compositions, so we are a part of this thing that is never changing and always changing. If you think you are a steamboat and can go up the river, you're kidding yourself. Actually, you're just the captain of a paper boat drifting down the river. If you try to resist, you're not going to get anywhere. On the other hand, if you quietly observe the flow, re-alising that you are part of it, realising that the flow is ever-changing and always leading to new complexities, then every so often you can stick an oar into the river and punt yourself from one eddy to another." [17]

Only now is the world of science catching up with what the ancients knew so long ago, that as Menelaus, in the myth of grief, struggles with The Old Man of the Sea, so he is propelled into disarray and chaos. All he can do is hold onto Proteus and be catapulted through the maelstrom of grief, for it is this maelstrom which awakens him to death and which, eventually, allows him to sail home to the safety of the Edge of Chaos and a changed world.

The shape of grief - rites of passage

Grief is a rite of passage and all rites of passage contain paradoxes: they celebrate changes and disruptions in a seemingly continuous life; and they acknowledge the fact that we are born and die alone, yet as a group we seek to find meaning in events which define birth, aging and death. Paradoxes can never be resolved but the in-built framework and safeguards that rituals provide allow us to experience their truth. It was Van Gennep, the pioneer in the structure of rites of passage who, in 1907, observed that a person or a group of people had to be separated from one role or rank in society before he, she or they could be incorporated into a new one. In this liminal phase between the two positions something extraordinary occurred. Native cultures employed sleep-deprivation and fasting to induce the extremes of emotional and physical stress and at the end of this transitional time, the individual or group of people emerged rejuvenated and was welcomed back into the community in a new role. Building on van Gennep's work, Victor Turner found that people who were in this liminal phase were not only out of place in the ordered structure of society but became mysterious and powerful as they underwent change. Mircea Eliade, philosopher and director of History of Religions department at the University of Chicago, suggests that rituals, along with myths, give us access to sacred or cyclic time. [18]

Paralleling this is the work of Joseph Campbell, American writer on mythology and comparative religion, who discovered that the journeys all central characters take in the great myths of the world contain three major phases: departure from the known world; initiation through isolation and encounters with dangerous elements; and the return to the tribe or the common world with a gift that will help those who have stayed behind. Given that journeys are undertaken to bring about change, this journey of adjustment and growth forges strength of character. However, this pilgrimage has its price, for "… every one of us shares the supreme ordeal … not in the bright moments of his tribe's great victories but in the silences of his personal despair." [19]

Rites of passage occur whenever we encounter life crises. They create anxiety by calling attention to seemingly irreconcilable human paradoxes. They shake us out of our mundane way of being, with our previous ways of acting, thinking and feeling and, separated from society, provide us with a new context for learning from which we emerge forever changed. The world is undone and the world is made new again. The same can be said of grief, yet in today's modern, industrial world, individuality is prized at the cost of experiencing life's transitions alone. We are, for the most part, born in hospitals and that is where most of us can expect to die. Birth and death are the two great portals of our lives, yet so often they are left unsanctified and uncelebrated. Grief, the hitchhiker on the same pathway as death, becomes not so much the great reflector of transition but an illness or sickness of which no-one speaks. Grief's shape shares this pattern:

- **Acute grief, the initial response**, where we are ripped from the world of common day and thrust into the turmoil and despair of grief;

- **Disintegration, the period of disengagement from the world** where we discover that the rules we have developed for living in the mundane world do not work in the land of grief and the mist in our head and the pain in our heart seldom clears;

- **Reintegration back into the community** after a passage of time but now in a new and productive role.

Grief pummels us from within, unplugging what was previously a highly active and capable intellectual capacity and leaving only pure emotion. However, whilst everyone's grief is unique and our personal expression of it depends on the relationship we had with the person who has died, the emotional and physical responses which wash over and around us are remarkably uniform:

Shock and numbness

Grief is an emotional wound; it causes pain in the same way as a physical wound. The body's response when we first hear of the death of a loved one is to produce powerful, pain-killing drugs similar to heroin and morphine known as enkephalins and met-enkephalins. These endorphins are natural narcotic-like chemicals produced at the level the body needs. [20] If you have ever jammed your thumb in a door or cut yourself with a knife, you will experience the same rush of chemical activity on a vastly reduced scale. This numbing effect is designed to enable the person to take action. A gashed leg, a wounded arm, a jammed thumb, all of these require attention NOW and our own natural pain-killers give us the time to attend to the wound, make a phone call for help or take action in some way. In such circumstances there is usually only a short delay before the pain comes rushing back. It is not so with grief. This numbness a person feels, this lack of physical or emotional sensation, and sometimes it is both, often misinterpreted as denial is, in reality, shock. Shock is the sudden disruption to our daily routines which causes a distressing effect on the mind and feelings and initiates suffering. Shock occurs whenever we experience pain or life-threatening situations. The associated numbness is one of a range of physical responses designed to decrease the immediate pain until it can be managed and it can last for hours, days and sometimes months.

Fear

Fear is an emotion triggered by the belief that someone or something is dangerous and likely to create pain. Fear causes our pulse to race and our blood to pump faster. It prepares us for fight or flight. Its origin is the Old English word "fær" meaning calamity or danger and "færan" meaning frighten, as well as reverence of the numinous. It is thought to be the first emotion to have evolved five hundred million years ago and it is as potent today as it was for our prehistoric ancestors. When someone we love dies, fear of the future and fear of not being able to deal with the huge emotional and physical change that has just entered our life are normal and natural responses. Such fears are designed to pinpoint areas in a person's life that have dramatically altered in order for the person to reset the parameters of their life. A reduction of financial income, for example, may be a real fear if the person has been relying on his or her partner to supply the weekly wages. Other fears may have little grounding in reality but impose an even greater emotional threat, such as the fear of living life without the partner. Although they may evoke panic, concern and worry, fears once named can be managed and the person in grief needs space to voice these concerns. However, we have been socialized to express fear indirectly as rage, revenge or self-loathing and these can have long-term consequences if they are allowed to define the person's life. Uncontrolled fear can be the underlying cause of anxiety disorders and some of the symptoms of depression.

Anger

Anger is a natural, adaptive response to threats. It inspires powerful, often aggressive, feelings and behaviours which allow us to fight and to defend ourselves when we are attacked. Like other emotions, it is accompanied by physiological and biological changes. When we get angry, our heart rate and blood pressure rise, as do the levels of our energy hormones, adrenalin and noradrenalin. A certain amount of anger is necessary for our survival but anger can vary in intensity from mild irritation to intense fury and rage, any of which can be triggered by external and/or internal events, such as a person, an event or concern with a personal problem. Memories of traumatic or enraging events can also release angry feelings. In the case of grief, anger may sometimes be associated with the circumstances of the loss. When someone has been prevented from being with the person when they died, they may experience anger at the turn of events. Katrina, one of our students, recently told me of this experience regarding her father's death:

> In November 1993, I left for a three-month trip to the Far East, partially motivated by a desire to consider some changes in my

life. The latter months of 1993 and the early months of 1994 were extremely difficult on a personal level. I do vividly recall about two months before I left getting an overwhelming feeling of "something bad is going to happen" but I could not pinpoint it. Not long before I left, my father had said to me that his desire was that I would be happy and I had the sense that he knew I was not entirely happy in the field in which I was working. In December, when I was in Nepal, I had a dream that my father came to me and told me that he had died. I thought at that moment that I should call home but didn't want to upset my mother. However, about two days later I was walking in the street and had a profound urge to call home and I did. My mother and my brother were just leaving the house for the funeral, having desperately tried to contact me in Nepal but to no avail because I was in transit when the event occurred. My father's death was unexpected, causing a deep emotional wound that motivated me to change my career and go back to school on my return to Canada. Due to the timing of this event, I did not return immediately. At the beginning of 1994, I was celebrating my birthday on the Ganges River in India. My whole focus at this time was turned towards broadening my horizons. When I returned to Canada in February, I had a big shock to the system as the reality of everything became quite imminent. Given the circumstances of the dream, I was not angry that I only found out about my father's death on the day of his funeral. In fact, I was relieved that I found out in the manner I did, seeing as my mother was having such a hard time contacting me. I was relieved mainly for her sake because I could imagine that it was particularly painful for her not being able to get hold of me. What I was particularly angry about is that, just when I felt I had found some freedom, I was suddenly decidedly restricted because I knew that when I went back to Canada, my responsibilities to my mother would be increased manifold. This was a most painful and confusing time because, just as I was liberated from one restriction, I was facing another. On the surface, this might sound callous but my relationship with my mother was exceedingly difficult, owing to her alcoholism throughout my childhood. So, yes, I was immensely angry because I felt that, just as I was beginning to fly, my wings were clipped or perhaps they melted because I got too close to the Sun.

If the relationship has been blocked or stifled in any way, then the client may be angry that the person has died before they have had a chance to mend the relationship. In such instances anger is often displaced onto a "safe" family member. Here's an example. My client lived in a different city to his father. In the midst of a telephone conversation, my client became angry at his father, swore at him and hung up. A month later his father died. My client's initial reaction to his father's death was: "I'm not ready for this!" Two months later, in another telephone conversation, his younger brother confronted him with their mother's now-restricted financial income. My client's parents had both been retired and living on pensions. They had lost their family home many years earlier through bankruptcy and my client and his wife had taken it upon themselves to buy his parents a small flat. He had used his parents' pension to help pay off the mortgage but had not thought to put them on the title deed alongside himself as security of tenure in their old age. Despite these changed events, he still assumed that his mother would continue to contribute to the rates on her now-halved pension. His younger brother suggested that his brother take on board a standard landlord's responsibilities and pay the rates himself. My client became enraged at what he thought was his younger brother's disrespectful way of treating him. He demanded an apology and when his younger brother refused, my client swore at him and slammed the phone down in his ear. In a letter he threatened to cut off all connection with his younger brother unless the apology was forthcoming. His younger brother maintained his position and my client held onto his anger for five years as a way of preventing him from confronting the pain of loss and the guilt of his last actions towards his father. In the course of the consultation he was able to come to the painful realisation that he had duplicated the circumstances of his last conversation with his father with his younger brother. At first he had tried to vindicate his actions and when that did not work, he had displaced his anger onto this safe member of his family until he was ready to look at it. The circumstances preceding the loss of my client's father had been unresolved and so he experienced anger but anger is not an automatic part of grief.

Reduced concentration

"No-one ever told me about the laziness of grief," writes C.S. Lewis in *A Grief Observed* [21]. "Not only writing but even reading a letter is too much." The reactions of someone in grief are slower than normal. A person's entire being in its emotional, physical and spiritual manifestation is trying to make sense of this painful situation. Lapses in concentration, such as walking into a supermarket without being conscious of how one has arrived there or making a phone call without being aware of picking up the telephone and dialling, are the hallmarks of this natural friend of acute grief. This inability to concentrate is felt at such a grass roots level that James and Friedman (The Grief Recovery Institute, USA) suggest not driving or avoiding work with tools that require concentration and mental co-ordination, since this is when a high percentage of serious and often fatal accidents occur. It is also another reason why it is important to let time pass before seeing a client for predictive work.

Being tearful

Tears play a vital role in our visual system. Physically the lachrymal gland of the eyes produces aqueous fluid in response to a sensation of dryness or irritation. These are called continuous or basal tears. Reflex tears or irritant tears are those which spring to our eyes in response to smoke, onion vapours or foreign bodies. They are produced by tiny glands on the underside of the upper eyelid and drain through a nasolacrimal duct into the nose where they are reabsorbed. When tears run down the face, it is because there are too many of them to drain. Tears are an efficient cleaning medium, washing foreign bodies from the eye and providing microbiological protection. They also produce a high quality optical surface which forms the major light-refracting element of the eye. Since the cornea has no blood vessels, nutrients and waste products are transported to and from it via the surface tear film. Tears contain immunoglobins and enzymes that protect the eye from infection. They contain oils and mucus that form a thin film which protects the surface of the eye. [22]

Continuous tears and reflex tears are fairly well understood and occur in other animals. Yet apart from a few reports in animals - an Indian elephant, an African gorilla, female seals, some species of dogs and others - humans are believed to be the only animals that shed tears when they are overwhelmed by intense emotion. We cry when we are joyful, in grief or despondent, tormented by hopelessness or overwhelmed with relief. We cry when exhilarated or creased over with laughter, when brimming with pride or beyond the limits of sheer ecstasy. These psychogenic lachrymations reflect the immense range of emotions of which humans are capable. Primal therapists understand that crying can be a catharsis for emotions. Cell biologists know that emotional tears have specific biological pathways although they still don't know whether they are caused by hormones or chemical messengers from nerves. Indeed little is known about these tears of emotions.

To explore this further, in the early 1980s, biochemist William H. Frey II screened the films *The Champ*, *Brian's Song* and *All Mine to Give* and asked a select group of viewers to collect their tears in test tubes. He also collected the reflex tears of people cutting onions. He discovered that emotional tears were chemically different from irritant or reflex tears. Amongst other things, emotional tears contained ACTH, a hormone indictor of stress and the endorphin leucine-enkephalin, part of the family of brain chemicals known as endorphins which are thought to modulate pain sensation. He also found high concentrations of manganese, suggesting that tears remove toxic substances from the blood or other body tissues. [23] His conclusion was that something truly unique happens when we shed emotional tears. Tears deal with stress, modulate pain and remove toxic substances, so crying is an appropriate physical response to stress. Indeed most people feel better after crying and regard it as a desirable and healthy release of tension. Mr Bumbles in Charles Dickens' *Oliver Twist* understood this when he stated:

> "It opens the lungs, washes the countenance, exercises the eyes, and softens down the temper. So cry away!" [24]

Alfred Lord Tennyson understood this when he penned *The Princess* (1847):

> "Home they brought her warrior dead.
> She nor swoon'd nor utter'd cry:
> All her maidens, watching, said,
> 'She must weep or she will die.'" [25]

Sir Henry Carr Maudsley (1859 - 1944) physician and pathologist understood this when he wrote:

> "Sorrows which find no vent in tears may soon make other organs weep." [26]

Too many tears, however, smokescreen the powerful depth of feelings containing the unresolved issues that must be completed with the person who has died. Tears drive a person to the location but words identify what is unspoken in the heart, and lay bare the raw material that lies behind the pain which produces the crying. Psychologist Jeffrey Kottler points out that people who are depressed cry all the time and feel worse. [27] Depression is an immobilized state whereas sadness offers one an acute sense of existence.

For the person in grief, the natural chemicals produced by the body to numb the pain begin to decrease as the weeks pass. Around four-to-six weeks after the death they are significantly low. As these endorphins start to wear off, the full extent of the pain filters through to reality. What seemed manageable before now seems worse than ever. Instead of decreasing, crying may increase as a way of producing more met-enkephalins, utilising the natural chemicals of emotional tears as a way of bringing the body back to a state of balance.

Disrupted sleep patterns

The death of someone close to us is now understood to be one of life's greatest stresses and one of the body's instinctive reactions is to produce adrenalin. This is a chemical secreted by the adrenal glands when the body believes itself to be under threat. It does this in order to provide enough energy to protect itself from danger or to run as far away from the danger as possible: the "fight or flight" response. Flooding the body with adrenalin creates an increase in blood pressure and heart rate and loads the body's muscles with tension. Think of any athlete on the blocks in the "get set" position before the gun is fired and you have an understanding of the state of the body at this time: totally primed with no race to run.

In previous generations and in other cultures significant amounts of this adrenalin would have been burned up by mourning, sitting around the body for three days and three nights crying, moaning, screaming and weeping. At the end of this time the person in grief would have been physically exhausted and collapsed with natural fatigue into deep sleep. Our modern western perspective teaches us to placate, patronise or modify such behaviour - "You must have a good night's sleep. Take a tranquilliser, you'll feel better in the morning" - but medications block the expression of pain. Acute grief is not concerned with "feeling better". Indeed the articulation of feelings, however they come, together with appropriate emotional support, is part of the rite of passage and of primary importance at this time, more so than the need for physical relief. Added to this is the serious side effect of prolonged dependence on the tranquillising qualities of drugs, for habitual use can lead to addiction.

When the doctor informed a client of her husband's terminal cancer in 1965, she refused to allow anyone to tell her husband that he was dying. When he died suddenly, she began taking the anti-anxiety agent Diazepam (Valium) as a short-term relief to help her sleep. She still takes a half of a tablet of Valium every night, now totally unable to sleep without it. This was a woman who took over her husband's business selling real estate after his death and succeeded as a woman in a man's world. This was a woman who travelled the world extensively, spending a year at a time with her family in Switzerland, her friends in England and her sister-in-law in America. Yet her history of denial of death, her fear of aging and her refusal to deal with the real and painful loss of her husband has followed her into her old age. When she was eighty and still actively flying around the world, she developed deep vein thrombosis, blood clots in the deep veins of her legs. This led to a series of operations and diminished movement. Now aged eighty five years, she has become frail and dependent and continues to be afraid of dying. This is a ripe and opportune time to allow those who love her to deepen their emotional ties to her by allowing them to participate in her natural process of aging and, eventually, dying. She, in turn, gains physical and emotional security as she journeys forth along that fearful pathway. Instead it has resulted in her becoming angry and embittered at her loss of mobility and her vitality, pushing away those who could help her deal with her fears.

Going to bed and sleeping for days at a time or staying awake for long periods of time are natural reactions to acute grief. The body has its own intelligence and will find a balance without the use of medication. Prescribed drugs cloud reality. They may work in the short term but as their effects fade, the person's awareness of the pain increases. They are most often prescribed for the sake of someone else rather than to cater for the needs of the person in grief. Indeed bereaved people unconsciously spend most of their time making other people feel better. "Have an injection/a tablet, it'll help you" in reality translates as: "We can't handle your emotions. Have an injection/a tablet, it'll help US."

A more positive expression for this trapped adrenalin is physical exercise such as long walks, swimming, gardening, housework, yoga or having a massage. After the sudden and unexpected death of her father at age seventy, the first of her parents to die, one client built a water garden in her back yard, spading the hard earth with her bare hands and installing a clever interconnection of ponds. She planted ferns and flowers around the ponds and added a floodlight and a garden seat for the evenings. The physical activity released her body from feeling continually pumped, the results of her labour gave her an environment from which she received great joy and pleasure and the end result established a living memorial to her father.

Planting a garden is a common female response to major change and reorganisation and indicative of moving towards a new life. When a person nurtures a garden, it nurtures them back. As seeds shoot into plants and buds into flower and fruit, so a woman, in effect, midwifes herself into healing. The thirteenth century Persian mystic, Rumi, said, "This outward spring and garden are a reflection of the inward garden." Contemporary Canadian symbolist painter and writer, Susanne Iles, expresses it this way:

> "Plants and flowers, trees and shrubs, have been our companions for eons. We grow gardens in our backyards, on apartment balconies, rooftops, and windowsills. We use plants not only to feed ourselves but also to nourish our senses and our connection to the earth. Deep within the roots of every plant dwell the seeds of myth, waiting to be reclaimed... the garden is a sacred place grown from the seeds of myth." [28]

Creating her own garden from nothing not only gave my client an outlet for her artistry and vision but the smells, sounds, colours, textures and energy of the plants and trees helped to ground her and ease the intensity of what was going on for her internally.

Changed eating habits

Loss of appetite is a natural reaction to grief, for the body's energy is directed elsewhere. However, feeling ravenous is also a normal reaction and someone in acute grief may swing between the two extremes. If this is the case, it is wise to have ready access to fresh fruit and vegetables, proteins and carbohydrates and to drink a plentiful amount of water.

Emotional highs and lows

People describe grief as "coming in waves" or "like walking through hidden swamplands". One client described her feelings "like taking an elevator straight from your head and intellect to your guts and heart". There is a difficulty in being able to maintain emotional stability and as a result, a person in grief will often feel emotionally and physically drained. Whilst the pain is at first intense and constant, moments occur where the pain recedes. As these moments increase to hours and then to days, a small and seemingly inconsequential action in the midst of a mundane event can trigger a memory and grief floods back in full three-dimensional colour and pain, as vivid and present as if it had occurred the day before. This was the experience of the man with the terracotta pot in the introduction of this book. Grief is an ever-changing, dynamic process and these are normal and natural reactions.

Bodily distress

Bereavement is a serious traumatic experience. As a result, any bodily system or organ can be affected to a greater or lesser degree. Bodily distresses can range from tightness in the chest or throat, backache and headache, mild gastro-intestinal disturbance such as indigestion, constipation, digestive disorders or heartburn or more incapacitating symptoms such as nausea, vomiting, diarrhoea, menstrual problems, migraine or acute chest pain. One woman found she couldn't stop trembling when her husband died but reaching out and touching someone would stop the trembling immediately. In this time of stress, the physical body is particularly vulnerable. Coupled with the production of adrenalin, the pituitary gland also produces an immuno-suppressant called cortisol which decreases the production of T-lymphocytes, the body's surveillance cells. T-lymphocytes are responsible for keeping infection and other abnormal cells in the body under control. When they are depleted, the body is defined as being immuno-suppressed, unable to fight infection or control the production of these abnormal cells. Viruses and bacteria gain the upper hand and the body can succumb to infections such as influenza, cold sores, upper respiratory tract infections, urinary tract infections, boils or conjunctivitis.

Sighing

The weight of grief can seem immense and a common, almost unconscious response is to sigh a great deal. The sigh, this audible exhalation, is the involuntary expression of exhaustion and lament. Deep sighing and frequent swallowing are ways the body releases tension.

"To sleep perchance to dream..."

Are dreams of the dead "real" contacts or simply images created by the dreamer to meet psychological needs? We will never know. What we do know is that many bereaved people actively dream about the one who has died and those dreams are vibrant, vital and deeply emotional and, in some instances, dramatically alter the way a person views death. At base their effect is healing and the dreamer almost always wakes with a sense of reassurance and exuberance. In the same way that not all people remember their dreams when life moves pleasantly forward in the normal course of events, so not all people in grief remember their dreams. My experience with clients who do dream, however, has been that, early in grief they will experience one of two types of dreams: the first is a series of dreams in a continuing narrative occurring within the first two-to-three months after the loved one has died. Such dreams include being with them, seeing them or having conversations with them at places of transition, such as on a bus or a boat, at a railway station, a wharf or an airport, by a door or gate, in a hallway or a tunnel, places which represent the boundaries between the two worlds. The final dream in the series usually occurs with the person who has died leaving for a distant land. The second type of dream is more of a one-off encounter and can occur at any time during the grief process. The one who has died is sighted in good health and full of vigour; sometimes they make contact with the dreamer, sometimes the dreamer glimpses them at a distance. In some instances the person may have been dead for some years and contacts a member of the family to look after another member.

I have also found two other types of dreams. Precognitive dreams occur as a series of dreams a few months prior to the death of someone close and alert the dreamer that the death is coming. The significance of such dreams only becomes apparent after the death has occurred. Claire had the following dreams which, in hindsight, made sense of her father's death:

> First, I dreamed I went to the garage and drove out my mother's vintage car which hadn't been driven for forty years. (My parents had been married for forty years.) Then I dreamed of a pavilion in a park: the blinds were shut and it was a place of extreme calm and peace. Indeed it was a place of such deep peace that I knew it was

where people go when they have just died and I was fearful I was seeing my own death, so I didn't say anything to my partner, although I dreamed of this place several times over the following weeks. The final time the blinds were open. Six days later my father died and it was then that I knew that what I had been seeing was the place where he would go on his death to heal. I was acutely aware of him in this place and felt a strong connection with him there. Four days after his death I started to lose him. The silver cord had stretched and he was moving off with his mother through some lawned gardens. It was dusk on the same day I had seen ten days previously. Three weeks later to the day I knew he had finally passed over, left the pavilion in the park and walked on - gone. The pavilion was now shut up, closed, private. The work was done.

Katrina, whose father died when she was in Nepal, maintained contact with him through her dreams after he died and it was he who told her of her mother's imminent death:

In the first dream my father described to me that he was in a plane of existence wherein all the senses were heightened. Everything looked and felt better there and he had discovered that beer tasted especially good in this place. He said that this plane existed parallel to ours, it's just that we on the earth plane couldn't see it. In the second dream, he was dressed in a formal outfit, like one might wear in the 1920's but somehow updated. He told me that after a certain period, those who die all receive an "assignment" which is much like a job or occupation. He had been assigned the task of librarian in this big cosmic library. People who have died have access to this library and can take out the books at their leisure. Apparently, these books contain all the information known in the Universe. The last dream I had was when he told me he was waiting for my mother and she died about two weeks later. I never had these sorts of dreams about my mother, nor any other dreams (of this nature) of my father since. However, when I sold my parents' house after my mother's death, something extraordinary occurred. My mother loved butterflies and collected images of them. On the day I moved everything out of the house, I shifted a dresser to the side and there on the floor was a tiny passport picture of my father. Then out of nowhere this beautiful butterfly, a variety that I have never seen here before or since, flew in through the window and alighted on the picture of my father. That was the very last "message" I had from either of them. I think that once my father died, they both moved on to wherever it is they needed to go.

The "extraordinary" dream which, if it occurs, appears to do so approximately three-to-six months after the loved one dies and is a final encounter in the grief season which leaves the dreamer in a state of euphoria. This was Claire's experience two and a half months after her father died:

> I dream of a young, handsome man who tells me he is leaving for Finland and that he has come to say goodbye. Between us there is a profound love that isn't sexual, an amazingly deep bond. He tells me he will send me letters from time to time but they will be anonymous and then he leaves and I realise this is my father and now he is leaving for "Fin" ("fin" means "the end" in French) land. I wake intensely and emotionally moved.

Ellen had this dream three months after her father died:

> I am with a friend I have known forever, a good childhood friend called Michael. We are in a gathering. There is a large crowd. Michael is singing a song to the tune of "Don't forget to remember me, my love". He is young, athletic, healthy, full of vigorous energy and has short, black, wavy hair. My relationship with him is extremely comfortable. Good friends. Non-sexual. As I watch him singing, his eye catches mine and I suddenly feel this enormous and powerful pain in my heart charka as we recognise each other. It is a deep connection. This energy is so powerful it wakes me up. It has literally taken my breath away and I think it has been a dream about my animus. Then I realise this was the man I had known as my father in this life and would know again as "Michael" in a future life when we met. I've often wondered how it is that you can be introduced to someone and have the sense of "knowing" them instantly, even though you've only just met for the first time. I had it when I met my partner, an instant "knowing" and recognition of each other. Of course the human part takes longer to understand what is happening but it suddenly made sense of my dream and I found it comforting. It didn't deny the father-daughter relationship we had had in this life and it didn't stop the process of pain and grief. It simply made sense.

Grief tosses time like a salad, mixing memories from the past with an echo-silent future. In the minute intervals, in the intolerable moments and the elongation of years that follows the death of someone close to us, the body and the mind continue to use their own intelligences to sort through the ideas, feelings and experiences of a lifetime of relationship. Some of these feelings may have lain dormant for many years, unconsciously hidden on the seabed of existence and only now exposed by the death. Others may involve the shocking recognition that words said in haste can now never be unsaid. However it occurs, if you are attending to the pain of grief and doing all that you can to acknowledge and give voice to your feelings in a way that brings completion, then you will heal on the far side of time.

Where grief can't flow - a sea with no tides

Society conditions us to avoid grief since the outward expression of it can make other people feel helpless and uncomfortable. How often do we hear of people in loss described as "putting on a brave face to the world"? We want the person in grief to change their behaviour so we can feel better, so we use intellect to couch the discomfort. Sarah Key [29] talks of "people's zippered mouths" when they didn't want to discuss her son's cot death at the age of ten-weeks old. Parents of a stillborn child are advised to "have another baby". Parents of a young child who has died are told they are "still young enough to have another child". Widows or widowers are told they can remarry. Such advice, whilst intellectually correct, is insulting and emotionally unproductive, for it ignores the emotional pain and does not offer a pathway for dealing with these feelings. This stems from an incorrect understanding of grief, underpinned by Replacement Theory.

What a person in grief wants most of all is to be heard without judgment and discrimination. However, what they need and what people tell them are in conflict, resulting in feelings of confusion, frustration and being double-bound. When we are socialised not to express what we feel, we are lead to emotional isolation. When we are expected to join in activities "as usual" without acknowledging the intensity of the loss, we are lead to physical isolation. We can't grieve alone, yet as a society we physically isolate those in grief because we can't handle their despair. Ignoring a category of people in society does not make them go away and treating grief as invisible merely pushes it underground. Normal and natural feelings of loss include shock and numbness, bodily distress, anger, idealisation, guilt, hostility, replacement and panic. Grief reactions that are stuck in a loop going nowhere include constant bodily distress, endless anger, constant idealization, continuous guilt, extended hostility, persistent panic, substantial emotional and physical isolation and the unending need to replace the dead with another baby/husband/wife/mother/ father, and so on. What someone in grief needs replaced is not the person who has died but some of the things that person may have contributed to the relationship had they lived, such as love, friendship, physical touch, emotional support, listening and acceptance. If the expression of grief is choked in this way, the natural healing chemicals produced by the body become choked along with it. The immune system remains dysfunctional and is more likely to produce illness and disease. If grief continues to be suppressed, these illnesses can turn into more serious conditions such as rheumatoid arthritis, ulcerous colitis, asthma, anorexia nervosa and neuro-dermatitis. All of these can be chronic, incapacitating and sometimes fatal.

Research has found that mortality rates are roughly the same for widowed as for married women but are considerably higher for widowed men than married men [30] ; that widows with acquaintances who made it easy for them to cry and express their intense feelings were healthier than those who experienced less encouragement from others to weep and discuss their feelings of grief [31] ; and that more men than women die following a distressing major life event and men died at an earlier age. [32] Beverley Raphael's study of widows in Sydney, Australia, showed that illness was up to ten times more frequent amongst bereaved women than non-bereaved and that the death rate increased markedly. [33]

When your body remembers

In his book, *Swann's Way*, Marcel Proust experiences "gusts of memory" as he dips a Madeleine, a small cake, into his hot tea. For a moment he is confused and then he remembers his aunt giving him Madeleines when he was small. Most of us have had a similar experience to this. Caught in the midst of the now, a particular aroma, flavour, vision, sound or even a movement can obliterate the moment and plunge us instead into three-dimensional sensations from yesteryear. Why is this so?

Sad, happy, traumatic or exultant experiences and the whole range of qualities in between shape our sense of who we are, what we do and how we do it on a moment to moment basis. These experiences are retained in the body and become part of the body's matrix of ongoing survival. If we have undergone traumatic experiences, they produce stress and suffering. It has long been recognized by alternative practitioners that stress can be released physically from the body through acupuncture, Rolfing, therapeutic touch, Reiki, polarity therapy and chiropractic work. Whilst working physically on the body, practitioners often describe clients having a similar experience to Marcel Proust, a phenomenon known as somatic recall, the recall of memories of traumatic or other events that are stored in or accessed by the soft tissues of the body. Hence touching someone can release memory traces and even communicate them to another person. Physiologist J.Z. Young [34] goes further and suggests that the ways the body has been used or misused are incorporated into the structure of connective tissue. The organisms of the body then make predictions or "forecasts" that promote future survival. Biophysicists Oschman and Oschman, exploring the scientific basis for these complementary healing methods and alternative medicines, suggest that connective tissue structure contains the history of what the organism has undergone in its existence. These are genetic, indicating ancestral physical survival techniques, and acquired, detailing the preferences, routines and adversities we have each undergone in our lifetime. Collagen fibres orient themselves on the assumption that we will continue following the same patterns. [35] Body memory thus takes the qualities of the experiences of past events which have become incorporated into the soft tissues of the anatomy, files them away and then under appropriate circumstance, makes predictions for the future and holds onto these predictions as a survival mechanism until provided with a new pattern. If these "memories" are released and their direction reoriented through the help of alternate therapies, the body can build newer and more successful pathways for sustaining bodily and emotional health. If trauma remains locked into body memory, it causes disease.

Personal time and cyclic memory

Whilst physical recall is triggered by the senses, emotional recall is triggered by time. "Personal time" can be defined as the time which belongs to the landscape we shape by the things we do in that time. If we have encountered anxious, upsetting or painful events, then those memories will be recalled when time meets that same date again in a future cycle. Some of the reminders are full of warmth and love. A young man sent the following email to A Word A Day [36]:

> Word: Avid
> Quick note to say how much I enjoy AWAD. My brother David set me up with a gift subscription about a year or so ago. He died of cancer six months ago, so in an odd sort of way I'm still getting emails from him. Better still, on his birthday, 16 October, the word of the day was 'avid' - four letters from his name!

As a society, dates hold particular significance in our memory. Anzac Day (25th April) in Australia, Remembrance Day (11th November) in England, Australia and the USA (where it is called Veterans' Day), and Holocaust Remembrance Day or Yom Hashoah, (27th of Nisan in the Hebrew calendar which corresponds to April-May in the Gregorian or civil calendar) are a few examples of society's need to remember and venerate the past. We do the same on a personal level and whilst some dates are overt, like the anniversary of a death, many dates are unconscious until events remind us of similar

₁ that occurred during the previous cycle of time. For whilst science
duce us into believing that time is linear, the bases of all time are,
mostly, the orbit of the Earth around the Sun which gives us the period of a
year and, secondly, the rotation of the earth on its own axis which gives us the
day. This cyclic nature of the universe is the fundamental principle of astrology
and the organ through which humanity operates. As Bernadette Brady says:

> "We are led to believe in our busy, self-absorbing world that time
> is linear, that it comes to us but once and once passed, is lost for-
> ever. This may be true biologically in terms of your age and body
> but it is not true in terms of how you experience the world. Time
> is not based on a linear concept, visiting but once like a finite
> piece of string stretching off into the distance. Rather it is circu-
> lar, a loop, and consequently visits again and again and again. You
> do get a second chance with time and events, sometimes even a
> third and fourth chance." [37]

If every Monday you do a particular task, it is easy for you to base your internal
clock on this regular repetitive event. As human beings we respond to rhythms
and cycles, from the beat of our heart to the rising and the setting of the sun.
In Hellenistic astrology, the concept of revolutions or returns, that is, a planet
or luminary returning to its place of origin and defining the next segment of
time by the chart it constructs, was so important that the technique has become
part and parcel of modern predictive astrology. It has its counterpart in cyclic
memory. Time, returning to a point where a distressing event has occurred
and which has been anchored in some way by the body's reactions, will
inundate the body with that emotional and sometimes physical memory. Thus
Time is a shaped terrain of unconscious impressions, remembrances and learned
responses to which we return cyclically and react accordingly and grief becomes
a landscape through which we walk in Time. We can chart that landscape as
follows:

"The dangerous and death-bearing day" [38]

News of the death, however it arrives, binds with the emotions and locks
itself into body and emotional memory. Whether the result of a long illness or
a sudden and unexpected death, the date, place and corresponding gut feelings
containing both shock and disbelief, are caught in the net of time and anchored
as a significant event for the rest of the person's life. We see this most clearly
with the death of public figures and major events of great note. People
remember where they were and how they were feeling when they heard the
news of JFK's assassination, or learnt of the death of Princess Diana, or when
they saw the Twin Towers fall on 9/11.

However, if you are lucky enough to be with your loved one when ╵.
whether at home, in hospital or in residential care, and to stay with them ╷╵.
an elongated amount of time afterwards, you will be gifted with an opportunity
and a life-changing phenomenon precious beyond measure and profound in
its illumination, for this is a time where death and love can meet. Hearing is
the last sense to go as we die. My mother told me how she held my father's
hand through the long night as he lay in a coma, dying. She told him that she
loved him and he squeezed her hand. My aunt, sitting with her, noticed the
green lines on the oscilloscope flatten and as they continued to sit with him,
they saw his face change. Even though the body cools and the skin colour
pales, the face takes on a radiance and beauty all of its own. There is a feeling
of completion and wholeness and an understanding of this exchange of life
for death that is beyond reason and logic. Indeed by placing one's hand lightly
on the crown of the person's head, it is even possible, though not always, to
feel the life force streaming out as it leaves the body for hours afterwards.
Attending the body in this way gives us an understanding of the process of
death that is rare in modern society. "To be able to be around the body of one
who has just died for four or five or eight hours afterwards allows an
understanding of the process of death unparalleled in our experience," says
Stephen Levine. [39] For those who have experienced this, it becomes clear
that death is not the end of life but a time when whatever we term the essence
of the beloved ceases to inhabit the body. Isabel Allende calls this "midwifing
a person into death", in the same way as we midwife an incoming soul into
birth, never more beautifully portrayed than in the feature film *Big Fish*.

The funeral
The funeral is a public statement of changes that have occurred within the
larger community. Whatever role the one who has died has played in society,
whatever their age, a shift occurs and that shift needs to be acknowledged and
the roles adjusted. Funerals are the time when we pay our last respects to the
one who has died and dispose of the body in a manner which reflects their
life. It is when we become aware of the finiteness of time and the fragility of
life. Above all, it is where we make the first public statement about this deep
loss. Whilst funerals contain the rites and rituals society or religion demand
for the appropriate disposal of the dead, funerals are not for the dead but for
the living, the ones who are left behind. Funerals facilitate the healing process
through how much they mean to the person in grief. They serve to bring
together friends and relatives to share in the experience and to re-establish a
network of support through the time ahead. Accepting help and support from
others is essential at this time, for it is difficult to move through grief alone.

The funeral is both a personal reminder and an outward signal that the one in grief is beginning a process of inward reflection. Since our senses connect emotions to events, the music one chooses for the funeral and the clothes one wears become anchors which flood the memory with recall. A client told me: "We chose a piece of music for my father-in-law's funeral and for years I could never listen to it again because it had been anchored to his death." Clothes worn at the funeral often never get worn again, for the same reason.

One week later

The history of the week is uncertain but once established, there is no record of the seven-day week ever being broken. Today it is enforced by global business, banking and the media, particularly television. A week, like a carousel, is a contained unit. Generally we know the form of what we will be doing on each day of the week but not necessarily the content. As a result, many people describe sunset on the day one week later as the time when they feel at their worst. The day and the time set off an explosion of emotional memory connected with the death, a cloudburst of "memory pain" which is intense and emotional.

Four-to-six weeks later

Four-to-six weeks later the body's protective devices start to wear off, revealing the depth of the pain, the loneliness and the intense sadness. By now society expects a person to have "got over" their grief and supportive people are usually physically no longer around to help. Friends and relatives will do many practical and caring actions in the short term but at such a critical point, when a person needs to talk about their feelings, their confusion and how upset they are over and over again and to be heard without judgement, people around them are less tolerant of any demonstration of sorrow and anguish. As a result, people often feel like they are getting worse, not better.

The prelude to the anniversary

At around eleven months after the death, people in grief describe being flooded by the same feelings and reactions they experienced immediately following the death. This prelude to the anniversary of the death activates the body's emotional memory and can manifest as minor or even major infections.

The anniversary of the death

Overall, the first year is painful and intense and its turning signifies a huge milestone, for Time has now touched all important shared dates: birthdays,

Christmas Day, and so on. Now the spaces between the pain grow
often it is in this second year that one gains the full impact of the
that time has stopped forever for the one who has died. Frc
"Anniversary reactions" will inundate a person in grief with reminders of the
one who has died. This often means painful memories and the grief can return
with a deluge of sensations as full as their initial impact. A female client in
Australia had this experience:

> I saw my father for the last time in September 1993, five months
> before he died. Just before my partner and I left the house he said,
> "I want you to have the grandmother clock", a request I had
> apparently made to him as a young girl. The grandmother clock
> had been in our family for several generations. It wasn't valuable.
> I just loved it. And then he continued, quite out of the blue, "Don't
> forget us!" meaning both my parents, something he had never said
> before to me. When he died there was a dispute over who should
> get the clock. My mother wanted it to go to my brother, the eldest
> son, since he was the one who, at that time, had children. However,
> since my father had made this statement in front of my partner,
> my mother grudgingly agreed that I was now the rightful owner.
> Since I lived in Sydney and my mother lived in Brisbane, it had to
> be carefully packed and shipped. The clock arrived at our house
> on the first anniversary of my father's death. That afternoon my
> partner and I were shopping in the supermarket. As I placed a tin
> of fruit into the trolley, I was galvanized to the spot. The song
> playing in the supermarket was Nat King Cole singing *Unforgettable*.

And Then?

There is no hard and fast edge to this chronology. The "forever-ness" of the
death becomes increasingly apparent around six weeks and the intense
expression of sadness and despair is most acute in the first three months. The
first year of bereavement is immensely painful. It may be intense for the whole
year but there will also be periods between the peaks of pain when the person
in grief can sustain themselves quite comfortably and even enjoy events.
Anniversaries, Christmas, a birthday or a significant date in the calendar for
the family may trigger the pain and this often carries through into the second
year of loss. Mal McKissock refers to a person in grief in the first two years
following the death as "the newly-bereaved". Two years appears to be the
minimum time that a person needs to come to terms with the loss of someone
close to us and five years appears to be long enough to integrate this. However,
some people may take longer; some may take less. Any number of events can
trigger memories, engulf the present and surprise us by the level of distress

produced by small things. In that moment, the pitch and power of loss is as acute, present and at the same level of intensity as when the person died. The difference is that, as long as it is not suppressed, the inundating emotion does not last as long, nor does it incapacitate in the way it did in the first two years. Given that Time is the medium grief uses to change chapters in a person's life, then five years is a short distance to travel in reorganising our life in a way that is as meaningful to us as it was prior to the death.

One Person's Pathway

Ewan's brother, Paul, died from cancer aged forty-one at Easter, 2000. Paul was sixteen months older than Ewan, and he describes it as a close relationship in a close family. The following are some of Ewan's email correspondence with me following Paul's death. They are revealing in the range and intensity of his feelings and offer his unique perspective in the rainbow of options called grief in the first three years after the death of his brother:

Seven months after the death

23rd November, 2000:

> Back from the first big family occasion without Paul, an aunt and uncle's fiftieth wedding anniversary. My aunt had her own scrape with cancer several years ago, before Paul was ill, and we worried, of course. She's one of my favourite people but... I don't know quite how to say it... somehow it would have been easier to understand if it was her rather than Paul that had lost the battle. I hate saying something like that but it is true. The day was a bit of a struggle. I didn't deal with it too well but my Dad opened up a little for the first time. We went through his diary of Paul's last few months. I'm intrigued and proud of the fact that Paul insisted on getting the bus in to hospital, rather than getting a lift, just nine days before he died. There are times when I wonder what more I could have done and then I am reminded what fierce independence we were dealing with. A year ago Paul had just spent a week in hospital, told a white lie to get out (that our younger brother would be at his flat to look after him) and then emailed us all with Martin Luther King's *Free At Last* speech. And I've just remembered this one. My younger brother was driving with Paul through the Devon countryside one night a couple of years ago when they saw a man with a scythe climbing over a gate. "Tell me," says Paul, "that you saw him too." I know I have to keep talking about Paul and writing about him. I'm terrified of boring my friends, although

to be honest they insist they understand. I can't bottle it up. I have his face beaming down from a photo among his music and his books and it takes nothing to set me off. What I wish is that Paul had been able to say to me that he didn't think he was going to survive. I would have done things differently.

27th November, 2000

I've been thinking hard about your question about what I would have done differently. It even kept me awake last night. About a year ago he and I went on a train journey to the place where we grew up (and left in 1973) and the only specific words I remember from all our conversations that day were him saying, "This isn't going to kill me." I'm sure he was convinced of that then. Five months later he was dead and somewhere in between I think he changed his mind but he never told me. His death shocked me because I still believed him. I knew he was really ill but I didn't think it was near the end. If I'd known, I would have told one of his oldest friends, his best man, who hadn't seen him for two years, to go and see him quickly. He lives the other side of the country and has lots of kids and money is tight but he's been so upset at not seeing Paul more recently, although they talked on the phone. If I'd known, I would have spent a pointless weekend with him in his flat. He loved his independence but he wouldn't have said no. I had saved my holiday allocation from work for later in the year in case he got ill and I needed to take time off but that seems silly now. I know that I had to devote time to Rachel and Brenna (my wife and daughter) too, but if you know someone's time really is so short, it would be understandable to see him more. If I'd known, I would have rung him every day, not once or twice a week. The last time I saw him alive, two days before he died, are two things that give me comfort. We were talking, alone, and he talked about what he wanted done with his ashes (we would talk about such things occasionally). For a second I wanted to rush to his side and grab him and tell him everything he meant to me, how I couldn't imagine things without him, no doubt getting highly emotional at the same time. But I stopped myself and I'm glad because it would have frightened the hell out of him (as well as me) and made him think I thought the battle was over. He knew how I love him anyway and he was so brave I just couldn't buckle then and I asked him if talking about his ashes meant he was pessimistic and he said: "Hell no, I've just bought my season ticket for Somerset Cricket Club!" We laughed and I felt better and now I wish I'd said, "But seriously Paul..." And, secondly, when we said goodbye,

Rachel, Brenna and I were getting in the car and Paul wasn't with us because he was so breathless he couldn't leave his flat and I got this sudden urge to run back to him, which I did, and I told him, as he lay on his new red sofa, that I would be with him as much as he wanted me to be, that he had to be honest with me and ask me to come even if he didn't think I'd want to and he agreed and seemed touched and I went and that was the last time I saw him alive. If he'd told me then (and it would have been an ideal time), what could I have done? The next day I spent with his children and he went into hospital, and the following one we were about to leave to visit him in hospital when the call came that he'd died. Honestly I don't know what I would have done differently. (This email could have started with that sentence and saved us both a lot of time.) Thanks so much for writing. I can't tell you how you've helped.

Nine months after the death

6th January, 2001

Rachel has been incredibly sick. She's eight weeks pregnant today. We've only told our families. We had a miscarriage before Brenna was born, so we're taking it cautiously. It has perked us all up a bit. "It's brought us some sparkle back," Dad said. I can't believe we're having a baby Paul never knew. I'm so happy about it, and Rachel, too, but I'm still mourning for Paul, so feel a bit mad, up and down but some sense of renewal I can't really express. Odd. I was born sixteen months after Paul was born, and if all goes well this baby will be born sixteen months after Paul died. I had an email from a journalist friend at Christmas saying her youngest sister was knocked down and killed by a van in the city. She was buried on her twenty-first birthday. Odd (again) how dealing with other people's grief somehow helps us come to place our own.

Paul came up in a conversation with a bloke at work the other day, someone I don't know that well, and he said, "Do you miss him a lot?" That is the dream question for me. I could have kissed him. A hard question to ask but the one I hope for. It's the people who have the courage to ask without thinking you're going to crumple in a heap on the floor, or not minding if you do. I've been going back over my time with Paul, looking at our relationship and crying like he died last week which is how it feels. I miss his wit. I miss his calls on Saturday morning with the kids. I miss his voice. I miss his enthusiasm. I miss his awkwardness. I miss the face he would make as he peeled oranges.

Ten months after the death

7th February, 2001

Looking at my history with Paul has made me realise we were re-ally OK with each other. We had always spoken honestly with each other. Did I tell you he wrote letters for us all for after he died? We had ups and downs but downs never lasted long. There's not an awful lot of baggage and I can say that honestly, having gone through things over and over. Maybe more will come up in time but that's really how it is now. Step by step. "You were bril-liant Ewan. You played a blinder," he wrote to me. Still wish I'd done more though. Rachel had her first scan today, and the baby is looking fit and well, which is a huge relief. Came out of the hospital and rang our families from the cafe nearby. Missed telling Paul terribly. He is so tied up with this new life, doesn't matter if it's a boy or girl, he/she will be forever linked with Paul.

18th February, 2001

Had my Dad on the phone last night. Somehow it opened it all up in me, immediately and deeply. All that new strength I felt was beginning to arrive has evaporated again. Missed Paul more last night than ever. Somehow. This grief thing is like nothing else, isn't it?? My birthday in a couple of weeks - when I reach forty-one, the same age he'll be for ever.

The anniversary of the death

12th April 2001

We're down to see my parents this weekend, along with my younger brother and his family. Rather like last year in fact. Except, ex-cept. Something slipping over me about Paul. Can almost physi-cally feel it. Thanks for helping me this last year.

Fourteen months after the death

28th June 2001

A beer with one of my oldest mates who spoke at Paul's funeral. Talk about work and babies and house prices and, inevitably, Paul. Sets me crying. Met another old friend the other day whose son was killed in a fire at the age of twenty-four a couple of years ago. No body for her to look at, he had to be identified by DNA. Paul's life is rich and full compared to him and I realise how lucky we were to say goodbye to his lovely crumbling old body. She remembers practically nothing of her son and I remember practically nothing of Paul. Is this at all common? Is it a human reaction in helping us to cope, because if it is, I don't want it. I want more memories please.

Seventeen months after the death

10th September, 2001

(In late August Rachel gave birth to a little girl, Celeste). If she had been a boy in some ways the connections to Paul may have even been too strong. I can sense the disappointment in some people's voices when they hear she is a girl, thinking perhaps that I wanted a boy. I didn't. I wanted a life, a new life that would breathe back happiness and renewal and corny-sounding stuff like that. When Rachel had gone with the nurse for a shower a few hours after the birth, I told Celeste all about her Uncle Paul and how I wish they could have met. I miss the enthusiasm and excitement he would have had at the news. On Thursday I will be exactly the age Paul was when he died. But he'll always be my big brother. Reading this I sound so glum but I'm fantastically happy about Celeste. Weird emotions.

Twenty months after the death

3rd December, 2001

George Harrison's death rather shook me. I'd say that it brought it all back about Paul's death, except it's never gone away. I knew Harrison was really ill but you hope it's not that. I had an hour or so out of the office but it was Paul that I was crying about, not Harrison.

Twenty-one months after the death

4th January, 2002

I hate the speed of time. 2001 is the first full year Paul never knew. I now cannot say he died last year. I don't want the waters to close over him. I want everyone to be shocked still that he can be dead at forty-one. That's what I hate about a new year.

The second anniversary of the death

9th April, 2002

I'm no monarchist but seeing the faces of the royal family at the funeral of the Queen Mother on the news today brought it home how grief touches us all. Nobody could have less in common than the Queen Mother and Paul - nobody - it makes me laugh thinking how on earth they could - but I was changing 'she' and 'her' to 'he' and 'him' in the funeral service and I liked what I heard.

Two years and three months after the death

2nd July, 2002

Just got through the second anniversary of scattering Paul's ashes. Made me feel quite aware that I'm going at a different speed to everyone else. I still want people to be shocked but realise that just saying "two years ago" makes it sound like an age.

Two years and eleven months after the death

3rd March, 2003

I got Tony Benn's [40] latest diaries for Christmas. His wife died of cancer a few months after Paul in 2000. Reading about it got to me. I wrote to him and had a good card back the other day telling me about his elder brother who died in WW2 aged twenty-two. He says he still misses him, nearly sixty years later. I realise I get some kind of comfort from writing to people Paul knew or admired to get some reaction. I still love telling people about him. The other day I was assembling Paul's rambling old sound system that I inherited and Brenna, who was "helping", said, "Do you wish Uncle Paul was here to help us?" (because he would have done it in two minutes) and I said I did and she said, "He would probably have forgotten how to do it by now because he did die a long time ago." To her maybe.

The third year

21st December 2003

I was talking to Brenna about my deputy editor who recently gave birth to a dead nine pound baby boy and she said how sorry she was that she didn't meet him before he died. I would sooner she and Celeste didn't grow up afraid of talking about death but it's hard to know the right way to go about it. I congratulated my deputy editor and her husband on their large collection of Christmas cards but she said most of them were bereavement cards she hadn't taken down yet!

o the Future ...

The future is a place which does not contain the beloved. This painful and often shocking fact takes time to comprehend. When we are used to our lives being witnessed by those close to us, when the slow build of history and the continuity of a life lived together ends, it seems impossible for life to continue on without one's loved one. Death freezes that relationship in the countryside of Time. A statement like "Had she lived, Anne Frank would have been seventy-five years old this birthday" may be true but it is irrelevant. Anne Frank will always be a young woman at puberty with all the potential of her life ahead of her untimely severed by the actions of World War II. So it is with those we love. We can only imagine the portrait time might have painted of their lives. The reality is that now they never change, neither in looks nor in temperament. Life no longer has any effect upon them. They remain "my older brother" or "my father who died when I was eleven" or "my two month old baby" no matter how old we grow. What does happen, if they are older than us, is that when we reach the age they were when they died, we realise just how young they were and how much more of life they could have had to live.

When I was in my late teens and still living in Perth, Western Australia, my home town, I read an article published in *The West Australian* newspaper announcing the death of a poet at the age of twenty-three and lamenting the end of his promising career. The family had published a book of his poetry privately in remembrance. The book was entitled *Light Me A Candle* and the poet's first name was Michael. Profoundly moved by the poem, I memorised it:

> Tonight there's a mother whose child has died
> rocking herself to sleep,
> With her fingers curled for the touch of her son
> who lies in a bloodied heap.
> She does not dream of a brave young man
> with a rifle, a curse and a girl,
> She dreams of a shy and loving lad
> who lived and was her world.

For years I kept the newspaper clipping until finally it became lost in the caravan of my life. Now Time has washed away the details, the name of the poem, his surname, and how and why he died. If anyone reading this can fill in the pattern, please let me know. In 2004 Michael would have been in his mid fifties. I can make that leap. Even knowing he died at twenty-three, I can imagine him a successful published poet climbing to the peak of his life. The family can't do this. Freeze-framed in memory, he stays that age. The home movie ends halfway through the first reel.

Death shakes us to the core of our being and puts us into a unique place with the one who has died. If the work of grief has been accomplished, then life re-establishes itself in concert with a newly-formed relationship with the dead, not forgetting them, not immobilized by the loss but embracing what has happened and moving on with life. It is an important step to reach. It means a person can start building a relationship with the beloved without expectation of their return.

Returning to the world

Grief is a powerful process which grips a person's life. It is painful and that is part of its unspoken contract with us. It lets us know that for a time, things have changed. Like a broken bone, grief must be properly set in order for it to heal and function with strength once more, so any action a person in acute grief takes to articulate the pain is healthy. Achilles' reaction when he heard the news of Patroclus' death was an expression of the intensity of the pain he was feeling on the inside. It was not a conscious decision on his part; it was helping him to survive. When someone yells, kicks, screams or howls, their behaviour is neither bizarre nor pathological, nor will they become violent, even though in Homer's work Antilochus held Achilles' hands "for fear of him cutting his throat." The person is simply doing what he or she needs to do in order to stay alive by expressing what they are experiencing and how they are feeling. However it is conveyed, people in grief are communicating their perception of reality. For them the pain is valid, physical and needs to be communicated. If we stop a person from doing this, it bottles up. If we impose a feeling of guilt on them for acting in this way, we encourage this suppression. Blocking grief can throw the person into secondary symptoms, such as depression or weight gain. There is nothing we can say that will take away this pain, nor does it need to be taken away. The pain "is". However, since we are unaccustomed to seeing the expression of grief in the community, because we placate it and hide it away, we are generally not aware of the intensity or duration of the pain involved unless we've experienced it ourselves.

Hamlet is the story of a man in grief for his murdered father. Through the journey of the play he is awakened to death and comes to realise that death makes life possible:

> "Not a whit, we defy augury. There is a special
> providence in the fall of a sparrow. If it be now,
> 'tis not to come; if it be not to come it will be now;
> if it be not now, yet it will come. The readiness is
> all..."[41]

"Readiness" allows us to fully participate in life and to wholly engage in the ritual of loss when it occurs. Further it allows us to return to a changed and different world, changed because we are changed, different because we are no longer responding in that way we did before the loss.

The process of grief takes time. Grief is the recognition of a deeply-felt loss, a necessary process for a person to go through in order to be able to collect the shards of life that fragmented with the death and to go on living fully again. The process of grief is one which heals and its expression should never be equated with weakness. It is a rite of passage.

✳   ✳   ✳

Endnotes

1. Homer. *The Iliad*, trans. E.V.Rieu. (1966) Harmondsworth: Penguin Books, pp.337-338.
2. James, J. W. and Friedman, R. (1998) *The Grief Recovery Handbook* (Revised Edition), New York: Harper Perennial.
3. Swan, Norman. 'Bereavement and Grief'. Transcript of a broadcast 14 January 2002, at http://www.abc.net.au/rn/talks/8.30/helthrpt/stories/s441997.htm - accessed 3rd February, 2003.
4. Population figure from the US Census Bureau: http://www.census.gov/ - accessed 28th April, 2004.
5. http://www.ifishoulddie.co.uk - accessed 3rd February, 2003.
6. ibid.
7. Bee, Peta, 'Love Drug: Why Women Are Getting Into Anabolic Steroids', *The Independent On Sunday*, London: 2nd March 2003.
8. http://www.grief-recovery.com/request_index.htm - accessed 13th February, 2003.
9. http://www.grief.net/Media/Wall_Street_Journal.htm - accessed 24th February, 2003.
10. Lockyer, Daphne. 'Falling Back On Hard Times'. *The Eye*. London: The Times, 10th - 16th January, 2004, pp.12-13.
11. Leunig, Michael. (1991) *The Prayer Tree*, Melbourne: CollinsDove.
12. Lamm, Maurice. (1969) *The Jewish Way in Death and Mourning*, New York: Jonathon David Publications, p.1.
13. http://www.globaleduc.org/Spretnak.htm - accessed 11th February, 2003.
14. Brady, Bernadette (1999) *Predictive Astrology: The Eagle and the Lark*, York Beach: Samuel Weiser. *Predictive Astrology* covers at length the nature of fate in a client's predictive work.

15. Kubler-Ross, Elisabeth and Warshaw, Mal. (1982) *Working It Through*, New York: Macmillan Publishing Company, p.134.

16. Waldrop, Mitchell M. (1993) *Complexity: The Emerging Science at the Edge of Order and Chaos*, New York: Simon & Schuster, p.295.

17. ibid. pp.330-331.

18. Rennie, Bryan (1998), 'Mircea Eliade' in *Encyclopaedia of Philosophy*. Routledge at http://www.westminster.edu/staff/brennie/eliade/mebio.htm - accessed 1st March, 2003.

19. Campbell, Joseph. (1988) *The Hero With The Thousand Faces*, London: Palladin, p.391.

20. McKissock, Mal. (1985) *Coping With Grief*, Sydney Australia: ABC Enterprises, p.14.

21. Lewis, C.S. (1963) *A Grief Observed*, New York: Bantam Books, p.8.

22. Frey II, William H. with Langseth, Muriel. (1985) *Crying, The Mystery of Tears*, Minneapolis: Winston Press, p.16 and passim.

23. Frey also found that both emotional and irritant tears contain about thirty times more manganese than is found in blood serum, suggesting while the lachrymal gland lacks the filtering apparatus of the kidneys, human tear glands can still concentrate and excrete substances from the blood or other body tissues. In sea birds like gulls, albatrosses and cormorants, and some marine animals, like seals and saltwater crocodiles, tear glands are more powerful than kidneys at removing toxic levels of salt from the body.

24. Dickens, Charles. (1907) *Oliver Twist*, London: Chapman & Hall Ltd, p.266.

25. Tennyson, Alfred, Lord. 'Poems Of Alfred Lord Tennyson.' *Great Literature Online*. 1997-2003 at: http://www.underthesun.cc/Classics/Tennyson/PoemsOfAlfredLordTennyson/Poems OfAlfredLordTennyson5.html - accessed 6th May, 2003.

26. op.cit. Frey (1985) p.108.

27. Kottler, Jeffrey A. (1996) *The Language of Tears*, San Francisco: Jossey-Bass.

28. Iles, Susanne. (2002) 'The Storied Garden: Planting the Seeds of Myth', *Spirituality and Health Magazine*, Summer 2002 at: http://www.spiritualityhealth.com/newsh/items/article/item_4577.html - accessed 26th May, 2003.

29. Physiotherapist Sarah Key is the author of *Body In Action, Back In Action* and *Sarah Key's Back Sufferers' Bible* (the latter two with forewords written by His Royal Highness The Prince of Wales). Her website is http://www.sarahkey.com. She was interviewed by Margaret Throsby on ABC Radio Classic FM, Australia, 7th February, 2000.

30. Helsing, Knud J., Szklo, Moyses and Comstock, George (August 1981) 'Factors Associated with Mortality after Widowhood', *American Journal of Public Health* 71 pp.802-9.

31. David Maddison and Wendy L. Walker, (1967), 'Factors Affecting the Outcome of Conjugal Bereavement', *British Journal of Psychiatry* 113, pp.1057-67.

32. Dianne Hales, 'Psycho-immunity', *Science Digest* (November, 1981), pp.12-14.

33. Raphael, Beverley. (1984) *The Anatomy of Bereavement*, London: Routledge.

34. Young, J.Z. (1975) *The Life Of Mammals: Their Anatomy and Physiology*, 2nd Edition, Oxford: Clarendon Press.

35. Oschman, James L. and Oschman, Nora H. (1995) 'Somatic Recall Part 1 - Soft Tissue Memory', *Massage Therapy Journal*, Vol. 34, No. 3. – at: http://hmrtec.com/somaticrecall1.html - accessed 16th February, 2003.

36. Word A Day is an online service which sends a vocabulary term and its definition to thousands of subscribers every day, providing them with the magic of words: http://wordsmith.org/awad/awadmail.html.

37. Brady, Bernadette. (2002) '2002 Cycles Within Cycles', *Wellspring Astrology Guide*, p.5.

38. Hermes Trismegistus. *Liber Hermetis*, trans. Robert Zoller. (1998) Brisbane: Spica Publications, p.28.

39. Levine, Stephen. (1982) *Who Dies?* New York: Anchor Books, p.220.

40. Tony Benn was born in London on 3rd April, 1925, the son, grandson and father of MPs. He is widely regarded as one of Britain's "greatest living Parliamentarians" (a Tory backbencher) and many polices he championed for which he was widely belittled, have entered the statue books. He retired from the House of Commons in May, 2001, after fifty years in Parliament. http://www.tonybenn.com/Biography.html and http://www.bennbiography.com/thebook.html - both accessed 20th May, 2004.

41.Shakespeare, William. 'Hamlet', (5.2.157-160) in *The Norton Shakespeare*, eds. S. Greenblatt, W. Cohen, J.E. Howard and K.E. Maus. (1997) New York and London: W.W. Norton, p.1751.

Encountering Proteus
The paradox of time without end and time passing

Time		Reaction	Feelings
ACUTE GRIEF: the initial response	THE FUNERAL / THE FIRST FEW WEEKS	Shock and disbelief. Fear. Reduced concentration. Numbness - may last moments, hours, days, sometimes months.	Tearful. Restless and agitated. Changed eating habits. Physical responses such as backache, headache, chest pain, diarrhoea. Emotional highs and lows.
DISINTEGRATION: the period of disengagement from the world	4-6 WEEKS	Pain. Intense sadness. General feelings of nervousness. Loneliness, isolation and despair.	Increased crying. Need to talk about feelings over and over again. Bodily distress. *Predictive work in this period will be acute and reflect these behaviour patterns.*
	THE FIRST 2 YEARS "the newly-bereaved"	Belief and disbelief. Extreme yearning, pining and anguish. Finality not yet real – hoping for a "return".	Overt grief. Preoccupation with the image of the one who has died. May hear or see them. Dreams of the one who has died are vivid and of a different quality to "normal" dreams. No major decisions. Healing process in action.
	Can last from 2-5 years	Sadness. Despair. Helplessness. Fact and permanence are real. "Anniversary reactions" will trigger reminders of the deceased.	Disorganisation of life style. Preoccupation with memories. Grief "comes in waves". *Predictive work in this period will allow the client to begin to reorganise their lives and be effective.*
REINTEGRATION back into the community in a new and productive role.		"Out-of-the-blue" return to feelings of sadness and despair.	Re-establishing previous relationships and activities but in ways that are irrevocably changed. Developing new friendships. Initiating a lifestyle that has reinvigorated energy and strength underpinning it.

2
Cultural Attitudes to Grief :
The Patterns of Childhood

My soul is a broken field, plowed by pain.
Sara Teasdale, poet (1884-1933)

The play *Kids' Stuff* by Ramond Cousse opens with an eight-year old boy who has just been to a funeral:

"And I lay down on the bench with my grey coat so as
not to catch cold and I said to myself let us try

Let us try to be dead

Let us try I lay down on the bench and I said to
myself it is so I am dead

I am dead as I had seen it in books on television in
the newspapers everywhere at war in the movies at the
cinema…" [1]

From this compelling opening we are plunged into the young boy's review of his eight years of life as he seeks to understand the death of his best friend, Marcel. His rich and vivid memories of their friendship, including both of them spying on Marcel's sister as she engages in sexual activities with the local butcher's apprentice and the impassioned speeches of their frenzied schoolmaster, captures the innocence, the wonderment and the sumptuous imagination of childhood. Finally the young boy's reminiscences bring him back to the funeral:

"The priest arrives everyone gets up but the priest says
You can be seated my brethren

He lifts his arms to the sky he sings he drinks from a big
glass

You must not weep my brethren

He says that if everyone weeps it is because everyone
believes that Marcel is dead

But rejoice my brethren I am going to announce the good news
Marcel is not dead he is in eternal life

I rejoice Marcel was not dead anymore the priest said it
in his church

Marcel is not dead anymore we continue anyway with the funeral..."

The funeral procession weaves its way to the cemetery. Marcel's coffin is lowered into the grave and people throw water onto it but witnessing this ceremony does nothing for the young boy's grasp of the situation:

"I went back the next day to the edge of the hole to help
Marcel come out but there was not any more hole just some
fresh dirt and white flowers

I was happy I said to myself Marcel got out all alone I run
to his father's house I go up to his room but Marcel's father
says to me

Where are you going my child

I am going to get Marcel

My child you know well enough that Marcel is no longer with
us that he is dead forever

I say no Marcel is alive the priest said so in his church"

This is the boy's first real encounter with death. Although he has seen hearses pass by his house and observed that only some of the people walking behind the hearses weep and whilst he has witnessed the butcher slaughter sheep and cattle and young calves and felt sadness at their demise, loss has not really impacted on his young world, for Marcel is his best friend and Marcel is the one with whom he fights and plays corks. Now Marcel is gone but where has he gone? They say he is dead but what is dead? They say he is in Paradise but where is Paradise? The young boy looks for understanding amidst his uncertainty. Instead the words of the priest only confuse and frighten him, for Marcel's father tells him that Marcel is dead forever. The young boy runs back to the church and confronts the priest. The priest lifts his arms to the sky.

"It is almost time for mass. Let us hurry my child if you
want to do your first communion someday to enter into eternal
life someday."

In trying to come to grips with his desolation and despair, the small boy has been cast aside by the religious adult world. All he can do is live with the bewildering torment:

"I did not know if Marcel was dead if Marcel was alive
I did not see him anymore ever in the street I did not see
him anymore ever in his room anymore ever at the cemetery
I did not see him anymore ever anywhere

I did not see Marcel anymore ever anywhere I only saw him
in my head at night when he told me to go wait for him in
his room."

So he visits Marcel in his dreams but in his dreams the young boy is placed into a coffin and carried through the streets in a hearse. His family and community follow in a line and he is lowered into an empty grave. At first he is joyous with the anticipation of seeing Marcel again "at the bottom of the hole". Instead he finds himself alone, abandoned alive in the grave in the darkness with dirt thundering onto the top of the wooden coffin and only the distant sounds of laughter to comfort him:

"I only hear from a distance the line that is leaving
having a good laugh and which says

How to answer my child those are words my child those
are words my child those are words my child those are words

those are words"

This work exemplifies how a young child is denied the opportunity to learn how to manage his pain and anxiety at the loss of his dear friend because no-one around him really knows how to deal with their own deep and immense sorrow. Instead what he learned about grief from this encounter was to not talk about death, to bottle up his feelings and to isolate himself. His young ship was suddenly idling in the bay on the isle of Pharos. What was he seeking that could have lessened his distress? What might he have learned from this experience which would have given him a firm foundation when he encountered loss the next time? For if statistics are to be believed and we lose someone through death once every nine-to-thirteen years, then this boy will surely come face to face once more with grief between the ages of seventeen and twenty one years, again (approximately) in his mid-to-late twenties, again (approximately) between the ages of thirty five and thirty nine and again (approximately) in his late forties. Unless informed otherwise, he will approach loss and grief in the same way as he has been taught to do here, here at its formation unfolding before us.

How Do We Learn To Grieve?

There are many ways we can, like Menelaus, founde in the bay and they occur extremely early in our lives. On many levels in western society we are taught to focus only on the surface of life and not to explore the depths. Through the circumstances of loss we rapidly learn that other people cannot or do not want to handle strong emotions and across our life we build up unconscious responses about how to deal with them. Sadly, within a short time after a death, even though we may be feeling the exact opposite, we are socialised to respond to the question: "How are you?" with the woefully inadequate term, "Fine".

Body Replication

If we examine body memory, touched upon in Chapter One, more deeply, we start to get a clue about what this young boy was patterning in this encounter with grief. Oschman and Oschman [2] describe the living tissue of the body as an interconnected molecular continuum or "living matrix" where a force introduced in one part of the body is rapidly transmitted throughout the entire system. This means that all systems within the body are aware of and in tune with all other systems and help sustain free movement and emotional fluidity. Restrictions occur when infection, physical injury and emotional trauma alter the properties of the fabric. These restrictions teach each cell of the body how to react. When faced with new problems or difficulties, our muscles and nerves scan for and use blueprints learned on earlier occasions. My teacher of directing and playwriting at NIDA (National Institute of Dramatic Art), Paul Thompson, drilled into us: "You only get one opportunity for a first impression." He was, of course, referring to someone seeing a production we had directed or reading work we had written but its application to emotional trauma is no different. The body gets one opportunity to be "impressed" and to lay down the ground plan for its future strategy of how to deal with emotionally-fraught issues. Unless consciousness is brought to bear, this ground plan runs ad infinitum: we repeat patterns which were established early in our lives when we were under extreme tension and our ability to process information effectively was weakened. Functions such as personal identity, the developing ego, our self-understanding and our perception of "the other", where we locate ourselves in the world and what we believe we can and cannot achieve are cross-referenced to what we have learned and remembered from previous encounters. If these references are to traumatic past experiences which resulted in pain, fear, anger, critical self-judgement, paranoia, false sentiment, guilt, restricted perspective or narrow interpretation, then, say Oschman and Oschman, they will be reflected in our physical and behavioural resilience:

how we move, how we walk and talk, how we react to the world, as well as how we respond emotionally. Freedom of movement and thought combined with awareness of our internal and external worlds will be dramatically reduced. Unless our small boy silently grieving for the loss of his dear friend, Marcel, finds a way to change his perception, he will use this same inadequate model to process and deal with later grief experiences, the results of which may be debilitating and occasionally lethal. *Kids' Stuff* was based on Cousse's own early experiences and adapted from his novel *Enfantillages*. Cousse was born on 20 April, 1942 at Saint-Germain en Laye in France.He wrote three successful dramatic monologues which he performed himself and took his own life on 22 December, 1991 at the age of forty-nine. [3]

Emotional Replication
We are a map of our parents, learning from them how to react emotionally and how to be in the world. One has only to observe small children and their parents together to see the patterns of mimicry that are unconsciously at work. Our parents teach us what they have been taught which is what our grandparents taught them and our great-grandparents taught our grandparents. This way of passing on information travels forwards through the generations. Our emotional history contributes just as much to our personal identity as our genetic makeup contributes to our physical stature. So it is with grief. Initially we learn how to grieve from our parents but if they have been taught incomplete ways of expressing and dealing with loss, they will pass on emotional replication. By refusing to talk about death with the young boy in *Kids' Stuff*, his family and his community were teaching him to repress his feelings. When we are discouraged from expressing strong emotions, our sense of isolation increases, for we are acutely aware of an undercurrent of disapproval and condemnation and sensitive to the fact that our actions are being judged and criticised. In a short time we learn superficial behaviour patterns that no longer exposes our vulnerability. What the young boy knew about death came from an illusion:

> "I am dead as I had seen it in books on television in
> the newspapers everywhere at war in the movies at the
> cinema..."

His community, the priest, continued that illusion:

> "Marcel is not dead he is in eternal life"

And finally not even his mother can help him:

> "I ask my mother loudly what does it mean eternal life
> but my mother says softly One must not talk at funerals"

As small children we all want our parents' love and approval. The young boy grasps from his mother's reaction that, even at the funeral, the place where it would have been at its most appropriate to talk about the death of his best friend, he must not do so. We assume adults know what they are doing. This is often a false assumption.

Society has developed the following injunctions to keep us from talking about our feelings of intense loss:

"Be strong. Your children need you."
"If you're going to cry, go to your room."
"Keep busy. You'll deal with it better."
"What's done is done. You have to move on."
"Put on a brave face to the world."

These statements do nothing to help us resolve the accumulation of emotions that arise as a result of the loss. The unspoken message is: "Don't show your feelings" but grief is, by definition, the emotional response to loss.

Annie, a woman now in her late forties, remembers an event from her past which illustrates this restrictive belief:

"In 1978, when I was twenty-three years old, my father committed suicide after my mother left him. We, as a family, drew together and didn't receive counselling. I couldn't talk about my father's death for many years. Even now I am greatly saddened by the whole event. My brother, who was the one who found him, was the most affected. I still can't watch movies where people shoot themselves. My husband advised me not to discuss this with anyone, so I didn't. It was only years later that I told my best friend what really happened."

"...Weep and you weep alone"

Grief is an experience with which we have been struggling for thousands of years. Throughout history the catharsis of crying has consistently been articulated in poetry and literature. Two thousand years ago, Horace, (Quintus Horatius Flaccus, 65 - 8 BCE) the son of a freed slave in Rome who became one of the nation's greatest poets, gave voice to this feeling:

"As man laughs with those who laugh,
So he weeps with those that weep;
If thou wish me to weep,
Thou must first shed tears thyself;
Then thy sorrows will touch me."

Ars Poetica (V. 102)

Ovid (Publius Ovidius Naso, 43 BCE - 17 CE), the son of an old land-owning class of equestrian rank and one of the most prolific poets of Rome's Golden Age, impassioned:

> "It is some relief to weep; grief is satisfied and carried off by tears."
> *Tristium* (IV. 3. 37)

And later:

> "Suppressed grief suffocates, it rages within the breast, and is forced to multiply its strength."
> *Tristium* (V. 1. 63)

Ovid's influence was felt from the Middle Ages to the Renaissance and his works shaped such Italian poets as Ludovico Ariosto and Giovanni Boccaccio and such English poets as Geoffrey Chaucer, John Gower, Edmund Spenser, William Shakespeare and John Milton. Egeon (5.1.298-300; *The Norton Shakespeare*, p.728) in Shakespeare's *The Comedy of Errors* declares:

> "O, grief hath changed me since you saw me last,
> And careful hours, with Time's deformed hand,
> Have written strange defeatures in my face."

Proverbs handed down from generation to generation resonate with the benefits of psychogenic tears:

> "Learn weeping and thou shall gain laughing." (*German*)
> "Tears soothe suffering eyes." (*Persian*)
> "What soap is for the body, tears are for the soul." (*Jewish*).
> "He that conceals his grief finds no remedy for it." (*Turkish*)

Yet how often did our parents tell us: "There, there, don't cry, it's alright." "You stop your crying or I'll give you something to cry about." "Please stop that crying, you're making your mother feel bad/upset/giving her a headache." Such unsupportive reactions manipulate a child into believing that crying is a sign of weakness, vulnerability and immaturity.

One way behaviour gets lodged into the culture is through popular song. An example of this is *Crying In the Rain*,[4] the battle cry of someone wounded by love who refuses to let anyone see them shedding tears. Even though their heart is broken, they have been taught that it is brave and courageous to hide their feelings, so using pride as a shield, they'll do their crying in the rain. We can perhaps trace this attitude back to the latter part of the nineteenth century, when American poet, journalist and free thinker, Ella Wheeler Wilcox (1850-1919), gained wide popularity with her nearly forty volumes of verse. Although never regarded as a major poet, she was widely published in women's magazines and literary magazines and by 1919 was sufficiently well-known to be included in *Bartlett's Famous Quotations*. [5]

She enjoyed favourable admiration and esteem and earned a comfortable living as a writer, a rare feat for women of her day. Her poetry was simple and mixed platitudes with sentimentality and though literary critics failed to be impressed, her messages of hope and comfort touched the hearts of readers of all ages and classes. Whilst her name may not be well-known, one of her lines of verse is now common parlance when it comes to grief:

"Laugh, and the world laughs with you;
Weep, and you weep alone."

Solitude

First published in *The Sun*, 1883, when Wilcox was thirty-two years old, thence in *Poems of Passion* [6] and in other newspapers in the years following, her poem continues:

"For the sad old earth must borrow its mirth,
But has trouble enough of its own…

Rejoice, and men will seek you;
Grieve, and they turn and go.
They want full measure of all your pleasure,
But they do not need your woe.

Be glad, and your friends are many;
Be sad, and you lose them all.
There are none to decline your nectared wine,
But alone you must drink life's gall…"

Wilcox had a mass following amongst the non-literary at a time when newspapers and popular magazines regularly published verse for the unsophisticated. She encouraged these people to struggle through dull, unrewarding lives for the greater good of what they could achieve on a divine level.[7] A sizeable audience sought comfort and wisdom from her words, so when this widely-read and well-received poem disseminated the idea that solitude and isolation were the appropriate solvents for the pain of grief, crying and grieving openly became unwelcome traits to cultivate, a social bias that has continued to this day. Yet research has found that healthy males and females are more likely to cry and have a more positive attitude toward tears than those with ulcers and colitis, two conditions thought to be aggravated by stress.[8]

Some years ago I was watching our (then) three-month old kitten carefully observing our older, head cat of some fifteen years. The older cat, who had a skin allergy around her mouth, was scrubbing her face vigorously with her paw after eating to alleviate the itch. Being young and impressionable, the small kitten also began to scrub his face, believing this was the way to wash on completion of a meal. After two or three scrubs he stopped. This action hurt his face and was uncomfortable on his whiskers. Not long afterwards I saw him wash his face with the soft, gentle action he maintains five years on in time. He had learned that if putting a deed into action hurts, he must change the action. Like other animals, we, too, copy the behaviour of our elders when we are young and looking for models by which to live. Considering our greater brainpower, it seems much harder for us to stop a learned behaviour when it hurts us. It takes an effort of will for us to consciously change a pattern of behaviour and often it is painful to do so, which may be why we continue to run that pattern, yet in the long run it is worth it, for the consequences of that change makes us free.

Avert-and-Smother

Misconceptions our parents, unconsciously and with deep care, teach us about loss and which become enmeshed into the matrix come in this form: "Don't feel bad, have a lolly." "Don't cry, we'll get you another... (animal)." "Don't worry, there are plenty more fish in the sea." On the surface these statements tell us to divert the pain by focusing attention elsewhere and then use a substance or an object to bury the problem. However, there are also unspoken commands embedded in communications such as these. Think back to a time when someone told you not to look at someone: your immediate reaction was to look at them. In order "not" to do something, a person has to know what it is they are not supposed to do. In telling someone "don't do X" they will automatically access the opposite command. So an instruction like "don't feel bad" is, on first impact, received as an injunction to "feel bad", "don't worry" is an embedded command to "worry", and so on. Such "double-messaging" results in a confused response. Our reaction is to reach for a short-term solution designed to bandaid or overarch the problem: Eat Something. Buy Something. Replace It With Something. Food, alcohol, prescription drugs, illicit drugs or narcotics, a shopping expedition ironically termed "retail therapy", one's work, one's anger or simply becoming lost in fantasy and illusion are amongst western society's temporary palliatives. Such words dismiss the value of the relationship and do nothing to complete the emotional pain caused by the loss. It also sets up a lifetime belief that feelings can be fixed by a short-term solutions. The truth is that our focus may have been distracted but such analgesics are not an answer. The loss and the network of feelings welded to it are simply smothered and entombed. We collude in the illusion that immediate release from pain gives us long-term underpinnings of consolation and ease. If we continue to use the "Avert and Smother" method with successive losses, life begins to implode. If no-one is willing to face the grief, it festers.

"What do I say?"

"There are so many people worse off than you." "You'll find each day will be a little easier." "So how are you managing without a husband?" "Separation is much more painful than bereavement." People are often immobilized with awkwardness when they hear news of a death. They have been taught that saying something totally inappropriate is better than saying nothing at all, so they offer the trite and the banal. However, what the person in grief hears is a tactless comment coming from someone completely unqualified telling them how they should be feeling right now. Ill-chosen words reduce the internal experience and stop communication. A person in grief needs to be acknowledged, not silenced. Worse still is when what is offered is a hackneyed and worn-out cliché. A cliché is a truth that began life as authentic but which has long since outworn its welcome. Often used as "plug and play" features in articles, they become inserted without thought as to their truth or appropriateness and sustained without the rigour of critical assessment. Why is glibness so excruciating? Because it clearly states that the person has no idea of what they are saying and has never allowed themselves to tackle the desolation of loss and to be truly insightful about it. Here's a recent and public example. In March, 2003, a twenty-six year old mother was paddling a canoe carrying herself and her three young children down a swollen river in Peru. When the canoe capsized, she managed to rescue all three of her children but before she could save herself, she was swept downstream by the rapids. One tribute to the family read: "She was an incredibly brave woman who died saving the things most precious to her." This accurate and warm-hearted statement was then diminished by the following platitude: "Let this be of help to you, knowing that she gave her life for the worthiest of all causes." Although well-intentioned, the message, placed on the Internet [9] where it can be accessed by many and rammed home as fitting, clearly disregards not only the inappropriateness of the canoe trip but also the crucible of mental agony in which the family now found themselves. It voids reality by putting illusion in its place, likening her to a soldier in combat.

In Series Three, Episode Four of the American television series *The West Wing*, [10] President Jed Bartlett (Martin Sheen) is given the task of informing the parents of two Americans that their sons, aged nineteen and twenty-one, have been the deliberate targets of a suicide bomber in Israel. What can he say? "My wife and I were terribly sorry to hear of the - ..." "Please accept our deepest condolences on the occasion of - ..." Finally he lifts the receiver to his ear: "Mr and Mrs Levy? This is President Jed Bartlett. I have three daughters. I have no idea what to say." Rather than cluttering the airwaves with unspoken fears, such communication opens a door to allow the other party to speak. People in grief need to ventilate what is happening on the inside of their reality without censure and without trepidation about the other person's reactions.

"I know how you feel!"

If you want to shrink the experience of the person in grief and deny the immediacy of the pain, tell the person in grief you know how they feel. If you want to kidnap the personal encounter of another as they confront loss or trivialise the unrepeatable and exclusive experience of their suffering, tell them you know how they feel. As each relationship is distinctively different, so no two losses are the same. The only common reality grief shares with each of us is the encounter with Proteus and any of the accompanying grass roots responses outlined in Chapter One but how each person engages with Proteus is their personal journey. It takes courage to realise that it is impossible to guess at the pain of another in grief, nor even to begin to imagine how they must be feeling. All we can do is remember a time when loss tore us to the quick and the desolation and heartache that stayed with us for months and sometimes years was almost unbearable. The word empathy comes from the Greek "empatheia" (from "em-" meaning in and "pathos" meaning feeling) and means the ability to understand and share the feelings of another, to be in-feeling with them. It was first used in the 1920's by American psychologist E.B. Titchner when observing one-year olds imitating the distress of another person. Empathy focuses the listener's attention on the inner feelings of the other and asks that they spend more time listening and less time talking. When you tell someone that you know how they feel, you indicate that you are about to replace their experience with yours, that the urgency of their pain and their need to put this into words are being hijacked by someone with little feeling for their circumstances. It takes boldness and daring to be with a person in the fullness of their grief, neither condemning nor condoning, neither afraid of their loss nor the fears inside us, accepting and observing, listening and loving.

Comparison

"Be glad you already have two other children." "Be glad you are still young enough to have another baby." Every loss is felt emotionally as a major loss. Author and humorist Mark Twain (1835-1910) observed, "Nothing that grieves us can be called little: by the eternal laws of proportion a child's loss of a doll and a king's loss of a crown are events of the same size." This is a truism through all time and in all cultures and such comparisons are odious: firstly, they fail to recognise that intense feelings are intense feelings for whomever or whatever they are felt and need to be dealt with in the moment they happen in order to facilitate healing; and secondly, that whilst the length of time required to complete any unfinished business may differ, it is the quality of the relationship and the deeply-felt separation that causes pain. The loss of an animal friend may be just as intense and painful as the loss of a human relationship. It depends on the age at which the loss occurs and the nature of that relationship.

"You never get over the death of someone close to you."
This belief is so ubiquitous one has to wonder about the nature of the secondary gain in saying this. Here's how it seems to work: the initial pain of the loss becomes anchored to the memory of the person who has died. Believing life is linear, we then, incorrectly, assume that if we stop the pain, we stop remembering. The fear is that if we bound back into our lives with our grief complete, we will lose the memory of the person forever, so we come to define ourselves by the pain of the loss and not by the memory of our relationship to the whole person. To add to the complexity, if the death has been the result of an accident or a long-term illness which has ravaged the body, many people remember the person they loved only in these final, difficult moments, freeze-framing their life on this image, despite the fact that the many years prior to this have been happy and joyful ones and running that loop time and time again.

Here are two examples: Jane, a female client in her mid-thirties, whose mother's family are extremely close, has lived in Birmingham all her life. Her Aunt Deirdre, her mother's sister, met Uncle Andrew when they were at high school in the 1940s. They were married after the War and stayed happily married. However, three years ago her Uncle Andrew, then aged seventy-two, died suddenly from a massive heart attack, the first of her mother's generation to die. "Aunt Deirdre has been in an awful state ever since," says Jane. "Not so long ago she broke down on the phone to my mother, confessing she still can't sleep because she keeps seeing Uncle Andrew collapsing in the doorway over and over again." When Jack, the male client in the case study in Chapter 5, offered to go with his ex-wife to the cemetery to visit his son's grave seven years after his death from a brain tumour, she replied that she appreciated his gesture but, unlike him, she had never been able to have any happy dreams or thoughts of their son, they were always nightmares. Her memory can only extend back as far as the last weeks, the horror of how he looked and the last moments of him dying. Such behaviour is the result of strong emotions caused by major and profound loss but the way the behaviour has been managed is inappropriate, for such memories are heavy burdens to carry for the rest of one's life. Inside us we carry many images of our loved ones in all their life expressions. My client whose father died unexpectedly at the age of seventy wrote this three weeks after his death:

> He was a King Lear
> An ancient Celtic King
> Who filled everybody's lives
> With tears and with joy,
> With sadness and happiness
> And anger and peace.
> In short, he was a total father.

Resolution does not mean forgetting. Through the work of grief what we are resolving and completing is our relationship to the pain caused by the loss. As James and Friedman note, pain does not equal love, love equals love.

Time and the Work of Grief

One of the most misunderstood clichés is that "time heals all wounds". In a radio interview, Gretel Killeen [11] tells of a key moment in her life when she was twenty years old. She and her boyfriend of four months were returning from the snowfields and were in a car accident. He died. She did not. "I didn't know how much that changed me," she says. "I felt his parents had the right to grieve and I didn't want to swan in and take the stage." So she buried her grief. Her next comment is revealing. She says that the common notion that time heals all wounds is incorrect. "Time," she says, "makes you realise you'll never find anyone else like that." Time itself does not heal anything, for Time is not an actor on the stage of life. Time is the medium through which we move and it dulls our memory the further we slide away from the event, adding a coat of dust on all the unspoken, uncompleted things we need to say, clogging, debilitating and finally choking our behaviour. We ourselves have to initiate and take action within a time frame in order for completion to occur. The action we take is the clutch plate between how things were and they way they can become. The work of grief is an active process, not a passive one, yet it requires nothing more than paying attention to the natural process that occurs inside a person when someone we love dies.

Memory, the natural process

Memory is the ability to retain an impression of past experiences. We build up memories of someone close to us through a life-long process which combines continuity and change through daily interactions. Over time the relationship embraces the whole ocean of gestures, signals, fine distinctions, subtle shadings

and individual idiosyncrasies of everyday living which Celia J. (
"tell me the other is who I perceive him/her to be, and which in turn, ᵢₑₜ
know he/she recognizes me." [12] Gradually knowledge specific to, and only
accessible by, each other is developed into a secret language understood solely
by the two people within the relationship. Each takes this so much for granted
that it is not even called "knowledge" by either person. The relationship
develops its own unspoken boundaries and newly formed boundaries have to
be renegotiated. This builds up expected ways of relating that are taken for
granted and sustains and maintains the other's identity. Relationships occur
in absolute, clock time and are calendar-specific in how they begin (the first
meeting, the birth of a child) and in how they continue (anniversaries and
celebrations, as well as routines such as dental check-ups or weekly coffee
meetings, and so on). The paradox is that whilst the narrative of the
relationship is expressed through the passing of objective time, the relationship
is experienced and undergoes change in subjective, "lived" time through
created moments which have significance and value and in which both parties
of the relationship place meaning. Memories, good and bad, sad and happy,
excruciating and exhilarating, are socially constructed within the context of
the two interwoven lives. The relationship also anticipates a future in which
events will occur and are part of the unspoken agreement between the two
people. This knowledge and identity of the other is processed into long-term
memory through encoded information but memories will always flush from
the brain unless some process attracts them to stay. Sleep is the mechanism
that appears to strengthen and integrate what we have learnt into our system. [13]
A full night of normal sleep is characterized by a succession of sleep states and
stages. [14]

Research at Harvard University revealed the following: the deep, slow-
wave sleep that occurs even in short naps allows recently-learned information
to be organised and digested in order for new knowledge to be acquired and
that training on a motor task and motor skill learning is maximised in the
critical final Stage 2 NREM sleep which occurs in the two hours just before
natural waking. [15] What this suggests is that people who sleep until they wake,
rather than being woken by an alarm or having their sleep time cut short in
some way, give their brains the optimum chance of learning and consolidating.
Healthy sleep must include the appropriate sequence and proportion of NREM
(slow-wave sleep) and REM (rapid eye movement or dreaming) phases, which
play a different role in the memory consolidation-optimization process [16] and
morning sleep and afternoon naps aid mental and physical functioning.

Sleep bolts into long-term memory data we have encountered in uptime.
Small children sleep so much because they are processing a glorious abundance

of original and fresh material. If you have ever visited museums or art galleries for the first time, studied different skills or moved into unfamiliar learning fields, you will do the same. Sleep occurs in direct proportion to the original information you are registering. The directive to "sleep on it" reflects the theory that restructured memories produce new creative associations in the morning. In the days, weeks, months and years of relationship, we not only witness the continuing identity changes of each other through the social construction of memory but consolidate these changes through sleep and build thousands of minutes of memories. When someone we love dies, this natural and ongoing process stops and another natural process takes its place called Life Review.

Life Review
In 1955 Robert N. Butler undertook the first long-term studies of healthy, older people aged sixty-five and above. [17] Similar studies were conducted at the same time at Duke University, Durham, North Carolina, USA. Both found identical results, that healthy older people in the community were mentally alert and active. As his studies progressed, Butler found a fascinating secondary phenomenon. He noticed that the imaginative faculty and memories of the past of these older people contained great power and luminosity and that their ability to recall early parts of their life, events and people which may long since have been sorted and filed, could come flooding back into the present with crystal clarity. When it did, there was a desire to complete the memory, rather like completing a jigsaw. Indeed the primary concern of this profound internal process appeared to be the desire to re-examine events in order to come to terms with what had happened in the past. Butler called this the Life Review and concluded that this was a normal function of later years. Using memories, reminiscence and nostalgia, it was neither the pathological condition of someone living in the past nor the confusions of a wandering mind. Instead it was an important psychological task of making sense of the life a person had lived as it neared its end. The life review can occur under peaceful conditions, remembering events with pleasure or communicated through storytelling, or it can contain regret, homesickness and sentimentality. It may be told to passers by, door to door salesmen, people in the street or to anyone who will pay attention or it may take the form of a personal interior monologue made audible to no-one's ears but the person's own. Life reviews can be convoluted, contain discrepancies and fallacies and are frequently filled with as much bitterness as humour. The aims of the life review are to smooth out past differences, to compensate and make amends for lost opportunities and to bring an end to hostilities with family members and friends, often after

years of lost time. It is designed to heal psychic pain through putting one's life in order and in so doing, take the necessary steps towards death by reducing any anger, fear or apprehension. It is most striking in old age and in recent years a variety of psychotherapeutic techniques have been developed using this natural process, including life review therapy, guided autobiography and structured life review therapy. As well, a number of life review and family history training manuals have been developed to guide older people on their journey. [18] The Reminiscence Centre in Blackheath, south-east London, UK, deems the memories of ordinary people and their everyday life in the first half of the twentieth century to be of such importance to the nation's heritage that they have established a centre, a museum, a theatre and an exhibition space in which to collate them. One of its functions is to act as a catalyst for groups of visiting older people to "stimulate long-since-forgotten memories and help them to learn more about one another's past experience." [19]

The life review and grief
This desire to form a complete picture in a way that gives new significance and meaning to one's life is exactly the same process that arises spontaneously when one is confronted by death. When a loss occurs, we are immediately flooded with memories of the entire relationship with all its positive qualities and all its difficulties. This is the raw material which the work of grief uses. Our memory searches for what was not communicated or brought to completion in the relationship and continues to work on evaluating this material from the unconscious until there is resolution. This review is at its most intense and most detailed immediately following the death of someone close to us. That is why most people in grief want and need to talk about the death, the circumstances surrounding the death and their relationship with that person or event immediately following the loss, for they are beginning their own automatic grief review process. The play *Kids' Stuff* is the grief review of the eight-year old friend of Marcel. Likewise, the feature film *Big Fish* [20] is both the life review of Edward Bloom (Albert Finney) and the grief review of his son Will, (Billy Crudup).

Why do we need to do this? As a species, we naturally seek completeness and whole pictures. The plays, films and literature from which we gain the most enjoyment are those that allow us to be actively involved. As playwright Jeffrey Sweet notes: "Our goal as playwrights is to engage the audience in our characters and their dilemmas. The way to get an audience engaged is to stimulate them to fill in for themselves what is left unsaid." [21] So it is with grief. Grief is an active process, not a passive one. As soon as a person in grief becomes aware of this natural review process going on inside them, the work can begin. [22] This work has been described by psychotherapist Alexandra Kennedy as a series of tasks, one of which is "to let the non-negotiable and excruciating reality sink in that you will never again be in the physical presence of your deceased loved one." [23] This work is necessary for our mental, emotional, physical and spiritual health. It ensures that we continue to remember our loved ones as we knew them in the fullness of their life rather than allowing painful memories of how they died or any anger at the circumstances surrounding the death to superimpose themselves upon happier recollections and consume us; it is designed to help us not be frightened of our grief; and it means that as we emerge from our period of mourning, we continue to have a life of significance, value and input, even though our lives have been radically, dramatically and irrevocably altered.

How do you know if grief is unresolved?

Unresolved grief is the sand still flying in your eyes from a loss that occurred many years ago. Unresolved grief, like other unresolved actions, takes a person out of the present moment into conversations with people who are no longer physically there, separating us from current circumstances by perpetually keeping us in a loop of the past. "Frozen sadness" is the term used by Pauline Boss.[24] If someone fears the intense torment of grief and is resistant to thinking or talking about the one who has died or any other trauma or adversity in their life, if they only want to talk about the positive aspects of the relationship or consider only the negative aspects, if thinking about the relationship brings up fears or affectionate recollections become distressful, then they may be experiencing unresolved grief. When a minor event triggers an intense grief reaction, when someone is unwilling to move any material possessions belonging to the deceased, when they convey a false euphoria or persistent guilt and lowered self-esteem after the death, when they make radical changes in their lifestyle following a death or when they exclude friends, family members, and/or activities associated with the deceased from their life, it is likely the person still carries unresolved grief. [25]

A sudden or traumatic death, a fatal accident, a terminal illness or murder, can evoke great rage, guilt, shock, disbelief or a desire for revenge. In such cases the process of grief can become obstructed and repressed and cause symptoms similar to post-traumatic stress disorder, including survivor guilt, extreme agitation, intense sensitivity to stimulus, and uncontrolled and unwanted thoughts. When death is connected to issues that are sensitive in the community, such as AIDS or suicide, the person can feel such extreme shame or confusion that they are unable to express what the loss means for them or even allow themselves to be conscious of their feelings. [26]

Unresolved grief is Menelaus unable to move from the bay. The solution is for the individual at some conscious or unconscious level to request to see Proteus, otherwise the grief becomes embedded and rigid or another death occurs, which gives the person a renewed opportunity to face Proteus.

Grief puts us through the meat grinder. It takes over and floods our lives. When we lose someone to death, observes psychologist Peter Marris, [27] we don't use the verb in the same way as when we "lose" our car keys. It is that the laws of gravity no longer work. In reclaiming a new centre of gravity, we encounter the work of grief.

❀   ❀   ❀

Endnotes

1. Cousse, Raymond. *Kids' Stuff*, trans. Katharine Sturak(1984) Melbourne: Australian Nouveau Theatre Publications. In programme notes for the Ensemble Theatre's 1998 season Sturak wrote:

> "Built like a mini-tank, a compulsive talker and hearty eater, he had just returned from the Avignon Festival in the south of France where he had had great success performing the boy in *Kids' Stuff*. I was instantly entranced by the profound simplicity of the character, and the universal experience of childhood that he had captured in this largely autobiographical work. The perfection of his text needed no interpretation, no adaptation. It simply is, like a prayer, like a mantra, and translating it was effortless."

2. op.cit. Oschman and Oschman (1995).
3. http://www.chez.com/raymondcousse/index.htm - accessed 9th March, 2003.
4. Words and music by Howard Greenfield and Carole King.
5. http://womenshistory.about.com/library/weekly/aa122900a.htm - accessed 2nd May, 2003.
6. Wilcox, Ella Wheeler. (1883) *Poems of Passion*, Belford, Chicago: Clarke & Co.
7. Garraty, John A. and Carnes, Mark C. (general eds.) (1999) *American National Biography*, Oxford: Oxford University Press. 23, pp.371-372.
8. op. cit. Frey (1985) pp.107-108.
9. http://news.bbc.co.uk/1/hi/scotland/2849095.stm - accessed 15th March, 2003.
10. *The West Wing* was created by Aaron Sorkin in 1999 and produced by John Wells Productions in Association with Warner Bros. Television.
11. Gretel Killeen is an Australian who started her career as a stand-up comic.

She works as a voice-artist in advertising and appears regularly as a humourist on Australian national TV and radio. She is a best-selling children's author and has written in excess of twenty-two books published in Australia, Britain, Europe, Asia and Canada. She was interviewed by Margaret Throsby on ABC Radio Classic FM, Australia, 1st December, 2000.

12. Orona, Celia J. (1997) 'Temporality and Identity Loss Due to Alzheimer's Disease' in *Grounded Theory In Practice*, eds. Anslem Strauss and Juliet Corbin, Thousand Oaks: Sage Publications, Inc. p.182.

13. Professor Gyorgy Buzsaki and his team at Rutgers University found that sleep "spindles" (bursts of activity from the neocortex) are followed tens of milliseconds later by "ripples" in the hippocampus. The team posits that this interplay between the two brain regions is a key step in memory consolidation. Sirota, Anton, Csicsvari, Jozsef, Buhl, Derek, and Buzsáki, György, 'Communication between neocortex and hippocampus during sleep in rodents' in *Proceedings of the National Academy of Sciences* 100, pp. 2065-2069; published online before print as 10.1073/pnas.0437938100 – accessed 4th March 2003.

14. In a healthy adult, the transition from wakefulness to sleep(Stage 1 NREM, alpha and theta activity) is followed by Stage 2 NREM (non-rapid eye movement) sleep (theta activity, sleep spindles and K complexes, both involved in keeping person asleep by decreasing sensory awareness). At this point, the person is sleeping soundly but if they are awakened, they will deny having been asleep. This is followed by Stages 3 and 4 NREM (delta activity, "slow wave sleep"). At this point, the person is in deep sleep and, if they are awakened, they will act groggy and confused. If nightmares occur, the person will not report a story but an emotionally-charged situation. This is followed by a period of REM sleep where dreaming happens. If they are awakened, the person appears alert and attentive and if they have been dreaming, they will recite a narrative-type story. This then completes the first sleep cycle. The two sleep states (NREM and REM) continue to alternate throughout the night with an average cycle lasting about ninety minutes. A full night of normal human sleep will usually consist of four-to-six NREM/REM sleep cycles. Stage 2 sleep represents about fifty percent of a full night of sleep. http://home.epix.net/~tcannon1/Physioweek7.htm - accessed 2nd April, 2003.

15. Sara Mednick and her colleagues at Harvard University investigated the role of sleep in perceptual learning in adult humans (July, 2002 *Nature Neuroscience*) and Matthew Walker and his collaborators at Harvard observed motor skill learning (July 3, 2002 *Neuron*): http://www.nimh.nih.gov/events/sleep.cfm - accessed 2nd March, 2003.

16. http://www.nature.com/nsu/010426/010426-15.html - accessed 2nd March, 2003.

17. http://www.hospicefoundation.org/laterlife/butler.htm - accessed 13th February, 2003.

18. In Great Britain, Age Concern England (http://www.ace.org.uk), the largest charitable movement in the UK concerned with the needs and aspirations of older people, offers: Gibson, Faith. (1998) *Reminiscence and Recall*, London: Age Concern England and Gibson, Faith. (2000) *The Reminiscence Trainer's Pack*, London: Age Concern England. See also: Lynn, Joanne and Harold, Joan. (1999) *Handbook for Mortals: Guidance for People Facing Serious Illness*, Oxford: Oxford University Press.

19. http://www.age-exchange.org.uk/htm/reminiscence.htm - accessed 7th March, 2003.

20. August, John (screenplay) 2003. From the novel by Daniel Wallace. *Big Fish*. Producers: Richard Zanuck, Bruce Cohen and Dan Jinks. Director: Tim Burton © Columbia Pictures Corporation, USA.

21. Sweet, Jeffrey. (1993) *The Dramatists Toolkit: The Craft of the Working Playwright*, Portsmouth: Heinemann, p.11.

22. op. cit. James and Friedman (1998) suggest asking the question: "What do you wish had been 'different, better or more' "? p.61.

23. http://www.alexandrakennedy.com/index.html - accessed 14th March, 2003.

24. Boss, Pauline. (1999) *Ambiguous Loss: Learning to Live with Unresolved Grief*, Cambridge, Massachusetts: Harvard University Press.

25. http://www.indiana.edu/~famlygrf/units/complicated.html - accessed 15th March, 2003.

26. *Sometimes Grief Becomes Complicated, Unresolved or Stuck*: http://www.4therapy.com/consumer/life_topics/item.php?uniqueid=5102&categoryid=438 - accessed 14th March, 2003.

27. http://www.indiana.edu/~hperf558/spring97/unit1.html - accessed 12th March 2003.

3
Proteus: Fight, Flight or Freeze

O, how shall summers hunny breath hold out
Against the wrackfull siedge of battring dayes…
- Shakespeare, Sonnet LXV

How does a chart encounter Proteus? How does a chart resolve and complete matters? What do we look for in the charts of other people to know how they will respond to grief? For grief is not just "the 8th house" or "a Pluto transit". It is a complex interweaving of responses which are both inherent within the chart and taught to us. The way we allow people, issues and objects to leave our lives is determined by the parental signatures in the natal chart, for these are the earliest messages we receive about how to let go. However, since grief is, by definition, the emotional response to loss and the process of adjustment to a new situation, it is the algorithm of the Moon in the first instance that gives us an understanding of how a person will process such an event. Added to this is our history, determined by our age and life experience, which defines the context we bring to the loss and which shapes the specific animals, monsters or demons into which Proteus is likely to turn.

The algorithm for how the Moon handles loss

+

Our history which impregnates Proteus

The algorithm for how the Moon encounters Proteus is described by the following:

- the zodiac sign in which it is placed natally
- the house it rules or in which Cancer is intercepted
- whether it makes any aspects to the Sun or other planets [1]
- whether via its zodiac sign it has any dignity (rulership or exaltation)
- whether it suffers any loss of dignity (detriment or fall)
- whether it has strength through being angular, succedent or cadent
- how it engages with the world through its modality - cardinal, fixed or mutable

- what it fears, for written into the Moon is the behaviour we
exhibit when we are feeling fraught or under stress.

Indeed Jan Hunt [2] argues persuasively for a return to attachment parenting, a natural child-rearing approach practised by parents for most of human history which stimulates feelings of self-worth, confidence and trust through extended breast-feeding, family co-sleeping and minimal child-parent separation. She asserts that the baby's ability to touch and hear their parents during the dark hours of the night is their only means of knowing that they have not disappeared, the presence of the parents helps to regulate the baby's heart rate, blood pressure, body temperature and sleep cycles and their breathing synchronises the baby's own breathing. Unfortunately this is not the experience of most babies born in the twentieth and twenty-first centuries where modern birth procedures combined with placing a baby in a crib at night often reinforces a difficult natal Moon configuration. When a baby embeds internal subjective hurt at or around birth, it gives rise to deep-seated, repetitive, destructive patterns and unconscious emotions such as shame, guilt, fear, distrust, a distorted reality and difficulty feeling and bonding, causing a person to build walls of emotional scar tissue which can take years to repair.

Using these technical details as a framework, the questions to ask on a psychological-behavioural level are:

- what is the initial expression (theme or issue) of the Moon in combination with the Sun or another planet?
- How is this behaviour maintained through early childhood, adolescence, young adulthood?
- Does this theme or issue have an option to change?
- If so, when and how?
- What are the behavioural difficulties or consequences in mature adulthood for the expression of grief?

Recognising that the most difficult aspects of the Moon in the natal chart will be with Jupiter, Saturn and the outer planets, as these represent encounters which take time and life experience to understand, we can look at how the Moon imprints nurturing at birth (and sometimes pre-birth) and as a consequence how a person bring those behavioural needs into play when it comes to expressing grief.

When the Moon encounters the Sun

Romeo: "But soft, what light through yonder window breaks?
It is the east, and Juliet is the sun."
- Shakespeare, *Romeo and Juliet* (2.1.44-45)

A Moon-Sun aspect describes a person whose emotions are intimately connected with their sense of self, their power and identity in the world. Mother and father theoretically carry this energy equally for the child; however, whilst the newborn displays their emotional needs, no matter how basic or unformed, they will project their Sun onto their father-figure to carry for them as they learn to become their own Solar Hero. This journey takes place slowly over some thirty-five years and is continually modified by the person's emotions. Hence in grief the person is more likely to identify purely with their emotional responses and leave functioning in the wider world to others. Forced to re-evaluate their sense of identity, they will readily abdicate their natural authority and look for someone else to take charge and, under the stress of loss, may become angry at God or religion. The angle between the Sun and the Moon will also identify the lunation phase under which they are born which will have a bearing on their desire to step forward into grief or to evade it. Someone born with a natal balsamic lunation phase can more readily understand and accept loss, for the background emphasis of their life is of letting go and shedding. However, the zodiac sign and house position will also have a bearing on how this is expressed. For example, if the Sun and the Moon are both in Aries, where impatience and anger flood the emotions, and in a natal balsamic lunation phase (Sun in 12th house, Moon in 10th house) this will express itself quite differently to them both being in Libra and where the Sun is in the 1st house and the Moon is in the 12th house.

When the Moon encounters Mercury

> Bassanio: "Madam, you have bereft me of all words,
> Only my blood speaks to you in my veins,"
> Shakespeare, *The Merchant of Venice* (3.2.175-176)

A Moon-Mercury aspect indicates an emotional communicator. Mother is seen as someone for whom thinking, writing and talking are a direct experience of how she feels and it is from her that the child learns to equate roving curiosity, knowledge for the sake of exploration or organised, factual knowledge with emotional security. However, with this configuration, emotions can cloud a person's judgement and reason. Under the pressure and tension of grief, they may sign documents in haste based on their emotions, such as putting a family house on the market too soon or selling personal items too rapidly, actions they may regret later. Thus when encountering the loss of someone close, they may need longer to process their grief in order to gain a clear-eyed perspective. This is the configuration of someone who can verbalise their emotions but in the sadness of loss they may also find themselves speaking out irrationally.

When the Moon encounters Venus

> But since she prickt thee out for womens pleasure,
> Mine be thy love and thy loves use their treasure.
> Shakespeare, Sonnet XX

A Moon-Venus aspect describes someone who relates on an emotional level. Mother is experienced as a person who achieves rapport with people through her feelings; the child learns that relating is both sensual and emotional and that their idea of beauty, harmony and what brings them joy, together with their socialising and networking skills, are conditional upon how they feel. Indeed with this aspect, emotions can often cloud a person's relationship needs, so that, when faced with the death of someone close to them, the cascade of feeling will propel them to seek greater support from their social network. It can also heighten their desire for sensual pleasure as a way of feeling emotionally secure. If they are fearful of delving into this emotional space, they may use sex, lust, passion and an over-indulgence of food as a stop-gap against the devastating pain of grief.

When the Moon encounters Mars

> Viola: "I have heard of some kind of men
> that put quarrels purposely on others, to taste their
> valour…"
> Shakespeare, *Twelfth Night* (3.4.216-218)

A Moon-Mars aspect describes someone who takes action based on their emotions. It is one indicator of a fast birth or where cutting is involved in the delivery and often designates the child who had fever as a baby, for these are the physical manifestations of the newborn's earliest experiences of mother, perceived as highly-energised and assertive or irritated and aggressive. From her the child learns that emotions fuel initiative and determination. In the chaos of grief, where emotions are erratic and unpredictable, insecurity can easily turn into anger and rage. If the person is unable to contain that rage through safe pathways, such as physical exercise, they will pick a fight or cause an argument as a way of dealing with their feelings. This can take the form of minor quarrels or major feuds which never get resolved.

When the Moon encounters Jupiter

> Malvolio: "In my stars I am above thee, but be not afraid of
> greatness. Some are born great, some achieve
> greatness, and some have greatness thrust upon 'em."
> Shakespeare, *Twelfth Night* (2.5.125-127)

A Moon-Jupiter aspect indicates confidence and optimism based on instinct and emotions. In a best case scenario mother is seen and felt as abundant,generous, loving and emotionally explorative; in a worst case scenario, as emotionally excessive. This is either the blessed mother who brings nobility, fame and glory to the child, the larger-than-life mother who is the great educating force in the child's life; or the reckless, wild and lavish mother. From her or from her father (the child's maternal grandfather) the child inherits a love of emotional risk, continually anticipating the possibility of bountifulness; or wasting time and money on gambles which never return their investment. The death of someone close to them will intensify the normal roller-coaster emotions of grief, bringing extremes of mood swings from over-excitement to depression. If this becomes uncontrolled, it can cause accidents through carelessness. Depending on the configuration of the Moon and Jupiter in the chart, the person may find they are over-indulging in food, alcohol, drugs, fantasy and betting as an avenue for expressing their emotions, or they may turn to religion and become enthusiastically devout.

When the Moon encounters Saturn

> Even so my Sunne one early morne did shine
> With all triumphant splendor on my brow;
> But out, alack, he was but one houre mine;
> The region cloude hath mask'd him from me now.
> Shakespeare, Sonnet XXXIII.

The background myth embedded in every Moon-Saturn aspect is the myth of The Expulsion From Paradise. Inside every human psyche there is the memory of a place where all one's needs are met, where there is no hunger or temperature change and where they are totally protected and sheltered from the outside world. This Garden of Eden is the womb and, whilst the power to recall this utopia and one's banishment from it exists for everyone, people whose charts contain a Moon-Saturn aspect feel it as a personal trauma. The post-birth procedure separates the baby from its mother in some way, denying the newborn immediate access to her touch, smell and heartbeat. Coldness and hunger set in and become anchored to isolation and rejection and, through no fault of the mother, the infant does not make an emotional bond with her. Instead what gets established is an unconscious separation anxiety and a profound well of loneliness, for the baby still seeks this mythic place of nurturing and protection and feels illogically wounded that they have been thrust from the source of it in this way. Without language these sensations are translated into insecurity, inadequacy and a deep-seated fear of rejection. Initially projected onto the mother (or mother-figure), the infant experiences her as emotionally austere and as someone who doesn't like being touched. As a consequence, the child has issues with hugging and touching, will not put themselves into situations where they are emotionally vulnerable and suffers unconscious abandonment issues. Hence they are often confronted with two irreconcilable demands: a dislike of being touched; and an acute "skin hunger", the instinctive need for physical human connection that remains unfulfilled, leading to feelings of anxiety, an inferiority complex, a fear of being ostracised and never feeling that they have enough. A person with a Moon-Saturn aspect is sensitive to cold and this is a clue as to when the person feels emotionally rejected, for when that part of the psyche that is cold, hungry and little reaches out to get its needs met, the natural response by the adult part is to copy what it learnt from its mother-figure which is to reject it.

The biggest obstacle for someone with a Moon-Saturn aspect is learning to give to voice their emotional needs, particularly when the person is in grief, for the death of someone close will intensify the isolation and separation and express itself as emotional restriction, loneliness, coldness, hunger and inadequacy. If the person is unable to surface from the chasm of loss and disconnection, emotional solitude may well become a habitual state; worse still, the issue may get driven into the "too hard basket" of their unconscious and become smothered with comfort eating and weight gain. The key as an adult is to find that tiny, emotionally-starved part of the psyche and to share with it the resources one has developed in maturity, in effect allowing it to grow up, for this small part that feels rejected has not previously had access to the adult's emotional resources. Metaphorically this small, rejected part of the psyche needs to be allowed to come in by the fire, to be cuddled, loved and nurtured. If such behaviour is going to emerge with some awareness, it will do so at the Saturn Return when skin contact through therapeutic massage or training the body in ways that allow it feel physically safe and in control, such as T'Ai Chi or yoga, can help that part to feel emotionally secure. Then the pain, pathos and emotional emptiness eases and as this tiny part of the psyche learns to resolve feelings of denial, low self-worth and being shunned, the coldness lifts. Any Moon-Saturn aspect brings emotional, gut-rending pain when young and needs to be reconciled before the adult can achieve emotional satisfaction but if this issue is not understood before the person encounters major loss, then loss exacerbates the emotional wound. In its mature form, the Moon-Saturn aspect gives the individual solidness and consistency of emotions and an ability to voice their emotional needs. This is one of the most painful aspects to have in a chart and it affects males and females in the same way without discrimination.

When the Moon encounters Uranus

> In faith, I doe not love thee with mine eyes,
> For they in thee a thousand errors note...
>
> Shakespeare, Sonnet CXLI

When a person has Uranus, the Sky God of freedom and intellect who does not understand emotions, linked with their Moon, the epitome of feelings and emotions, they experience nurturing through the lens of the frozen wastelands of emotions. The issue becomes embedded at birth when the newborn either receives technological intervention with the delivery or else inconsistent emotional messages from the nurturing figure after birth (reaching for the baby/pushing it away; wanting to feed/unable to feed). In this pre-verbal level of language, the newborn rapidly learns that the body and all things to do with the body, including emotions, are unpredictable and unreliable and they unconsciously label emotions and feminine energy as illogical, irrational, weak and destructive. In a best case scenario they may be surrounded by "many mothers" (grandmothers, aunts, cousins) at the birth and in the months following and so learn to gain emotional nurturing from many sources, not just one. Initially projected onto the mother (or mother-figure), in worst case scenario the child sees her as strange, eccentric or bizarre and, fearful of her erratic emotions, develops a detached bond with her. In a best case scenario mother is seen as independent and intellectual, able to keep a cool head in intense situations and who may be involved with technology or fringe areas. Puberty, that time of intense body change and extremes of emotions, can cause tremendous difficulties for the young person who may be attracted to another physically and sexually but yet feels uncomfortable about emotional commitment and bonding and may only do so when it is emotionally safe and where they retain emotional independence, such as when the relationship is about to split up or when the other person is involved with someone else. Parenthood, which represents the antithesis of freedom, for children tie one down and force one to confront emotional issues, may also be met with resistance or escape. Indeed a woman with a Moon-Uranus aspect will be ill at ease with the intense, emotional process of being a woman and for this reason may not want to biologically encounter her body in this way and follow the traditional, expected child-bearing pattern of her mother. This may express itself through infertility, frigidity, continual miscarriages or no sex life at all. A man may end up having many lovers as a way of escaping commitment.

Often described as emotionally tone-deaf, a person with a person with a Moon-Uranus aspect unconsciously recognises that strong emotions freeze them and prevent them from thinking or acting and learns to approach intense emotional experiences with the intellect and head rather than the heart. So when someone close to them dies, they may seem to be dealing with the loss but are, in reality, refusing to acknowledge the pain, pulled between the logic of what they know intellectually and the irrational, unfounded roller coaster of emotion into which they find themselves propelled. In denying their feelings and only focusing on the intellect, this can cause a mind-body split. Depending on the sign of the Moon, they may swing between anger and rage and ice cold intellect and displace unresolved grief onto others through fury, hostility or blame; or apply a well-reasoned or scientific solution to their feelings which in no way deals with their feelings of loss.

The key as an adult is to recognise that there are many ways to approach their feelings through the intellect, often called mind-mapping, including such disciplines as neuro-linguistic programming or gestalt therapy, which allows them to maintain control over their emotions in a way that isn't suppressing and so to stay present and continue to act in the world. Indeed the powerful emotions of grief can thrust them into realising that emotions need not be a hindrance but a way of locating concealed feelings which gives them leave to make their emotions practical.

When the Moon encounters Neptune

> Shall I compare thee to a Summers day?
> Thou art more lovely and more temperate...
> Shakespeare, Sonnet XVIII

When Neptune, the desire in all things to move towards oneness, makes an aspect to a person's Moon, the epitome of emotions and nurturing, the infant blends these two components via the aspect into a deeply intuitive and boundless connection with the nurturing source, creating a total merging of emotions and a lack of discrimination over who is infant and who is nurturer. This connection begins whilst the child is still in the womb and is reinforced at the birth when, as the result of a drug-induced delivery, a water birth, a music-filled or candle-lit birth or a birth where the child is given into the care of its grandmother, there is confusion over who is mother and who is child.

One of the greatest things for an infant to recognise is bodily integrity, that they are a being separate from their mother. However, a Moon-Neptune aspect does not offer this clarity for the person. Body recognition lacks sharpness and definition and there is doubt over whose emotions belong to whom. If not tackled appropriately, the infant can feel emotionally invaded, a "psychic vacuum cleaner" subject to the emotional temperaments around them, unconsciously doing what pleases other people instead of what pleases them. On a physical level this can express itself as an addictive personality, ranging from a susceptibility to allergies (the result of a confused immunological system), drug sensitivity (anything from chocolate or coffee to western medication used in operations) or drug addictions (alcohol, cigarettes or hard drugs).

In its best expression, a Moon-Neptune aspect offers the person an emotional rapport not only with mother or the nurturing figure but with the world at large, someone who has great receptivity, immense compassion and considerable intuition about other people's emotional states. However, this manifestation comes at a price and that price is the necessity to develop clear boundaries between themselves and other people and they will be continually confronted to draw clear lines in the sand about how far they will allow themselves to be intruded upon emotionally. As a result, the person with the Moon-Neptune aspect will instinctively seek space and reclusion. They will also be drawn to the arts, painting, music, singing, travel, the healing fields, metaphysics, meditation or spirituality where they can safely merge and lose themselves in the work and where emotionally there is the least confusion.

Unless they have developed these clear boundaries, then when they encounter the death of someone close to them, the deluge of other people's emotions may cause immense bodily distress, increasing their tearfulness and the extremes of emotion. They may experience a loss of energy. They may seek and use alcohol and/or drugs as way of numbing the pain. They may unconsciously choose confusion as a way of not dealing with their emotions or refuse to deal with the situation by becoming a dreamer and a drifter, lost in fantasy. They may idealise and romanticise the one who has died. They may turn to religion for support. Depending on the relationship, they may even duplicate the physical signs and symptoms of the one who has died. However it is expressed, and depending on what sign and house the Moon is in natally and its orientation n the chart, the sensitivity of the Moon-Neptune will be heightened under stress of grief and large groups of people can distort and contaminate their emotional wellbeing.

In a best case scenario grief asks the person with a Moon-Neptune aspect to maintain their faith and integrity in the grief process and to gain clarity around their feelings through an avenue that is both imaginative and structured, maintaining a practical hold on reality. This may take physical expression, such as yoga or T'Ai Chi, as a way of keeping the person grounded and focused, or artistic such as drama, music therapy or spontaneous drawings. They may also find their dream life increases and that dream analysis can give insights to their emotional turbulence.

When the Moon encounters Pluto

> For I have sworne thee faire, and thought thee bright,
> Who art as black as hell, as darke as night.
>
> Shakespeare, Sonnet CXLVII

When Pluto makes an aspect to the Moon in a person's chart, the fusion of intense, transforming energy with emotions and nurturing forms a behaviour pattern which is deeply passionate and non-superficial. Forged in the crucible of birth, experienced as dramatic, violent or crisis-filled by the neo-natal, he or she creates a powerful emotional bond with the giver of life, the mother, as a survival mechanism. For the delivery itself may have produced life-and death complications or the need for an operation or intensive care afterwards; mother may have been contending with powerful adult emotions, such as being in grief, dealing with an adulterous partner, giving birth in a war zone, and so on; or - its most difficult expression - mother may have died whilst giving birth. In whatever shape or form these come, at the pre-verbal level of communication the newborn neither understands nor possesses the resources with which to process and handle these acutely-overwhelming sensations. Pushed into the unconscious and revealed as intense emotional insecurity, the child grows up loving mother but also hating her for the powerful hold she exerts, for mother is the one who activates the same instinctive feelings of agitation in the child as she did when the behaviour was first generated. As a consequence, the person will often experience power struggles with mother in order to create the same intensity that was created at birth as a way of feeling connected to her, for the underlying fear is that the bond with her might be broken and she will die.

As the male or female child grows up this gets projected onto other women/nurturing figures and meaningful emotional relationships are all experienced as intense. Indeed any strong emotional bond will activate this insecurity and express itself as issues of paranoia, trust and betrayal. In the initial stages of getting to know someone, the person with the Moon-Pluto aspect may appear secretive and superficial. However, in their intimate circle, they will be considered extremely emotional and not superficial at all, for they feel that once the emotional bond is made, it is there forever and if it is broken, then it is severed eternally.

Unless this behaviour pattern of seeing the world in emotional extremes has been worked through, the death of someone close to them will only intensify this black and white spectrum. They will feel the loss as a personal breach of trust, the ultimate betrayal, and may initially express their feelings as anger at close family members. In a worst case scenario they will seek intensity from someone emotionally close to them and project all the ferocity of their grief onto them. This can give rise to power struggles, fights and lifetime vendettas which serves to fuel the intensity of feeling but blocks them from having to face the underlying issues, enjoying the drama of grief rather than its resolution. What the person seeks most of all is someone to replace the loss on a professional level until they can complete any unresolved issues. In a best case scenario, the person can use the grief process to sort through their deepest feelings and slowly make sense of the profound deluge of emotions, recognising that loss of life does not necessarily mean the end of the relationship but rather a change in how that relationship is articulated.

If loss occurs at puberty and the adolescent is given no help in how to handle it, then it can ricochet throughout the person's life as further loss or health issues until they are forced to deal with it. For both men and women, birth and mothering contain strong emotional undercurrents. A female with a Moon-Pluto aspect in her chart has to recognise that it is possible to have strong, connected bonds with children without necessarily fighting with them. A male with a Moon-Pluto aspect in his chart may find he is relating to an extremely emotional, possessive woman or that he is afraid of women. In its best case scenario, this is a strongly focused, emotionally-empowered person who is not afraid of their emotions and who has distilled levels and degrees of trust in the people around them, with clearly defined opposing principles, rather than judging people as for or against them.

Additional Encounters with Proteus

Other planetary combinations will meet grief in their own unique way and will be helped enormously by life experience, wisdom and personal growth. In their simplest forms they encounter Proteus with three distinct motifs:

Fight

Charts with a predominance of planets in angular houses describe people who will successfully produce an intended result. Shown a pathway forward through the challenging situation of grief, they will take action and often respond to predictive work as a way of future-pacing. If there is a 7th house emphasis such people will be more reliant on friends and intimates than if they had planets in other angular houses. They may seek an immediate replacement for the one who has died, being drawn into relationship as a compulsive relator and therefore unable to operate in the world without a partner.

Charts with a predominance of planets in succedent houses will handle the emotional extremes of grief most effectively when surrounded by others, at times relying on their own skills, at times needing help and input.

Charts where the main thrust of planets are in cardinal signs actively seek challenge and encounter. When someone close to them dies, they will be proactive in their approach to dealing with loss.

Charts with 8th house planets indicate someone who is not afraid of confronting life, birth and death and feels comfortable with crises and turning points in their lives. They will probe beneath the surface of events and prefer to know the underlying motives behind events and/or actions. If the death of someone close occurs while they are young, going through the grieving process, rather than being shielded from it is necessary in the understanding of how to utilize that 8th house.

Pluto conjunct the Ascendant or in the 1st house suggests someone who doesn't shy away from deep emotions and is naturally confronting, who feels at home with profound intensity and may confront death and grief as a way of understanding themselves.

Pluto conjunct the MC or in the 10th house indicates someone who wants to work on projects with large groups of people which change the wider community in some way. This may express itself in any number of forms from undertaker to grief counsellor.

Venus-Pluto combinations in a chart describe a person who is an intense relator and networker, whose alliances and connections are passionate, vibrant possessive and monogamous. Unless experience teaches them otherwise, such people will not be afraid of encountering or working with the intensity of grief.

Flight

Charts with a predominance of planets in cadent houses describe people who are at their most functional and fruitful when working for the good of other people. When faced with the death of someone close to them, they may stay lost in the obligations and demand of others for years, avoiding their own needs.

Charts with 12th house planets may have been unconsciously struggling for years to articulate family fears, and phobias. In grief the individual may therefore seclude and isolate themselves from the family in order to avoid the title of scapegoat. If the individual can be mindful of the role they play within the family structure, the period of grieving can be a time of immense clarity, allowing the individual to take on the burden of these blood-fears and heal them for the family.

Charts where the main thrust of planets are in mutable signs in grief may avoid facing and dealing with their feelings, sometimes for years, moving from one job to another, one group of people to another as a bandaid cure, never really coming to grips with the issues at hand.

Sun-Neptune combinations in grief will tend to romanticize the memory of the person who has died, often preoccupied with their image and sometimes duplicating their physical symptoms. They may hear the dead person's voice or see them in their environment. As a way of avoiding the pain and desolation of grief they may become lost in fantasy through books, television, cinema, drugs, alcohol or the extremes of exercise. They may turn to western medication as a way of dealing with sleeplessness and find they have become dependent upon it. They may also open themselves to deception and disillusion, continually seeking for answers in the world of charlatans and frauds.

Saturn-Venus combinations describe someone who feels restricted in their ability to merge with and relate to other people pre-Saturn Return. Encountering grief can compound this fear of being hurt in a relationship and cause them to isolate themselves or shut down on their feelings. This combination can translate into long-term committed relationships after the Saturn Return but, if grief is not understood, it can cause the person to focus heavily on work as a way of avoiding the pain.

Freeze

Charts where the main thrust of planets are in fixed signs in grief will find it more difficult to allow introspection and change, for grief is the antitheses of permanence.

Saturn-Sun combinations under the stress of grief and in the realm of tumult and upheaval, can assert rigid control over their world. Death may feel like failure and guilt may be an overwhelming reaction. Over-control can manifest as problems with knees, neck, shoulders, back, skin, hair or teeth, the boundaries and the structural parts of the body.

Saturn-Mars combinations encountering grief may feel rage at the loss but not necessarily be able to express it. Anger turned inwards is depression. If a person has not been given clear pathways for expressing the fury of their grief, then the bottled frustration can lead to stiffening of the joints, such as arthritis and rheumatism, and a lack of flexibility in both body and mind.

Saturn-Pluto combinations describe the generation that is sensitive to the unexpressed drama and violence in the community and who will experience grief as a difficult and arduous journey, often accompanied by nightmares and powerful dreams, increased anxiety, wariness and paranoia.

Saturn conjunct the Ascendant or in the 1st house in grief will want to be seen as responsible, committed and in charge. Grief may exacerbate an inferiority complex and feelings of failure and, as a way of compensation, they may become over- domineering and plagued with control.

Saturn conjunct the Descendant or in the 7th house in grief will seek to fill the gap caused by the death with people who are older and wiser than them or who limit or restrict them in some way.

Saturn conjunct the IC or in the 4th house in grief will feel blocked and restricted from the warmth of the home or family, feeling there is little or no room for emotional expression.

Saturn conjunct the MC or in the 10th house in grief will want to maintain a position of control, status, dignity and respect and will see crying and feeling emotionally distraught as a sign of weakness.

Sun-Pluto combinations may result in the individual perceiving the death of someone close to them as an act of betrayal: if the one who dies has been under medical supervision, then the betrayal will be by the medical profession; if a sudden death or a young death, then the betrayal may be by God. Forced to embrace drama, crisis and rapid change, and fearful of taking action, the person may project anger and resentment onto those around them. Unless they have learnt to trust themselves, they can retreat from life becoming a colourless, disempowered individual.

Pluto in the 12th house describes a particularly intense connection with the individual's family and the objective psyche, revealing itself as an immense fear of death, violence and loss of control. The death of someone close to them can evoke extreme fear.

Pluto conjunct the IC or in the 4th house in its extreme configuration can signify the death of the mother at birth or the death of an immediate family member. If this occurs in childhood and is not adequately reconciled, the person can carry this wound with them for years, replicating the unresolved grief as a cyclically-recurring pattern of loss.

Pluto conjunct the Descendant or in the 7th house in its extreme configuration can signify the death of a parent and continual intensity or drama in the area of intimate or business relationships. The person therefore may never commit to an intimate relationship, since to do so means they must allow these intense emotions into their lives. If this is the case, then grief can seem overpowering, terrifying and destructive.

When there is a connection between the 4th, 8th and 12th houses: Rulerships connect houses like underground rivers of behaviour which surface in surprising ways. When a person is in grief and under pressure, the family may reveal these hidden patterns as issues from past generations. These combinations are as follows:

- when the ruler of the 4th house is in the 12th house or the ruler of the 12th house is in the 4th house;
- when the ruler of the 12th house is in the 8th house or the ruler of the 8th house is in the 12th house;
- when the ruler of the 4th house is in the 8th house or the ruler of the 8th house is in the 4th house;
- combinations where the rulers of these houses form aspects, such as the ruler of the 8th and the ruler of the 12th forming a conjunction in the 4th house.

When these rulers are initially difficult combinations, such as Venus-Saturn or Saturn-Pluto, the strain becomes immense. The individual is under pressure to resolve not only their own grief but the grief of previous generations of their family and whether or not they are successful, such a configuration often describes lasting and enduring changes to the family structure as a result.

Finally...

Theatre citric Kenneth Tynan (1927-1980) humorously wrote: "A neurosis is a secret that you don't know you are keeping." When we are confronted with Proteus, he shows us this secret through the behaviour we manifest. This behaviour can be traced back to the patterns with which we are impressed as we begin this life. When grief takes us on its night sea journey we revert to these early patterns but there are other ways to express them. Clients in grief can be helped greatly by this understanding.

Endnotes

1. I prefer to use in-sign Ptolemaic 4th harmonic aspects: the conjunction, the sextile, the square, the trine and the opposition.
2. Hunt, Jan. (2001) *The Natural Child: Parenting from the Heart*, Gabriola Island: New Society Publishers.
3. See for example: Symes, Mary. (1987) *Grief and Dreams*, Melbourne: René Gordon Pty. Ltd.

4
A Normal Life

If we could read the secret history of our enemies, we should find
in each man's life sorrow and suffering enough to disarm all hostility.
Henry Wadsworth Longfellow, poet (1807-1882)

In an effort to find out what a "normal" life looked like astrologically, in
March, 2000, I set up a voluntary questionnaire based on the one used in
The Grief Recovery Handbook [1]. Given that the way we handle loss and grief is
determined by the parental signatures in the natal chart, I was looking for a
correlation between behaviour and astrology. I used a qualitative methodology
in the following manner: as a starting point I went to our astrology students
and then gave questionnaires to people who attended my lectures on grief. I
stressed that their history, their feelings and their precious memories were
valuable to me and that there was no judgement involved. I asked those who
wished to partake in the questionnaire to write down their earliest memory.
This was a starting point only to stimulate recall but I was surprised when
this, too, yielded useful information. Next I asked them to identify their most
painful loss and to write a paragraph on the circumstances surrounding the
loss and their responses to that loss: How did people try to help them through
that experience? Did they? Could they? Were there any behaviours they may
have used to gain short-term relief? Were there any beliefs that had become
embedded at the time of the loss? The next step was for them to revisit their
past and recount loss events as they remembered them. I asked them to use a
horizontal line to represent linear time and vertical lines to establish the
relative degrees of their losses. I also asked them to list any substances they
used for short-term relief or any short-term behaviour which covered the pain.
I was aware that I was getting a biased sample, as only those people who were
prepared to consider their history of loss and grief would be interested in
completing such a survey. Nevertheless this provided me with valuable results
and insights. What follows are some of the responses I received.

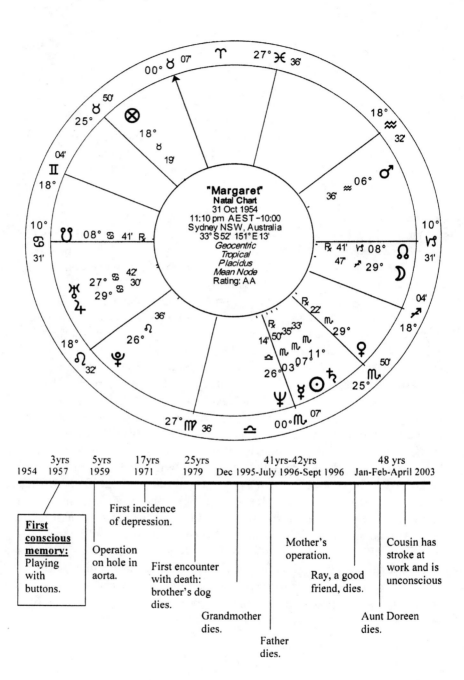

3yrs	5yrs	17yrs	25yrs	41yrs-42yrs	48 yrs
1954 1957	1959	1971	1979	Dec 1995-July 1996-Sept 1996	Jan-Feb-April 2003

First incidence of depression.

First conscious memory: Playing with buttons.

Operation on hole in aorta.

First encounter with death: brother's dog dies.

Grandmother dies.

Father dies.

Mother's operation.

Ray, a good friend, dies.

Cousin has stroke at work and is unconscious

Aunt Doreen dies.

MARGARET

Parental signatures in Margaret's chart and what they might say about grief:

Father-figure: *Mercury-Sun-Saturn in Scorpio in the 4th house (Mercury rules 3rd and 12th houses, the Sun rules the 2nd house, Saturn rules 7th and, by old rulerships, the 8th house) conjunct the IC square Mars in Aquarius in the 8th house, (Aries is intercepted in the 9th house and Mars by old rulerships rules the 4th house).*

From her father-figure Margaret imprints sensitivity to issues of trust and betrayal (Sun in Scorpio and an emphasis of planets in Scorpio) which are helped after her Saturn Return and once she forms a committed relationship (Saturn natally in the 4th house rules the 7th house). However, combined with a fear of intimidation and an ensuing inferiority complex (Sun conjunct Saturn), Margaret learns not to talk about her feelings (Mercury conjunct Saturn) and to withhold her anger (Saturn square Mars in mutual reception, strengthening this aspect). Blending with the myth of Scorpio (the myth of Medusa falsely accused), this is a recipe for rage and emotions that become jammed over time and which can, in turn, develop into depression. Mercury conjunct the IC and the ruler of the 12th house suggests that the inability to express what is occurring internally is an inherited family motif.

Mother: *The Moon in Sagittarius in 6th house (Moon is void of course and rules the Ascendant) trine Pluto in the 2nd house (ruling the 4th house) and sextile Neptune in the 3rd house (Neptune rules the 9th house). Pluto square Venus in Scorpio (in detriment) in the 5th house (Venus rules the 10th and 11th houses and Libra is intercepted in the 3rd house). Venus trine Uranus conjunct Jupiter in Cancer (in exaltation) in the 1st house (Uranus rules the 8th house, Jupiter rules the 6th house and, by old rulerships, the 9th house). Uranus conjunct Jupiter square Neptune.*

From her mother Margaret learns emotional independence (Moon in Sagittarius) underneath which sits a strong, intense bonding with mother emanating from an early pattern of crisis (Moon trine Pluto). As she begins to socialise and network with others, she quickly learns to trust few people (Pluto square Venus, Venus in Scorpio). This is at odds with her need to encounter all manner of people (Venus trine Uranus, water trine) and to take risks with such encounters (Uranus-Jupiter), risks which succeed only as long as she keeps her finger on the pulse (Jupiter in exaltation). This aspect is underpinned by hard work (Jupiter rules the 6th house), a clear philosophy (Jupiter rules the 9th house) and crisis and change (Uranus rules the 8th house) and if it has no way of expressing itself in Margaret's life, it will explode randomly,

' or enthusiastically in her life and force social change upon her.
itive to pain (Moon sextile Neptune) this blend, in its worst case
fers isolation, addictive substances or food as solutions to grief.

Other issues:

The Nodal Axis: *North Node is conjunct the Descendant in Capricorn. The dispositor, Saturn, squares Mars. The South Node is conjunct the Ascendant in Cancer. The dispositor, the Moon, is void of course, trine Pluto and sextile Neptune.*

As Margaret reaches for and forms a committed relationship in her early twenties (North Node in Capricorn conjunct the Descendant), she encounters issues that were shaped and imprinted from her father-figure (ruler of Capricorn is Saturn conjunct the Sun and Mercury). As this early dream of relationship fades, she is forced to return to the South Node (in Cancer conjunct the Ascendant) and relook issues of emotional independence and trust that are shaped by her mother (ruler of Cancer is the Moon).

MARGARET
Answers to Questionnaire

First conscious memory - 1957. Playing with buttons.

December, 1959:

Operation on aorta. I was born with a hole in the aorta, near the heart. This caused a lack of oxygenated blood circulating. Consequently I was exceptionally weak. Towards my fifth birthday it became clear I was dying but an operation had been developed in 1958 to correct the condition. I'm aware now that my parents did all they could to explain it to me but I must not have understood. I thought I'd been left at the hospital for punishment and didn't know what I'd done wrong. I was scared but, more than anything, I was sad that I wasn't good enough for them and when they came to visit me I tried my hardest to be good. I remember lying to a nurse who asked me what was wrong. I don't think I could have put it into words and I know I said nothing to my parents because my mother cried when I told her about it many years later. I remember being given ice-cream if I was good about being in the oxygen tent. A theme of self-medication with food is recurrent in my life.

1971. First incidence of depression:

I was working in the Candy Bar of the theatre where my mother worked as an usherette. I had my long hair up and Mum was looking down at me from the upper level. When I got home she told me not to wear my hair scraped back because I looked so plain. I went and looked at myself in the mirror, and she was right. I was, and am, a short, fat, plain person who wears glasses, not at all what any teenage girl wants to be. I was rigid with anger for the next two days because I thought it was so unfair. I hadn't really thought much about looks before but once I did, I started to hate myself. The anger subsided into depression because I thought that how I looked was going to blight my life. I thought I was unlovable. What I felt I lost was an image of myself as a reasonable looking person. How do I respond to grief? Well, self-pity is one of my strong suits. I went on one of many diets. I still looked like me, only a bit thinner. I don't think anyone knew how I felt and I didn't tell anyone.

April, 1979. First encounter with death:

This was the first death I ever experienced. She was my brother's dog but I loved her and could express it by patting her and looking after her. I felt she loved me, too, and all she asked was to be fed, walked and loved. In a way she was my first love, the first living being to whom I felt I could show affection. Mum rang me at work. I had to behave properly, so I don't remember crying for her then. I tend to bottle things up, eat too much and get depressed in response to loss. After eighteen months, I finally told someone. I went to the Doctor and received anti-depressants.

December, 1995. Grandmother dies:

My grandmother was ninety-five when she died. Up until a fall at the age of ninety-two she had been wonderfully fit, active and witty. She kept all her senses up until the day she died but she couldn't walk for the last three years. In those three years I watched Nanna die by degrees. My grieving for her was done before and after each visit to the Nursing Home. Watching someone you love humiliated, humbled, incapacitated, bullied and frightened by those supposedly caring for them is hard but far harder for the person living it. She bore it with grace and dignity. I felt guilty that I wasn't caring for her, I hated having to go and see her in the home and I became frightened of growing old. These were all part of grief. I discussed it with Mum sometimes and she felt the same. When she died, I was calm because her death had been happening

in front of our eyes for so long and it was finally ended. I hope she
is at peace. My response was to eat. I put on twenty pounds.

July, 1996. Father's death:

Dad had suffered a series of mini-strokes since mid-1990. After a
major stroke left him unable to walk and without much speech, he
had to go into a Nursing Home. How I hate those places! Dad
sometimes believed he was back in the Army and he wanted to be
demobbed or he'd cry to come home. I watched a man I'd feared as
a child and despised as a teenager become helpless, lost and
miserable. I stopped hating him. I pitied him and then found I
loved him. When he died, my grief was different. I got to know
about how hard his upbringing was and why he'd been the way he
was. I was and am sorry that I spent so much time hating an
extremely unhappy man. This sounds so arrogant but I think I
learned about understanding and forgiveness. I told my friends
that my Dad had died and many came to his funeral to support
me. I don't think I'd realised what good friends I had. After my
father's death I ate.

September, 1996. Mother's operation:

For over thirty years Mum has been ill with tachycardia (an
abnormally rapid heart rate) due to extra "wiring" to the heart.
There had not been a cure until about 1994. Mum said that she
felt she couldn't go on, that her heart was failing, so she underwent
the operation to burn away the extra nerves to the heart. It had
considerable dangers and I was afraid I'd lose her. I started to grieve
when I saw her in hospital because I didn't know if I'd see her
again. The illness made her thoroughly irritable and naturally she
was afraid, too. It was like a reversal of my operation as a five year
old. I felt helpless that there was nothing I could do to influence
that most important outcome. I didn't say much to anyone about
it but boy, I ate a lot.

In April 2003 I asked Margaret if she would like to update the graph and she replied as follows:

Mum is now in better health than she has enjoyed in thirty years
which she freely acknowledges. Mum and I are close but still many
things go unsaid. She is an unsentimental person and I'm all watery
emotion, so sometimes we don't quite mesh. Still, couldn't get by
without my Mum, as the ads say! However 2003 has not started
well.

January, 2003. Ray, a good friend of many years, died suddenly at home at the age of eighty one:

His death is the "best" I have experienced, in a way. He was at home and though physically rather frail, was still in full command of body and mind. He sat down to address an envelope, wrote on the front, then turned it over to put the sender address and died. He was an old fashioned gentleman and scholar and his dying at home, in the company of his devoted wife, with no great indignities of body and mind attendant upon his death, to me is the best way anyone could go. Whilst I was surprised by his death, I felt philosophical. He'd reached a good age and lived a good life and was happy with his life. I feel the usual regrets that I had not made more time in the usual "busyness" of life to listen to him more but I'm glad I knew him. What has been surprising is his wife's reaction and how I react to that. She is hysterically, furiously angry at him for leaving her. She is eighteen years younger than him and has been deeply devoted, to the point where her life has been curtailed by his weakness and inability to do much. She had spoken of the minor irritations and limitations of her life with him and I knew she resented it somewhat but had no idea she would be so angry. Her words on trying to find something amongst his many collections: "I shouldn't have to do this! It shouldn't be like this!" What's relevant here is that I have little understanding of her reaction and, I regret, little sympathy. Whilst I say all the formulaic things to her and generally just provide a listening ear, privately I think she is being ungrateful. She has been left extremely well provided for, he expressed his love to her every day, he always thanked her for her good care and took the greatest interest and pride in her activities outside the home. I know I don't know everything about their life together but, deep down, I find her reaction somewhat repugnant.

Rage has been an odd theme of reaction to the death of such a gentle man but it has had this affect on me, too, in another way. At work (I was working in Payroll), it was made extremely difficult for me to attend Ray's funeral. I had no choice but to shut the office and put a sign on the door (in my view, tantamount to deserting the ship!) The other three work colleagues were either on leave or insisting they had to be somewhere else and this time I refused to carry the can. As usual, the rage burned brightly inside but was not expressed externally until later. I wrote out my resignation and held onto it until I could arrange my finances. Although I intended to give five weeks notice so they could employ a replacement, in the end I couldn't contain the anger and left after three weeks. I'd started to tell friends how annoyed I was and, encouraged by their support, just left. Drawing a not-too-long bow, I ran away in response.

February, 2003. My Aunt Doreen (father's sister) died, after a year of suffering pancreatic cancer:

Like my father, she was an unhappy and bitter person all her life. She used to terrify us kids with sudden inexplicably screaming rages. I know now that her parents visited their sins upon the children: their father was a brute and their mother embittered and vindictive. The sudden rages were a feature of both Dad and Doreen and I'd say rage is a big theme in the family: depression is submerged rage. I'm ashamed to admit I was sick of visiting hospitals and Nursing Homes, and was (unexpressedly) angry that, for the third time in six years, I had to do it all again. I struggled with the sense of duty and some empathy, against the wish for a life where this wasn't the pattern. Oh, yes, I ate. Put back the stone in weight I'd lost.

I had spoken to friends about Doreen and they were sympathetic but there's a lot you can't say, like: "God, please, no one else is allowed to die!!! I never want to see another @#*&! ruddy Nursing Home again, I'll kill myself before I get too old, so it can't happen to me." Fear of getting old is a boiling undercurrent in how I felt. When she died, I was sad for her wasted life but relieved that it was over. Mostly I feel sorry for her. She never enjoyed her life and I don't want to be like that. Doreen left me her house which I am selling. I know I should be grateful and I'm sure I will be when I realise the money. I am, however, deeply ashamed that I resent the burdens attendant upon this, as the house is something of a white elephant. While I discuss practicalities with friends and they have been extremely helpful and kind, which is much appreciated, there is a lot left unsaid.

For a while I was in stasis, in a way, just waiting for the next blow to fall. Then it fell.

April, 2003. A good friend was diagnosed with cancer and then my cousin Sally, fifty-two years old, had a major stroke at work, is on a ventilator, and still unconscious after four days:

In this case I have less obligation to visit the hospital and haven't gone. What can I say or do for her in this state? I'm forty-eight years old. Sally's situation is a much closer object lesson for me. I know I should be working on making my life worthwhile but I'm stuck. Every muscle is tense and I'm so tired I find moving an effort. My feelings are: "Please can this stop? Please can there be some fun and happiness? No more dying."

Right now I'm a lady of leisure and though I've been invited to return to my old job, am doing some serious thinking on how to make more out of my life, to put meaning into the experience of working. Doreen's and Sally's examples are strong in my mind.

HARRY

Parental signatures in Harry's chart and what they might say about grief:

Father-figure: *Sun in Virgo in the 12th house (ruling the 11th house) square Uranus in the 8th house (ruling the 5th house).*

From his father-figure Harry learns that identity is bound up with rules and criticism (Sun in Virgo), solitude (Sun in the 12th house), the intellect (Sun square Uranus) and irrevocable change (Uranus in the 8th house). Indeed the 12th house is a place where father-figure is experienced as weakened or lost to Harry in some way. The square causes tension in his life but as it is mutable, once he has acknowledged the problem he solves it rapidly, flexibly and creatively.

Mother: *Moon-Jupiter-Neptune triple conjunction in Libra in the 12th house (Moon rules the MC, Jupiter rules the 3rd house and, by old rulerships, 6th house and Neptune rules the 6th house) square Mars in Cancer (in fall) in the 9th house conjunct the North Node (Mars rules the 7th house and, by old rulerships, the 2nd house). This triple conjunction is also at The Bends (that is, square the nodal axis) which highlights and stresses its function in his life.*

From his mother Harry learns rapport and harmony that began in the womb (Moon in Libra conjunct Neptune), followed by a drug-induced birth (Moon conjunct Neptune) which causes confusion over emotional and physical integrity. This can manifest either as a susceptibility to allergies, drug addictions or excessive health difficulties (Mars in Cancer in fall square Neptune, Jupiter and Neptune both ruling the 6th house) resulting in a term in hospital or a strong desire to isolate oneself and escape to an emotionally safe place (Moon-Jupiter-Neptune in the 12th house). There is also a strong connection to a grandmother (Moon-Neptune). Emotionally motivated or driven (Moon square Mars) through alternative avenues (Mars in fall) of education via travel or study (Mars in the 9th house), mother and women are also the great educating forces in his life (Moon-Jupiter-Neptune triple conjunction). Thus

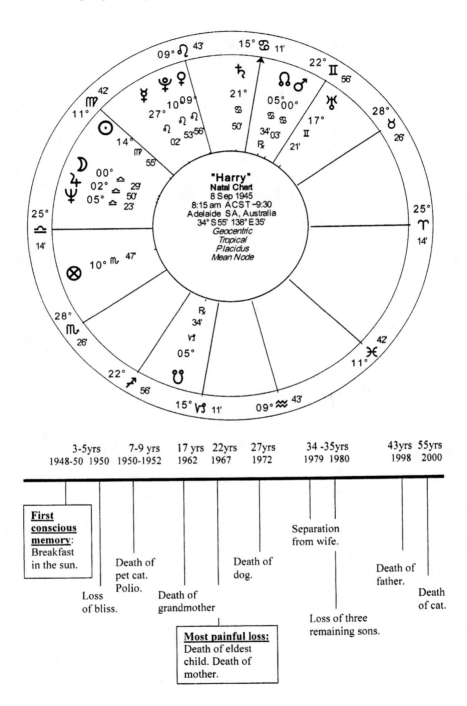

"Harry"
Natal Chart
8 Sep 1945
8:15 am ACST −9:30
Adelaide SA, Australia
34° S 55' 138° E 35'
Geocentric
Tropical
Placidus
Mean Node

3-5yrs	7-9 yrs	17 yrs	22yrs	27yrs	34 -35yrs	43yrs	55yrs
1948-50	1950 1950-1952	1962	1967	1972	1979 1980	1998	2000

First conscious memory: Breakfast in the sun.

Loss of bliss.

Death of pet cat. Polio.

Death of grandmother

Death of dog.

Most painful loss: Death of eldest child. Death of mother.

Separation from wife.

Loss of three remaining sons.

Death of father.

Death of cat.

emotional security is not only linked with calmness (Moon in Libra) but with spirituality, metaphysics, fantasy, the arts, music (Moon-Jupiter-Neptune) and solitude (Moon-Jupiter-Neptune in the 12th house) in its best case scenario but also with alcohol, drugs or dreaminess. So he may be taught to use isolation, fantasy, western medication, alcohol and possibly illness as a way of coping with loss.

Other issues:

There is a predominance of unaspected planets in Harry's chart:

> **Unaspected Saturn in Cancer (in detriment) conjunct the MC** *(ruling the 4th and by old rulerships the 5th house)*.
>
> **Unaspected Mercury in Leo in the 11th house** *(ruling the 9th and 12th houses)*.
>
> **Unaspected Venus-Pluto conjunction in Leo in the 11th house** *(Venus rules the Ascendant and the 8th house, Pluto rules the 2nd house)*.

Unaspected planets are like pure colours in a chart, unmodified by any other planet or luminary; they function erratically in a person's life, either fully and potently or not at all, until the person becomes conscious of this behaviour. They also describe unresolved inherited family issues. In Harry's case, these are: issues of public responsibility or lack thereof, modelled by the conditional parent (Saturn in Cancer in detriment in the 10th house); issues of how he communicates to groups or carries out mercantile business practices (Mercury in Leo in the 11th house); and issues of group networking and relating which revolve around themes of trust and betrayal (Venus-Pluto in the 11th house).

HARRY
Answers to Questionnaire

First conscious memory - 1948-50:

> Each morning I would sit outside our house near my pet cockatoo in the garden and eat toast and vegemite and "Weetbix". Then I would climb the old plum tree and converse across the six foot high galvanised iron fence with my only known childhood friend, Denise, the girl next door. We loved each other but weren't allowed to play together. Her father was "away" (in jail) and they weren't "good enough", so I stole early morning moments to talk with her.

Around 1950 - Loss of bliss:

From as early as I can remember when I went to bed I wouldn't go to sleep. Instead I would become my thumb which would swell and become as big as the room. At that point I would be free, out amongst the stars but "with my father". I loved this time more than any other and felt extremely safe. I distinctly remember the night I tried to get out but couldn't because I had a new feeling, one I didn't like. I felt "shame". I didn't know why. I hadn't done anything and hadn't been blamed for anything. The best guess I now make is that I tapped into the cloud of "shame" around family secrets and most likely around my step-grandfather from whom I was kept away "for my protection". He lived alone in his room, not part of the family but always "there" That terrible feeling of "shame" and not being able to go out to "my father" made me cry. From then onwards I didn't want to go to bed, began to wet the bed, cried myself to sleep, had to have a night light and began years of nightmares. I really was problem child, getting sick, being naughty, clinging to parents, living in fear. No-one knew what the matter was and I felt too much "shame" to even try to communicate.

1952. My pet cat, "Snowy", was run over:

I cried for two weeks exactly. The pain was horrendous. I was inconsolable.

1962. My grandmother died in hospital from cancer:

I sat with her for several weeks as she died and held her hand. I loved her dearly and didn't want to let her go. When she died, I was greatly upset and became angry. My anger lasted for thirteen years. No-one knew I was grieving, not even me, but I was angry with God and stopped going to church, becoming an avowed atheist. I became an angry workaholic and burnt myself out with work and sex and fantasy, reading voraciously. These comforts did not originate at seventeen. They just became more extreme. I already used them, as well as sugar and chocolate and I turned into an arrogant, loud, self-indulgent person.

Most painful loss. 1967. Eldest child died from SIDS (Sudden Infant Death Syndrome)/Mother died from cancer:

My eldest child died from SIDS at age one. Once again I felt terrible grief and went into the lowest depression I have ever experienced. Although I didn't contemplate suicide, it was close and lasted exactly a year. I didn't cope with life at all. I clearly remember painting an aunt's roof and feeling totally bereft, at the bottom of a dark pit. No-one could help. I didn't use any means to get relief but I mentally and emotionally shifted gears during that year from atheist to agnostic for a while. I became extremely close to my surviving son (who was three weeks' old at the time of my first son's death) and am sure that the love between us pulled me through. Shortly after the death of my son, my mother died of cancer. I was upset and cried but was still numb from my son's death. I felt sad that my mother and I, although on good talking terms, had never been able to touch or hold each other. She was an extremely detached person and I had become the same. We just talked in our relationship. I always felt her love was unconditional, whereas my father thought I was "bad". So her loss was significant but somehow it was swallowed up in the larger grief of my son's death.

1972. My dog died of throat cancer:

It was a deeply sad moment. I didn't want another dog. I just felt immensely sad. After my first son died I didn't want any more children, mainly because our marriage was in such a disastrous state. However, two more children were born (my third son on 25th March, 1969; my fourth son on 23rd March 1970) and while my wife was in hospital to have her wandering copper loop removed, I fell in love, platonically, with one of my students. For the first time in a long time I felt loved. This student was the catalyst for turning things around for me when she and I read Dag Hammerskjold's book *Markings* together and I started to become open to some new ideas. The infatuation soon passed but its consequences did not. I began reading voraciously and slowly, step by step, I discovered a broader way of looking at things. By the age of thirty my anger had passed.

1979. I separated from my wife:

This was a loss of family but a finding of freedom.

1980. Loss of three remaining sons:

A year later my wife prevented my sons from seeing me. This was a great loss. It was her only way of getting revenge for my leaving her. Friends helped me cope and I only had to wait six years to be reunited with my three sons again.

1998. Death of father:

My father, who had remarried and lived interstate [2], died of asbestosis. I saw him twice before he died and went to his funeral. I didn't feel much at all. He had died to me so many times that his leaving was a non-event. I felt sad that we hadn't been able to be close but I couldn't be a "born again Christian". Having experienced my own rebirth in another way, in his eyes I belonged to the Devil. It's hard to be at ease with someone who does that to you. The sadness I felt was not grief at his death but grief at the distance apart that we had been ninety-nine percent of the time.

2000. My twenty-year old cat died:

I cried as I buried her. She had been a wonderful animal friend, a person in every sense and part of my life for so long. Tears come as I write about her. She was a stray named "Katmando" or "Catmantoo", as I called her. I'll go and make a cup of tea now to console myself. Sex, drugs and work don't do as much as a good cup of tea these days - I must be getting old!

Afterword:

The night after completing the Grief Questionnaire I remembered the first great grief of my life. I had totally forgotten it and failed to indicate it in the time line. It was this:

1950-52: Polio. Starting school was a huge loss: home, mother, grandmother, normal routines and connection with nature. I cried all day the first day, making a complete nuisance of myself. After a few days I responded to the friendly gestures of a few older children who had obviously been asked to be the "caretakers of the new babies". I made friends in my class but experiences of a toilet variety caused embarrassment a few times and every morning was a drama. I didn't want to go to school and tried every "sick" trick in the book. Then one morning in winter I felt too tired to go to school. Mum tried but I just lay down on the floor. They called the doctor and found out I had polio. Dad was called home. Mum nursed me and Dad drove me to Northfield Infectious Diseases Hospital. They couldn't come in with me and I was left there alone. I was freaked out beyond belief. I refused to eat. I wet the bed. I cried and screamed and drove everyone nuts. Eventually, weeks and weeks later, long after I had given up and didn't care what happened, I was taken out to Mum and Dad. Apparently I said: "I thought you didn't want me anymore!"

I went home. I had a new bedroom, new toys. I was sort've happy but kept pushing Mum and Dad to their limits, I suppose to find out if they really loved me or not. My great-grandmother died and that was cool as she died so peacefully with a smile on her face. They found me sitting on her bed talking to her. They explained she was dead and led me away. I didn't mind. I loved her and she was nearly a hundred years old. It all seemed okay to me but I became deeply unhappy at school. I had missed so much time that I was a class behind my friends. I don't remember making any more friends for at least five or six years and probably no real friends until high school.

This was an extremely frightening period for me. Fear was the ever-present undercurrent. I had nightmares, nightlights, the lot. Around this time I began to have a rich "fantasy" or "day-dream" life which didn't really help schoolwork much. It lasted for about ten years but it was my refuge. My fantasies were full length movies. (Guess who was "Superman"?) So this was a period of major grief. I relived it in the dream state for several hours after doing the questionnaire. I felt as though a burden had been lifted by the time I awoke. So many memories all keyed into the grief of loss in hospital, so totally forgotten for fifty years.

NETTE COSTERIS

Parental signatures in Nette's chart and what they might say about grief:

Father-figure (almost a Kite pattern): *Grand trine in earth between Sun in Capricorn in the 3rd house (ruling the MC), Jupiter in Taurus in the 7th house (ruling the 3rd and, by old rulerships, the 5th house), Uranus-Pluto-Mars in Virgo in the 11th house (Uranus ruling the 4th house, Pluto ruling the 2nd house and Mars, which is too wide by orb to trine the Sun but part of the triple conjunction, ruling the 7th house and, by old rulerships, the 2nd house).*

Jupiter opposite Neptune in the 1st house (ruling the 5th house) and Neptune conjunct the Moon in Scorpio in the 2nd house (Cancer intercepted in the 9th house) although the Moon is too wide by orb to oppose the Jupiter. (Note: Pluto sextiles Neptune but the Sun is too wide to sextile Neptune to complete the full Kite pattern.)

From her father-figure Nette learns that the gift of practicality (Grand Trine in earth) comes through facing family issues. However, they come at a price: control and domination (the myth of the Sun in Capricorn), questions of freedom and difference (Sun-Uranus), paranoia and lack of trust (Sun-Pluto), matters of education and grandfather, as well as excess (Sun-Jupiter), a love of power (Jupiter-Pluto), a desire to take risks (Jupiter-Uranus) and an immense amount of physical energy (Mars-Uranus) which can explode as a volatile temper (Mars-Pluto). All of this becomes a resource once she recognises that she is her own best teacher and judge (Jupiter opposition Neptune).

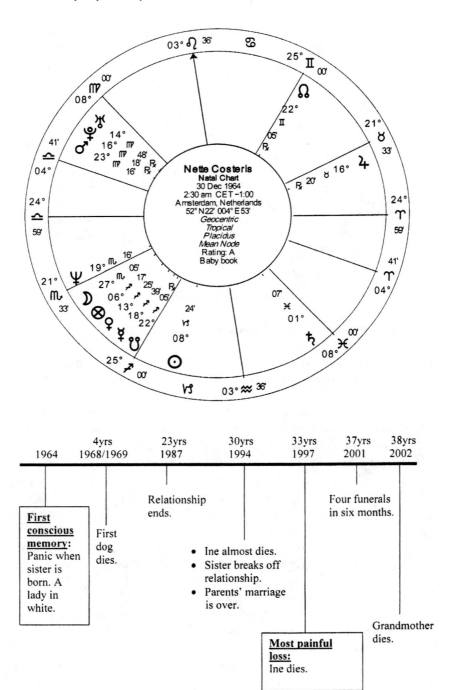

1964	4yrs 1968/1969	23yrs 1987	30yrs 1994	33yrs 1997	37yrs 2001	38yrs 2002

First conscious memory: Panic when sister is born. A lady in white.

First dog dies.

Relationship ends.

- Ine almost dies.
- Sister breaks off relationship.
- Parents' marriage is over.

Four funerals in six months.

Most painful loss: Ine dies.

Grandmother dies.

Nette writes: "When I was young my father broke off contact with his family (you see a clear family pattern) because his parents did not accept my mother, so most of my family experiences are from my mother's side of the family. A lot of the things I am supposed to have learned from my father I learned from my mother."

Mother: *Moon-Neptune in Scorpio, Moon sextile Mars, Neptune opposite Jupiter.*

From her mother Nette learns that emotional needs are a struggle between drama and crisis (Moon in Scorpio) and compassion and rapport (Moon conjunct Neptune) and that there is a deeply intuitive bond between mothers, grandmothers and grand-daughters (Moon conjunct Neptune). Mother/grandmother is also seen as a spiritual teacher (Jupiter opposite Neptune, Moon conjunct Neptune).

Other issues:

Uranus-Pluto-Mars square Venus-Mercury-South Node in Sagittarius in the 2nd house *(Venus ruling the Ascendant and the 8th house and Mercury ruling the 9th and 11th houses).*

This aspect indicates a struggle between freedom (Uranus square Venus) and commitment (Pluto square Venus) in relationships, between thinking differently (Uranus square Mercury, Mercury in Sagittarius and Mercury in detriment) and thinking obsessively (Pluto square Mercury), between being locked into rules and regulations (Virgo) and seeing the bigger picture (Sagittarius). Indeed this issue of thinking outside the square and at the same time her thinking being clouded by relationship issues is an inherited family issue (Mercury in Sagittarius conjunct the South Node).

Mars at The Bends (square the nodal axis) stresses an erratic, volatile temper and deep, immense rage (the triple conjunction of Uranus-Pluto-Mars) which if blocked or checked in any way, can cause immune system health problems such as cancer.

Unaspected Saturn in Pisces in the 4th house *(Capricorn is intercepted in the 3rd house and, by old rulerships, rules the IC.)* This is an aspect that is either fully functional, allowing her to take on a great deal of family responsibility, or else she feels that she has no ability to do so whatsoever. When made aware of these two states of being the person is usually able to begin to work more consciously with the unaspected planet.

NETTE COSTERIS
Answers to Questionnaire

First conscious memory - Sister born:

I remember the panic in the house when my sister was born on May 30th, 1967, because (I heard when I was much older) my mother nearly died. I recall a lady dressed in white with a white hat.

1968/1969: My first dog died:

My parents bought him in a pet store and his health was extremely bad. My father took him to the vet and my mother, my sister and I were crying. We called the vet one more time to ask if it was really necessary.

1987. My relationship ended:

My in-laws and I could not get along and I was so fed up with it, I broke off the engagement. After three months my future husband wanted to talk with me and we decided to try again.

1994. Ine almost died before my eyes:

Ine is my grandmother's sister but she was like a grandmother to me. It looked like she choked but afterwards she couldn't remember a thing. Because I thought she would die, I called my sister, who had broken off contact with our parents at the end of 1993 but who still had contact with Ine and me, and explained the situation and told her that if she wanted to see Ine, she could come to my parent's house which is where Ine lived. My sister sent me a goodbye-letter in which she accused me of making up Ine's health situation in order to make her talk with our parents. Until today I'm not seeing her but I don't miss her which is strange because we were always extremely close.

I also started to lose my father bit by bit through Alzheimer's Disease, we think, but he refuses any medical help because he feels nothing is wrong with him and Alzheimer's Disease can appear in many different ways. That hurt a great deal. He is aggressive towards my mother and he loses interest in most things, even in his grand-daughter. What also played a part is the fact that he drank too much alcohol for years. The most difficult thing is that he has his good moments when he seems interested and caring again. Every time you hope, against one's better judgment, that he will stay this way. Before he got ill he was the best father a child could have. My parents' marriage became worse but they did not get divorced. Instead my mother leans on me because she misses a partner.

Most painful loss. 1997. Ine died:

As a small child she was greatly important to me. As I grew up she was always nearby and for several years she lived in our house. At the end of her life my mother bought her a new house and I took care of her every day for four months. Ine's health was not good but she always pulled through and in the mind of my mother as well as mine the idea rose that she would not leave us for some time because we put so much energy and money in her new home and she was so happy here. Strange how the mind works. After four months of living there, Ine died suddenly in the presence of my mother, my husband and myself. At the moment of her death a piece of me died with her. I was grateful that I had her for thirty-three years but because we were so close, it caused great pain. My days felt empty. Although I do have the tendency when I'm grieving to seclude myself from the world, what helped after she died was the support of friends and the fact that my mother and I designed her grave and paid for it together. The funeral was also highly personal. We go every week to Zorgvlied, a beautiful cemetery near the Amstel River, to take care of her grave. We left Ine's house in its old status for forty days. This is an old Indonesian tradition and I like old traditions but because she had been so happy there, my mother and I could not sell the house then. Instead we kept it for a year. Then we could let it go, although not easily.

2001. I had four funerals in six months:

At the first three funerals, the feeling that it was better for the person that died dominated. The last one had the greatest impact. He was the father of my daughter's girlfriend and was only thirty-nine years old. He died of a heart attack. When I saw his wife and children mourn, I felt terrible, for it has always been my biggest fear that something like this can happen to me (my husband is forty-one years old).

June, 2002. My grandmother, Olly died:

Ine and Olly were sisters but I have always been closer with Ine. I come from a family with exceedingly difficult relationships and many arguments. Jealousy played a great part. When my grandfather died in 1990 we had no contact with him. He had asked for my mother when he was dying but one of her sisters refused this. Ine also lost contact with her sister because my grandparents made her choose between them and my mother. In 1997, just before Ine died, Olly came back in my life. She apologized to my mother and we all saw it as a new beginning. Her other children were angry with her for seeing us again and they came less and less. Olly's health decreased. In March, 2002, she was at my home because she had a doctor's appointment the next day. He was worried when he saw her and spoke of an operation. This was upsetting for her, so I proposed that she stay the weekend in order to deal with this. My mother looked for alternative ways and she found a specialist in pain-treatment who was willing to help Olly. It was a beautiful period. She talked a lot about her childhood and Indonesia and we shared things, we never shared before. She became a real grandmother (isn't it beautiful?!).

On May 17th she got a severe haemorrhage from the stomach. I informed the rest of the family. Hell broke loose. This was the first time they saw her that year. They argued with the doctors and told Olly that she had to go to the resthome when she came out of hospital. She was afraid and we told her that this would not happen, that she would come home with me. It turned out that she had cancer (we never told her) and the wound did not heal. The rest of the family threatened to kill us, interrupted when we were with Olly and were talking about the inheritance. The worst thing was that they stripped her house. It was an awful three weeks. When you lose someone you love, it's terrible but now we felt we played a part in some kind of horror movie. It felt so unreal. To make a long story short, on June 6th she passed away and we could take her home. She stayed in my living room until we burried her next to Ine together with my grandfather (we put his urn in her coffin). She had a beautiful funeral.

All of this had a great impact on me. A great one. Olly lived with us for almost ten weeks. Now the house felt so empty. My daughter also needed extra attention. She loved Olly immensely, so she had to deal not only with the loss but also with the fact that she had not seen me for three weeks. I visit their graves at least one time a week with my mother. I had a close relationship with my mother but now we only got closer. Although it was difficult, I look back on the whole period with a smile and a really warm feeling. She is still nearby and gives us lots of signs. Since her things were here when she died and we had almost the same size, I wear her clothes. She was so proud of me for studying astrology and often when I go to classes, I wear something of hers and I say to her, "Are you coming with me tonight?" This has helped me a lot.

How do I deal with grief? In general, when I'm emotional (cheerful or sad) food plays a role. Mostly I'm eating extra, not candy but hearty things but when I'm sad, I don't eat. When I'm

sad I don't want to have sex. This can take weeks. I isolate myself.
I live a great deal in my own world at such a time. Another relief
is shopping. I always feel better after shopping when I'm sad.
Another great comfort is that I believe in an after-life and I believe
they still look over my shoulder and support me.

What do these loss histories tell us about the natal chart?

Firstly, in reading other people's histories of loss and the circumstances around
which loss becomes lodged into the psyche, one recognises a universal truth,
that whilst life may appear to deal more harshly with some people than with
others, all lives are filled with losses.

Secondly, when people recalled these sad events, it was with intensity,
vividness and great emotion. These memories were as alive and painful as if
they had happened last week, an indication of unresolved grief.

Thirdly, the reactions of parents to a child's early losses such as the
death of a pet or a grandparent decided the pathway for future losses. Rather
than parents seeing such events as the natural completion of cycles and
allowing them to be portals through which grief and the corresponding
emotions that accompany it can be discussed and managed, the common
response was to suppress or silence them.

Fourthly, when issues inside the family unit became too "hot", they
were projected onto a member of the family and splits occurred. A "normal"
family in the twentieth and twenty-first centuries means one that contains
cut-offs, detachments, splits and the withheld anger of generations past.

Finally, in most cases, it is not until the years following the Saturn
Return and sometimes well into the Mid-Life Crisis years, that a person can
start to gain some sort of perspective on how they have been suppressing
feelings of grief.

Parental signatures in a chart offer us a spectrum of possibilities from
best-case scenario to worst-case scenario and teach us how to manage emotions
and relate to others (the internal pathway learnt from the mother through
the Moon and Venus in a chart) and how to be in the world and take
responsibility for our lives (the external pathway learnt from the father-figure
through the Sun and Saturn in the chart). Whilst most of our behaviours fall
in the centre of this bell-curve, some slip towards the worst-case scenario end
and cause us difficulties. Knowing the range of expression can help us to shift
towards the more fulfilling best-case scenario end. However, the manner in
which early losses are handled can seriously retard this expression. As well,
there is no guarantee that the natural maturation process of the adult human

will alter the way they handle their grief unless they actively engage with the process.

In these case studies Margaret was able to find a way through the maze of patterns of how to fully grieve when, at forty-one years old, she finally saw her father through adult eyes. She was able to talk about the death with her friends and allow them to support her. Harry's friends helped him cope with being prevented from seeing his three sons when he was thirty-five years old. Nette became much closer to her mother between the ages of thirty-three and thirty-eight through the deaths of her great aunt and grandmother when caring for these women in life and through the rituals of their deaths gave them common ground to share their feelings. For her part, by reuniting with Nette and her family from whom she had been estranged, Olly was able to complete her own life review. Other questionnaire answers give different insights. One woman's father died when she was seven-and-a-half years old and she was "excluded from the process by my mother and therefore the rest of my family, thinking that I did not understand what was happening". At the age of seventeen she watched her mother struggle through her step-father's death; at the age of eighteen she experienced the death of her sister's youngest child just after childbirth; and at the age of nineteen she had to handle her uncle's death alone as the family no longer kept in touch with him. It wasn't until the age of thirty-two that she began to recognise the pattern:

> On 19th July 1987 my nephew was killed in an accident. My brother and wife and two of his three daughters, along with his son, were in the car. This was a highly traumatic time for the whole family and I had difficulty dealing with this as no-one was prepared to communicate their grief. For the first time I realised that this was how we dealt with tragedy, by pretending it wasn't happening. My role with my mother reversed and I became the nurturer, trying to help her come to terms with the situation. As I was unable to discuss the situation within my family, I turned to reading books as I struggled to understand why a ten-year old child could be taken from us so suddenly and this is about the time I started to delve into astrology, looking for the answer to: - why did this happen? There must be a reason.

Another woman began studying astrology when she was thirty-five years old and used this model of behaviour to illuminate why she felt and acted the way she did:

> It was the first time in my life that I used a positive thing rather than a destructive one in order to give myself a purpose.

She also realised that exercise was a useful valve to release anger and she began attending counselling sessions. Yet another woman was in her late-thirties before she felt able to resist previous patterns of getting drunk and stoned to deal with her grief and face the feelings inside her. This gave me a clear picture of what was occurring at the natal chart level but what was unfolding in time?

Time from an astrological perspective

Astrological time is governed by cycles. If we develop and grow as a result of learning from and modifying the actions we take as time passes, then predictive astrology allows us to recognise cycles and prepare for the future. In order to gain a deeper understand of these Loss Histories, I took one I had not already considered above and looked at it through the lens of predictive astrology. I correlated the story I had been told with three astrological predictive tools:

> 1. **Fidaria** (also spelt Firdaria, see Appendix 1) - a system of planetary periods where the life is divided into irregular periods of years with each period being ruled by a planet, luminary or nodal axis. I have found Fidaria almost overwhelming in their ability to dominate, flavour and underpin all other predictive patterns.

> 2. **The Secondary Progressed Lunation Cycle** (see Appendix 2) - to show the seasons of a person's life.

> 3. **Transits,** the major predictive tool of modern dynamic astrology, for detail. The meaning of transits and progressions throughout this book are taken with kind permission from Bernadette Brady's *The Eagle and The Lark: A Textbook of Predictive Astrology.* York Beach: Samuel Weiser, 1992, as an unbiased source of delineation.

Here is what I found:

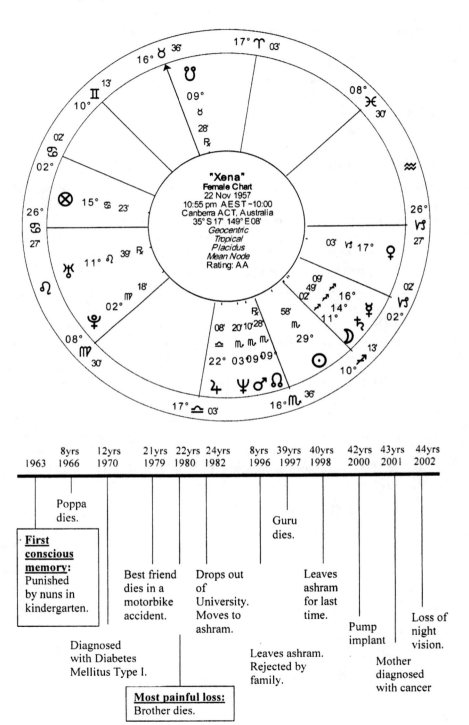

CASE STUDY : XENA

Chart Pattern - Themes and issues

Parental signatures in Xena's chart and what they might say about grief:

Mother: Nurturing and Communication

Moon-Saturn-Mercury conjunction in Sagittarius (Moon ruling the 12th house and the Ascendant; Saturn ruling the 6th and 7th houses and Aquarius intercepted in the 7th house; Mercury ruling the 2nd and 11th houses); Moon square Pluto in the 1st house (ruling the IC); Moon-Saturn-Mercury trine Uranus in the 1st house (Aquarius intercepted in the 7th house).

The Ascendant which describes the Primary Motivation [3] or "the will to survive", designates the background theme of the chart. With a Cancer Ascendant, the primary drive of Xena's chart is the need for emotional security, articulated through the Moon: a crisis at birth (Moon square Pluto) possible technological intervention (Moon trine Uranus) and some form of separation from mother after birth (Moon conjunct Saturn). Xena sees mother as emotionally independent (Moon in Sagittarius), emotionally austere (Moon conjunct Saturn), emotionally inconsistent (Moon trine Uranus) and maintaining a powerful and intense emotional hold over her (Moon square Pluto).

If unable to express any of this, Xena grows up believing she is mentally inferior (Mercury conjunct Saturn) and struggles to express an exceedingly bright mind (Mercury trine Uranus) in a precise, clear and structured manner (Mercury conjunct Saturn). For whilst there is a quick-thinking ability and the capacity to see the big picture (Mercury in Sagittarius), there is a difficulty with details or language in some way (Mercury in detriment), compounded by having to painstakingly structure her thinking and her communication (Mercury conjunct Saturn). Social or group interaction feeds this creative thinking (Mercury rules the 11th house) but she needs to value the way she thinks first (Mercury rules the 2nd house), a situation which is helped tremendously once she is in a business partnership or a committed relationship (Saturn rules the 7th house and Aquarius is intercepted in the 7th house).

In its worst-case scenario, whenever Xena seeks emotional security (the Primary Motivation), what she encounters is drama and crisis (Moon square Pluto) fuelled by unknown fears (Moon rules the 12th house). She feels mentally inferior (Mercury conjunct Saturn) with low self-esteem (Mercury rules the 2nd house), little support from her family (Pluto rules the 4th house), partner (Saturn rules the 7th house), groups (Mercury rules the 11th house) or work (Saturn rules the 7th house). Feeling rejected (Moon conjunct Saturn), she counters this with a strong desire to pull away from everyone (Moon in Sagittarius), using intellect to give distance to feelings (Moon trine Uranus) and health as the catalyst for withdrawal (Saturn rules the 6th house). In situations of tension or stress, the areas that incapacitate her are the structural parts of her body: hair, teeth, nails, bones, skin.

In its best-case scenario, whenever Xena seeks emotional security (the Primary Motivation), what she becomes aware of is an ability to deal with strong emotions or crises (Moon square Pluto) through following her own intuition (Moon rules the 12th house) and supported by those she calls family (Pluto rules the 4th house). Health and emotional well-being improve once she is in a committed relationship (Saturn rules the 6th and 7th houses and Aquarius is intercepted in the 7th house) and this most likely occurs after her Saturn Return. Indeed through the support of a partner (Saturn rules the 7th house), groups (Mercury rules the 11th house) and work (Saturn rules the 6th house), she learns to respond to life creatively (Moon is in the 5th house, mutable square) and with emotional consistency (Moon conjunct Saturn), valuing her own clear, practical thinking (Mercury conjunct Saturn, Mercury rules the 2nd house), unusual solutions and a high level of independent thought (Mercury in Sagittarius, Mercury trine Uranus).

Father-figure: Identity
Unaspected Sun in Scorpio in the 4th house (Leo intercepted in the first house).

Unaspected planets or luminaries do not get the chance to blend and harmonise their energies in a chart via aspects to other planets or luminaries, so the person has conscious experience of two states of being: the energy of the unaspected planet and the rest of the chart separate to it. As a result they feel as if the unaspected planet or luminary either works to capacity in a chart or doesn't appear to be there at all. This can feel highly unsettling and throughout the course of the person's life their aim is to build a bridge between the two states so they can utilize the energy at will, rather than randomly. Unaspected planets or luminaries also point to inherited family patterns or traits which have, in past generations, been a useful way of solving problems but which have now become stuck. The current family members now unconsciously request the one with the unaspected planet or luminary to solve the dilemma for the family, a situation which can cause polarisation and scapegoating.

Xena sees her father-figure as the parent most dominant in her home as a child (Sun in the 4th house). Intense and often unforgiving (myth of Scorpio), he teaches her about issues of trust and betrayal by bringing such issues into the domestic environment. She models her ego, her identity, her vitality and power in the world on her father-figure but finally sees him as unable (unaspected Sun) to teach her how to turn her rage and sense of injustice into something that is creative (myth of Scorpio). The pathway that Xena walks in her lifetime is to learn detachment in order to see situations more clearly and, as a consequence, to get in touch with her own uniqueness. In so doing she changes the themes of intensity and betrayal in her family. Whilst the Sun is unaspected, it does aspect the Cross of Matter (trine), meaning it is are effective and engaged. (The angles of the chart complete a cross inside the circle of the horoscope and a cross in the language of symbolism is representative of the world of matter. The angles of the horoscope can therefore be called the Cross of Matter.)

Other Issues:

Motivation and drive

Neptune (ruling the 8th house) conjunct Mars in Scorpio (in rulership) in the 3rd house (ruling the 9th house and, by old rulership, the 4th house) conjunct the North Node square Uranus in the 1st house; Uranus at The Bends (that is, squaring the nodal axis); Mars-North Node conjunct the IC.

The North Node, by house and sign and any planets conjunct or square it, offers early success. By the late twenties that success is felt to be unfulfilling and this dissatisfaction forces the person to return to their South Node to encounter issues that have been neglected and which need to be embraced. This then allows the person to re-encounter their North Node later in life, now informed with issues articulated by the South Node. Xena's early success not only contains issues of family intensity and revenge (North Node in Scorpio conjunct the IC) but an abundantly high libido and a quick, fast, chaotic temper (Mars in rulership square Uranus) which arm-wrestles with a loss of energy and hence an inability to maintain initiative and impetus (Mars conjunct Neptune). Motivated by feelings (Mars in Scorpio), Xena pours energy into her early education (Mars in the 3rd house) only to find herself feeling drained, unfocused and weak (Mars conjunct Neptune). She is forced to consider tertiary education, teaching in some capacity, publishing, the law or travelling to other countries or foreign communities (South Node in the 9th house) in order to help ground her philosophy and make it practical (South Node in Taurus). Once this is done, she then gains an understanding of what drives and motivates her (Mars rules the 4th and 9th houses) and can return to the North Node and the fulfilment of house, home, hearth and family (North Node conjunct the IC) without acromonious issues clouding the matter. She is also continually forced to understand her own independent pathway (Uranus at the Bends) and is most successful when supported by a business relationship or an intimate partner (Aquarius intercepted in the 7th house).

The best-case scenario is for her to direct her energy into artistic, spiritual or alternative healing fields such as mediation, yoga or T'ai Chi (Mars conjunct Neptune). Then she finds an immense storehouse of energy that can be applied to her work (Mars conjunct Neptune) through short-term projects (Mars square Uranus).

Relating, socialising and networking

Jupiter in Libra in the 3rd house (ruling the 5th and 8th houses) square Venus in Capricorn in the 6th house (ruling the 3rd and 10th houses).

This aspect suggests Xena is initially fearful of relating (Venus in Capricorn) and of expressing herself (Venus rules the 3rd house). However, her world is expanded through a love of communication (Jupiter in the 3rd house) coloured by creativity (Jupiter rules the 5th house) and change (Jupiter rules the 8th house). As she actively resolves the tensions between learning and labour (cardinal square between the 3rd and 6th houses) by working for and on behalf of other people (cadent houses), so she finds that her daily work environment (Venus in the 6th house) gives her a career (Venus rules the 10th house) and brings her joy (Jupiter-Venus is the signature of "The Optimist"). Helping her may be a beneficial relationship with a brother or a grandfather. As she matures, she learns how to maintain strong, solid, (Venus in Capricorn) joyful relationships (Jupiter-Venus). Whilst these two planets only aspect each other and no other planets or luminaries, they do aspect the Cross of Matter (Jupiter squares the Ascendant and Venus trines the MC), meaning they are effective and engaged.

All four of these complex issues will compete for attention in Xena's life and, depending on how she was taught by her parents to handle loss when young, can cause havoc in her adult years if unattended. Here is how Xena gained an understanding of how to manage loss in her life.

Xena's history of loss

Earliest memory, 1963 (6 years old) – *Moon Fidaria (Moon/Sun period). Crescent Secondary Progressed Lunation Phase. Transiting Pluto square natal Moon. Transiting Saturn square the MC:*

Half the class got strapped by the nuns because we accepted lollies
from the local priest. I remember being confused and upset because
I couldn't work out what we had done wrong, since we'd all been
laughing at the tricks the priest was doing for us.

Emergent Pattern
Xena's earliest memory is one of active punishment and pain for accepting
emotional nurturing (the lollies). Unable to defend herself verbally (natal
Saturn-Mercury), she experiences rejection (natal Moon-Saturn). In her Moon
Fidaria, and in the phase where how she is nurtured affects her ego and identity,
(Moon/Sun period) and coupled with the vulnerable, emergent phase of the
Secondary Progressed Lunation Cycle (the Crescent phase), transiting Pluto
squares her Moon, (the ruler of the Ascendant and the Primary Motivation of
the chart) and transiting Saturn, moving through her 7th house, squares her
MC. The nurturing aspect in her chart is under heavy threat and leaves an
indelible memory of betrayal by an authority figure for an act of innocence.

29th September, 1965 (nearly 8 years old) - Grandfather dies
*Moon Fidaria (Moon/Mercury period). First Quarter Secondary Progressed Lunation
Phase. Transiting Saturn square natal Moon-Saturn (retrograde hit in October)
and Mercury (retrograde hit in August).[4] Transiting Uranus square natal Mercury
(first hit). Transiting Pluto square natal Mercury (third of five hits in September):*

> Mum told me that Poppa, her father, had died and that she and
> Dad were going to Berry, a little town on the south coast of New
> South Wales, Australia, where Mum was born and brought up, to
> go to the funeral. I wondered why I couldn't go and I remember
> Mum being sensible about the whole thing but I also remember
> sensing her grief, though I didn't understand it at the time. My
> mother adored her father.

First encounter with grief – what is being implanted
Xena encounters her first experience of how adults grieve: her mother is
"sensible about the whole thing". Xena says her mother "adored her father"
but they do not talk about the loss that Xena instinctively feels from her
mother. Nor do they involve her in the funeral. So Xena learns to disregard
her feelings (natal Moon-Saturn-Mercury triple conjunction) intellectualise
by "being sensible" (Moon partile trine to Uranus) and to isolate herself (Moon
conjunct Saturn).

A hole in the pattern of Xena's psyche is formed. A matter of deep
worry and anguish rises to the surface with her grandfather's death (transiting
Saturn square natal Moon-Saturn) and as she enters the First Quarter
Secondary Progressed Lunation Phase, the time when she seeks challenges,

and now in the Moon/Mercury period of the Moon Fidaria where she is learning to articulate her feelings, silence surrounds her (emphasised by transiting Saturn, Uranus and Pluto all aspecting her natal Mercury.) The boat slows, the wind dies. Menelaus is becalmed in the bay.

1970 (12 years old) - Diabetes Mellitus type "I"

Saturn Fidaria (Saturn/Mars period). Gibbous Secondary Progressed Lunation Phase. Transiting Neptune conjunct natal Sun (begins in January). Transiting Saturn opposition natal Neptune (completes in February). Transiting Saturn conjunct MC (begins in June). Secondary Progressed Moon conjunct MC (exact in June):

> In Australia, primary, secondary and tertiary school years begin in February. When I was about to start high school, I developed diabetes mellitus type "I". I was so sick and out of it that I didn't really realize what was happening to me. I just did what I was told, as I'd always done because I was always scared that I would do something wrong. I do remember the shock, though, of a nurse walking in one day and telling me I had to give myself injections from now on. (Since I'd been a small child I've always been terrified of injections. I still am which is pretty bizarre when I have more than eight needles going into my body each day and, to put it bluntly, I suppress all the emotion around this particular can of worms. I'm scared that if I think about it too much I will give up.) I'm sure people tried to help and my parents probably were there for me, or at least Mum was, but I don't remember them being there. I don't remember being comforted or held as all these terrible things were happening to my body. I just remember always being alone with this trip.
>
> How did I gain short-term relief? There is no short-term relief with this. It's with me every second of every minute of every day and night of my life. I suppress my feelings towards it, I try not to think about it, I try to be sensible, I try not to become obsessed, I try to be "normal", I try to be brave and strong just like my mother taught me - and this doesn't work. At that time I would have been confused and I would have tried to be a brave little girl.
>
> In the winter (June-July-August) I was so sick I started to go into a death coma. Mum and Dad were about to go overseas. I tried to tell my mother all winter that something was wrong. It was a truly horrible time. Anyway nothing happened until one day I couldn't walk anymore and my parents rang the doctor and I remember Dad carrying me into hospital. I was drugged and out of it and that in itself was a relief for awhile, until I was back in the real world again.

Loss of health

The potential health difficulty of the natal chart (natal Mars conjunct Neptune) becomes apparent as the transit of Saturn opposing Xena's natal Neptune completes and the transit of Neptune conjunct her unaspected Sun begins. About to start high school, with its offer of authority, credibility and respect in the wider community (transiting Saturn and the progressed Moon both conjunct the MC), instead her change of status is to "diabetic" and her separation anxiety (natal Moon-Saturn) becomes exacerbated: "I don't remember being comforted or held as all these terrible things were happening to my body." Scared that she might do something wrong, she suppresses her feelings and does as she is told. The pattern of how to deal with loss is reinforced: "I try to be sensible, I try not to become obsessed, I try to be 'normal', I try to be brave and strong just like my mother taught me." (natal Moon-Saturn-Mercury conjunction/Moon in Sagittarius/Moon trine Uranus). In the Gibbous Secondary Progressed Lunation Phase of adjustment and in the Saturn/Mars period of her Saturn Fidaria, a hole called "loss of health" forms in her psyche and it connects with the first hole called "don't talk about Poppa's death", only now the consequences take one step closer to her, in her own body. The first piece of the jigsaw puzzle falls out of the pattern, and the ship does not stir in the bay.

6th January, 1979 (21 years old) – Death of Best Friend
Jupiter Fidaria. Disseminating Secondary Progressed Lunation Phase. Transiting Saturn square natal Moon. Transiting Pluto square natal Venus:

> I lost one of my best friends, Paul. (My other friend at the time was my younger brother, Patrick.) Paul's death was a rather remote event. He was killed in a motorbike accident. His parents rang to let me know what had happened but there was no funeral or wake or anything. Paul's family closed down and kept everything within the immediate househ
> 0.old. I didn't get to see his parents until much later.
>
> At this time I was in a highly destructive relationship that had begun in 1978 with a man called Thaddeus. In the period after Paul's death, Thaddeus' father had repeatedly attempted to commit suicide and Thaddeus was getting fed up with picking up the pieces afterwards to the point where he wished that if his father was going to kill himself, then the least he could do was do it properly. I was now drinking heavily and occasionally smoking dope and hashish.
>
> I can't remember what I did about Paul's death, however, and it wasn't until a few years ago that I went and found where his

ashes were buried. I probably suppressed it all, as was my habit well and truly by then – like, I'm standing here functioning in the world like a socially and politically correct robot because my feelings and my emotions and my real thoughts are well buried and by this stage in my life what's buried has become too, too threatening.

Loss of companionship

In a Jupiter Fidaria and the Disseminating phase of the Secondary Progressed Lunation cycle, one would expect a person to be reaping the benefits of their hard work. The Great Benefic, Jupiter, always promises success. Even if it is in difficult condition in the natal chart it will still give success, albeit diminished. In Xena's chart, Jupiter aspecting Venus and the angles suggests it can fulfil this promise - once she is past her third Jupiter Return and has a better understanding of wisdom. But Xena is twenty-one years old and still completing her second Jupiter cycle and Paul's death is announced by transiting Pluto squaring Xena's natal Venus: "the sudden and emotionally-packed ending of a relationship". Not helped by Paul's family physically and emotionally distancing her from the event, once again Xena suppresses her emotions. The natal pattern of rejection and isolation is reinforced with transiting Saturn squaring Xena's natal Moon. Xena learns to put on a socially acceptable face to the world but underneath, the real issues are hidden and strangled. She learns not to ask for help to deal with her unresolved grief which is now beginning to compound. More holes are formed in the jigsaw. More pieces of the pattern are lost. No wind is predicted in the bay.

24th February 1980 (22 years old) - Most painful loss

Jupiter Fidaria (Jupiter/Mars period). Third Quarter Secondary Progressed Lunation Phase. Transiting Jupiter conjunct Pluto. Later that year transiting Pluto conjuncted natal Jupiter:

> I was with my younger brother, Patrick, when he was killed in a motorbike accident on the 24th February, 1980. It was a strange day. Patrick was helping Thaddeus and I move house. We had just finished the move and had decided to go to a local pub for a counter lunch in the early afternoon. Patrick was on his red motorbike in front of our white Valiant station wagon. The road we were travelling down was a dual carriage way and there were no trees or buildings on the corners which meant the area of vision at each intersection was clear. I was lighting a cigarette when Thaddeus said to me, "Patrick has been hit", so I didn't see the actual moment of collision. A young man had just finished work and was going home in his car and he didn't see Patrick as he came through the

intersection. There was no speed involved in the accident. It was just the way the contact happened and the way Patrick fell on the ground - his head hit the edge of the concrete curb. I figure he must have broken his neck on impact because when I got to him there was no visible damage, just a trickle of blood coming out of his nose but I knew he was dying. The strange thing is that if he had fallen about an inch or two further onto the nature strip he would have been okay, if a bit battered and bruised. The poor young man that hit him came up to me and asked me who I was and when I told him, he cracked up. I remember my heart breaking for him because he was young and all he had been doing was going home after work on a Saturday afternoon and I couldn't imagine what it would be like to know that, for the rest of your life, just because you didn't check an intersection properly, you ended up killing someone. I sometimes wondered how it affected his life. So there was no blame, only grief and sorrow.

My immediate emotional response was, "This is not true, this is not possible, this sort of thing doesn't happen to me, it only happens to other people". And then this circular steel wall came down through the centre of my being and I went numb. I went to the hospital in the ambulance. I went to the morgue to identify the body. Then I went to my parents' house and I realized so clearly that there would be no support or refuge there and that, for the first time in my life, I really was on my own to get through this. People were kind and generous, doing the Irish Catholic thing. I am the eldest child in the family but Patrick was the eldest son but all I remember is being told I had to be strong and brave, for my parents and for my siblings and all I wanted to do was scream, "Don't you realize what I've just seen?" (and as I write this I can still feel it inside me).

I remember seeing the photographs from the funeral at dinner at my parents' place one night and I began to cry and my mother told me to stop … and now, twenty years later, I realize that if I had have cracked that night, the dam of grief and unexpressed emotion that the family was holding back god only knows for how many generations would have burst and that was too terrifying. So I tried to get relief by trying to live life, trying hard to function normally and I began to die inside. How did I deal with it? I didn't. I drank, Thaddeus used to roll me a joint at night to help me sleep, and sex.

My parents seemed to separate out of their relationship after Patrick died. Both of them locked themselves into their own world of grief. I remember talking to Dad one night out on the driveway, just before I went home to my place. I asked him why he and Mum didn't talk to each other about what had happened to Patrick and share their grief and support each other emotionally. He told me that Mum had her way of dealing with things and he had his. I remember feeling incredibly sad at this and thinking that a marriage, a relationship, should be more than two emotionally separate individuals living together under the one roof. Dad and Mum are both extremely devout Roman Catholics. After Patrick died Mum went right into her faith and drew strength from it, and Dad almost lost his faith in the church and God.

Death of brother

Xena's initial responses to her brother's death are normal and natural: pain, shock, numbness and disbelief. The problem occurs when the family has the opportunity to express their shared grief and it is suppressed: "I had to be strong and brave ... and all I wanted to do was scream." Later when she attempts to express grief with her mother (seeing the photographs from the funeral at dinner at my parents' place), her mother suppresses her. In her Jupiter Fidaria, new learning and growth is manifesting through assertion and/or anger (Jupiter-Mars period/Mars in rulership) except that natally the empowered Mars is conjunct Neptune. Life demands that she change and redefine her philosophy (transiting Jupiter conjunct Pluto, reinforced later that year by transiting Pluto conjunct natal Jupiter) but does not take into account the constraints of a family who do not want to deal with grief. Struggling to be heard, Xena's emotions are blocked and smothered with alcohol, drugs and sex in an effort to stop the pain. By now the jigsaw has many holes missing. The unconscious picture is fragmenting badly and Menelaus is slowly starving in the bay.

1982 (24 years old) - Leave family

Jupiter Fidaria (Jupiter/Sun period). Third Quarter Secondary Progressed Lunation Phase (approx twelve months from being Balsamic). Transiting Saturn square natal Venus and conjunct Jupiter. Transiting Jupiter conjunct natal Mars-North Node:

I dropped out of university. I failed myself, I failed my mother, I failed my father. By this stage of my life depression had become a constant companion. I was sick all of the time because my diabetes was out of control (my diabetes has always been unstable, it's just a matter of degrees), therefore I was on an emotional roller coaster and some part of me knew I was dying because parts of me had stopped working: digestion, menstrual cycle, lymphatic and elimination systems. Still I kept trying to be normal and get it together ... I just kept working and drinking.

I left Canberra and went to live in an ashram. In retrospect this was a huge move. I left my family, I left my culture, I left my socio-economic group and I left my religious upbringing (which had pretty much gone by that time anyway). I found short-term relief in dealing with the new environment, especially as an insulin-dependent diabetic, and work, and I worked between twelve and twenty hours a day for the next thirteen-to-sixteen years.

Two side effects of diabetes mellitus are hair loss and retinal haemorrhaging. At that time my hair was falling out in clumps, so in 1983 it was easy to decide to have my head shaved as I thought it would help my hair grow. Retinal haemorrhaging means the cells on the retina leak blood into the vitreous fluid in the eye, and so the space between the lens and the retina becomes opaque. For quite a few years the ophthalmologists who were treating me thought I was going to lose my eyesight. It was horrible because I'd wake up each morning and be too scared to open my eyes just in case I couldn't see anything. The treatment is to burn off the cells that are leaking with laser in order to arrest the development of the haemorrhaging. I got to the point where I hated the treatment as much as my fear of going blind. The haemorrhaging increased from 1986 onwards and reached its climax during 1991-1993. As of late 2000 that is now in recession and has been for five or six years. One thing I learnt in this period is that the medical profession rarely tell the whole truth. People kept telling me that it was all going to be okay and to just keep on going as if nothing was happening and to think beautiful thoughts (this one came from my father) but it was pretty hard when I only had partial vision in either one or both eyes and no sense of depth.

Secondary symptoms

The suppressed and denied grief now develops secondary symptoms: depression, problems with digestion, menstrual cycle, lymphatic and elimination systems. Only twelve months away from the Secondary Progressed Lunation cycle becoming Balsamic and as if sensing the changes ahead of her, Xena breaks her commitment to University education (transiting Saturn square her natal Venus) and seeks a new teaching body (transiting Jupiter conjunct the North Node) in the shape of an ashram, an arena of controlled spiritual study (transiting Saturn conjunct Jupiter). In this Jupiter/Sun period of the Jupiter Fidaria, she uses a guru (Jupiter) to understand her own identity (Sun) but instead of dealing with her suppressed emotions, she goes into overdrive with work (transiting Jupiter conjunct Mars). Hard work and drink, however, are only short-term reprieves, the ill-informed ways of a world focused on visible productivity and, in the final analysis, powerless to compensate for buried issues.

1996 (38 years old) - Leaves ashram/undermined by family
Mars Fidaria (Mars/Jupiter period). First Quarter Secondary Progressed Lunation Phase (the New Secondary Progressed Lunation Phase began at 29° Sagittarius in the 5th house in August 1986). Transiting Pluto square natal Pluto. Transiting Neptune conjunct the Descendant:

> I was in India for about a month at the end of 1995 for a tantric ceremony that extended over two weeks, devoted to the feminine force of the universe. At the same time I witnessed the ceremony of initiation of a tantric guru. By the time that I returned to Australia I knew that I could no longer remain in the ashram because I couldn't handle the hypocrisy anymore. This loss was a way of life that had held so much potential for me, yet the underbelly of the spiritual world had been so disillusioning. So in January or February 1996 I asked my mother and father if I could stay with them for a while until I sorted myself out. My father wanted to help me. My mother didn't want to know about me. And so began a devastating seven-to-nine months living with my mum and dad and a sister who had never moved out of home. The loss this time was my already non-existent sense of self-worth. It was a nightmare. It was a nightmare that I intellectually knew I could get out of, yet some part of me couldn't or didn't want to. The situation culminated with the four of us sitting down and my father telling me I had to leave because I didn't fit in and that all the tension in the house was because of me. This was the most devastating thing that has ever happened to me and I still cry when I think about it. I felt I had no place in the world or in the universe and that I was worthless. I felt so unloved. What did I do? I shut down emotionally yet again and just kept going because that was what I had always done. If I thought beyond what I had to do next, then I think I would have killed myself, that's how much this one got to me, even more than being with Patrick while he died.
>
> About four weeks after this discussion I visited the ashram because someone was out from India. Four weeks after this I had packed up my life in Australia and went to live and work in India indefinitely. As far as I was concerned, the further away I was from my family, the better. In India any lingering illusions I had about gurus and spiritual life were destroyed. I worked and tried to keep my diabetic body together. That took most of my energy until I

realized that if I stayed much longer I would not survive another summer over there. Part of me really wanted to die and part of me really wanted to live and part of me was addicted to the drama of all this.

Loss of self-worth

Now in the Mars/Jupiter period of her Mars Fidaria, the inverse Fidaria for Xena of when her younger brother Patrick was killed (Jupiter/Mars period of her Jupiter Fidaria) she is once again having to deal with her siblings and family at a close level (Mars and Jupiter are both in the 3rd house, Mars is conjunct the IC natally and, since Jupiter rules the 8th house, it will always bring change in some form when being activated in Xena's chart). The Descendant, initially how we view our parents' relationship, represents the template we use for our own intimate relationships. However, instead of protection, she becomes the family scapegoat and encounters despair (transiting Neptune conjunct the Descendant), the worst-case scenario expression of all Neptune transits. Isolation has now become Xena's permanent way of dealing with grief: "The further away I was from my family the better." Amongst this devastation (natal Neptune also rules the 8th house) the background theme of the first of her mid-life crisis transits (transiting Pluto square Pluto) attempts to make itself heard: the recognition that all life is finite and that we are mortal; that this present moment is the life we thought we would lead "in the ever after"; and the fairytale of "one-day when I grow up -... " is over, for this is "one-day".

1997 (39 years old) - Death of "spiritual" teacher
North Node Fidaria. First Quarter Secondary Progressed Lunation Phase. Transiting Saturn square natal Venus. Progressed Moon conjunct MC (exact in October):

> My first "spiritual" teacher, Swami A., died in June 1997. I heard about his death in India and my reaction to it was anger and rage. I met Swami A. in my early twenties and it was an interaction with him in November 1982 that precipitated my decision to leave Canberra and my family and go and live in an ashram. He promised that he could help me deal with the diabetes. In retrospect this was the beginning of sixteen years of broken promises and shattered dreams, yet paradoxically it probably saved my life, that is, the yogic practices probably saved my physical life but there was a high price to pay. Swami A. was an exceedingly charismatic teacher and he had what it took to become great but the charisma evaporated when money and power gained an upper hand. He blew it all in about 1986 by embezzling company funds and seducing

underage girls and he ended up in prison. Eventually he became
an alcoholic and this was the cause of his death. I obviously
suppressed my rage and anger at his betrayal of my faith and trust
in him for many years until I heard of his death in India in 1997. I
was getting out of the lift in the library on my way to work one
morning and Jyotirmayananda rushed up to me and said, "Swami
A. has just died." I just shrugged my shoulders and kept going. A
few minutes later when I walked into my office and began sorting
through the work for the day, the rage erupted from the pit of my
abdomen. I was immensely angry at Swami A., ashrams, gurus and
the whole "spiritual" trip. The setting was appropriate because there
I was in India in an ashram working for a guru, when the guru in
question, Swami N., walked through the door. All I remember is
looking at Swami N. and thinking really clearly, "You and your
guru and your ashrams are nothing but a con!" It still took me
another year to extricate myself.

Anger

The event that precipitated Xena's decision to leave her family and go and
live in an ashram was meeting Swami A. which occurred the last time Xena
experienced transiting Saturn square to her natal Venus in 1982. Saturn-Venus
transits bring either commitment to or destruction of a relationship. In this
case it is the realisation that this powerful shaping relationship in her life is
finally dead. Now in her North Node Fidaria, she is forced to face and define
what she considers will give her fulfilment or completeness (the journey of
the North Node). Helping this is the fact that she is in an action-oriented
period of her life (First Quarter Secondary Progressed Lunation Phase) and
aware of the need to change her standing in the community (progressed Moon
conjunct MC). The last time Xena's progressed Moon conjuncted the MC
she was twelve years old and developed Diabetes Mellitus Type I: "I'm sure
people tried to help and my parents probably were there for me, or at least
Mum was, but I don't remember them being there." That immature but totally
understandable sense of betrayal at the age of twelve is now played out in
maturity.

1998 (40 years old) - Leaves ashram for the final time
*North Node Fidaria. Gibbous Secondary Progressed Lunation Phase. Transiting
Uranus square Mars. Transiting Uranus square the nodal axis. Transiting Uranus
opposition natal Uranus. Transiting Saturn opposition Neptune (begins in late July):*
I left the ashram for the last time in May, 1998. This loss took
awhile to filter through to my consciousness. When I had arrived
back in Australia, the chairman and treasurer of the ashram

organisation asked if I would help the board of directors restructure it administratively and legally. I agreed to help for 6 months which I did. However, the politics in the ashram, which make federal and state politics look like child's play, reached a point where I resigned my position and left. This time I didn't go anywhere near my family. However, learning to survive in the real world when you are a forty-year-old, single woman with no material resources and an unstable physical body doesn't leave much time to grieve for a way of life that has consumed sixteen years of your life. In November or December 1998 I went to the doctor because of the shocking pains I was having, and am still having, while I menstruate. At that time the tests showed atypical cells on the walls of my vagina and cervix. These were frozen off and recent tests are clear. However the menstrual cramps continue, with vomiting and diarrhoea each month and the allopathic doctors suggest having a hysterectomy which I'm not going to have.

Changes

This is a year of "haste, accidents, anger, sexual energy and passion" (transiting Uranus square Mars) underpinned by the "blinding flash of the obvious" (the second of Xena's mid-life crisis transits, transiting Uranus opposing Uranus). Uranus transiting through the seventh house gives her freedom from her business relationship (the ashram) and the opportunity to adjust the course of her life (North Node Fidaria and the Gibbous Secondary Progressed Lunation Phase - see also next entry). For Xena this is a major loss of a way of life but this time she chooses not to look for emotional support from her family. Instead her body expresses this loss through a health crisis (transiting Saturn opposing Neptune: "illness, tiredness, depletion of resource, despair, to be without hope)".

2000 (42 years old) - 15th February 2000.

South Node Fidaria. Gibbous Secondary Progressed Lunation Phase. Transiting Saturn conjunct the MC (ends in April). Transiting Pluto conjunct natal Moon. Transiting Jupiter conjunct the MC (once only in May). Transiting Saturn opposition natal Sun (begins in August):

> This was the day that Dr White told me that the insulin injections weren't really effective and asked whether I could find $6,250 (AUD) to have an insulin pump installed. The pump costs about $250 (AUD) a month to maintain with tubing and catheters and batteries and swabs - all the paraphernalia. Dad paid for the pump and my friend Chris, the man with whom I now have a relationship, helps me out with my medical costs. I love them both dearly but I

was really hoping to become financially independent at some point in the near future. Maybe it would be a good idea to let that dream go for a while.

My relationship with Chris began to take on a "courting" flavour in March 1998 and by the end of that month we had slept together. (In 1998 transiting Uranus squared Xena's natal Mars, expressing the sexual energy and passion of that transit). To put this in perspective, I had known Chris for many years prior to this and had worked with him at different times when he was involved with ashram affairs - even though he has never lived in the ashram. When I got back from India he was one of the two people who approached me to do the secretarial work for the organisation while they were restructuring. This time there was a definite spark between us and he was the person with whom I had to work most closely - although I'm sure both of us engineered it that way. The rest, as they say, is history. As much as any of us can be certain of life's unfolding, we are both in this relationship for the long haul.

17:55 on 17th April, 2000 (final touch of transiting Saturn conjunct the MC). At Prince of Wales Hospital, Sydney, the catheter was inserted into my body and at 18:00 the pump began pumping - my little lifeline. It has transformed my life.

Early November, 2000 (final touch of transiting Pluto conjunct the Moon). I knew this would be a huge change for me and it proved to be much bigger than I anticipated. Six months after going onto the insulin pump I've become used to the whole thing and so has my body. So the diabetes is easing but from July onwards (the retrograde hit of Pluto conjunct the Moon) I kept getting viral infections and felt exhausted all the time. I had tests done and found out I was anaemic. I hadn't eaten meat for about twenty years and although I'd been taking iron supplements for a couple of years, I hadn't been absorbing them. Things reached such a crisis point that I was prepared to do about anything and last weekend (second touch of transiting Saturn opposition natal Sun and third and final touch of transiting Pluto conjunct natal Moon), I went and bought a kilo of beef, a cast iron pot and a bottle of red wine (for me to cope with eating the meat). I braised a big beef stew and I've been eating it each day. I'm beginning to feel much stronger physically and I'm even beginning to enjoy eating it.

The one thing that has kept me going this year is my astrological studies (begun in February 2000). It's the one thing that I can feel passionate about and focus on and it helps keep my head out of trouble.

Irrevocable adjustments
The South Node Fidaria often brings up health issues from the past and so it has for Xena, only this time it gives her solutions. The natal configuration of rejection, isolation and her inability to discuss how she feels is emphasised with transiting Pluto conjuncting her natal Moon. Physical and emotional changes to her body force her to take on a new level of responsibility (transiting Saturn opposite natal Sun): the insulin pump and eating meat. Finally she gains stability for her body, a stronger sense of self-worth and a relationship that is both loving and understanding.

In March 2003 I asked Xena if she would like to update the graph and she replied as follows:

26th July 2001 (43 years old) - Mother diagnosed with breast cancer
South Node Fidaria. Gibbous Secondary Progressed Lunation Phase. Transiting Saturn opposite natal Moon-Saturn. Transiting Pluto conjunct Saturn.

> My mother rang from Canberra to say that she had been diagnosed with cancer in her left breast. I flew down to Canberra on 28 July and stayed until 30 July and it was a truly horrible time because all the dysfunctional family dynamics were in full swing, along with all of the unexpressed unresolved grief in my family. It took me weeks to recover from this trip emotionally. Eventually I valued the insights I gained into my own behaviour within my family unit through being there and watching how I reacted to the extreme stress at that time. This, in turn, triggered me into working again with my own dysfunctional behaviour in relationship and now (March 2003), I feel like I am making some headway in being able to hold my own space even when I am with my family. Mum ended up having a lumpectomy. There was only a little bit of cancer there and it had not spread to the lymph nodes.
>
> What did I do to help deal with this internal distress? Telling my story to you and then going through *The Grief Recovery Handbook* took the lid off everything that I had blocked out. I thought about this last night after sending off the last bit of information to you and I feel how important it is to be able to tell my story of my experiences, to have it heard and acknowledged. This is so essential. Beginning to work through my grief has helped to loosen me up a lot, especially my emotionally reactive patterns to people and life. So because I am a little more open now, I begin to notice when I react strongly to certain situations and I begin to wonder why I do so. After that visit to Canberra my naturopath recommended that I see a particular healer in order to start working

on an emotional level, mainly because I was feeling really, really stuck with my teaching, despite naturopathic treatment and having acupuncture every week. This, in turn, has led me to work on an energetic level with my relationship with my mother and the rest of my family. The knowledge that I gain from this, along with the astrology, are powerful tools that help me to shift belief systems and behaviour. I now feel that I am able to respond to people and situations rather than being extremely reactive all the time. In other words, I now tend to ask why I think the way I do and why I believe the things I do and whilst this is an ongoing process, last year and this year there have been subtle shifts in my relationship with my family and especially with my mother. It's all slow work and intense but that's part of the journey, I suppose. I hang in there as best I can. I feel deeply and strongly that filling out your grief questionnaire was the beginning of this healing process for me. Telling stories is such a powerful medium, as you no doubt know.

June, 2002 (44 years old) - Loss of night vision
Sun Fidaria. Full Moon Secondary Progressed Lunation Phase. Transiting Pluto conjunct natal Mercury (retrograde hit in June). Transiting Neptune square Mars-North Node (retrograde hit in August). Transiting Jupiter conjunct the Ascendant (once only in July):

I began to notice that it was becoming harder and harder for me to drive at night. I reached the point where I didn't think it was safe, so I made an appointment with my optometrist for 1 August, 2002, and asked him whether I was being fanciful or was something happening to my eyes. He was horrified that I was driving at night at all and then explained that because the surfaces of both my eyes have been completely lasered in order to prevent me going blind, I am now reaping the side effects of this treatment and have begun to develop something like blind spots on parts of my retina.

This felt like a punch in the stomach at the time. How could I go out socially at night and how could I teach yoga at night unless I had someone to ferry me about? Loss of independence is a scary thought to me. It also brought back all of the years I lived in fear, when the possibility of losing my eyesight altogether was really high. Luckily I will always be able to read but I have lost some of my peripheral vision. It is as if my retina has difficulty receiving images at night if it is happening quickly. If I go from bright daylight into a dark room it takes quite a while, relatively speaking, for my eyes to adjust and the same going from dark into daylight which is painful for me at times.

Once I have adjusted it is usually okay. However, at night it is difficult for me to distinguish objects. It's like there is not enough contrast for the objects to register on my retinal surface and this, combined with my reduced peripheral vision, makes it dangerous for me to drive. Chris would drive me, even though it is a fair distance from his place but I am kind of relieved not to do the class at the moment. I am happy to do the two classes I have during the day on Wednesday. This, with the study and clients is enough for me at the moment - along with arranging to move in with Chris.

Afterword: 2nd April, 2004 (46 years old) - Move in with Chris

Sun Fidaria (Sun/Venus period). Full Secondary Progressed Lunation Phase. Secondary Progressed Sun conjunct natal Venus (exact in March). Transiting Jupiter square natal Moon-Saturn-Mercury (retrograde hits in February-March). Later in the year: Transiting Saturn opposition Venus (one touch only in July). Transiting Saturn conjunct the Ascendant (begins in October):

31st March: Well, I passed the astrology exam with a credit which I am kind of happy with. It was really strange adjusting to life without the study but I'm enjoying getting used to it. The relocation took up a lot of that space. Yes, as of a week ago, the event that has been going to take place for years happened: I moved in with Chris. I thought the equinox was a good time to take the plunge. Chris is surrounded by two hectares of bush and sandstone on a hill that overlooks eucalypts and bays of water in one direction and out to the ocean in another. I know I will be happy here. I feel settled. Our first week of living together was rather traumatic as both Chris and I went into our dysfunctional behaviour patterns, provoking and bouncing off each other. However, even going through that and even thinking "oh my god what have I done?", I did, and do, feel like this move is right and appropriate; and when I stop still and feel deep into the relationship and the land on which we dwell, I do feel settled. I feel it in my body and my bones and I feel it in my inner being - and the feeling is so sweet and pure - I can't ever remember feeling like this.

 2nd April: Yesterday, not long after I sent my email to you, I was sitting on the train going down to Sydney and began reflecting again on the move and the past six months - and I was really proud of myself. Over the past two years I seem to have travelled an extremely long way because not only had I managed to sit the AGE Int. Diploma exam and pass (which to me was a huge achievement, given my past history at achieving for myself) but I have also developed enough sense of confidence, self-esteem and self-worth to actually move in with and engage in a full relationship with someone. I can feel my faith in myself welling up inside me and the belief that I have a right to be here on this Earth. Two years ago, four or five years ago, such things would have been inconceivable to me. So as I travelled through gorges and watched the Hawkesbury River slip by, I really did think, "Wow, well done!" And that's the story up until today, a happy ending and a new beginning.

Conclusion

We breathe in to bring oxygen into the system and we breathe out to release harmful carbon dioxide. We eat and drink to energise and nourish our body. We urinate and defecate to release detritus. The excretory processes of exhaling, urinating, perspiring, defecating and crying play a vital role in maintaining homeostasis by removing waste and harmful substances and it is no different on an emotional level: we take in sensory experiences by living them but talking about them, thinking about them and shaping them into a story that has meaning for us is the way we contain that which sustains and stimulates us and allows us to let go of that which does us harm. The inability of her family to adequately deal with loss when Xena was young, the pattern she internalised and adopted, anxious to be accepted, and which kept being reinforced every time she encountered loss as an adult, was a metaphorical landmine destined eventually to explode.

Breath, like air, has heat energy, kinetic energy and pressure. For Menelaus and his wind-starved sailors, there was nothing lyrical about the lazy slap of wave against hull, the rock of a ship going nowhere. The leap from stranded to lifeless is only a matter of breathing. It is one of the body's vital signs. Marooned in the bay, the pressure rises from miserable to intolerable but to whom could Menelaus turn? In this commercial and industrial age we have learnt "lean-back technology". We distance ourselves and use clichés and platitudes to push away from people in grief. "Lean-forward technology" is the demanding skill of listening with an open heart, without judgment or blame and with consideration. It is a simple enough statement: "... how important it is to be able to tell my story of my experiences, to have it heard and acknowledged." In *Macbeth* (4.3.209-211; *The Norton Shakespeare*, p.2607), when Macduff learns of the savage slaughter of his wife and children, Malcolm implores him:

> "What, man, ne'er pull your hat upon your brows.
> Give sorrow words. The grief that does not speak
> Whispers the o'erfraught heart and bids it break."

To allow someone in grief to give voice to their experiences is not just being kind. It is saving their life.

❊   ❊   ❊

Endnotes

1. op.cit. James and Friedman (1998), Chapter 5, pp. 85-102.

2. Australia is divided geographically into six states and two territories. Therefore in Australia the term "interstate" refers to someone or something being located in a state separate from the one in which one is currently living.

3. Zoller, Robert. 'Medieval Delineation of Character', in *Astrology: An Ancient Art in the Modern World*, ed. Mari Garcia (1998), Adelaide: Australis '97 The Congress Papers, pp.170-172.

4. Against other background themes, transits dance a pattern all of their own. Unlike natal aspects with which we live our whole life and come to know and finally appreciate, transits come in from the cold for a short period of time and so feel raw and unformed, even feral. The beginning of the transit can be likened to The Stranger who knocks on the door, offering us a gift in the shape of an event. The event may come out of the blue or appear to be the next step along a pathway we are following and whilst we respond with a range of behaviours to the event, from joy and excitement to wariness, resistance, apprehension and even devastation, The Stranger remains a stranger, different, new and separate from us. When the retrograde touch of the transit occurs it can be likened to The Stranger coming to live with us. We struggle to accommodate their demanding ways and assertive needs and fight against the complex knots this master-mistress ties around our lives. By the end of the transit, as we find we are doing what we thought we could never do, the outcome of the transit leads to greater clarity and with a shock we realise we are The Stranger. That which we thought had nothing to do with us at the beginning of the transit has now been learnt, incorporated and welded into the matrix of our behaviour and would not have happened without the struggle. The choice is always to accept what is being offered or to turn away from the knowing, to stay in the safe, secure world of the familiar or to go through the new doors that are being opened for us at the time.

5

In the Consulting Room -
A Way Through the Dark

> When it is dark enough, you can see the stars.
> Ralph Waldo Emerson (1803-1882)

An astrological consultation is a highly-focused, qualitative interview in which the astrologer listens to the history and context supplied by the client, correlates that with the bell-curve of possibilities for the issues described by the natal chart and then projects that pathway ahead in time using predictive tools. When the client has experienced loss, that same process is woven with an understanding of the process of grief and the client's relationship to the one who has died. We cannot change events that have already taken shape and passed the client by. What we can offer are options which will allow them to change their attitude towards the past which then changes their attitude towards future events. In such a way clients come to have mastery over their future. So "when" a client comes to see us for a consultation is as much a factor in the consultation as "why".

A client in grief will come to an astrologer because they want someone who can tell them when their feelings of aloneness and pain will end. Unconsciously they may demand a great deal but the three things they have the right to request and receive are that the astrologer will be someone who can hear their story, won't patronise them and will understand the excruciating pain they are now feeling. They want the astrologer to be personally present and standing behind them in the experience from which they've come and also able to see the wider field, for Proteus will take many shapes through a client's predictive work.

About age

From my work with clients, it is clear that the client's age is a vital ingredient in an astrological consultation. If clients are to fully appreciate and comprehend grief in a way that can be applied meaningfully to their lives, then they have the best chance of doing so after the Saturn Return. The Saturn Return recolours the life. Often it is about letting go - of a job, a marriage, a country, a single life or even a death - and redefining life by a new benchmark of responsibility, so loss takes on a totally new meaning by such life experience.

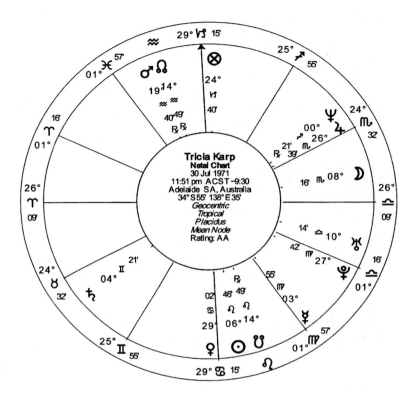

Tricia Karp was originally a client and subsequently became one of our students. She answered my Grief Questionnaire in early 2000 when she was twenty-eight and a half years old. She has her natal Moon in Scorpio in the 7th house ruling the IC square to her natal Sun in Leo in the 4th house with Leo intercepted in the 4th house and conjunct her South Node. Tricia chronicled her most painful loss as follows:

> In early 1987 I broke up with my first "serious" boyfriend. We had been together for nearly one year. He was older than me (he had left school and I was in Year Ten when we started seeing one another) and our relationship not only impacted on me but my whole family. For reasons I couldn't understand, he broke off the relationship and I was absolutely devastated. He was my first true love and I adored and worshipped him. Without him I was nothing. I couldn't even begin to imagine how my life could possibly continue without him. I was just fifteen years-old and remember vowing to never again allow anyone to hurt me the way he did, to

never let anyone get that close to me ever again. My mother was almost as upset as me and I clearly remember her crying, too. The departure of my boyfriend affected my whole family and became the major focus at that time. I remember being outside talking to Mum while she was watering the garden and she suggested that perhaps my boyfriend had left because he was eighteen years-old and was looking for someone more mature. She mentioned that he may want to have sex and perhaps I should think about that if I wanted to get him back. I'll never forget her saying that. She wanted him back in the family almost as much as I did and she did what she could to help. While I'll never forget her words, she was certainly well meaning. It wasn't as though she was forcing me to do anything I didn't want to do. It was more like we were having a discussion about the birds and the bees. My friends couldn't understand what I was going through which wasn't surprising because none of them had had a relationship like I'd had. I felt so alone, like no-one really cared or understood, except for Mum. But I knew, at the end of the day, only I could really deal with the situation. I spent a lot of time alone in my bedroom.

During the time we were apart (we did get back together again), I felt like my lifeline had been cut off. With my boyfriend I could go out and do things that my other friends didn't get to do. Our relationship gave me a certain freedom because he had a car and my parents trusted him to take me out. After the break-up, all of a sudden I was stuck at home, devastated and bored. I don't remember anything that helped me to gain short-term relief but it was common for me to go off my food at stressful times. It was almost like a hunger strike. I used that as a control mechanism, although it never lasted long.

A year later, in January 2001, when Tricia was twenty-nine and a half, her predictive work was as follows:

- **Saturn Return** (one touch only in May): Learning at ground level the meaning of responsibility.
- **Transiting Neptune square natal Moon** (beginning in early February and completing in early December): a visionary drug sensitive time, spiritual time where the individual experiences the dissolving of emotional responses. Time out from the world to unconsciously reorganise one's emotional reality.
- **Transiting Neptune opposing natal Sun** (beginning in late March 2001 and completing in early November 2002):

confusion about one's role in the world; desire to escape, travel or recluse while one reconsiders – possibly on an unconscious level - the way in which one exists in the world.

- **Secondary Progressed First Quarter Lunation Phase** (beginning in February): a time of action, pushing forward, manifesting the energies of the New Moon (seeded in Leo in the 4th house in 1992).
- **Secondary Progressed Moon in the 8th house in Sagittarius:** life events become more intense with a focus on beginnings and endings in order to allow change into a person's life (8th house) through an expansion of the unexplored world (Sagittarius).
- **Secondary Progressed Mercury square to natal Neptune** (exact in May): being forced to take action involving clear communication, paperwork, study, movement.
- **Jupiter-Moon sub-period of her Jupiter Fidaria** (which changes in early November to Jupiter-Saturn). Jupiter's natal placement in Tricia's chart is in Scorpio in the 8th house ruling the 9th and 11th houses, trining Venus in Cancer in the 3rd house conjunct the IC, and sextile the MC. Jupiter as the Great Benefic wants to expand and change her world through other people's resources (8th house). She gains wisdom through overseas travel (Jupiter ruling the 9th house) and new groups (Jupiter ruling the 11th house) and this raw material is shaped into showing her what her emotional needs are in relationship (Moon in Scorpio in the 7th house ruling the 4th house).

This was how the year unfolded:

In January 2001 I met "Andnej", a European man who literally swept me off my feet. I was certain he was the ideal man for me - my soul mate - the man I'd been waiting for all my life - the "One". I broke off my relationship with my fiancé, packed my bags and left Australia to live with Andnej in America. In March, just seven weeks after I'd left home, Andnej and I travelled back to Australia. He was caught importing drugs at Sydney airport, arrested, charged and thrown into jail. I was also questioned by the police and arrested. I spent two weeks in jail before being allowed out. My parents posted bail against their house and I returned home to live with them in Adelaide. I had to report to the local police station three days a week.

I was absolutely devastated and didn't know how I could possibly live without Andnej in my life. My solicitor advised me not to have any contact with him, so I began writing letters to him every day that I planned to send to him later when we were allowed to have contact again. I started working part-time at a health centre and slowly began to piece my life together again. I cried every day for months. I would eat dinner and then lock myself in my bedroom at night, spending a lot of time taking a good hard look at myself! When I was in jail I knew that everything would have to be different in my life from then on. I felt as though whatever I had thought my life was about was all wrong. It was like I was starting from the beginning - from "square one" - and I didn't really know how to do that. All I knew was that I had to, and with a criminal charge hanging over my head, it was extremely serious.

The Department of Public Prosecutions withdrew the charge against me in August. I was incredibly relieved. I felt like justice had been done because I had had nothing to do with Andnej's illegal activities. As soon as I was able to, I flew to Sydney to visit him and we continued our relationship as best we could until the end of 2001 when I decided it was just too difficult and too painful and I cut off the relationship. I then became quite resentful and angry and continued to grieve for another year. At times I felt like I wasn't just grieving for my "lost love" but for many other things in my life, some of which were quite old. I realised I hadn't grieved about or processed them properly before. It was like I was having a massive emotional clean-out.

In March 2003, after much work on healing the trauma, for the first time I felt that I could truly accept what had happened. I knew I needed to visit Andnej to tell him that. It felt important for me to bring the situation into present time because it had had so much power over me and I wanted to be able to honestly tell him that I had forgiven him. I needed to complete this chapter in my life and I knew he did, too. I could feel that he was still clinging to the hope that we would be together again.

In April 2003 I went to see him. It felt confronting and overwhelming to walk into a jail again and I was extremely emotional. I was also incredibly grateful that I had had the courage to face my demons. Through many tears I told him that I now accepted the situation and that I had moved on in my life, that what we had shared was a magical time which also caused me the most intense pain I had ever experienced.

I had a lot of clarity and I reflect on the visit now as the biggest thing I have ever done in my life. In my heart I will always feel love for him and I have no doubts as to why I fell for him the way I did. He is a beautiful man and immensely charming. During the visit, he did his best to try to "win me back" but I now see that men like him just aren't good for me. I imagine I'll always be attracted to this type of man but now I know better. I was so proud of myself to be able to sit with him and be absolutely clear inside about where I stand in my life now. I realised how far I'd come and I felt a strong sense of dignity and self-respect. I saw his manipulative ways but there was no bitterness left inside me, just acceptance.

I can honestly say that what I went through was the most amazing experience, filled with many opportunities for growth and I can answer one question with a definite "yes" - my Saturn Return loss combined with those bloody Neptune transits was certainly the biggest grief event in my life so far and far overtook breaking up with my first boyfriend!! As difficult as it was, I pounced on those opportunities and my new life is wonderful! I am so thankful for my journey.

Terminus, in Roman mythology, was the god of boundaries, the protector of limits both of private property and of the public territory of Rome. Sacrifices of blood, incense, fruits, honey and wine were poured into a ditch and lit. When they had been totally burnt, an anointed stone crowned with garlands was positioned into the hot ashes and secured into the ground. Anyone who removed this boundary stone was damned and could be killed with impunity until a fine eventually replaced the death penalty. Terminalia was the name of the festival held at the boundary of the old and new (Roman) years on the 23rd of February. We see this ancient Roman custom in the stones (not flowers) placed by Jews on graves, acknowledging the boundary between life and death. The Saturn Return is a Terminalia. It defines a boundary of experience. Values change and we see life through a more practical lens. It allows us to process grief in totally different ways to someone pre-Saturn Return, to make sense of it, to ground it and make this a practical application of life.

The design of the matrix
How do you talk to a client in grief about their future? What do you say? As an example of how life can blossom or implode for a client, depending on how imprisoned they are by their previous decisions, with Margaret's permission I have taken her Loss History from Chapter 4 and looked at the predictive work asking: "How might a consulting astrologer have helped her if she had rung for a consultation at that point in time? How might it have changed her future?"

Margaret

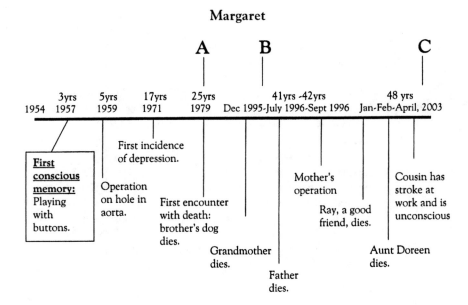

If Margaret had come to see you at point "A" in April 1979 after her brother's dog died (aged twenty-five), the first death she had experienced and the first living being to whom she felt she could show affection, you would note her predictive work for 1979 was as follows:

- **Jupiter-Sun period of her Jupiter Fidaria** (since April 1978): education which shapes her identity and vitality.

- **Second Jupiter return** (begins in September 1978 and completes in April 1979): a year of growth and education. Her natal Jupiter is exalted in Cancer and hence promises benefit and success as long as she is prepared to apply effort and energy. Being natally conjunct Uranus suggests the benefits come to her as long as she is taking risks. However, without life experience under its belt, Jupiter rarely fulfils its promise prior to the third Jupiter return.

- **Secondary Progressed Moon enters the 5th house** (in late March): a focus on personal creative skills, children, lovers and recreation.

- **Balsamic Secondary Progressed Lunation Phase** (completes in October 1979): a period of shedding, letting go, releasing.

Since August 1975 Margaret has been in this process of recalibrating her life, sifting through that which is no longer needed and holding onto foundation stones that would form the basis of the incoming cycle being seeded at 2^0 43' Sagittarius. For the last Secondary Progressed New Moon phase, seeded before she was born, began at 2^0 47' Scorpio, conjunct her natal Mercury. Since the Mercury is also conjunct the Sun and Saturn and in a fixed square to Mars, this means she has been evolving and maturing how she expresses issues of trust and betrayal (Mercury conjunct the Sun/Scorpio myth), a fear of intimidation (Sun conjunct Saturn), inherent rage and anger (Saturn square Mars) and an inherited family motif of inhibition of blocked communication (Mercury conjunct the IC and the ruler of the 12th house and conjunct Saturn). So it would have been appropriate to talk with her about this major cycle in her life that was ending and how she was being asked to allow change into her life, how the next cycle was bringing in a desire for expansiveness and greater independence. This would have given her the space to talk about her brother's dog and her illogical feelings of loss and rage and may have averted the period of depression into which she fell. Dealing with her grief clearly and openly at this stage, in keeping with the Balsamic Secondary Progressed Lunation Phase, may well have unlocked other issues hidden deep within her about feeling intimidated and unloved. Being taught techniques for handling her emotions at this stage of her life may well have meant she reacted to her grandmother's death (when she was forty-one) in a totally different manner. By then, well past her Saturn Return, she may have felt better equipped to understand the affection she felt for her grandmother, clearer in her ability to discuss the contradiction of emotions she felt and, finally, less frightened of growing old.

The loss of an animal friend is a grief many people encounter, yet do not pay it the attention it deserves. When we have lived with and cared for an animal for a number of years and been the recipient of its unconditional love, its playfulness and its companionship, the loss of that component in our lives will be deeply felt. This has begun to be recognised by the pet insurance industry. On Friday, 3rd May, 2002, More Than, part of The Royal & Sun Alliance insurance group, announced its new policy on pet insurance.[1] Already claiming twelve percent of the UK pet insurance market and offering acupuncture and herbal remedies for pets as part of its cover, More Than now added a free, twenty-four-hour counselling service staffed by twenty-six counsellors trained by the British Association of Counselling and Psychotherapy specifically for cat and dog owners whose pets became seriously ill or died. Recognising that people share their lives with an animal friend for approximately ten to fifteen years and sometimes longer, the company understood that the serious illness or death of such an animal friend was an extremely traumatic event, particularly if the person lived alone. Indeed one in ten claims on More Than's pet insurance products related to an animal's death.

However, none of this happened for Margaret at age twenty-four and the unarticulated feelings, recognised as powerful and intense, were categorised as trivial by her mother and so repressed by the Sun-Saturn-Mercury part of Margaret's chart. Although conscious of how large a part of her twenty-four years of life had been enriched by the unconditional love she had received from her brother's dog, still she was unable to talk about this to anyone for eighteen months. When she did finally visit a doctor, that natural urge to talk and discuss was treated with anti-depressants. It could be argued that Saturn won the battle for her self-expression through fear and intimidation, exacerbated by Margaret's lack of understanding of the need to articulate her grief. As a result Jupiter's expansion occurred through her body instead of her well-being.

If Margaret had come to see you at point "B" in February 1996 (aged forty-one), after her grandmother's death, her predictive work would have revealed a different focus. Her grandmother had fallen over in 1993 at the age of ninety-two and for the following three years had been confined to Nursing Home care. Slowly Margaret watched her grandmother's life ebb away, hating the situation of powerlessness in which both she and her grandmother found themselves, yet unable to change things. Her predictive work for the three years leading up to her grandmother's death reveals the following:

1993:

- **Secondary Progressed Moon moves into Gemini** (in March): a focus on data and information-seeking.
- **Transiting Saturn opposition natal Pluto** (begins in April and completes in December): blocked energy, melancholy and attrition; the necessity to work hard and be productive.
- **Transiting Saturn square natal Venus** (begins in May): the making or breaking of commitments in relationships and/or financial restrictions.
- **North Node Fidaria** (begins in October 1993). To change Fidaria means that a person experiences a change in the substance of their life. Since Margaret's North Node is conjunct her Descendant, this period of time forces her to relook at relationships, both intimate and business. The dispositor of Margaret's North Node is Saturn which not only conjuncts the Sun and Mercury but squares Mars and forms a mutual reception

to it. This period of her life demands slow persistence in the achievement of her goals.

1994:

- **North Node Fidaria** continues.
- **Transiting Pluto square natal Pluto** (begins in December 1993 and completes in October 1994): a mid-life crisis cycle, a crisis of mortality, the recognition that life is finite.
- **Transiting Jupiter conjunct natal Sun-Saturn** (begins in December 1993 and completes in September 1994): expansion of responsibility.
- **Full Moon Secondary Progressed Lunation Phase** (begins in April): a time of reaping rewards, of harvesting what has been produced at the summit of the cycle, rather than starting new projects.
- **Secondary Progressed Moon moves into her 12th house** (in May): Usually this would be described as a time of retreat in order to explore one's inner life, to work quietly on one's creativity or to sort out hidden issues. However, since it occurs whilst the Secondary Progressed Lunation Phase is Full, then what Margaret is work hard at or reaping the benefits from are inherited family issues.

1995:

- **Transiting Pluto conjunct natal Venus** (begins in late December 1994 and completes in October 1995): the sudden or emotionally packed ending of a relationship; matters involving large sums of money.
- **Transiting Uranus opposition natal Uranus** (begins in February and completes in late November): a mid-life crisis cycle, a crisis of individuality. The blinding flash of the obvious.
- **Transiting Uranus opposition natal Jupiter** (begins in March): being confronted to take risks.
- **Transiting Uranus square the MC** (begins in March): sudden changes to job, career or social status through risk-taking action.
- **Secondary Progressed Moon moves into Cancer** (in March): a focus on nurturing and growing in a safe environment.
- **Secondary Progressed Moon conjunct the Ascendant** (in November): propelled into an active visible phase, the person can now take effective action and push forward with their life.

The options are these:

If Margaret had come to see you at point "B" and had already acknowledged her feelings of loss when her brother's dog died, then her grandmother's death, whilst sad, could be seen within the context of the natural life changes that we all encounter, the passing on of an older generation and the recognition of the impermanence of life, as well as the role that Margaret plays in her family carrying the genes and wisdom from one generation to the next.

If Margaret had come to see you at point "B" and had buried those feelings through isolation and anti-depressants, wondering now why she felt outraged by the treatment her grandmother received and betrayed by her death, then it would have been clear that this was a time to begin to unravel those difficulties in order for her to see her grandmother's death as an organic cycle and begin to approach her feelings of guilt. It would have been appropriate to talk with Margaret about the nature of the changes that confront a person during the mid-life crisis years, asking them to reconsider their priorities and refocus their attention on what will fulfil them in the second half of life. If Margaret took that opportunity to define her own needs and patterns of security (Secondary Progressed Moon moving into Cancer) and to look at them within the framework of how her family dealt with loss (Secondary Progressed Moon in the 12th house), she may have gained clear insights (transiting Uranus opposition natal Uranus) which would have allowed her to gently open the door to grief and helped her to rebuild an image of herself as loveable. Now seen and visible, (Secondary Progressed Moon conjunct the Ascendant), she would then have been able to take a risk and reach for what it was she felt would fulfil her (transiting Uranus opposition natal Jupiter and square the MC). The change to her North Node Fidaria would have helped her as she found more effective ways of managing any issues associated with anger, frustration and intimidation. Unpacking those issues would then have influenced how she handled her father's death in July 1996 and her mother's operation two months after that. Looking ahead at what 1996 held for her, you would have noticed the following:

- **Transiting Neptune square natal Neptune** (begins in February and completes in December): a mid-life crisis cycle, a crisis of faith, learning to have faith and trust in the area of the chart in which Neptune sits natally.
- **Transiting Jupiter conjunct the North Node-Descendant** (begins in February and completes in October): encountering new groups and new relationships/business partnerships from which she gains wisdom and insight.

- **Transiting Uranus square natal Mercury** (begins at the end of March): the sudden encountering of new ideas through intimate relationship or business partnership; changes in one's communication.

In this first year after her grandmother's death, in a time of disorganisation, it would have been appropriate to talk with Margaret about the journey of faith that lay ahead of her (transiting Neptune square natal Neptune) as she encountered new groups and formed new relationships (transiting Jupiter conjunct the North Node-Descendant). The unfolding of events tells us that her unexpressed anger at the domineering repression she experienced as a child (ruler of the Descendant is Saturn conjunct the Sun and Mercury) had, through a crisis of faith, been allowed to soften and gave her insight and compassion:

> I watched a man I'd feared as a child and despised as a teenager become helpless and lost and miserable. I stopped hating him. I pitied him and then found I loved him. When he died, my grief was different. I got to know about how hard his upbringing was and why he'd been the way he was. I was and am sorry that I spent so much time hating an extremely unhappy man. This sounds so arrogant but I think I learned about understanding and forgiveness.

and she learns to express herself differently (transiting Uranus square natal Mercury): "I told my friends that my Dad had died and many came to his funeral to support me. I don't think I'd realised what good friends I had." Transiting Neptune square Neptune continues to bring in loss with her mother's illness:

> I started to grieve when I saw her in hospital because I didn't know if I'd see her again. The illness made her thoroughly irritable and naturally she was afraid, too. It was like a reversal of my operation as a five year old. I felt helpless that there was nothing I could do to influence that most important outcome.

Still fearful of turning the key in the lock of her grief, Margaret's reaction is to close down on communication and to eat.

If Margaret had come to see you in May 2003 at point "C" (aged forty-nine), her predictive work for 2003 reveals the following:

- **Third Quarter Phase Secondary Progressed Lunation Phase** (since May 2001): a time of taking action to restructure old skills.
- **Secondary Progressed Moon in the 3rd house** (since August 2001): seeking knowledge and activity and wanting to express ideas.

- **Secondary Progressed Moon in Libra** (since October 2001): a time of socialising, relating and communicating.
- **Sun-Moon period of her Sun Fidaria** (begins February 2003): identity and vitality shaped into emotional fulfilment.
- **Transiting Neptune square natal Saturn** (begins in late February and completes in late December): illness, tiredness, depletion of resources; the major signifier of health problems in predictive astrology.
- **Transiting Uranus square natal Venus** (begins in late February and completes in mid-December): changes to socialising patterns; changes to financial situation.
- **Transiting Saturn conjunct South Node** (begins in August): an increase in responsibility in the family or "tribe".
- **Transiting Saturn conjunct the Ascendant** (begins in late August): being seen as capable of handling authority.

The year commences with the death of an old friend, Ray, at the age of eighty-one. From Margaret's perspective, this was a good death, since he died at home "in full command of body and mind", yet she feels intense rage when her colleagues make it difficult for her to attend Ray's funeral. This catalyses a chain of events that ends with her resigning from work. When her aunt dies in February (transiting Neptune square her natal Saturn: a depletion of resources), Margaret's unexpressed anger is again smothered using food. She gains financial freedom as the inheritor of her aunt's house (transiting Uranus squaring her natal Venus: unexpected changes to one's financial situation) but resents the unwanted responsibility, "sick of visiting hospitals and Nursing Homes, and ... (unexpressedly) angry that, for the third time in six years, I had to do it all again." In April a friend is diagnosed with cancer and a cousin, only a few years older than her, has a stroke and is left in a coma. The physical manifestations of this transit are tense muscles and tiredness (transiting Neptune squaring Saturn: illness, tiredness, depletion of resources; the major signifier of health problems in predictive astrology.)

Proteus has visited Margaret in many different forms in her life. Sometimes she was able to move towards him as he lay down with the seals but mostly she pulled away and placated her emotional distress with eating: "I know I should be working on making my life worthwhile but I'm stuck." This is Menelaus in a windless harbour; grief immobile and untrained in the ways of finding a solution.

Since both Saturn (by old rulerships) and Uranus rule Aquarius which forms the 8th house cusp of Margaret's chart, all Saturn and Uranus transits will cause lasting, permanent changes to her life. With Saturn transiting the

South Node and crossing the Ascendant in the middle of 2003, irrevocable changes to her life are inevitable. It would have been an appropriate time for her to look deeply at what governs her life, to shake loose the coils of rage and bitterness and approach ageing in a constructive and joyful way. With her Secondary Progressed Lunation Phase in its Third Quarter, she can take action to reshape her life and hone old skills in order to gain success, for this is a highly productive phase of her life. The danger is that the lack of air in the bay is now oppressive and blinding and the urge to continue as a by-product of her family rather than as freshly-generated blossom is overwhelming.

Family dynamics and life expectancy

There are two other factors that enter the world of clients in grief: the first is family dynamics and what happens to these when death strikes; the second is an understanding of life expectancy.

Kin

Familes are naturally fractured units. They gather for a time and condense around a central core but like gravel they are also composed of different material: some parts mix well, others don't. Eventually like all living things that produce seeds, those seeds fly in the wind. The core of the family separates and forms a nucleus elsewhere. The notion of "happy families", dynasties that live forever, is a misnomer. It is not in the nature of life to stiffen and spread as one entity but rather to form a focal point for a time from which issues, neuroses, fears, complexes or psychoses arise. These take on their own life and in any given family, each member of the household will be dealing with different parts of the issue. Some will be willing to look inwards at their behaviour and make adjustments and change while others look outwards and deny or blame.

This coagulation around a central nucleus which fluxes for a time and then breaks apart and begins the dance elsewhere is mirrored in a mathematical creation called The Game of Life, invented by mathematician Dr John Conway in 1970. [2] He developed this game as a simple way of studying patterns and behaviours in complex systems. The Game revealed whether a pattern will die out completely, form a stable population or grow forever.[3] It is a simple example of "emergent complexity" or "self-organizing systems" and shows how elaborate patterns and behaviours can emerge from extremely simple rules. As such it has helped scientists and mathematicians understand such diverse effects as how the petals on a rose or the stripes on a zebra can arise from a tissue of living cells growing alongside each other. It also helps explain the multiplicity of life that has evolved on earth. Indeed scientists and mathematicians have now discovered that diversity is essential to life on this blue planet.

We can apply The Game of Life/complexity theory to families. Each of us belongs to clusters or structures we call families. These clusters or structures form patterns which maintain a particular stability and equilibrium by each member playing a specific role. This gives rise to a paradox: we want to maintain the closeness established in the family unit when we were children but each of us is a developing human being reaching for our own independence and empowerment as we move from childhood to adulthood. The way we attain this independence and empowerment is through change but the unspoken dictates of families is to stay the same, for if we alter our unconsciously-designated role in the family, and change our patterns of silence or vagueness or blaming or anger or however that role has been shaped for us, we will automatically be met with strong opposition and a refusal by members of the family to accept it. Harriet Lerner calls this a "Change back!" reaction.[4] It is an explosive situation in which to find ourselves. Lerner maintains that in order for us to make changes within a family, they must be done slowly, in small steps, so that we have time to observe and test their impact. If too much changes too fast, it stirs up too much anxiety and emotional intensity and either old patterns and behaviours from the past are unconsciously imposed once more or the member of the family bringing in the change is expelled from the family unit. The Game of Life allows us to better understand the spectrum of difference that naturally occurs within families. Clients often observe how different they are to their siblings or parents, cousins, nephews or nieces. We accept variegation when it comes to flowers, dogs, cats, birds, yet somehow feel guilty when we see it in families. So we can define a family as a subgroup in which each member sustains and supports a particular role in order to run a particular pattern.

When someone in the family dies, all the family dynamics transform. A client in grief is not only dealing with the loss of their relationship to the individual who has died but also the ripples of metamorphosis in the family caused by that death. Like a planet that suddenly leaves the solar system, all positions shift to fill the gap. There are conscious and unconscious bids for rank and jockeying for position. Changes can and need to occur to allow the family to resettle into a position of safety. However, under the stress of the situation and without objective external support, often these changes occur too quickly and cut-offs and splits in families occur. The Game of Life shows this as a naturally occurring pattern: members peel away from the main branch, separated from touching or shaping the lives of their descendants and affect other people instead, starting a whole new stream elsewhere, a reflection of the Game of Life. We may never know exactly why and there is no blame in this. The one thing we do know is that this is the pattern of families.

Life anticipation

A hundred years ago, infant mortality was the expectation. It was common practice for a woman to bear many children, as it was a given that a number of children would not live to full maturity. A walk through the cemeteries of the eighteenth and nineteenth centuries reveals a large percentage of graves of the very young. Prior to the emergence of twentieth century improvements in sanitation and living standards, children had a high death rate in their first seven years of life. The most life threatening diseases were measles, scarlet fever, diphtheria, whooping cough and the common, unnamed pneumonias and diarrhoeas. These have been the greatest threats to children throughout history and are still threats in developing countries. Whilst these common dangerous infections of childhood now only account for about one percent of children's deaths in today's western world, medicine continues to be vigilant, as a sign common in doctors' surgeries clearly understands: "Childhood diseases haven't died. Children have."

Medieval astrology understood this, also, when it formulated the ability to read the length of life in a newborn's chart. Should a child be named, educated and trained in a profession or simply allowed to enjoy a short and happy life without schooling or expectation of adulthood? Bernadette Brady writes:

> "These may seem offensive questions to our modern expectations but when resources were limited and one's safety and quality of old age depended upon one's ability to produce and rear heirs, these were vital questions concerning the chart of the new born child. Thus Hellenistic, Arabic and Medieval authors devoted large sections of their writings to this subject and although modern medicine buys for us a certain comfort zone and we find death an offensive thing to acknowledge, the fact still remains that some of us are born with greater vitality than others...
>
> Techniques to determining life expectancy are really concerned with questions of the vitality and life force in a chart rather than the timing of a person's death. This is evident by the fact that calculations give the length of life provided the person is not killed in a sword fight, run over by a speeding chariot, pushed off a cliff or lost at sea. In other words, the methods were for looking at how much "life" or power was given to a chart provided you were not accidentally killed beforehand and this length of life was considered to be when your life energy would wind

down. So these techniques are about judging the vigour and physical resilience of a chart, how strongly a chart claims life and therefore how strongly it will hang onto it." [5]

Thus a medieval parent would want to know whether the child dies at birth or shortly thereafter, dies before he or she has taken any form of nourishment, takes nourishment but dies later, dies before the age of twelve, lives to adulthood but dies before reaching old age or lives to old age. In our contemporary world we know that science can step into the hall of death and halt disease to a certain extent. Translating this medieval technique into the present-day consulting room, one knows that if the planet that allocates the years of life runs out of time, it does not necessarily mean death but may mean a time of crisis after which the person's energy is diminished, or they undergo such an alteration to their lifestyle that their life work is complete and the pathway less action-driven. Studies show it is a normal feature of childhood for a child to experience a raft of diseases in the first seven years of life in order to build strength in their immune systems.[6] In the last thirty years we have grown so accustomed to medicine winning the war against death that we are shocked and horrified when death occurs in childhood, adolescence or teenage years. An ancient Chinese saying embracing the meaning of life highlights this: "The grandmother dies, the mother dies, the daughter dies." This is the natural order of life and when that order is changed, this tiny glitch on the surface of life causes undercurrents for years to come. Today we are told seven percent of deaths in the USA in children aged one to nineteen years old are from cancer, seven percent are from suicide and fourteen percent are from homicide.

Many scholars consider Shakespeare wrote King John in 1596, based on the belief that Constance's lines (3.4.93-97; *The Norton Shakespeare*, p.1054) reflect Shakespeare's own grief at the death of his son Hamnet in August, 1596:

Constance: "Grief fills the room up of my absent child,
              Lies in his bed, walks up and down with me,
              Puts on his pretty looks, repeats his words,
              Remembers me of all his gracious parts,
              Stuffs out his vacant garments with his form;"

A story from the Buddhist tradition tells of Krishna Gotami whose only son had died. Devastated, she carried her son to the Buddha and begged for a medicine that would bring him back to life. The Buddha nodded. It was indeed within his power to fulfil this wish but first he must have a handful of mustard seeds. Krishna Gotami was overjoyed and immediately made plans to leave.

The Buddha raised his hand. There was one proviso: each mustard seed had to come from a house where no-one had lost a child, a husband, a parent or a friend. After a long day of fruitless searching, pleading and, finally, despair, Krishna Gotami understood at last that birth and death are the inverse sides of the same coin. They cannot exist without each other and both are dependent upon each other to make the other real. She buried her son and returned to the Buddha to gain further wisdom from his teachings.

Jack - A Father in Grief

The tapestry

When Benjamin was born on 29th May, 1973, in London, England, Jack (aged thirty one and a half) already had two daughters. With enthusiastic Jewish aplomb, his aunts flourished a ring and a thread and came to the decisive conclusion that this child, too, was going to be a girl. Jack thought no more of it until the time of delivery when the doctor, who was a great soccer fan, exclaimed, "Oh he's a big boy. He'll be a midfielder for Manchester United for sure!" Jack's knees buckled beneath him. He struggled for the door, certain he was going to faint. This was the son who would carry on the family name. The family business that had been passed on to Jack would now be passed on to Benjamin, the boy with the cheeky smile, the infectious laugh and the quick grin, for these, Jack felt, were the right qualities for the next caretaker of such a prestigious commerce. However, it was more than this which drew Jack to his son. Benjamin was a great mimic and constantly had people in fits of laughter, quite often at his own expense. This meant that Benjamin was vulnerable and it was this quality of openness and receptivity that Jack loved most of all. "I hug him often," Jack writes in his diary. "I want him to know that he is so incredibly special to me. We laugh, we play pranks. He is the most beautiful boy I have ever seen. His beauty is much deeper than just the physical. We do so many things which we take for granted. Can father and son have a spiritual umbilical cord?"

In 1992 when Jack was fifty, his predictive work was as follows:

- **Balsamic Secondary Progressed Lunation Phase** (began in July 1989 and completes in October 1992): the end of the cycle, a period of letting go.
- **Secondary progressed Moon in Capricorn** (since January 1991): a focus on order which springs from the fear of chaos.

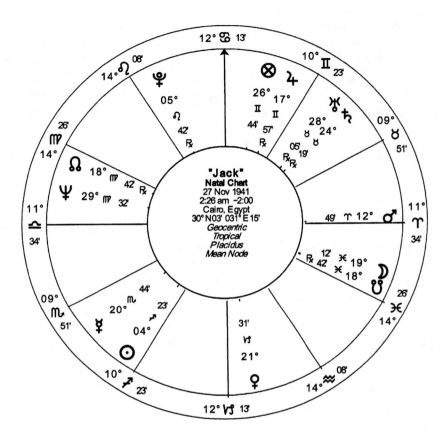

- **Sun-Saturn period of Sun Fidaria** (since August 1991): vitality, energy and identity shaped into responsibility.
- **Secondary progressed Moon in the 4th house** (since November 1991): a focus on house, home, family.
- **Transiting Pluto conjunct natal Mercury** (since late November 1991): a year of worry, concern and obsession.

In January 1992, Benjamin was eighteen years old, a six foot three inch athlete with the most engaging smile in the world. He was an extremely good tennis player, had already won several major tournaments on the ITF Junior Circuit and had been competing at Junior Wimbledon since he was fifteen. It was Jack's opinion that Benjamin could become a Wimbledon champion but one thing bothered his coach. He could not understand why, with all his latent skill, lately Benjamin had stopped playing to his full potential. One moment he would be challenging with brilliant shots, a moment later he would be fumbling and groping at the ball as if it was beyond him to play the shot at all. Benjamin also began acting erratically, jumping up and down on the spot in the kitchen as if limbering up on the tennis court. When Jack questioned this behavior Benjamin looked at him curiously. "What behavior, Dad?" With Benjamin's GCSE A levels looming and pressure mounting, the doctor attributed it to stress before exams, and indeed when Benjamin received his final results, he found he had failed his A levels by one subject. Despite this, Jack was dissatisfied and he and his wife, Val, decided it was time for Benjamin to see a neurologist. The neurologist also connected this fluctuating behaviour with stress, yet MRI tests revealed another cause: a tumour on the right side of Benjamin's head. Uncertain as to the cause, it appeared to have been there for about six or seven years. The doctors reassured Jack and Val that it was readily removed by an operation and radiotherapy and this is what came to pass. Benjamin ended up with a scar across his forehead but recovered satisfactorily from the operation and with Val being the major breadwinner at that time in their lives, Jack was able to spend every day of the next few months with him.

Benjamin returned to the tennis court and within months, looking the embodiment of health, he began playing competition tennis. He and his girlfriend, Jenny, were a striking pair, soul mates sharing countless moments of happiness. Jack could see how much Jenny meant to Benjamin, how he was maturing and how all his tennis pupils adored him and he felt immense pride and happiness for "his boy". One night Benjamin sat down with his parents and told them he wanted to get back onto the European circuit to advance his ranking. Jack and Val looked at each other. Both of them knew this was an important step for Benjamin to truly develop the raw talent they saw in him but he was still on specialised medication and they were reluctant to let him travel on his own. Tennis life was hard, Jack argued. You could end up sleeping anywhere: in a garage, in a pig-sty, on hay with the animals in a barn. Benjamin agreed. He knew the situation. He also knew that, given his age and recent history, it was now or never for him to make a serious bid at professional tennis. Neither Jack nor Val wanted to stop him from achieving his ambition, so they agreed to let him go.

Benjamin packed his bags and booked a flight. As the tapestry of his life became woven with French verbs and grammar and rapidly became a living language, so his tennis, hewn and polished with regular challenge, became fluent on the court. In those days before the Internet he spoke with his parents often by telephone. During one such conversation, Jack realized Benjamin was slurring his words. Hesitantly he asked if he was okay. "I have a headache", was Benjamin's reply. "Are you taking your tablets?" Jack continued.

Benjamin couldn't tell him. Jack's response was immediate. He asked the French family with whom Benjamin was lodging to take him to hospital. The hospital ran tests and found the tumour was back, not only back but growing at an alarming rate. Jack arranged for a doctor to fly Benjamin back to London and a recommended surgeon operated with laser. In the aftermath of surgery they waited for the results. The surgeon arrived surrounded by his entourage. Brutally and without compassion he told them Benjamin didn't have long to live. Outraged, Jack and Val flew Benjamin to Edinburgh to a doctor who used thermal heat treatment against cancer cells. The intervention helped but time was against them. Benjamin's brain began to swell and for several days he lay in a coma. Specialists advised them to take Benjamin off the life-support system and, heavy of heart, they concurred. The green lines faded but Benjamin's soul clung on. His mother and sister visited him and quietly offered their goodbyes. Then Jack was alone with his son, in the austere privacy of a sterile hospital room, facing the moment all parents dread and none believe will ever happen to them: the child of his loins untimely ripped from the net of life and time. In a sandpaper voice he told Benjamin how proud he was of him and what a wonderful son he had been. As the toll of minutes passed he knew he was to be Benjamin's Gate Keeper. "Now," he whispered. "Now it is time for you to relax and let go." He joined Val waiting patiently outside the room and in silence they found their way home. A few hours later the phone rang. Benjamin had died. It was 24th November 1992 and Benjamin was nineteen years old.

1993: The First Year

- **New Secondary Progressed Lunation Phase in Capricorn in the 4th house conjunct Venus** (since October 1992): new beginnings, new responsibilities, new groups, new ways of socialising, relating and networking.
- **Transiting Pluto opposition natal Saturn** (begins in December 1992 and ends in October 1993): melancholy, darkness of feelings, being in a "black hole", attrition, feeling miserable.
- **Transiting Jupiter conjunct the Ascendant** (begins in December 1992 and ends in August 1993): changes in what one is learning and that other people now see.
- **Sun-Jupiter sub-period of the Sun Fidaria** (begins in January): the life force, the vitality, the sense of self and identity is being shaped into new knowledge and growth.

- •   Transiting Uranus conjunct natal Venus (begins in March and completes in December): changes to socialising patterns; falling in or out of love; changes in financial situation.
- •   Transiting Saturn squaring his natal Saturn-Uranus conjunction (begins March): frustration; slow progress in achieving new goals.

"Suddenly we are childless. The new and total silence in our lives is unbroken."[7] Jack and Val flew Benjamin's body back to London and both of them underwent a short period of grief counselling. However, Benjamin's death had changed the family dynamics totally. Where previously the family had felt balanced with Jack, Val, their two daughters and Benjamin, Jack now felt completely swamped with female energy. He and Benjamin had shared common interests, cemented with a special bond of understanding. Jack describes it as "losing my best friend, the source of my joy, the comedian in the family."

An astrologer would most certainly expect the predictive work to express the black melancholy of grief (transiting Pluto opposition natal Saturn), the recognition that life erodes all that is important, along with the slow progress in achieving any goals (transiting Saturn squaring his natal Saturn-Uranus conjunction). Chaos and disorganisation had now descended upon his life (transiting Uranus conjunct Venus) and he was being asked to lie down with the seals. However, whilst the pain of the loss was clearly the overwhelming emotion with which he was dealing, the astrology also describes new beginnings, new foundations on which to build his life (Secondary Progressed New Lunation Phase in Capricorn) and an expansion of his world which other people see (transiting Jupiter conjunct the Ascendant).

Isolation

The death of a child creates an unforeseen stress in marriages. There is a Jewish saying: "Love is like bread, it must be made new each day." All intimate relationships require this consistent vigilance, yet when a child dies from illness, an accident, murder or suicide, not only will each partner express their distress differently but grief is exhausting and will often take the form of withdrawal, leaving little room for either partner to attend to the other's needs. Some parents, heavy with torment and the onward echo of endless time, even consider taking their own lives in order to end their suffering and be reunited with their dead child. After Benjamin's death, Jack isolated himself. He went away on his own and he read books on grief but felt that nothing could help him understand the vale of sorrow into which he had been plunged. He became religious and attended Orthodox Jewish services but on the Day of Atonement the words of the liturgy only inflamed him. How could God decide who would live and who would die? What right had God to take on that mantle of omnipotence? Jack had felt good about being able to pass on to Benjamin the values he had learned in life. They did "boy" things together and Benjamin listened to him. One day when Jack had walked Jenny home after services, she had told him how proudly Benjamin had talked about the things Jack had taught him, the small courtesies of life, such as when being introduced to someone, how important it was to shake their hand firmly, look them in the eye and call them by their name. Now there was no-one to teach:

> No more fond admiration or encouraging words of praise
> "That's awesome Dad! You're a champ!"
> Now only memories to cherish for a lifetime
> filled with infinite images of those dreams of what might have been. [8]

Jack did not sleep well and he developed acute headaches. He dealt with Benjamin's death by writing him letters and poems:

> ...My son, my most precious promise of tomorrow...
> I feel so alone.
> Who will now look up to me, who will ever compliment me,
> who will admire me ...
> who will need me that way ever again?

As part of the grieving process, Jack and Val joined a group for parents who had lost children but it did not really achieve what he wanted. However, whilst he was there, he was told that the statistics of parents who break up after a child dies is exceedingly high. This frequently-quoted fact ranges anywhere from between fifty-to-eighty percent. Is this true? In 1998, in an effort to find the source of these statistics, Dr Reiko Schwab conducted a review of the literature to find just such evidence.[9] She found no verification whatsoever in holding the death of a child liable for such a high rate of divorce, nor did she find that the rate of divorce among bereaved parents was any higher than that of the general population. If marital stress was apparent in the relationship prior to the child's death, then the death itself can further complicate the problems, leading to the conclusion that there is no reason to put further effort into solving a relationship that is no longer viable, resulting in divorce. However, those couples whose relationships are well-established with ways of solving disagreements and differences of opinion prior to their children's deaths are more likely to continue the everyday spadework necessary to finding solutions and hence keep their relationships intact. In the same way as a person may feel anger at the circumstances surrounding a death, so it is possible that the rate of divorce may be affected by the circumstances of death, for example, if one of the parents believed the other parent contributed to the child's demise. It can be argued that statistics such as those quoted above, passed on by professionals who omit to examine the cited sources and who then use them to predict a likely outcome, are somewhat alarming. They add an unwarranted layer of anxiety onto the shoulders of bereaved parents who may be concerned that their marriage won't survive the loss. Schwab's research showed that the majority of marital relationships not only outlast the severe demands on the marriage brought about by a child's death but may even be strengthened by it in the long run.

Jack was aware that Benjamin had been his ally. When he turned to Val, he felt only her distance and detachment (transiting Uranus conjunct natal Venus). Val had never really been able to talk about deep, personal issues and now, more than anything else, Jack wanted honesty. If he could not have a close relationship with his wife, then what was the point in them being together? Faced with his own mortality, feeling Time to be at its most potent now, he understood, in a space deep within him, that for however long the rest of his life promised to be, he wanted quality in those remaining years. With Benjamin gone and Val unreachable and withdrawn, Jack hated coming home (transiting Pluto opposition natal Saturn). With a shock, he realised that their marriage had been a shell held together for the sake of the children. Six months after Benjamin died, Jack and Val separated.

For most of 1993 Jack attended personal growth groups. They were not necessarily connected with grieving but were groups which helped Jack express his feelings: one was on intimacy; another was on breath work, encouraging people to release emotions through exhalation. It was in these groups that Jack began to realise that many people carry pain and for quite different reasons. From the space of "I am the one suffering and feeling sorry for myself", he became empathic, open and able to talk about what happened, an expression of the new growth and learning that was entering his life (transiting Jupiter conjunct the Ascendant).

At that point Jack began to dream of Benjamin. His initial response on waking was distress, knowing that time in the dream with Benjamin was limited due to his illness. Jack's words were: "There is always the concern, the fear, the sorrow of knowing. It's never a dream like a normal dream. There is always the component of knowing that he's going to be here for just awhile and then he's going to be gone." Even when Jack dreamed that Benjamin was fully recovered, there was pressure to appreciate the moment and enjoy what was happening. It wasn't until he became aware of how much joy he gained by being with Benjamin in his dreams that he really began to look forward to them. Meanwhile he was experiencing a long and drawn out divorce with Val (another expression of transiting Pluto opposition natal Saturn). Jack had always said he would split everything fifty-fifty with Val, even the family business which had been passed on to him by his father. However, Val and her advisers valued the business unrealistically and she became bitter, suspicious and extremely antagonistic towards Jack. It took two years for the divorce to be settled.

Jack's social patterns also took a surprising turn (transiting Uranus conjunct natal Venus). In March, 1993, Jack met Carol at one of his personal growth groups. It was a time when people who had completed such workshops would give each other a hug when they met again, something people never used to do before this. At a wedding later that year, the last function Jack attended with Val, he again encountered Carol and she threw her arms around him. As he hugged her back, Jack felt a spark between them. Only four months since Benjamin's death, getting involved in a relationship was the last thing he wanted. However, by now insomnia was wracking his body and Carol was a body worker who specialised in releasing emotional blocks held in the muscles. Jack decided to see Carol professionally. After one session, Jack slept soundly for the first time in months. When Jack separated from Val, he and Carol started seeing each other as friends but Jack found himself in emotional turmoil: he was not ready to get involved in a relationship and yet he enjoyed her company, so they decided to keep meeting and talking but did not go out together socially.

Family dynamics
As always, a change in one part of a family causes changes elsewhere. His younger daughter, Kathy, asked Jack if he thought he would ever remarry. No, said Jack. However, in December, 1993, when Jack had been on his own for six months, he told his older daughter, Amanda, that he was starting to see somebody. "That's a bit sudden, isn't it?" was her immediate response. Jack was taken aback and yet he could understand her reaction. Amanda was Val's daughter from her first marriage and she had experienced the marriage break up at the age of four. Now the same event was happening all over again. Jack trod carefully. Yes, it was sudden, he said, but he had no intention of getting seriously involved. He really liked Carol and he would probably start going out with her. From that moment on Amanda stopped speaking to Jack. Jack has tried several times to re-establish a relationship with Amanda but each time he has been unsuccessful. To add his pain, Amanda's first son, Jack's first grandchild, was born the day after Benjamin died. To Jack it seemed that everything had a price. Not only had he lost a son, now he had lost a daughter and a grandson. Here was transiting Pluto opposing Saturn in the 8th and ruling the 4th and 5th houses at its blackest. Jack's grip on Proteus tightened.

1994: The Second Year

- **Secondary Progressed Moon moves into the 5th house** (in January): a focus on personal creativity, lovers and children. New relationships may be formed or the person engages in new activities or hobbies.
- **Transiting Neptune conjunct natal Venus** (begins in late January and completes in early December): illusions in love relationships; romantic love which may be wonderful or may leave the individual to deal with cold realities after the contact has finished; confusion in financial maters; being conned.
- **Sun-Mars sub-period of the Sun Fidaria** (begins in June): the life force, the vitality, the sense of self and identity shaped into motivation and drive.
- **Progressed Sun trine natal Uranus** (exact in September): a redefinition of the sense of self without obstacle where the person is no longer afraid to rebel against what other people think.

Given the above, an astrologer would expect Jack to express the predictive work this year either by feeling confused and scattered, allowing other people to take advantage of him and being deceived by them or else by moving into a more metaphysical stage of his life and walking down a pathway in the enchanted world.

In 1994 Jack began working as a healer and a counsellor in earnest. He specialised in massage and esoteric healing and he tailor-made audio meditation tapes to help his clients with specific areas of concern in their life. He found he was extremely good at this work. He was developing his ability to understand and share the feelings of another. Sensitive and open about her emotions, Carol formed a stark contrast to Val. It was in this year that they began courting each other seriously and transiting Neptune conjunct Venus expressed itself as "Romantic Love". Carol wanted to get married but Jack felt it was too soon. Two years after his son's death, he was still in a state of disorganisation.

1995 : The Third Year

- **Secondary Progressed Moon moves into Pisces** (in March): reconnecting with the deeper or higher self. An increase in sensitivity which can cause a desire for reclusion.
- **Transiting Saturn conjunct the natal South Node-Moon** (begins in April and completes in December): loneliness, isolation, feeling unsupported; needing to consolidate resources along with

an increase in responsibilities to do with family or "tribe"; fated karmic bonds are changed in such a way that the person has to carry a greater load.

- **Venus Fidaria** (begins November 1995): a focus on socialising, networking and the world of sensual delights and pleasures. Venus in Jack's chart is angular and the ruler of the Ascendant and the 8th house, in Capricorn and trine the Saturn-Uranus conjunction. This suggests that Jack has the ability to form long-lasting, committed relationships which have a degree of difference to them and which are underpinned by change, growth and development.

Jack's and Val's divorce became legal in June 1995 (transiting Saturn conjunct the natal South Node-Moon). Jack and Carol travelled overseas to attend an advanced course in esoteric healing (secondary progressed Moon in Pisces) and here they got engaged. In December 1995, Jack and Carol were married (the other face of transiting Saturn to the natal Moon and the Venus Fidaria). Proteus was now vanquished and gave Jack the answers he was seeking: he had successfully reached the safety of the shores of home and home lay with Carol.

1996: The Fourth Year
- **Venus Fidaria continues.**
- **Secondary Progressed Sun trine natal Neptune** (exact in February): a redefining of the self as spiritual and creative.
- **Secondary Progressed Moon moves into the 6th house** (begins in March): a focus on duty, service and follow-through.
- **Crescent Secondary Progressed Lunation Phase** (begins in April): the new direction of life becomes apparent.
- **Secondary Progressed Sun moves into Aquarius** (in July): this is a move that all people born with the Sun in Sagittarius will eventually encounter through the progression by secondary direction of their Sun. Being born with his Sun at 4° Sagittarius, at around age twenty-five Jack would have experienced a change from independence and overview to one of responsibility, achievement and outcomes. Now at age fifty-four he was again experiencing a maturing of his Sun as it moved into the sign of Aquarius, allowing team-orientation and the needs of the group to become a dominant focus.

- **Transiting Jupiter conjunct the IC and square to natal Mars in rulership conjunct the Descendant** (begins in March and completes in late October): the expansion and joy of the new home life and relationship.

Joy and expansion

1996 was dominated by the flavour of expansion, change and an enriched lifestyle. Transiting Jupiter conjunct Jack's natal IC and square to natal Mars conjunct the Descendant underscored the happiness and joy he had been craving as the underpinning to his life: a partner with whom he could communicate freely (Jupiter rules the 3rd house) and joy in their everyday life together (Jupiter rules the 6th house). The Crescent Secondary Progressed Lunation Phase tells us that Jack was now ready to reach outwards in his world, that the new roots he was putting down were starting to take hold. In this current year, free from major external transits drawing his focus and nearly four years after Benjamin's death, Jack continued to process the grief. Counsellors said he held deep-seated anger at Benjamin's death. Jack didn't feel that. He never felt that there was anger with Benjamin's death and indeed anger doesn't have to be part of the grieving process. Always aware of his shortcomings as well as his strengths and now defining himself as more intuitively aware (Secondary Progressed Sun trine natal Neptune), Jack felt he had a good grasp on what was going on inside himself. There was pain and sorrow and the difficulty of understanding why but never anger.

If "working through" the grief means "not feeling any pain", then Jack admits he has not worked it through. He has come to accept there will be pain and there are moments when memory overtakes him and the emotions surface, as deep and profound as when Benjamin first died. "Sometimes weeks can go by and you think that you've come to terms with it but every now and then something happens and it just reaches right deep within you and you know that you'll always have that deep, deep pain." Although Jack cried for his father when he died and was extremely upset, this sorrow for Benjamin contained a far different quality. Jack now came to understand that loss held many flowers in its bouquet and the death of a parent is what's expected in time. Nevertheless through Benjamin's death Jack has been able to see other people's pain and this has allowed him to become a lot more accepting and a lot less judgemental.

1997: The Fifth Year

- **Transiting Pluto conjunct natal Sun** (begins in January and completes in late October): irrevocable change to one's identity.
- **Venus-Mercury sub period of his Venus Fidaria** (begins in January): socialising and networking are shaped into communication, paperwork, contracts and ideas.
- **Secondary Progressed Moon moves into Aries** (begins in June): a focus on independence and clarity of action, confrontation and challenge.

Metamorphosis

1997 was the fifth year after Benjamin's death. For a number of years Jack had neither ambition nor drive. He would "just get by day by day". Now the astrology tells us that he was reorganising his identity (transiting Pluto conjuncted natal Sun), looking outward for new challenges (secondary progressed Moon in Aries) and allowing his social network to shape itself into new ideas (Venus-Mercury sub period). This was the year Jack took over as Chairman of the business in London and committed to it in a whole new way.

1998-1999:

- **Secondary Progressed Moon conjunct the Descendant** (exact May 1998): a re-evaluation of what one requires in relationships.
- **Venus-Moon sub period of his Venus Fidaria** (begins in March 1998): socialising and networking are shaped into emotional completeness.
- **Transiting Jupiter conjunct the natal south Node-Moon** (begins in May 1998 and completes in December 1998): expansion, benefit and wisdom that is gained from re-evaluating emotional issues of the past.
- **Secondary Progressed Mars square natal Pluto** (exact January 1999): large projects that take a great deal of energy.
- **Venus-Saturn sub period of his Venus Fidaria** (begins in May 1999): socialising and networking are shaped into communication, paperwork, contracts and ideas.
- **Secondary Progressed Moon moves into Taurus** (exact November 1999): a focus on consolidation, patience and persistence.

An astrologer evaluating Jack's predictive work for these two years would recognise a hiatus of activity. From the year of worry and concern prior to Benjamin's death through the grinding abrasion of the five years following, the cosmos was now giving Jack "time off", suggesting that this interval could be more profitably spent weighing up, judging and assessing his place in life rather than having to face external pressures. Such times of evaluation in the waxing cycle are necessary periods when life continues externally whilst rest and recuperation occur internally. Indeed Jack describes the last few months of 1999 as bringing with it a sense of re-emergence in the business and of him having more of a corporate profile.

2000:

- **First Quarter Secondary Progressed Lunation Phase** (begins in February): a time of action and personal achievement, a deep need to physically materialise the desires planted seven years earlier.
- **Venus-Jupiter sub period of his Venus Fidaria** (begins in June): socialising and networking are shaped into wisdom and expansion.
- **Transiting Uranus square natal Mercy** (begins in May): sudden ideas, encountering new books, new thoughts, new ways of doing things.
- **Second Saturn Return** (begins in June): the second great cycle of authority and responsibility.
- **Transiting Jupiter opposition natal Sun** (begins in July): being confronted with expansion and new growth of identity.
- **Transiting Saturn conjunct natal Uranus** (begins in July): slow progress in achieving new goals.
- **Secondary Progressed Moon moves into the 8th house** (in September): issues of money and power, big business, taxes, wills and inheritances; a time of allowing change into one's life.

In 2000, Jack and Carol bought a large country property in Gloucestershire with various farming activities (Secondary Progressed Moon moves into Taurus) stimulating new challenges (First Quarter Secondary Progressed Lunation Phase), new subjects to learn (transiting Uranus square natal Mercury) and further changes (Secondary Progressed Moon moves into the 8th house). Ever since Benjamin died Jack no longer considered himself to be religious. Now for the first time in seven years, Jack attended services. He is less angry with God and more accepting that Judaism is his faith. He accepts what he can and feels free to dismiss or reject what is not acceptable to him. Before Benjamin's death Jack described himself as being "decidedly closed, a bit of a poker face". Through the courses he attended, he learned to express his feelings and to become aware of other people's torment, allowing him to see life from a quite different perspective.

Jack doesn't go to the cemetery much now because, he says, "Benjamin's not there." Instead it is in his dreams where Benjamin is alive. Sometimes Benjamin is six or seven years old and Jack is teaching him to play tennis. Sometimes he is fully recovered and a teenager. Often no words are spoken. However the dreams manifest, they are always happy times. Jack wakes filled with Benjamin's love and joy and the happiness stays with him. In late 1999, on the anniversary of Benjamin's death, Jack offered to go with Val to the cemetery. Val declined. Her memory of Benjamin's death remains centred on that last week, the distress of his condition and his moribund form. Despite years of happiness, some people only remember the person they loved in these last difficult moments, such as Jane's Aunt Deirdre who can't sleep for "seeing Uncle Andrew collapsing in the doorway over and over." This is a heavy load to bear for the rest of one's life.

The astrology tells us the most difficult times for Jack were the first three years after Benjamin's death. Jack's Balsamic Moon swept away the last vestiges of a life in which he had hermetically sealed his feelings. Benjamin's death was a lever on the lid of Jack's emotions and like a cyclone they rushed in to fill the gap of loss. As this life at sea settled to a steady rhythm, Jack found himself breathing new air. What he has learnt from Benjamin's death now underpins the next thirty years of his life.

Hannah - A Mother In Grief

I saw Hannah as a client in 1999. The question with which she came to me was, "I want to look at my relationships. Should I get involved with this man from my past?" This was her predictive work:

- **Transiting Pluto opposition the natal Moon** (begins in January 1999 and completes in early November): Emotional distress; issues with mother or mothering; issues with groups of women; stress on the emotional bonds that bind lovers/family together.
- **Saturn-Mars sub period of her Saturn Fidaria** (begins in February): responsibility and authority are shaped into motivation and drive.

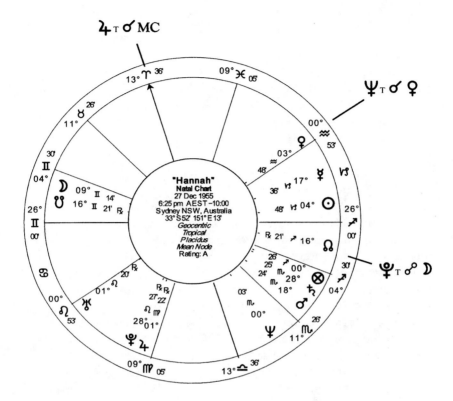

- **Transiting Neptune conjunct natal Venus** (begins in March 1999 and completes in October 2000): Illusions in love relationships; romantic love which may be wonderful or leave the individual to deal with the cold realities after the contact has finished. Confusion in financial matters; being conned.
- **Transiting Jupiter moves into the 10th house** (in April 1999): A change in what one is learning or mastering expressed through career or how society classifies you.
- **Her Secondary Progressed Lunation Phase is Balsamic** (began in June 1998 and does not become new until July 2002): A time of release and endings. Clearing old ground. Clearing a space for new things to enter.

Transiting Pluto opposition the natal Moon describes a deeply hidden issue connected with the women of her family (the Moon is natally in the 12th house) that Hannah sees clearly (the opposition). The issue is part of her physical, emotional or spiritual make-up which expresses itself either as a genetic weakness or an inherited family pattern through illness or allergies (the Moon is conjunct the South Node).

Saturn-Mars sub period of her Saturn Fidaria. Natally Hannah's Saturn is square to Pluto and makes a wide conjunction to Mars in rulership in the 5th house in Mars's sign, so there is reception. So this time period is one of a great deal of hard work that can be highly creative or involve children (the 5th house).

Transiting Neptune conjunct natal Venus alerts one to the fact that, for these two years, Hannah is being called to an enchanted world, a world of illusion and romantic love in order to break down any rigid, intellectual thinking around relating (natal Venus is in Aquarius). Hannah has natal Venus square Neptune as part of her T-square, so there is already an embedded issue of valuing variety and spontaneity in relationships or unusual and different relationships (Venus opposition Uranus across the 2nd-8th house axis, Venus in Aquarius) and resolving the chaos this brings through gullibility, idealism and a lack of discrimination (Venus square Neptune). With transiting Neptune now swimming over her natal Venus, this was not the time to make any hard and fast commitment to a relationship but simply to enjoy what was being offered and not to believe that it will last. Indeed fairy tales tell us that the way to survive Neptune transits is to continually revisit the mundane world, the world of practicality, in order to stay grounded - do the shopping, clean the house, balance the books, dig in the garden - so that when one returns to the broad light day after the transit is complete, one does not feel confused or deceived. So she has to wait until the transit has passed in order to see what, if anything, remains.

The Secondary Progressed Balsamic Lunation Phase forms the background theme to this time period. When Hannah came to see me, only one year of its four year duration had passed. With another three years of change ahead of her, clearly this was not the time for Hannah to enter into a relationship but rather to deal with issues from the past and to let them go.

This is what emerged in the consulting room
In 1971, when Hannah was nearly sixteen, her maternal grandfather died, "the one person in my life who seemed to love me unconditionally" (natal Sun trine natal Jupiter). By the time this occurred, she had already, at age five, moved with her family from the city to the country, at age ten experienced

her friend killed by a car (February), the death of her cat (November) and death of her paternal grandmother (December), at age eleven she had been sexually abused by a friend's father at her friend's birthday party (loss of innocence and trust) and at age fourteen developed anorexia (loss of a perspective on reality). Many patterns of how to deal - or not deal - with loss had already taken hold and were deeply routed in her psyche.

Hannah's grandfather still lived in the city. Knowing he was dying and believing he would not see Christmas, he asked Hannah to come down on the train from the country and visit him. Hannah's parents did not take his request seriously and refused her permission to go. Her grandfather died at five minutes to midnight on Christmas Eve, collapsing on the bathroom floor from an embolism and falling against the door. Her grandmother couldn't get him out of the bathroom and the ambulances had chosen that night to go on strike. Hannah says:

> I believed for years that, had I gone down, I could have helped. I felt I had let him down. My father wouldn't let me tell the other kids until after Christmas Day. I remember that day being the longest of my life - and I ran away from home that afternoon. I took the phone call in the evening about him dying. No one really helped me through it. No-one helped me with my grief. My father is uncomfortable about expressing emotions and I make him uncomfortable because I have always been the opposite. Just like the anorexia, no-one seemed to notice anything. After Pop died, my Grandmother became an incurable alcoholic. No-one dealt with or addressed that, either. I felt terribly abandoned and terribly alone, cut off from people and not part of the world.

Hannah's way of coping was through isolating herself, through reading books walking and being on her own. Hannah was at the end of her previous Secondary Progressed Balsamic Lunation phase. Within a year the phase had turned New, seeded at 21° 54' Capricorn, conjunct her natal Mercury in the 7th house. She was being given the next twenty-nine years or so to find her voice.

In 1975, when Hannah was nineteen and now a gifted violinist, a friend asked her to put down a couple of tracks on a record with a guitarist. When she arrived at her friend's place, she was introduced to Art, the young man playing guitar. They fell desperately in love (transiting Neptune was opposing her natal Moon) but her father did not approve of the relationship and when he told Hannah she had to make a choice, she felt it was an easy one to make. She left home with Art the next day and not long afterwards they married (transiting Uranus was squaring her natal Uranus). Despite mixed feelings about her parents, Hannah felt a great sense of loss and sadness but time had to pass before she was ready to see them again. Seven years after they married, in 1982 when Hannah was twenty-six, her predictive work was as follows:

- **First Quarter Secondary Progressed Lunation Phase** (since August 1980): a time of action materialising desires planted with the New Moon cycle in Capricorn in 1972 and now visible to the world.
- **Secondary Progressed Moon is in the 11th house** (since June 1981): a focus on social interactions.
- **Mercury-Mars period of the Mercury Fidaria** (since June 1981): ideas shaped into action and drive. Mars is in rulership in Hannah's chart.
- **Transiting Saturn square natal Mercury** (began November 1981): serious decisions, burdensome paperwork, study.
- **Transiting Neptune conjunct the Descendant** (begins late January 1982): dissolving relationships; new type of relationship needs surfacing in the individual.
- **Secondary Progressed Moon moves into Gemini** (begins in October 1982): seeking a greater and wider knowledge base through books, courses, languages, conversations and people.

Hannah's natal Sun is in Capricorn and hence responsive to seven-year cycles. The dispositor, Saturn, was squaring her natal Mercury and she was in the Mercury-Mars period of the Mercury Fidaria. She was also pre-Saturn Return and there were clearly unresolved issues in the relationship. As worries came to a crescendo (transiting Saturn square natal Mercury) she and Art split up (transiting Neptune conjunct her Descendant) and Hannah fell head over heels in love with Sean, a man with whom she played music and who had been married but was now separated. During the time of his affair with Hannah, Sean vacillated between staying with her and going back to his wife. Fed up with being the patsy, Hannah forced his hand. She removed herself from the situation, in effect making the decision for him, and Sean went back to his wife. On the rebound, feeling miserable and unloved, Hannah briefly became involved with someone else and fell pregnant. At six weeks she made the decision to have a termination. The operation proceeded without a hitch and two weeks later she returned to have an IUD inserted.

Some weeks passed and she felt really off-colour. She rang her doctor and told him that she still felt sick, that in her opinion she didn't think she had recovered from the operation and furthermore, she didn't understand why she was feeling like this. The doctor told her it had been a difficult time, that it was logical she would feel this way and not to worry, that things would get better in a few more weeks. A few more weeks passed and she didn't feel better. Now deeply concerned, she made another doctor's appointment. "Look," she asserted, "I've got all the symptoms of pregnancy. I still feel pregnant". Her doctor replied: "You can't be!" He carried out some tests and sent Hannah to have some scans which she was given in a packet without explanation. A good deal more frightened and placid than she was now, she did not ask what they revealed. Instead she returned them to her doctor who informed her that she was seventeen weeks pregnant. There had been a twin pregnancy. They had removed one of the embryos and not the other.

Hannah was appalled that this could have happened, particularly with the insertion of the IUD. The doctor defended himself by saying that, since they weren't expecting anything, they didn't know to look for it. To them it would simply have appeared to be a swelling from the operation. Hannah had two options: to go ahead with the pregnancy or to have a mid-trimester termination. Hannah didn't want to have a mid-trimester termination but neither did she want to have another baby. She was completing her Dip.Ed. (Diploma in Education), she was not in a relationship, she already had two little girls and she had no money. She had arranged her life so she could start teaching by the end of that year with the aim of earning a decent enough income to give her young girls what she thought they needed. She was also pulled by the little soul growing inside her.

She decided to go ahead and have the baby (transiting Saturn square natal Mercury) but the underlying feeling was shame. It wasn't Art's baby which would, in some way, have legitimised the pregnancy and it wasn't Sean's baby, the person she had really wanted to father it. At the end of the day, it was a mistake. She didn't really want it and what was more relevant, she didn't want other people to know about it, so she hid it. In those days this was an easy thing for her to do. She knew from both her previous pregnancies that she never showed much until about seven months, so when she did, she wore baggy jumpers. She also avoided running into Art, who had access to the children every second weekend, by taking them to child care and letting him collect them. That suited both of them, since they were still intensely angry with each other and didn't want to spend any time at all together.

When Hannah was just under eight months pregnant, she felt the world become exceptionally quiet, free from ripples or splintered time. She thought nothing of it, went to bed and slept through the whole night. As she prepared for bed the next evening, she realised what was wrong. The reason she had been able to sleep was because she hadn't been woken up. In pregnancy both her other two children had woken her around three by kicking in the morning

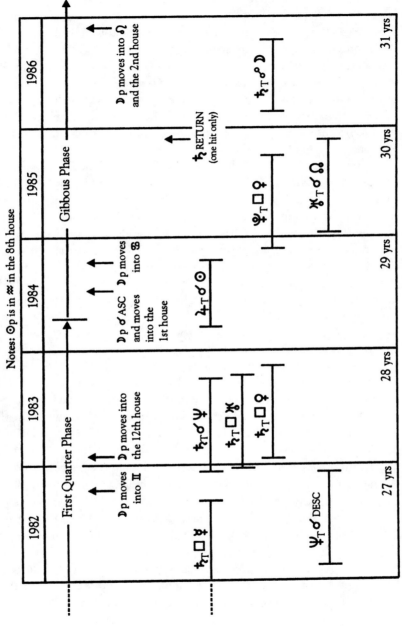

Time Map for Hannah 1982-1986

Notes: ☉p is in ♒ in the 8th house

and this one was no different. Tonight there was nothing, no movement, no activity, only stillness. The next day in surgery the doctor couldn't pick up a heartbeat and tests on her amniotic fluid showed that the baby had died somewhere in the previous twenty-four to thirty-six hours.

Hannah describes her response as "incredible guilt". She says, "It was obviously something that I had willed. I didn't want it and so therefore I was going to make damn sure I didn't have it one way or the other." The next step was to induce the baby before the placenta began to decay. Her previous children had been easy deliveries, birthed quickly without delay: Lizzie, her eldest daughter, born sixteen minutes after Hannah went in to hospital; Stella, her second daughter, born after forty-six minutes of labour. This induction took twenty-seven hours, a total shock to Hannah but then part of her felt that this was not a birth. This was something different and Hannah was hanging on, not wanting to let go, not wanting to face events. Hannah describes the birth as "dreamy, surreal. I wasn't conscious. I went into some kind of respiratory -... not failure but I remember being extremely light-headed and losing consciousness." In reality it was a type of shock connected with her heart and respiration. Hannah has an irregular heart beat which only surfaces in times of severe stress and labour is the most stressful event a woman can encounter. The same reaction had occurred during both her daughters' births but since they were uncommonly quick, it hadn't been a serious issue. Hannah had spoken to the doctor about this after the first birth and his reply was that if this only happened when Hannah was in severe stress, then it wasn't something with which she need concern herself on a daily level. However, inducing this baby turned into a long and protracted process and although it wasn't a matter of life and death, Hannah passed out. When her body had been stabilised and she had regained consciousness, the baby was gone.

This action raises some interesting questions, such as what right did the hospital have to confiscate the child without the mother's permission? When a woman has carried a child nearly full term and built a relationship with the growing soul, despite what Hannah felt about the way it was conceived, why would anyone expect that such an action of removal was ever going to be the resolution to losing this significant relationship? One of the women who answered my Grief Questionnaire had a miscarriage at the age of thirty-five. Ten years later, in the year 2000, this was how she remembered it:

> Miscarriage at twelve weeks. A voice in my head telling me I had
> to let go, that this chid was not meant to be. Insisting that I be
> taken to hospital, even though there were no strong physical signs
> of a miscarriage. Calmness and a sense of dissociation when the
> miscarriage happened after a day in hospital. Sensation of coldness,

emptiness, numbness, total removal of the senses. The next day physical after-effects, like I had been kicked in the stomach. Rawness, like physical pain but not physical. Nausea, bitter taste, blackness. I can remember these things. And then crying - I am not a cryer by nature - crying and crying and crying like never before. Totally untouchable - no-one could get near me. Rage and then emptiness. Depression. Removal from everyone - loss of direction, difficult, prickly, inconsolable, exhausted.

The length of a pregnancy is not a measure of the depth of grief. Grief has an existence all of its own. Each year in Australia approximately 58,000 couples experience reproductive loss: around 55,000 experience early pregnancy loss, 1,750 babies are stillborn and approximately 900 babies die in the first twenty-eight days after birth.[10] Spending time with the stillborn baby, seeing the body, naming it and taking photographs is now considered a healthy way of dealing with the grief. These small gestures allow the development of memories and provide a focus for the parents' feelings. No matter how painful, these simple acts provide the reality and context to enable a person to grieve. Again it didn't occur to Hannah to assert her rights and ask for her baby, so she didn't see the body and she had no idea what had happened to it once it was delivered. She didn't know how to deal with her feelings and, since Art was not around to help, her overriding motivation was to stay strong for her girls.

With her Dip.Ed. safely in place, Hannah rang the Education Department two days before placements went out: "Send me to the outback. I'll go anywhere." In December, Hannah left the city with her two little girls and severed all connections with anyone she knew. In the outback she made an abundance of new friends who did not know her and did not know her history but she thought about it all the time and she felt a terrible guilt that somehow She Had Done It. With no outlet for the expression of her pain, it became jammed in her unconscious and a deep depression set in for roughly seven years. Like Menelaus was captain of a ship going nowhere.

If Hannah had come to see you in 1983, in her first year of grief, her predictive work suggests a year of quietness and slow, inward processing (Secondary Progressed Moon in the 12th house, First Quarter Secondary Progressed Lunation Phase, transiting Saturn conjunct natal Neptune), allowing time to deal with the death (transiting Saturn square natal Venus) and moving forward slowly but thoroughly (transiting Saturn square natal Uranus). In this year of confusion and disintegration, without major external events jostling for position in her life, Hannah was being given a chance to integrate the loss and make adjustments to her life. If she had embraced her grief, then the astrology for 1984, in its best-case scenario, suggests that, whilst the process of her grief continues, Hannah's world is also expanded through a new business association or intimate alliance or, since she was a teacher, then possibly a new teaching position, through which she learns about how she functions in relationship (Secondary Progressed Moon in the 12th house, transiting Jupiter conjunct her natal Sun in the 7th house). Building on this in 1985, again in its best-case scenario, the astrology tells us that Hannah is entering an active, visible phase (Secondary Progressed Moon conjunct the Ascendant), stepping away from inward processing and encountering an intense, fated, committed relationship (transiting Pluto square natal Venus) which brings sudden, unexpected changes to her life path (transiting Uranus conjunct the North Node). This is her Saturn Return year and for Hannah Saturn visits but once, suggesting that she has already been confronted with a great deal of change. In this period of expression (Gibbous Secondary Progressed Lunation Phase) 1986 offers her the opportunity to consolidate the intimate relationship of the previous year through greater commitment (transiting Saturn opposition natal Moon).

However, this was suppressed grief and none of this happened. Instead in 1984 (transiting Jupiter conjunct her natal Sun) Hannah experienced excessive trauma and crisis when her house, which she had rented out, got trashed so badly she had to sell it. In 1985 (transiting Pluto square natal Venus) she began a new, intense, intimate relationship which polarised her friends, some of whom she lost as a result. In 1986 (transiting Saturn opposition natal Moon) Hannah fell off her verandah and shattered her elbow so badly that she lost the use of her right arm for four months and had to have a plate inserted which stayed in her arm for seven years until the bones knitted:

> I also injured my back and was in physiotherapy for a long time. I lost a great deal of mobility including the ability to play my violin, to swing a golf club or to lift a tennis racquet. I couldn't play netball anymore because I was afraid of falling over. I also lost a lot of money in medical bills until some compensation money, just enough to cover the bills, came through five years later.

Fourteen years after her baby died, when Hannah was forty, she moved back to the city. Her predictive work for 1996 was as follows:

- **Third Quarter Secondary Progressed Lunation Phase** (since April 1994): New ideas concerned with old issues. This is the time when the person begins to review their life situation and rearrange it accordingly. It is a highly productive phase where the person takes action based on wisdom learned earlier in the cycle.

- **Secondary Progressed Moon in Sagittarius** (since August 1995): the impulse for new exploration and new encounters, coupled with the desire for greater independence.
- **Saturn Fidaria** (since late December 1995): responsibility, authority, duties, burdens, accountability.
- **Secondary Progressed Moon in the 6th house** (begins in January): issues of duty, service and follow-through; the hard work and daily grind of health and routine.
- **Transiting Uranus opposition natal Uranus** (begins in February): "The blinding flash of the obvious".
- **Transiting Uranus conjunct natal Venus** (begins in late March): changes to socializing patterns; falling in and out of love; changes in financial situation.
- **Transiting Saturn square natal Sun** (begins in late May): increase of responsibility.

Once again Hannah was in a relationship with someone that she cared about greatly. Once again she found out she was pregnant. This time she felt as if she had been hit over the head with a hammer. She couldn't see this relationship being permanent and she didn't want to go through another pregnancy alone a second time. Once again she decided to terminate the pregnancy. Some weeks' later she still felt really off-colour. This time she knew! She went back and had a second termination two weeks' later. Her past experience had given her the insight to understand the physical nature of what was happening (transiting Uranus opposing natal Uranus) and she was correct, it was a twin. The same thing had happened!

Hannah's grandmother had been a faith healer, detached and slightly other-worldly in many ways, yet always kind. She had half-terrified and half-amazed Hannah but after her death, when Hannah was nearly eleven, Hannah missed her greatly and wished she had been able to see more of her. As a child Hannah had thought faith healing so odd she had ignored it but when the same pattern of pregnancy surfaced, Hannah went see a clairvoyant. This was the first time in fourteen years that Hannah had talked to anyone about what had happened. The woman told her it wasn't her fault, that it was the child who had changed her mind, that this little soul trying to come through was born into the wrong generation and it wasn't meant to be like this. Hannah didn't believe her. She thought it was a really convenient psychological model that people could believe if they wanted but in her case it didn't work like that. A few nights later Hannah saw her mother. She said nothing about going to see the clairvoyant, nor anything of what she had been told. Of her own volition her mother told her that when she was first married she had fallen pregnant and the baby had died in the womb. Some months' later, feeling most unwell, her mother had gone to see the doctor. The doctors were of the opinion that Hannah's mother could not possibly still be pregnant but she was - with Hannah. Hannah was one of a twin. The other twin had died in the womb. Not only that but her grandmother and her great-grandmother had also lost babies. Four generations of women had a repeating pattern of infant loss.

Hannah's Moon is in Gemini in the 12th house conjunct the South Node. In Hannah's chart her emotional wellbeing was intimately tied up with this inherited family pattern of the lost twin, reverberating like an echo through the generations, a pattern looped in time trying to resolve itself. Hannah was nineteen when she married. Seven years later she was divorced. Fourteen years passed between the first aborted twin pregnancy and the second one. Hannah was clearly responding to the myth of her Sun in Capricorn, the myth of domination and suppression as a way of controlling her life, and the cycles of Saturn as its dispositor. Now she was piecing together another myth - a puzzle that involved four generations of the women of her family and a pattern of twins - the myth of Gemini.

Suddenly this answered a whole lot of questions for Hannah. She had always felt like she had no clear identity, no lucid memories of childhood or adolescence: "Like, it didn't happen. I can't put borders around it." When Hannah found out she was pregnant again, all the old emotions resurfaced: "It wasn't like this event had nothing to do with anything else. It's not in little bits. It all flies back in." This was unresolved grief as potent and powerful as it had originally expressed itself. So Hannah began talking to her unborn daughter at night, letting her know that again the time was wrong. Communicating in this way, consciously acknowledging the history of which she recognized she was now an important part, Hannah began to feel her twin around her less and less.

Lone twins

Joan Woodward, now a seventy-eight year old psychotherapist working in Birmingham, England, lost her identical twin sister from meningitis at the age of three. Since then she had been acutely aware of having distinctly different feelings to her singleton friends. In order to understand this further, in the early 1980's she interviewed two hundred and nineteen volunteer lone twins, both men and women, in England and Wales, ranging in age from eighteen to ninety-two. Some had lost their twin at or around birth, some in childhood and others in adult life. Ninety of them were identical (monozygots), one hundred and eleven were fraternal (dizygots) and eighteen did not know their zygosity. [11] Eighty-one percent of the lone twins interviewed described their loss as having either a severe or a marked effect on their lives, the severest felt by those who had lost a twin of the same sex, whether identical or not, and those who had lost their twin before the age of six months. Woodward believed this was due to the fact that their experience of loss was at a pre-verbal age when they were unable to express what they were feeling and separation anxiety became locked in to the behaviour sequence, giving rise to such symptoms as depression, fear, feelings of inadequacy, extreme anger and violence. As well, the surviving twin not only had to cope with their own feelings but with their parents' emotional anguish as well. No research work at all had been carried out in this field until Woodward's study was published in 1988, the most controversial part of which was the area that focused on twin loss in the womb or at birth. Most psychiatrists and psychoanalysts doubted whether memories in the womb or at birth could contribute to the surviving twin's sense of loss. Attachment theorists believe attachment behaviour comes into being around six months of age. Woodward believes otherwise and cites the work of Pionelli who, in 1992, observed the behaviour of twins in the womb via scans and discovered that how twins related to each other in the womb was reflected in how they related to each other as babies. Woodward has sighted videos of Pionelli's work and been impressed with the evidence which not only suggests that twins in the womb respond to each other but that the death of one of them and their subsequent removal from the womb will have serious consequences for the twin remaining behind. Woodward's study confirms that the loss of a twin, at whatever age, is a profound experience, leaving a relentless feeling of incompleteness and that possibly because twins are only noticed when they are seen together, such feelings are often diminished as invalid. Her work shows that this loss is significant and needs to be endorsed and acknowledged as a crucial experience which affects the lone twin's whole life. [12]

The case of Samuel Armas

In support of this idea are the somewhat controversial photographs taken during a revolutionary operation on 19th August, 1999, to fix the spina bifida lesion of a twenty-one-week-old foetus, Samuel Alexander Armas, in the womb.[13] Julie Armas, a twenty-seven year old obstetrics nurse in Atlanta, Georgia, USA, and her husband Alex, a twenty-eight year-old jet aircraft engineer, had been desperately trying to conceive a baby. Julie had previously suffered two miscarriages, so when, at fourteen weeks, she began to experience appalling cramps, she was given an ultrasound scan to observe the shape of the developing foetus and its position in the womb. The scan revealed that Samuel had a misshapen brain and that part of his spinal cord was exposed after the backbone failed to develop. He had spina bifida.[14] Julie and Alex were devastated. They were offered the routine, and perfectly legal, procedure of termination and many parents would have accepted. However, Julie and Alex were deeply religious and it was not a course of action they wished to follow. Instead Julie's mother found a website on the internet which detailed the pioneering surgery of neurologist Dr Joseph Bruner and his team at Vanderbilt University Hospital in Nashville, Tennessee. Although the results have not yet been endorsed in medical journals, the surgical team had developed a technique for correcting foetal problems in mid-pregnancy by temporarily removing the uterus, draining the amniotic fluid, performing surgery on the tiny foetus entirely through a tiny slit in the wall of the womb, then restoring the uterus back inside the mother. The instruments had to be specially designed to work in miniature and the sutures used to close the incisions were less than the thickness of a human hair. Controversy surrounds surgery like this because it opposes the general medical rule that risk should not outweigh benefit. Julie and Alex were fully aware that if anything went wrong, no attempt would be made to deliver Samuel by Caesarean section, since medical science does not yet have the capability of keeping a twenty-one-week-old foetus alive outside the womb and that, as a safety precaution, a crash-cart would be on standby for Julie throughout the operation. Julie's response was clear: "The worst thing might be if we don't do this and this is standard treatment when he's twenty one years old, and he says: 'Why didn't you know about that?' and we say, 'We did but we didn't do it for you.' "

Samuel Armas was the fifty-fourth foetus operated on by the surgical team and the entire surgical procedure was completed in one hour and thirteen minutes. Bruner says that both Samuel and Julie were under anaesthesia during the operation and could not move. Michael Clancy was the veteran photojournalist in Nashville, Tennessee, hired by *USA Today* newspaper to photograph the operation. This is what he saw:

> When it was over, the surgical team breathed a sigh of relief, as did I. As the doctor asked me what speed of film I was using, out of the corner of my eye I saw the uterus shake but no one's hands were near it. It was shaking from within. Suddenly, an entire arm thrust out of the opening, then pulled back until just a little hand was showing. The doctor reached over and lifted the hand, which reacted and squeezed the doctor's finger. As if testing for strength, the doctor shook the tiny fist. Samuel held firm. I took the picture!...

It was ten days before I knew if the picture was even in focus. To ensure no digital manipulation of images before they see them, *USA Today* requires that film be submitted unprocessed. When the photo editor finally phoned me he said, "It's the most incredible picture I've ever seen. [15]

Bruner's account is that he saw the hand "sort of pop up in the incision" from the womb and he "reached over and picked it up." Clancy shot a couple of frames and Bruner tucked the hand back into the womb. "Why did I pick up the hand?" Bruner says. "I have no idea why I did it. I looked and I saw this hand and I guess that to me it was just a very human thing to do to reach out and shake somebody's hand."

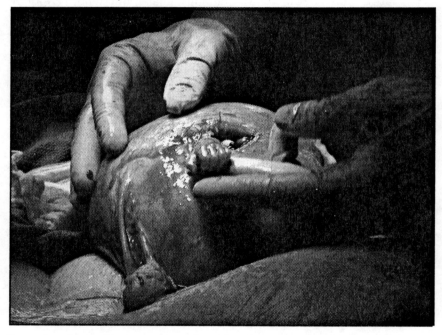

Reproduced with kind permission from the photojournalist © Michael Clancy, 1999.

The surgery was successful and Samuel was born at thirty-six weeks on 2nd December, 1999, at 6:25 pm at Northside Hospital weighing five pounds eleven ounces and measuring twenty-and-a-half inches long. He did not have to spend any time in a neonatal unit and an ultrasound showed he did not have any hydrocephalus and the brain malformation had resolved. He moved his legs well from the hips and some from the knees. Although a frank breech (folded in half) in the womb, the orthopaedist was confident Samuel stood a good chance of walking. Whilst pro-life and religiously conservative groups have been quick to embrace Clancy's photographs as indications of the conscious action of a twenty-one-week-old foetus, Bruner maintains both Samuel and his mother were anesthetised. Clancy's stance is simple: "The picture is proof that at twenty-one weeks in utero, the child is a reactive human being and that anesthetising a foetus is the most experimental thing about this surgery."

Until further work is done in this field, it will always spark controversy. Nevertheless reactive or conscious, life is clearly formed and functioning at this time. Its implication for a lone twin in the womb, in such a confined space, is unsettling. The constant, unprocessed, sensual feel of "the other", known and understood as a given, the eternal movement, the transmission of touch, the sharing of instincts as defined for a foetus plunged suddenly into aloneness, such a loss so early in development, understood at a pre-verbal level and imprinted onto the psyche, must be excruciating.

At what point in time parents tell the lone twin of the situation, how they tell them and their attitude afterwards all play a vital role in their acceptance of the loss. Most lone twins on hearing their story feel they have found a missing link. So it was with Hannah. Hannah says:

> I have this extremely social side that fills in all the gaps and people have this perception of me being such an open person and I'm not. I'm remarkably private. I have this part of me that's totally intimidated by the dark that's inside me and so only goes to this line and no further. It's not that I do it deliberately. It's just that I don't quite know how to get my tongue around the words, like it won't come out. That's why I get all these chest infections and can't breathe.

In 1998 Sean finally left his wife for good. Hannah had been extremely angry with him over a whole range of issues and didn't respond when he contacted her. Six months into the year, his daughter, aged eighteen, crashed a car into a tree and was killed instantly. This child was Hannah's god-daughter, a child she had fed as a baby when Sean's wife was ill and raised as one of her own for the first few years of her life. All Hannah's anger at Sean dissolved. All that was on her mind was that Sean needed support but his daughter's death brought up a great deal of guilt connected with all her unresolved issues of grief. Sean told Hannah that as soon as she said the word, he would be there to form a committed relationship with her. Now at the beginning of 1999, this was the question on her mind: should she be with Sean or not?

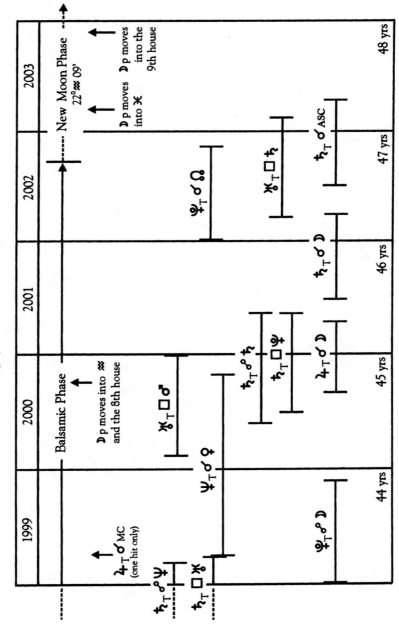

Time Map for Hannah 1999-2003

Hannah did no bereavement counseling in 1982. She did a little after the termination in 1996 but didn't feel it was useful because she still felt ashamed and couldn't tell her whole story. Hannah saw me as a client in 1999 and that was the first time she had ever told anyone the whole story. For the first time she began to get a handle on the emergent patterns. Underlying this time of enchantment there were clear messages: it was time to deal with her unresolved grief and it was time to be clear about her relationship with Sean. Hannah knew Sean was desperate to replace his daughter. She also knew that that, for her, this was now totally out of the question. Knowing she had to maintain her integrity and draw a clear line in the sand (transiting Neptune conjunct natal Venus), once more she sent him packing.

In her Secondary Progressed Balsamic Lunation phase, Hannah started to re-establish links with the people she had known before her pregnancy in 1982 and slowly and painfully, started to speak out about her history. In mid-2000 she wrote to me:

> I have had what I regard as an extraordinarily rich and full life. Along with all these losses I feel quite blessed. I have an amazing network of loving friends, wonderful kids, a brain that seeks out and desires new things and that will never stay still and generally good health. I love my life and wouldn't want another. I would never make the same decisions now as I may have five years ago. I am a much stronger individual who is able to prioritise her own needs more effectively than before, although some of this still fails me from time to time. Those boundaries have been hard won but I know my limits and I know the things that hook me into situations that I can do without. Even my relationship with my parents is much more grounded now, although I will probably never be close to them.
>
> My earliest memory is trying to get the sun out of my eyes. I remember not being able to do this. I must have only been a year or so, just a baby, and the dominant feeling was discomfort. Perhaps that's been a theme in my life that is now finally starting to change. My own involvement has prevented me from seeing the relationships between events and perhaps, truthfully, my hesitancy to deal with parts of my strange life. I want to thank you for helping me to do this. It made me reflect a lot at the time and I really enjoyed working with you; your patience and care, and sensitivity was immensely special.

The Secondary Progressed Lunation cycle which began at 22⁰ Capricorn conjunct natal Mercury in her 7th house in 1972, offered Hannah as its prelude the death of her grandfather. That cycle was now completing with this Neptune transit and the encrusted layers beginning to dissolve, exposing the heart of the matter. In the myth of grief Proteus had spoken and Hannah had found her voice. She was now free to sail home to her changed world. With the Secondary Progressed New Moon phase beginning in July 2002 at 22° Aquarius in Hannah's 8th house, square to natal Saturn and opposite natal Pluto, this next period of her life offers her a thirty year cycle of a completely different texture and fabric.

In October 2003, well into the first year of her Secondary Progressed New Moon phase, with the Secondary Progressed Moon in Pisces in the 9th house and in the Saturn-Mercury sub period of the Saturn Fidaria, Hannah's new life had already begun to take shape:

> I'm looking at the psychology behind anorexia at the moment, the idea that the impulse doesn't leave but that it shifts sideways into something else. I have been speaking with a lot of women recently who also were anorexic teenagers and working with a number of students who I find myself understanding on a particularly dark level. It's got me fascinated. There are remarkable similarities in our thinking. One belief is that family systems contain a lot of grief and sometimes one person in the family manages that collective grief and taps into it. It may roll over some generations and come out in certain types like yours truly. Would be very interested if there was an astrological correlation of which you were aware. Otherwise life continues as normal. I have finished the first draft of my film script and am now going through the process of editing which is pretty astounding really. Loving it and wish I had more time to put into it. My girls are well. Lizzie's partner had cancer last year and we had a lot of growing to do through that. He has an extremely strong life force and a lot of positive self talk and will be around for a good while yet, I think, although I had to face the final realisation that I couldn't save everyone. That was a right angle rather than a learning curve. Stella is fine, has a super well paid job and is shifting up the corporate ladder in leaps and bounds. Such different characters. Oh, and by the way, I don't know if I told you - Sean became a grandfather last year and, you guessed it: twins! A boy and a girl born under Gemini. My God, I get blown away. The music of the cosmos really.

Conclusion

What is the client in grief seeking from the consultation? Often the client doesn't know that what they desperately want is a benevolent heart and a stay of time, a place where the world will not collapse in on them and a place where they do not have to pretend. If grief has been suppressed, what emerges in the safety and security of the consulting room is the sound of a broken heartstring as it tries to keep playing the tune of life. With clarity, empathy and solid astrological technique, the client can walk away from the consultation bearing the gift of their future. It may take many more months, perhaps years, of walking through the unique topography that is their grief but at least they understand there is a pathway to walk. If you have done your job well enough, you will have flashed a light onto their way through the woods, revealing that through the prickly branches and the mist, life waits them at the edge of the forest, dressed in cloths of gold and sustained with love and warmth.

> The wind brings
> enough fallen leaves
> to make a fire.
>
> Ryokan (Japanese poet, 1758-1831)

❋   ❋   ❋

Endnotes

1. http://news.bbc.co.uk/1/hi/business/1966635.stm - accessed 12th February, 2003.
2. http://www-gap.dcs.st-and.ac.uk/~history/Mathematicians/Conway.html - accessed 4th April, 2003.
3. It comes from a field of mathematical research called "cellular automata" in which rules are applied to cells and their neighbours in a regular grid.
4. Lerner, Harriet. (1985) *The Dance of Anger*. New York: Harper Collins.
5. Brady, Bernadette. (1997) 'Life, Death and the Whole Damn Thing!' in *Astrology: An Ancient Art in the Modern World*, ed. Mari Garcia, Adelaide: Australis '97 The Congress Papers, p.15.
6. http://www.mercola.com/2001/oct/31/childhood_diseases.htm - accessed 20th May, 2003.
7. This quote from The Compassionate Friends website sums up the stark and terrifying reality that floods many parents faced with the death of their child. The USA website states: "It is estimated that more than 200,000 infants, children, teenagers, and young adults will die this year. Nearly 27,000 families will face a stillbirth and 900,000 families will suffer an early pregnancy loss." The Compassionate Friends is a national non-profit, self-help support organization offering friendship and understanding to families grieving the death of a child of any age, from any cause. There is no religious affiliation.

Their websites are: (UK) http://www.tcf.org.uk/ and
(USA) http://www.compassionatefriends.org/ - both accessed 20th May, 2003.
8. My sincere thanks to Jack for allowing me to publish his poetry.
9. Schwab, Dr Reiko, (1998) 'A Child's Death and Divorce: Dispelling the Myth' in *Death Studies*, Vol. 22, No. 5, pp. 445-468.
10. http://www.sands.org.au/ - accessed 28th May, 2003.
11. The study was presented at The International Congress of Twin Studies in Amsterdam in 1986 and published in the Journal of their Proceedings a year later.
12. In May 1989 Woodward set up The Lone Twin Network (originally called the Lone Twin Register) to offer a network of contacts and support to anyone whose twin has died, at whatever stage of life. They can be contacted by post only at: Lone Twin Network, P O Box 5653, Birmingham, B29 7JY, England.
13. I am indebted to Michael Clancy for information on this story, as well as the following sources:
http://www.michaelclancy.com/story.html - accessed 29th May, 2003;
http://www.usatoday.com/leadpage/indexusa.htm - accessed 31st May, 2003;
http://www.truthorfiction.com/rumors/babysamuel.htm - accessed 31st May, 2003;
http://www.snopes.com/photos/thehand.asp - accessed 31st May, 2003.
14. Spina bifida is a congenital neurological disorder marked by underdeveloped vertebrae that leave the spinal cord exposed. It occurs in about one in one thousand pregnancies. Though not always fatal, the most severe form, myelocele, involves a physical change in the spinal cord itself and can result in severe physical handicaps if the child survives and is untreated.
15. Clancy asserts that, for legal purposes, it must be stated that this "Story Behind the Picture" is his opinion of the events as they took place during the surgery for Samuel.

6
Children and Grief

A torn jacket is soon mended; but hard words bruise the heart of a
child.

Henry Wadsworth Longfellow, poet (1807-1882)

When children experience loss, we are not dealing with a
one-to-one interface as we would be doing when an adult seeks
astrological help. Indeed over the years of consulting and teaching, it has
become evident that a change in attitude occurs in a person around the age of
twenty-three. This may be due to the waning Saturn square which offers a
person the opportunity to take on more responsibility with their life or it may
be that now the person has a degree of life experience under their belt.
Whatever the case, when it comes to students and clients around this age,
they seem to hear more clearly what is being said to them, to better understand
the complexities of the natal chart and to be more willing to take charge of
their learning than someone of younger years. As a result Astro Logos has a
policy of only educating students and taking on clients who are twenty-three
years or older. However, a large part of our caseload involves reading children's
charts and their predictive work for the parents of children who may be aged
anywhere from birth to twenty-two. When it comes to loss and children, the
following factors come into play: the knowledge of how children grow and
learn about the world and hence how will they react to loss; the emotional
connection the child had to the person who has died; the circumstances of
the death; and the willingness of the parent to also deal with the loss and
truthfully express what they themselves are feeling.

How do we learn and grow? How do we gain understanding about the world around us?

Jean Piaget [1] (1896-1980), one of the most influential researchers in the area
of developmental psychology during the twentieth century, was deeply
interested in the biological influences on how children come to "know", how
language develops and how children recognise people and objects. He was
conscious that cognition or the acquisition of knowledge is not innate, nor is
it developed through our senses as the end product of environmental input.

Instead he believed that people actively seek out knowledge, organise it, assimilate it and build on it and that this is an ongoing relationship between the child and their environment. As a result of his research, and recognising that individual children develop at different rates, he formulated that cognition occurred in the following ways:

The first month of life is characterised by instinctive reflexes such as sucking and grasping. The infant is only aware of themselves and their environment and learns about the world through the objects they put into their mouth. **From one to four months** infants start to look, grasp and turn their head in the direction of a sound. They learn that different parts of the body belong to them and that they have control over them. They like to be held and rocked and notice bright colours and patterns. They also learn repetitive activity. In his work with tears, William Frey found that newborn humans produce continuous and irritant tears from the time of birth but it takes several days, weeks or in some cases up to three months before the human infant develops the ability to shed tears in response to emotional stress. **From four to eight months** the infant begins to jabber, coo, and laugh aloud. They can hold their head erect and sit supported for brief periods. They are able to distinguish between self and objects but believe an object that is out of sight does not exist. As a result, they also believe that their actions cause external events. **From eight to twelve months** intentional behaviour emerges. The infant reaches for objects that it wants, anticipates people and searches for partially-hidden objects. Memory or what Piaget calls "object permanence" begins to enter awareness. A one year old infant begins to show affection, anger and jealousy. They are able to express fear of strangers, fear of heights and fear of separation from parents. They cry when scolded, resist having toys taken away and physically express frustration.

A one-year old may not have memory recall but as we saw in Chapter Two, the body will pattern and lock in all sorts of messages. In this first year of life the infant is developing trust, so any predictive work in this year will reveal events that affect this part of the infant's life. If mother dies in childbirth, in the first weeks or the first year of an infant's life, one would expect this pattern to show up in the birth chart and in the predictive work as the infant being forced to deal with intense emotional stress and a loss of trust in some way whilst it is developing sensory-motor skills and intentional behaviour.

In its first year of life a baby is also totally dependent upon a nurturing source, so the mode of knowing astrologically comes through his or her Moon, initially projected onto mother as the source of nurturing as outlined in Chapter Three. By house, sign, rulership and aspects this emotional lens acts as the conduit through which the baby receives nourishment and learns to express its emotions. Sometimes the thoughts and feelings of the mother impact upon the developing foetus as early as conception onwards and the boundary between child and mother remains open. An example of this is a Moon in Pisces or a Moon in aspect to Neptune. For others this connection may be shattered during the birth process when the Moon stumbles into the territory of Saturn, Uranus or Pluto and produces birth trauma. Here is an example of birth trauma which continued to play itself out in the child's early years of life. Kevin [2] was delivered by emergency caesarean and had lifesaving surgery within twenty-four hours of his birth. At the age of three, Kevin's parents were concerned at his "autistic-like" play. He would repeatedly lie on the floor, stiffen his body and pretend he was dying, then slowly return to life wailing, "Save me!" He was experiencing life as if the event was still happening, trapped in an emotional loop that begged to be heard so it could be attended to and healed.

Babies understand language long before they can speak, so a baby in the preverbal first year of life will also be contending with issues of communication. Joseph Garcia [3] became fascinated with sign language and learnt how to communicate with the deaf in order to better understand it. He observed that the hearing babies of his deaf friends were extremely adept at sign language at around nine months of age, yet the nine-month old babies of his hearing friends were communicating little, if at all. The difference intrigued Garcia so much that he made it the subject of his Master's thesis at Alaska Pacific University in the USA in 1987 and carried it further into doctoral studies in adult learning and education. Garcia's research revealed that hearing babies of hearing parents who are exposed to signs regularly and consistently at six-to-seven months of age began using signs effectively as early as eight months, with some exceptional children as early as six months. This new discovery seriously challenged the opinion of many child development experts, including Piaget, who theorized that babies can't mentally represent symbols until they are almost two and therefore can't learn to talk until then. Instead, it appears that young infants simply lack the fine motor skills necessary to produce spoken language, not the conceptual ability to understand and use it. It is now thought that, in the same way that crawling stimulates a child's interest in walking, signing provides a bridge to verbal communication. A growing body of research has shown that babies who sign can communicate before they can speak, speak earlier than non-signers, experience less frustration, have IQ's that are ten-to-twelve points higher, have a better grasp of grammar and syntax, past and present tenses and of language in general, demonstrate a greater interest in books, have better imaginations, possess greater self-confidence and experience a closer bond with their parents and siblings.[4] By the age of two they had a vocabulary of fifty more real words, on average, than their non-signing counterparts. By age three, children exposed to signing had language skills approaching that expected of four year olds. Garcia's system, *Sign With Your Baby*, teaches parents how to empower babies as young as eight months old with expressive communication skills, including initiating conversation and problem solving.

From twelve to eighteen months Piaget found that the infant now develops insightful thinking (Mercury by house, sign, rulership and aspects). For example, a child wanting to obtain a thimble in a slightly open matchbox after fruitless attempts by groping, will stop and closely examine the box, at the same time opening and closing its mouth or hand, as if paralleling the result it wants, leading to success in opening the box. The infant recognises familiar people and objects and follows simple verbal instructions.

From eighteen to twenty-four months, the child is mentally inventive, developing what Piaget terms the semiotic or symbolic function. This function has to be modified by Garcia's work which clearly shows that babies form symbols extremely early in their lives. Suffice it to say that it is in this period that memory and imagination expand in understanding, the spoken word blossoms, deductive thinking and reasoning begins and trial and error is used on a physical and mental level. Symbolic play situations are a necessary part of the child's assimilation and reinterpretation of events and help the child deal with unsatisfied needs and issues of authority and obedience. For example, a fight at lunch may find its way into the afternoon play with dolls but now ending in a happier conclusion. Symbolic play may also be used as a defence against anxiety, phobias, aggression, withdrawal from fear of risk or competition, and so on, and the child will create as many symbols as it needs in order to express everything in its life that cannot be formulated and assimilated by language. Indeed the symbolic world of play strongly resembles the symbolism of dreams, for the dreamer is also without the rational use of language, the sense of reality and deductive or logical reasoning.

In these first two years of life, infants will not understand death as a concept but they do experience intense subjective images.[5] So the loss of the sight, smell, feel and voice of a familiar person in their family unit can cause strong symbolic imagery which may be frightening. If this is a grandparent who has lived in the same house as them, the infant will not only be dealing with their own reactions but the emotions of the parent who has lost their mother or father. This may reveal itself physically as irritability, clinginess, eating or sleeping problems, emotional outbursts, nightmares, bed-wetting or an increase in colds or indigestion. Predictive work for this period of time will show the impact of the loss on the infant's growing and developing sense of themselves and the world.

Drawing is an intermediate phase between symbolic play and mental image and rarely appears before the ages of two or two and half. At this age, given a crayon or pencil, a child will initially draw a set of scribbles. Shortly after this, however, they will see form in the scrawled lines and attempt to draw an image from memory. The drawing, however poor in form, immediately becomes an imitation, a bridge between what is seen externally and what is visualised internally, for until they reach the age of eight or nine, a child's drawings are essentially realistic in intention, representing what they know about a person or an object long before they can depict what they actually see.

Symbolic play, dreams and drawings are all an expression of the unconscious. In 1996, researchers surveyed one hundred children from primary care paediatric clinics with a history of headaches spanning longer than three months. The researchers wanted to determine the type and associated features of the children's headache and their reasons for wanting to see a physician. The children's ages ranged from three to seventeen years. The children were also asked to draw pictures of how they felt when in the grips of a headache to assess their nonverbal perceptions. Over ninety percent of the headaches were found to be migrainous and third of the children's illustrations showed helplessness, frustration and anger, with over one fifth of the adolescents depicting themselves as dead, dying or about to be killed by their headache.[6] Spontaneous drawings can also reveal a great deal about the unspoken caverns of confusion felt by a child tossed on the waves of grief. Allowing a child to draw spontaneously unlocks unconscious psychic energy that may have been repressed in order to handle the loss and Gregg M. Furth's work has done much to further to voice of grief on this level. [7]

From age two to four (Piaget's preconceptual period), the child is unable to distinguish one member of a class from the class itself (all women are "mummy") and cannot see the world from other than their own point of view. They believe that everything that lives has feelings and intentions, that inanimate objects can move, think, feel and rest and that dead people are not really dead but continue to live under changed circumstances. Hence death is merely a deep sleep and a child will worry that the dead person might be hungry, cold or lonely. They will also employ magical thinking, believing everything is under the power and control of someone else's will: a person can die as a result of someone else's wish and return to life just as readily. One client distinctly remembers her sense of omnipotence as a child: "When I was younger, I used to think the world was activated by my eyes. I thought I caused all sorts of things to happen." At this age children begin to experiment with their independence through walking, running, climbing and jumping. They learn to feed and dress themselves, develop bladder and bowel control and eat solid foods. They begin to talk in simple sentences. If this is inhibited in any way, they may develop a sense of shame and doubt and learn to accept defeat in battles of will. According to Harvard researchers, by the age of two, children have developed memories strong enough to repeat tasks shown to them months earlier. [8] Even so, most adults can only remember as far back as ages three, four or five.

Predictive work in this period of time will indicate the impact of events on the infant's growing and developing sense of independence and will. In this age group a child may not understand the concept "dead" but they will most certainly sense the magnitude and depth of feelings when someone close to them dies. They may feel abandoned and express that emotion through the concrete items in their life, for example that Daddy can no longer play trains with them. They will need comforting, touching and frequent verbal repetition from an adult that the event has occurred so they can integrate it. At this age they will see death as reversible and believe they have the power to make things happen. This may express itself physically as regression to earlier behaviours such as bedwetting and thumb sucking, they may feel guilty that they have caused the death, they may appear not to care, exhibit fear of separation from significant others or re-enact the death or the event prior to the death through play. What they need most is consistency and reassurance.

From age four to seven (Piaget's preoperational period) the child experiences kindergarten and the early years of primary school. This time period is distinguished by semi-logical reasoning, with the child only able to deal with one variable at a time: a cup cannot be both blue and made of china. The child now remembers, imagines and pretends and employs precausal reasoning: any two events that occur together are causally related. Elisabeth Kubler-Ross believes that up to the age of three, a child is only concerned with separation and it is only later that they develop a fear of mutilation when, for example, they see, a pet that has been run over or a bird that has been torn apart by a cat. At this age, when the child is worried about the integrity of the body and feels threatened by anything that can destroy it, they need to be allowed to express their fears and encouraged to do so. Whilst death is not a permanent fact for a three-to-five year old, after the age of five, death is seen as a man who comes to take people away. One client whose older brother died when she was five, thought death was a man in a brown suit and, as she watched the car taking her brother's body, away she thought that heaven lay over the brow of the hill. Predictive work in this period of time will indicate the impact of events on the child's growing and developing sense of resourcefulness and as they begin primary school, their developing competence and the ability to work together with other children.

From age seven to eleven (Piaget's concrete operations period, the period that relates to objects rather than hypotheses) the child learns how to handle the basics of reasoned thought, coherency and sequence. By applying logical abilities, the child learns to understand fundamental, specific and concrete ideas of conservation, number, classification, and so on. Understanding that matter is conserved, regardless of change in form and size, allows the child to develop reversibility, that is, the ability to transpose the process back to the original form of the object. This ability to think backwards and forwards in time means the child is capable of filing thought patterns in memory; the child now understands the idea of today, tomorrow and the future. Around the ages of nine or ten death is recognised as a permanent biological process. The child may personify death as the bogeyman or a ghost but if the child's magic is strong enough, death can be overcome, for death only comes for the sick or the old, not the young and healthy. Believing it is their fault that the person died, a child needs to be encouraged to express the full spectrum of their feelings, as well as being allowed to spend time alone. Symbolic play and spontaneous drawings can describe many feelings that they child is unable to put into words. As part of the normal course of development, they may want to know all the details of dying and what happens to the corpse after death. They may have nightmares or anxiety attacks about being trapped in coffins and there is often an overwhelming concern for the child's own body. They will be concerned with proper procedure, how others respond and how they should respond. Reaction to the death may be physical (stomach ache, headache, nausea, vomiting, diarrhoea, constipation and fever) or behavioural (withdrawal, aggression, insomnia, refusing to talk about the person or expressing fear of their own death or the death of the caregiver). Predictive work for this period of time will indicate the impact of events on the child's growing and developing sense of peer support.

Here is an example of an Australian woman, Lizzie, now in her forties, who experienced the first death in her life when she was ten years old. Lizzie has a natal Moon-Neptune conjunction in Libra in the 8th house, with Cancer intercepted in the 4th house and Neptune ruling the 12th house cusp. The only aspects the Moon-Neptune makes are sextiles to Pluto in the 5th house and to the MC. In January 1968, transiting Uranus was about to retrograde back over her Descendant (exact in February). Her natal Uranus is conjunct Venus and Mars in Leo in the 5th house, trine Saturn and ruling the 11th house. The Secondary Progressed Moon was in its Full Phase in Pisces in the 12th house. She writes:

> In January, 1968, my oldest sister died from an asthma attack. I
> was ten years old. I was with her when she collapsed but she was

kept on life support for one week. This was never discussed, as we were supposed to keep going as if nothing was wrong. My mother was determined to be the perfect 1950s/1960s housewife, so we were taught early in life not to rock the boat. We never spoke about her death in our family. It occurred during school holidays, so it was as if it never happened at school. I don't remember changing my behaviour at all. None of the family did.

Lizzie developed diabetes when she was fifteen and at twenty-six had a coronary artery bypass graft surgery. She continues:

I thought once I was over the operation (three months) I would be back to "normal". This did not happen and I did not deal with (and was not encouraged to recognise) the loss of my health and my future. Six months after the operation I was in a depressed state which required treatment. My friends were supportive but my family did not understand depression (especially my parents, who prayed for me). Because I was young, it was expected I would get over the surgery and because it was not obvious I had a problem, there were no allowances made. I was extremely angry and sad. I spent a lot of time reading, sewing, knitting, watching TV and visiting my friends. Anti-depressants helped my mood. I did not really come to terms with the loss of my future until 1988 when I started Feldenkrais Training and then in 1994 at the age of thirty-seven, when I began a search of New Age ideas and Mind-Body Therapies. By this time I'd had my second coronary bypass surgery (1990) been diagnosed with unstable angina (1992) and suffered a heart attack and depression (1993). This heart attack was *not* a loss for me. It allowed me to stop all intervention and accept where I was. Work was supportive. My partner was struggling with my ill-health and was sometimes supportive. My family still didn't understand what I was going through. My mother was still praying for me.

It was not until she reached the age of forty in 1997, and suffered her third heart bypass operation that Lizzie had completed enough physical, emotional and spiritual work to come to terms with what her future held.

From ages eleven-twelve to fourteen-fifteen (Piaget's final period of formal operations) the young person is now an adolescent and capable of thinking rationally and systematically about abstract concepts and hypothetical events, although it is now thought that not every child reaches this formal operation stage. As part of thinking more abstractly, adolescents develop images of ideal circumstances - the ideal parent, the ideal career - and the waxing Saturn opposition will bring a natural sense of rebellion into their thinking and actions. By now the adolescent understands that death is permanent and universal, even though they still believe that it won't ever happen to them, for time in adolescence is centred in "the now" and death is a remote concept that cannot affect them or interrupt their ongoing plans. As if to thumb their nose at death, adolescents frequently take unnecessary risks, pitting themselves against the elements for an adrenalin hit and as a way of impressing friends, unwilling to accept the reality of personal danger. If a peer dies, they will often concentrate on the glory of the death and idolise their colleague, at the same time manifesting depression, repression, denial or anger at parents, religion or their friends, fearing the future and fretting that they have been forced to grow up. Some may turn to drugs and alcohol to numb the pain. Others may shut down areas of themselves they consider to be vulnerable or confusing. What they need most is an adult who is able to give them the space to articulate their feelings, a point clearly understood by shock-rock singer Marilyn Manson in the documentary film *Bowling for Columbine* directed by Michael Moore.[9] Manson was blamed by the media and the community as being the cause of the shootings at Columbine High School, so Moore sought him out and asked him what he would have said to the students. Unhesitatingly Manson replied: "Nothing. I would listen to what *they* have to say."

Adolescence is a phase generally unknown to aboriginal cultures, for once sexual maturity is reached, marked by the onset of menstruation in females and by a culturally significant rite of passage for males, children are treated as adults, with the gradual increase of responsibilities through childhood now acting as a bridge to a more mature contribution. This doesn't happen with such clarity in western cultures. Of all the rich and varied forms of life on planet earth, human beings are the ones who undergo the longest period of dependency. Many animals reach maturity and are able to be self-sustaining within the social unit within a year of being born. A few take as long as four or five years, with sexual or reproductive maturity following several years afterwards. Human beings are the only species to reach reproductive maturity well before social maturity - and this in itself heralds its own degrees of difficulties. Predictive work in this period of time will indicate the impact of events on the adolescent's growing and developing sense of identity through puberty, rebellion, achievement and ideals.

Piaget's timeline ends at adolescence but we can continue this into young adulthood: **the ages of sixteen until the waxing Saturn square at twenty-three.** The task of young adulthood is to develop a life of one's own and in this period of time, able to vote, drive a car and be served alcohol at a pub and seeking a mate who will fulfil their childhood dreams of the perfect partner, the young person is desperately trying to wear the mantle of adulthood.

Now physically mature, this is the time when young adults complete their education and begin to earn money, yet few are given the fundamental skills of how to take care of their feelings and the feelings of those around them, nor how to manage relationships. Young adults are expected to be financially, and personally successful, yet if they fail, society deems them to be flawed, rather than recognising it has ill-prepared them for these functions. Young adulthood can be a time of loneliness, emotional turmoil, and confusion. It can also be a time of mental and emotional growth, self-analysis and clarification of one's values. Encountering death at this time can bring new understandings of one's mortality, the nature of religion and spirituality and what constitutes the soul. Predictive work in this period of time will indicate the impact of events on the young adult's growing independence.

The emotional connection of the child to the person who has died.

The relationships we have with one another across our lifetime are unique and totally different in flavour and texture for each and every person and the emotional responses we have when they die will be in proportion to that relationship's depth and value. If a child's attachment to their grandparent or aunt or uncle was strong and a powerful bond has been forged, then their death will produce a powerhouse of emotional energy. If that grief is unexpressed, then they will experience sympathetic behavioural and physical symptoms. If the child had little contact with that relative, then their death may produce few emotions. As well, not all children love the relatives their parents love. It may also be the case that a parent has a difficult or awkward relationship with a relative whom their child loves. By maintaining a neutral stance in the situation, a parent allows their child to discover what is unprocessed or fragmentary in that relationship without adult agendas confusing the issue. The emotional bonds children make and their need for relationship and intimacy are crucial for their emotional security and in contributing to their happiness and wellbeing. The successful conclusion to these bonds and attachments is just as significant.

The circumstances of the death.

Death comes as a shock at the best of times. That loss will be compounded if the death is sudden and unexpected or if there is mutilation or disfigurement, such as from a car accident, a murder, a suicide or a long, drawn-out illness. In this extreme situation, without opportunity to prepare for the loss or say goodbye, the child not only has to process the separation from parent or relative but also the complete visual transformation of someone they loved. The trauma of the mismatch, the incongruity between form and function, the integrity of the body and its frailty in the face of machines, guns, medication, disease and clinical depression amongst other things, can stimulate intense reactions such as shock, anger, guilt, sudden depression, despair and hopelessness, as well as Post Traumatic Stress Disorder, all of which may take years to reconcile and cause the child to step away from life as a survival mechanism.

The pitch of the family also changes. Along with the devastation of the primary loss there may also be unforseen secondary losses: lost income, loss of home, loss of social status or parental marital problems, all of which will affect the child. If the child was also involved in the disaster or was physically injured, further difficulties occur, resulting in "survivor guilt," feelings of numbness, unreality and fear and a closed loop of virulent memories.[10]

The ability of the parent to express truthfully what they are feeling.
Children need others to mirror as they grow and will follow role models on a consistent basis without question. In the feature film *The American President*,[11] the character of Lewis Rothschild, the American President's Chief Domestic Policy Advisor, puts it this way:

> People want leadership. And in the absence of genuine leadership, they will listen to anyone who steps up to the microphone. They want leadership, Mr. President. They're so thirsty for it, they'll crawl through the desert toward a mirage, and when they discover there's no water, they'll drink the sand.

Whilst Lewis was referring to adults, children are no different. If parents shut down on expressing emotion, the child will copy this. When it comes to grief, the most precious gift a parent can give a child is to tell the truth about how they are feeling without assigning blame to any external mechanism or judging their own feelings, no matter how difficult they are to express. Children think literally and need concrete terms in order to be clear about the situation. Answering their questions simply and honestly and using the word "death", rather than euphemisms like "passed away", sets a clear framework for them. They don't need great detail and if you have shown willingness to engage with them about the situation and your feelings, they will ask if they want to know more. You will be able to tell by their body language if they are listening because it is a new situation with which they are trying to grapple (focused, attentive, eye contact) or if they there for your benefit (agitated, fidgety, little or no eye contact). In this way a child learns that it is safe to reveal any and all of their feelings about their relationship with the one who has died without the confusion of adult approval. This allows them to build their self-confidence in expressing emotional truth in the face of future losses, both large and small.

This is called managing emotions and educating a child on how to do this begins early. Continually feeding children statements of value ("you are bad") wedded to statements of blame ("you make me angry") means they constantly learn to hand over responsibility for how they feel to other people and become endlessly manipulated by other people's needs. Statements that place the person in the centre of their emotional world (statements that begin with "I feel...") allows the person to take responsibility for their feelings and to manage their emotions. When a parent tells a child, "I feel angry at your behaviour" and discusses that behaviour with them ("This is what occurred when you took this action and next time I would like you to think more carefully before you do that") the child learns that it is their behaviour that is under discussion and not their inherent right to be loved. It also allows the child to modify their behaviour next time and empowers the child who learns that it is appropriate and satisfactory to access their own internal states ("How am I feeling?") rather than having feelings assigned to them by others who may not have their best interests at heart or who may not understand their situation ("They are angry" = "It is my fault" = "I am powerless to feel other than angry"). This has immediate benefits when connected with grief. When a child feels safe enough to tell a parent, "I feel angry that my brother died", this means the parent can guide the child to explore this feeling more fully whilst keeping the child in the centre of their universe and find ways to bring these feelings to a satisfying conclusion. It may take days, weeks, months and years for all the other emotions connected with this statement to be fully fleshed out but now their feelings have a pathway for completion, it is no longer a closed system.

Staying alert to how we, as adults, send these messages to children takes focus. A good example of this is the experience of a recent client who was saying goodbye to her sister who was moving to another country. It was clearly an emotional time for her, and her two small children, sensing her distress without understating why, expressed this by demanding her attention. When Trent, her four-and-a half year old, inadvertently bumped her and the plate she was holding dropped and broke, my client's reaction was to sit heavily in a chair, sigh vigorously and put her head into her hands, indicating she was holding back her temper. With his Cancer Ascendant and seventh house Capricorn Sun, Trent immediately broke into tears for fear he was going to be blamed and punished. Dorothy, his younger sister aged two-and-a-half year, with her Cancer Ascendant and Leo Sun rising, immediately pointed at the broken plate and said to Trent in clear mimicry of her mother in anger: "Look at what you've done!" My client came to recognise that under stress she had reverted to patterns that her mother had used, that of blaming external causes for her emotions. If she had defused the situation by telling Trent that she loved him, that she was angry at his behaviour and that this room was not the place in which to run around and let off steam and could he suggest a better place to do that, she would have empowered him, teaching him about the appropriateness of space and how to handle his emotions. Indeed if she had explained to both Trent and Dorothy before the arrival of her sister that this was probably the last time she would see their aunt for a long while and that she was feeling deeply saddened by this, she would have given them a clear template for expressing sorrow at loss.

In 1964 in her work with an emotionally disturbed five year old boy called Dibs, Virginia Axline,[12] the originator of play therapy, recognised that Dibs could only grow in confidence if confidence was shown in him and that this could only be achieved in a two-fold process: firstly, by her understanding that every action he undertook had reason behind it; secondly, in her having no hidden agendas in her actions towards him. This meant that she did not expect him to read her mind and come up with answers which met her unstated standards, as my client above had been taught to do by her mother. This then gave Dibs the opportunity to see and feel the effects of his own reactions and in so doing, make them clear for himself, become conscious of them and finally accept them.

How can a parent help a child deal with grief?
Grief is a confused jumble of complicated and painful memories. Children, like adults, will have things they wished they had said to the person who has died, things they regretted saying and the desire to continue to experience the future with that person. With the chance to say or correct these things gone, the emptiness that is left has emotional value for the child and needs to be given voice. If that is stopped by adult intellect, then like Kevin's memory of his caesarean birth, these unexpressed emotions will continue to revolve as unconscious loops inside the child's head, stockpiled just below the conscious Plimsoll line and requiring energy to prevent them from escaping. The truth is that children will respond fully to grief experiences until they are taught to do otherwise. They will express a range of emotions, evaluate and conclude what is unfinished for them and then move on. They also imprint adult reactions with alarming speed and begin to shut down on this ability to grieve fully anywhere from ages three to seven.[13] Knowing a child's predictive work helps to understand the shape of their future and how they are likely to respond.

Loss as path-finders in adolescence

Sean Kane suggests there is an unseen balance between the Otherworld, the world of the enigmatic and the mundane world where life takes shape and form. We need boundaries between these worlds in order to avoid contamination. Where any two worlds meet the point is sacred, the boundary often marked by stone or ritual. In the secular world these two worlds come together most clearly when we encounter death. The guardians of the threshold demand our attention and if it is difficult enough to pay those dues as an adult, how much more difficult is it to do so when a child and still unformed. However, in its best expression, these early losses can become the catalyst for that person's contribution to society.

In the documentary film *Me and Isaac Newton* [14], two scientists came to an epiphany through such losses. Dr Karol Sikora, Professor of Cancer Medicine at Hammersmith Hospital, London and (then) Chief of the World Health Organisation Cancer Program, was encouraged by his father, an electrical engineer, to read science books at the age of eight or nine. Since children's science books were not then available, Sikora set up his own experiments, making bombs as a way of finding out how the world functioned. His father was Polish and whilst his extremely heavy Polish accent embarrassed his son, he was, like all other immigrants, extremely ambitious for him and insisted that he go to Oxford or Cambridge, after which he could do as he pleased. Sikora secured a place at Cambridge at the age of sixteen. Not long afterwards his father died from lung cancer. "He was a great friend," says Sikora who felt extremely relieved that his father knew he had made it into Cambridge but deeply regrets the fact that he can never have a beer with him in a pub and enjoy the adult conversation that he now has with his own son. From his first year at medical school Sikora knew that he wanted to be a cancer specialist, even though he could not foresee then that cancer going to become one of the dominating illnesses of the twenty-first century. "I don't think (my father's death) influenced me going into cancer specifically," he says. "but it influenced me about medicine and communication with patients because communication in the '60s was really poor with families, with patients, and so on."

Dr Gertrude B. Elion (1918-1999), Pharmaceutical Chemist for Glaxo-Wellcome and 1988 Nobel Prize Winner, became interested in science at the age of fifteen, an age she considers fairly late in a young person's life. As she was getting ready to enter college, her grandfather, to whom she'd been extremely close as a child, died "pretty horribly". As she watched him die, she had the sudden realisation that what she wanted to do with her life was to become a chemist and find a cure for cancer. Once set upon this course, she never wavered from it. Later she recognised her pathway in life had been wholly determined by family loss, for she was engaged to be married to a man who developed a bacterial endocarditis and who died two years before the advent of penicillin. "Everything seemed to say to me, if you do research and you discover cures for diseases, this is what your life is about."

Not every young person has experiences such as these, yet all encounters with the boundary guardians are there to feed and nourish us, if we let them.

Astrological Tools
In working with children's charts anywhere from six months onwards, I will use the same predictive tools as for an adult: transits and progressions, Fidaria and the Secondary Progressed Lunation Cycle, along with identifying the cognitive and developmental needs of the child at their various ages. It's also important to recognise that some of the demands of the child's heavier transits will be handled by their parents and when the relative who has died is also closely connected with the parent, it is useful to consider the parent's predictive work as well. In the following case study I have only focused on the child's natal chart and predictive work.

Edward
A Child In Grief

The following case study concerns one of our former students, Julie, and her son, Edward.

Parental signatures in Edward's chart and what they might say about grief:

Father-figure: *Sun in Pisces in the 8th house* [15] *(ruling the 2nd house) conjunct Mercury in the 9th house (ruling the 3rd and 12th houses) The Sun-Mercury forms the apex of a mutable T-square with the Moon in Gemini in the 12th house (ruling the Ascendant) opposition Uranus in the 6th house (ruling the 8th house).*

The Sun trines Pluto in the 4th house (ruling the 5th house). Uranus trines a Venus-Mars conjunction in Aries conjunct the MC in the 10th house (Venus rules the 4th and 11th houses and Mars rules the 5th and 10th houses.) Pluto squares Jupiter in the 8th house (ruling the 6th and 9th houses).

Unaspected Saturn conjunct the South node in Scorpio in the 5th house.

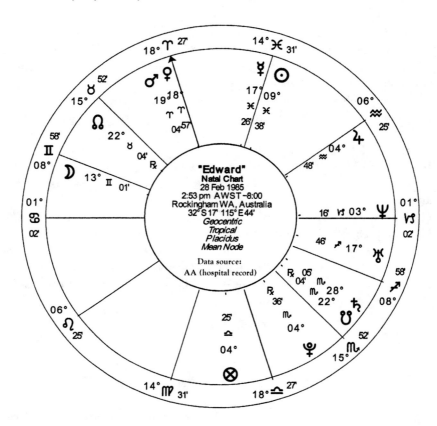

Mother: *The Moon in Gemini in the 12th house is part of the mutable T-square.*

Grandmother: *Neptune conjunct the Descendant ruling the 9th house.*

Edward learns how to solve problems (the T-square) from both his parents (the Sun and the Moon are both involved with the pattern), for they are teaching him how to differentiate between being emotionally overwhelmed by people and situations (Moon in the 12th house, Sun conjunct Mercury in Pisces) and being able to maintain emotional objectivity (Moon opposition Uranus, Mercury square Uranus). Since this is a mutable T-square, a problem is not always going to be readily apparent to Edward until it is right in front of him, when he solves it quickly, rapidly and creatively.

He is seen as someone who needs emotional security (Cancer Ascendant) and he learns how to do this from his mother (the ruler of the Ascendant is the Moon and its aspects). Sensitive to all of her emotions and the tide of feelings around him (Moon in the 12th house), he seeks nurturing and security through information and data, such as books, television and the Internet (Moon in Gemini) and to process his emotions in solitude (Moon in the 12th house). Under stress or when confronted with strong emotions, he comes to rely on his intellect to solve these issues (Moon opposition Uranus). He continually struggles with the need to be both visible (6th house) and invisible (12th house), to enjoy change and daily social interaction (Uranus in the 6th house, Uranus trine Venus-Mars conjunct the MC in the 10th house) and to have enough space and privacy for himself (Moon in the 12th house).

The apex of the T-square (Sun-Mercury conjunction in Pisces) describes how he solves this dilemma. Edward experiences his father-figure either as a yin or gentle man who in a best-case scenario, finds total unity and ecstasy through his faith, his beliefs or his creativity through the arts (the sacred theatre); or, in a worst case scenario, as a dreamer, an alcoholic or an invalid reliant upon drugs and with little regard for his physical body. Hypersensitive to the people around him, empathic without necessarily realising it, from his father-figure Edward learns to value (Sun ruling the 2nd house) this creative side of himself (Sun in Pisces) and to express his feelings (Mercury ruling the 3rd and 12th houses). Slowly and painfully he has to learn self-reliance without the strong role model of his father (Sun trine Pluto, Sun in Pisces); Edward's thinking is visual, creative and often out-of-consciousness (Mercury in Pisces) and there is a sharp and ingenious mind at work (Mercury makes a partile square to Uranus). However, he may struggle with the more linear demands of communication such as spelling and grammar (Mercury in detriment and fall), and under stress he may battle to express his thoughts and ideas. His chart also contains an inherited family issue (unaspected Saturn conjunct the South Node) regarding commitment and accountability by the disciplining force in his life towards children or creativity (in the 5th house). Under stress this may express itself through the structural areas of his body: his bones, knees, shoulders, hair, skin or teeth. Edward also has a strong and vital connection with his grandmother (Neptune conjunct the Descendant and the Pisces Sun).

Background

Julie was married to Daniel, an Anglican priest. Both were born and educated in Australia but moved to England when Daniel was offered work there. Julie describes Daniel as "an absolutely *excellent* father" in the first three years of Edward's life and in the next nineteen months as "an *extremely good* father". In September 1989, when Edward was four-and-a-half years old, developing the shoots of his resourcefulness with semi-logical reasoning powers, yet still only able to deal with one variable at a time, Daniel acknowledged that he was gay and left them both. More than his confession, what shocked Julie was Daniel's lack of contact with Edward. Missing arranged meetings without explanation, Daniel simply disappeared from Edward's life.

Although mobile phones were first invented in 1985, in 1989 they were nowhere near as prolific as today and there was certainly no such thing as text messaging to maintain contact. It was also to be another ten years before *Queer As Folk* [16] appeared on television giving an establishment voice to the gay scene. Indeed at that time all the gay discos in Brighton were in basements, so with transiting Pluto conjuncting Daniel's IC, he literally went underground. It was a vastly different story for Julie who, with transiting Pluto conjuncting her Descendant, just felt devastated. Edward's first experience of loss and grief took them all to the sharp end of difficulty.

Edward's predictive work for 1989 was as follows: *Sun Fidaria (Sun/Moon period). Secondary Progressed Gibbous Lunation Phase. Transiting Jupiter conjunct the Ascendant.*

One would delineate this as a year where Edward was having to make adjustments to his world (Gibbous Lunation Phase) as it expanded (transiting Jupiter across the Ascendant) and where his energy and vitality were being expressed through his emotions (Sun/Moon period of his Sun Fidaria). If Daniel had not left them, this could have been seen as an emotionally satisfying year. However, under the given circumstance, Edward's bodily response took over as a protective mechanism and whenever he became emotionally upset (Moon in the 12th house, Sun in Pisces), he lost his vision. For their own survival Julie moved them both into a shared house with a family who, with love, understanding and homoeopathic medicine, helped nurture them through the next three months. It was, on the one hand, a busy, happy time for Edward, who Julie says loves living with people and the stimulation that this brings (natal Uranus in the 6th house trine Venus-Mars in the 10th house). It was also a time of deep grief.

Edward's predictive work for the next five years when he is learning how to handle the basics of reasoned thought, coherency and sequence, developing peer support and at the same time coping with his father leaving him, shows the following:

1990 - 5 years old:

- **Secondary Progressed Sun moves into the 9th house in January:** a change of philosophy through encountering new communities and ways of doing things.
- **Transiting Saturn square natal Venus-Mars (February-October):** restrictions and hard work, coupled with changes and endings or new commitments in relationships.
- **Sun Fidaria** (Sun/Saturn period begins in November): identity being shaped by restriction.
- **Secondary Progressed Moon moves into Virgo in November:** focusing on detail and perfection.

1991 - 6 years old:

- **Transiting Saturn square natal Pluto (March-December):** attrition, lack of money and feeling miserable.
- **Transiting Saturn conjunct natal Jupiter (March-December):** consolidation.
- **Secondary Progressed Moon moves into the 3rd house in November:** the desire to learn new things.

1992 - 7 years old:

- **Secondary Progressed Full Moon Lunation Phase (begins December 1991):** the culmination of the cycle, the harvest.
- **Transiting Pluto conjunct the South Node (begins December 1991-October 1992):** encountering an intense family issue/health issue from the past.
- **Sun Fidaria (Sun/Jupiter period begins in April):** identity being shaped through education and expansion.
- **Secondary Progressed Moon moves into Libra (in November):** socialising, relating, communicating, trying to keep things calm.

1993- 8 years old:

- **Transiting conjunction of Uranus-Neptune square MC-Venus-Mars (January-November):** sudden and unexpected losses and changes to a parent (MC), a great deal of socialising, anger and passion, romanticism along with feeling confused and drained of energy.
- **Transiting Saturn square natal Saturn (April 1993 - January 1994):** being forced to encounter responsibility.

- **Sun Fidaria (Sun/Mars period begins in September):** identity being shaped through action or anger.

1994 - 9 years old:
- **Secondary Progressed Moon conjunct the IC (begins in February):** issues of home, hearth and family become important, changes of residence or issues to do with mother.
- **Transiting Saturn conjunct the natal Sun (April 1994 - January 1995):** increase in responsibility or feeling pressured.
- **Secondary Progressed Moon moves into Scorpio (in November):** the expression of strong emotional needs.
- **Transiting Pluto conjunct natal Saturn (begins November):** attrition, lack of money, feeling miserable.

This can be laid out on a Time Map as shown on the following page.

No body
If Julie had come to see you at the beginning of 1990, you would have noted the flow of Saturn transits in the two years following Edward's father's disappearance signalling a great deal of change and anxiety as he is building his initiative and resourcefulness. So it would have been appropriate to talk with her about letting him take up some form of sport or physical activity (transiting Saturn square natal Mars in rulership in the 10th house) in his pre-school year, 1990, and as he begins primary school in 1991 (transiting Saturn square natal Pluto) as a safety valve for any frustration or anger. You would also have noted 1992 as a year of intense emotional change connected with family or someone from the past (transiting Pluto conjunct the South Node) and identified this as an echo of the issues of late 1989 (since natal Pluto is natally sited in the 4th house) bringing possible re-contact with his father or an issue to do with his father.

The consequences of this, as he begins to develop reasoned thought, logical abilities and peer connections, ushers in unexpected changes (transiting conjunction of Uranus-Neptune square the MC-Venus-Mars) in his third year of primary school, 1993, along with the first flickerings of him having to shoulder responsibility in some way (transiting Saturn square natal Saturn). This responsibility is emphasised in 1994, his fourth year of primary school (transiting Saturn conjunct the natal Sun) and linked with changes or some form of consolidation connected with home, hearth and family (secondary progressed Moon conjunct the IC).

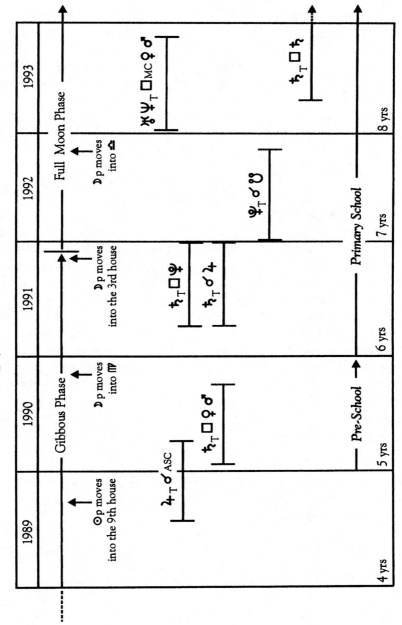

Time Map for Edward 1989-1993

It is likely that Julie will carry a great deal of the demands of these Saturn transits for Edward in this time period. Nevertheless, the fact that there is a predominance of Saturn transits tells you that the pattern of the natal Saturn (unaspected Saturn conjunct the South Node) is about to unfold early in Edward's life. As far as they were both concerned, without any contact whatsoever from Daniel, they had both been plunged into sudden loss. Proteus had come to call with a form of grief that is possibly the most punishing of sorrows, the lament for an intimate still alive but not around physically, for without a body to view to make the event concrete and final, there is always hope that the person will return.

This is what happened
In mid-January 1990 Julie and Edward returned to Sydney, Australia. Edward was due to start school and the Australian school year begins in February. As well, a lawyer had advised Julie that, unless she took action as soon as possible, then under the Hague Convention, there was a chance Daniel could force her to stay in England at his whim once he re-surfaced. It was a turning point for both of them. With no financial or emotional support from Daniel, Julie found work and endeavoured to hold things together. Later she reflected: "I thought that I was doing the right thing bringing him back to a supportive family and in some ways it was the right thing - but it was too much too soon." A change of residence for a child is a loss of basic bricks-and-mortar security. A change of country is a loss of environment, culture and friendships. Connected with the loss of his father, the number of external changes that were occurring in such a short period of time for Edward was disproportionate. The return to Australia proved to be the moment of impact. The key to living in England is to dress in layers (vests, shirts with buttons, coats with buttons, scarf and gloves), all of which required dexterity, a task Edward managed easily. In Australia he was unable to perform even the simple action of pulling on a T-shirt and shorts. Engulfed with unexplained emotional pain at the loss of father, house, home and friends, Edward's way of coping was to throw massive tantrums, the primal cry for help from someone drowning in their own confusion, frustration and sorrow.

In mid-1990 Julie moved into a share house with another mother and a young boy the same age as Edward. It was a happy household and Julie felt that life was secure enough for her to begin studying astrology. In class she met Alexander, another student, and they fell in love. Slowly that year they got to know each other. Julie would visit Alexander after Edward was asleep and on the one or two occasions that she spent the night with him, she made sure she was home by 6.30 am. Mostly Alexander stayed at their house and slowly Edward got to know his new step-father, (one expression of transiting Saturn square natal Venus-Mars). Julie thought she was being a responsible parent and Alexander a thoughtful partner. Edward's perspective, however, was quite different, as she found out some years later.

In 1991 the unexpected happened. Daniel returned to Australia and once more became part of their lives. Edward began seeing his father once a fortnight when, as Julie put it, Daniel would do all the "fun" stuff with him but without any real sense of responsibility. Nevertheless life settled into a pattern and Edward's transits reflected these changed family circumstances. In 1992 Julie and Alexander moved in together (one expression of Edward's transiting Pluto conjunct the South Node) and they have been together ever since.

Then in February 1994, Daniel remembered Edward's ninth birthday. This puzzled Julie, for it was not like Daniel to be so thoughtful. She looked at Edward's chart and saw that he was about to have transiting Saturn conjunct his natal Sun, followed by transiting Pluto conjunct his natal Saturn in 1995. In addition, Edward's Progressed Moon, which had just crossed his IC, moved into the sign of Scorpio in November 1994 and stayed there until December 1996. Shortly afterwards Julie visited Daniel, sharing her curiosity at the birthday card and alerting him to the fact that Edward had some difficult astrological configurations in the next two years which could possibly involve his father. Daniel went white. He suggested she pour herself a glass of wine and sit down. Then he told her that he had AIDS and that he had known this for about a year. Julie felt her stomach fall away. Apart from her own feelings, she was faced with a dilemma: should she tell Edward or not? Tossing the problem around in her mind she finally decided that telling him was the best possible solution given his upcoming Saturn transits.

Normally it is impossible to predict death for a healthy person with certainty from a chart. However, once Julie knew of Daniel's diagnosis and Edward's forthcoming predictive work, she and Alexander could begin to plan how to deal with the situation. In April 1994, on the first touch of Edward's transiting Saturn to his Sun, Julie told him that his Daddy was extremely ill. Edward asked if he was going to die and Julie said, yes, eventually, and it's going to be difficult. Julie, Edward and Alexander discussed the situation extensively. They made a list of the people they wanted to tell, double-checking that Edward felt secure discussing it with them. With natal Neptune conjunct his Descendant, this also included his grandmother. Julie's family and some of her friends were furious with her for telling Edward, saying he was too young to cope with death. Julie thought otherwise.

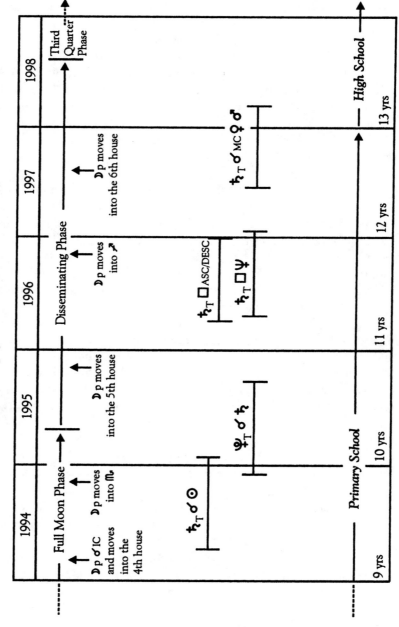

Time Map for Edward 1994-1998

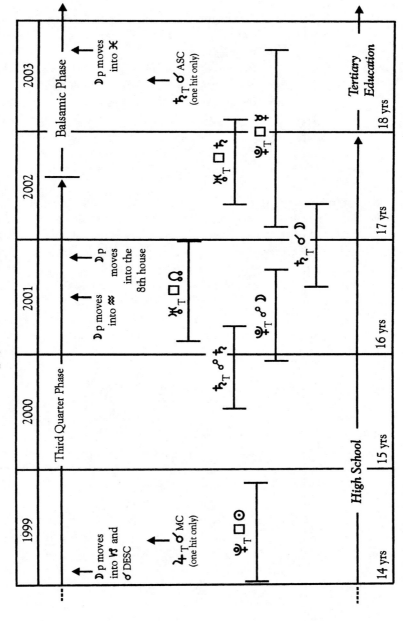

Time Map for Edward 1999-2003

1995 - 10 years old:

- **Venus Fidaria (begins in March):** learning socialising and networking skills which are of a different or alternative nature (Venus in detriment).
- **Secondary Progressed Disseminating Lunation Phase (begins in March):** the beginning of a more internal, reflective and productive period based on the harvest that has just occurred.
- **Transiting Pluto conjunct natal Saturn (December 1994-September 1995):** melancholy, attrition, feeling miserable.
- **Secondary Progressed Moon moves into the 5th house (in December):** personal creativity, new activities or hobbies.

In the intervening months left to them, Edward saw a great deal of his father. It was an extraordinarily close time and they told each other often how much they loved each other. Daniel wore an amethyst pendant and he told Edward that after he died, Edward could keep it as a communication memento between them. In August, 1995, Daniel made the decision to go to Melbourne in order to be near a priest who was like a father to him. He booked himself into a hospice and kept in constant contact with Edward by phone. Five hours before his death he said a final, tearful good-bye to Edward. The date was 6th November, 1995. Edward was nearly eleven years old and he had reached out to Proteus.

Edward asked if he could see his father's body, so Julie booked train tickets for them both and together they travelled from Sydney to Melbourne. Julie had seen a dead body before and described it "like seeing a waxworks body." However, AIDS is an extremely cruel disease. Not only was she shocked at the deterioration in Daniel but she could see that Edward was stunned and overwhelmed. Yet by viewing his father's body, Edward was expressing the physical manifestation of transiting Pluto to his natal Saturn, the black hole of attrition formed from the knowledge that death was a permanent, irreversible, biological process.

The priest who had been with Daniel when he died said to Edward: "I know it's a shock to see your Daddy like this but don't get caught up in the adult world. It's just a body and your daddy is with the angels. Let yourself feel what you're feeling and then talk about it because talking is a way of dealing with it and it will help." So over the next two years (1996 and 1997) Julie, Edward and Alexander agreed that whenever Edward wanted to talk about his feelings, his father, his death and all that had happened, he could and they would listen.

1996 - 11 years old:

- **Venus Fidaria (Venus/Mercury period begins in April):** socialising and networking skills which need expression or communication.
- **Transiting Saturn square Ascendant-Descendant (April-December):** handling responsibility in relationships.
- **Transiting Saturn square natal Neptune (May 1996 - January 1997):** illness, tiredness, depletion of resources, to be without hope.

If Julie had come to see you in early 1996, with Edward in the early embrace of grief, you would have noted the two years of continuing Saturn transits through 1996 and 1997. So it would have been appropriate to talk with her about how 1996 would reveal to Edward the hopelessness of loss, how weak life was and how it eroded all that was important (transiting Saturn square natal Neptune). There were two expressions of this in Edward's life. Firstly, he began having a difficult time at school. Julie went to see the teacher and explained that Edward's father had just died. She was dismayed when the teacher replied: "I don't care whose father's died, I treat all children equally." Julie had no more joy with the headmaster, so they decided to change schools. This proved to be a wise decision but it was a hard and difficult year for Edward. Secondly, to the absolute rage of all concerned, they found that Edward's grandmother had taken the amethyst pendant from Daniel's body. With an aversion to squabbling, Julie remained detached from the process but others fought successfully on Edward's behalf and retrieved the amethyst. A great deal of emotional trauma was expended in the process. This was transiting Saturn square Neptune expressing itself as confusion over the ownership of a stone which Edward considered to have spiritual or metaphysical properties. Edward now has the amethyst next to his bedside and he still wears it.

1997 - 12 years old:

- **Secondary Progressed Moon moves into Sagittarius (since December 1996):** the desire for greater independence and to broaden one's worldview.
- **Venus Fidaria (Venus/Moon period begins in June):** socialising and networking skills which are of an emotional nature.
- **Progressed Moon moves into the 6th house (in July):** the hard work and daily grind of health and routine.
- **Transiting Saturn conjunct MC-Venus-Mars (begins June):**

greater responsibility and learning to stand on one's own feet; making or breaking commitments in relationship; physical restraint, hard work, being exhausted.

If Edward was not in grief, this year's predictive work may have been expressed by Edward taking on some household responsibilities and feeling more grown up as he approached puberty. However, Edward was now in the centre of his grief and one would expect his life to continue to be confused and disorganised. If Julie had come to see you in 1997, it would have been appropriate to suggest that this is a year where Edward feels that authority figures have let him down in some way (transiting Saturn conjunct MC-Venus-Mars). Edward desperately wanted Julie and Alexander to get married but this was not in Alexander's plans, so Edward showed Alexander the brunt of his temper. From mid-1997 to early 1998, Julie describes Edward as "a particularly angry child", yet anger as an expression of untangling grief will often be projected onto a safe member of the household who can carry it for the person until it can be understood. This was Edward being tossed by the changes embodied by Proteus.

1998 - 13 years old:

- **Transiting Saturn conjunct MC-Venus-Mars (completes March).**
- **Venus Fidaria (Venus/Saturn period begins in August):** socialising and networking skills which contain responsibility.
- **Secondary Progressed Third Quarter Lunation Phase (begins August):** a productive phase of reorientation where one reviews one's life situation and takes action accordingly.

In 1998, the third year after his father's death, Edward's desire to constantly talk about his father began to peter out naturally. Edward became a little more "romantic" about Daniel, remembering only the good times and Julie had to work hard at grounding this "romanticism" with the reality she knew to be Edward's father.

In this year Edward started senior school. With the final touch of transiting Saturn conjunct the MC-Venus-Mars, Julie deliberately chose a Catholic humanistic school that contained a stricter, more authoritarian framework than the more relaxed State/public school system of his primary education. She also took into consideration that his father had been a priest and hoped the religious nature of the school would be beneficial to Edward's Sun in Pisces. As transiting Saturn moved to conjunct his Venus, Edward also became aware of girls.

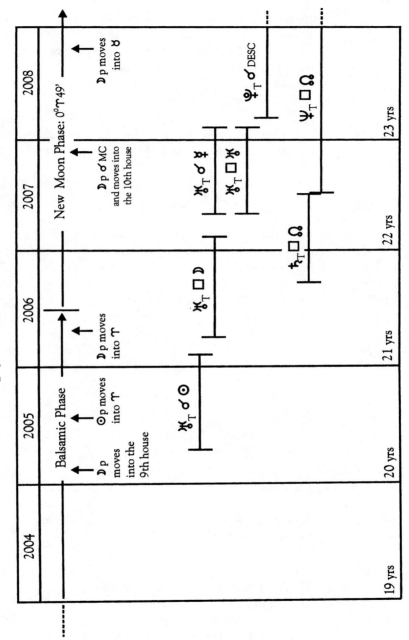

Time Map for Edward 2004-2008

1999 - 14 years old:

- **Transiting Pluto square natal Sun (January- November):** irrevocable change to one's sense of identity.
- **Progressed Moon moves into Capricorn (in February):** the desire to control one's environment.
- **Progressed Moon conjuncts the Descendant (in March):** recognising what it is one requires in a relationship.
- **Transiting Jupiter conjunct the MC (once only in May).**
- **Venus Fidaria (Venus/Jupiter period begins in September):** socialising and networking skills which expand one's world.

In 1999, as he turned fourteen, the fourth year after his father's death, the astrology tells us that Edward was reorganising his identity (transiting Pluto square his natal Sun).

Julie says that everything unresolved re-surfaced with this transit and many hidden emotions were revealed. It was in this year that Edward confessed to Julie that during the first year of her relationship with Alexander, when he had woken in the night and needed her warmth and found instead her empty bed, he had felt abandoned by her. The depth of his feeling surprised her. It was so different to her experience of events that she found it hard to believe and yet she acknowledged that this was how he had experienced it and she felt upset about her past actions: "I was his only continuum in his little life - the only person who had been there from babyhood to age five-six."

Into the future

If Julie had come to you in 2000, it would have been appropriate to alert her of any other big years around which she and Alexander might need to guide Edward. Clearly transits to Edward's Sun are going to be important, for he was in his Sun Fidaria when Daniel first left them. Saturn transits will also be important, for this is when Edward first learnt of his father's terminal illness. Pluto transits will also regurgitate feelings of unrest and upheaval (Pluto is natally in the fourth house, as well as trine his Sun, bringing in unconscious issues of trust and betrayal). One would also be looking for the "gear change" years of the Fidaria and the Secondary Progressed Lunation phase, the Secondary Progressed Sun changing signs or the Secondary Progressed Moon crossing the angles. So one would note the year **2001** (when Edward was sixteen years old) bringing emotional intensity (transiting Pluto opposing his natal Moon) along with loneliness, isolation and feeling unsupported (transiting Saturn conjunct natal Moon) as possibly the year when he falls in love for the first time; **2002** (when he is seventeen years old) when there is an intense focus on thinking, writing and communication (transiting Pluto square natal Mercury) and letting go (the Secondary Progressed Balsamic lunation phase) coinciding with the end of his secondary schooling and continuing into 2003 (when he is eighteen years old) when there will be significant changes to Edward's study routines and ways of communicating (the Mercury Fidaria begins) coinciding with the beginning of his tertiary education; 2005-2006 (when he is twenty and twenty-one years old) when he gains a new found freedom and independence, possibly coinciding with the completion of his tertiary education (transiting Uranus conjunct natal Sun and square natal Moon, combined with the secondary progressed Sun and Moon both moving into Aries and the secondary progressed Lunation phase becoming New); 2007 (when he is twenty-two years old) when sudden changes bring early success, new ideas and a new career direction (transiting Uranus conjunct natal Mercury and square natal Uranus, transiting Saturn and transiting Neptune both squaring the nodal axis and the Secondary Progressed New Moon conjunct the MC); 2008 (when he is twenty-three years old) when there are irrevocable changes to his intimate relationships and he encounters the enchanted world for the first time (transiting Pluto conjunct his Descendant and transiting Neptune square the nodal axis). With Edward now in his Secondary Progressed New Moon period, this is much more likely to be describing love and marriage, than death and grief. In May 2003, Julie wrote to me:

> Now that Edward is eighteen, he is treated pretty much like an adult in this house. I was greatly impressed with his school last year because their graduation ceremony was a real ritual into adulthood. It was such an appropriate time to use as a launch into me playing a different role in his life, that is, him having more freedom and independence. I also used it as an opportunity to hand over the responsibility of maintaining connections with his father's family. I have been doing this on his behalf since his father died. (Of course I will still have some connections). I encouraged him to make contact with his father's family in his own right. So he spent Christmas with them! Extremely different for me and totally healing for him. Although he got into Wine Marketing at a traditional style university, he chose a Technical College course which is in line with his passion - sports! He is doing really well, studying a Certificate in Sports (Coaching and Development). He has been having lots of fun exploring his new-found freedom, although as transiting Saturn emerges from the 12th house and crosses into his first house, I am starting to step in a little again by emphasising the need for him to start earning his own way in this

household. One of his favourite songs is *Cat's in the Cradle!* [17] I must admit that this brings a few tears to my eyes.

Templates of completion

How a child reacts to the loss of their intimate kith and kin is influenced by many factors which include the child's age, the child's relationship to the person who has died, the strength and attachment of that relationship, the circumstances of the death, the child's perception and awareness of life and its process and their understanding of death. It also depends on the willingness of those close to the child to talk freely and truthfully about their own emotions in order to help to create a safe place in which the child can express confusion and pain. Depending on the child's age, their predictive work may well be handled by their parents in some way. A Saturn transit for a four-year old will express itself differently to a Saturn transit for a ten-year old. The worst case scenario will manifest as the child being blocked from expressing their feelings about the loss. The best case scenario will allow the child to take on new responsibilities in the light of the death. In Edward's case, by telling him that his father had AIDS and was going to die, Julie consciously allowed Edward's Saturn transit to mirror a shift of responsibility which in turn enabled Edward and Daniel to determine the shape of their remaining time together. Clearly the way Julie and Alexander guided Edward as he dealt with such intense loss at so young an age gave him a tremendous advantage in handling crises he may yet encounter as an adult.

On top of all this, a direct family member for a child - a grandparent, parent, sibling, spouse, aunt, uncle - will also be a direct family member for the parent, so the parent will not only be supporting the child's emotional landscape but dealing with their own grief as well. Under such circumstance it is all too easy to push the child aside. The more complete path is to allow the child to be part of the circle of loss. It takes courage to stay open to a child's grief.

Endnotes:

1. Piaget, Jean and Inhelder, Barbel. *The Psychology of the Child*, trans. Helen Weaver. (1973) London: Routledge and Kegan Paul.
2. http://www.mothering.com/10-0-0/html/10-9-0/trauma.shtml - accessed 15th September, 2003.

3. http://www.sign2me.com/joseph.htm- accessed 23rd May, 2003.

4. http://www.sign2me.com/science.htm - accessed 23rd May, 2003.

5. Bonertz, Camara. *Developmental Concepts of Death*. Vancouver: Canuck Place Children's Hospice at: http://www.canuckplace.com/PDF/Dev_Concepts.pdf and *Children's Concepts of Death*. Washington: National Education Association at: http://www.nea.org/crisis/b4home16.html- both accessed 14th March 2003.

6. Lewis, Donald W., Middlebrook, Margaret T., Mehallick, Lissa, Rauch, Trudy Manning, Deline, Carole and Thomas, Elise F. (1996) 'Pediatric Headaches: What Do the Children Want?' in *Headache: The Journal of Head and Face Pain* 36 (4), pp. 224-230.

7. Furth, Gregg M. (1989) *The Secret World of Drawings: A Jungian Approach to Healing through Art*. Inner City Books: New York.
See also: http://www.arttherapyincanada.ca/pages/BKSbereavement.html - accessed 9th February 2004 - for further art therapy resources for children in grief.

8. http://www.cnn.com/2002/TECH/science/10/30/coolsc.kid.memory/ - accessed 23rd September, 2003.

9. *Bowling for Columbine*. Written, produced and directed by Michael Moore. © 2002 Iconolatry Productions Inc., an Alliance Atlantis Company and VIF Babelsberger Filmproduktion GmbH & Co. Zweite KG. The documentary utilised the 1999 gun massacre by eighteen-year old Eric Harris and seventeen-year-old Dylan Klebold on their classmates and teachers at Columbine High School in Littleton, Colorado, as a bounce board to examine the legal, cultural, political and media contexts for gun violence in the USA. The massacre resulted in the deaths of twelve classmates and one teacher and Harris and Klebold committed suicide after they killed the students. When Moore posed the question of who was to answer for episodes of school violence, a repetitive subject of blame was shock-rock singer Marilyn Manson. When questioned by Moore, Manson intelligently observed the perpetual "campaign of fear and consumption" by which Americans are convinced to buy products in order to stave off attack.

10. http://www.journeyofhearts.org/jofh/grief/accident2 - accessed 12th February, 2004.

11. Sorkin, Aaron (1995) *The American President*. © Castle Rock Entertainment and Universal City Studios, Inc. at: http://plaza26.mbn.or.jp/%7Ehappywel/script/apresident.htm - screenplay downloaded 9th November, 1999.

12. Axline, Virginia. (1964) *Dibs: In Search of Self*, Harmondsworth: Penguin Books.

13. An extremely useful guide for parents helping their children to deal with grief is: James, J. and Friedman, R. with Dr Leslie Landon Matthews. (2001) *When Children Grieve*, New York: Harper Collins.

14. Apted, Michael (writer/director). (1999) *Me and Isaac Newton*. Producers: Jody Patton and Eileen Gregory. © Clear Blue Sky Productions Inc. Seattle, USA.

15. Traditionally most ancient and medieval authors used orbs in working with house placement (unless they were those who worked with Whole Sign houses). In his 1997 medieval coursework lectures Bob Zoller has quoted Bonatti, saying that, if a planet is 8° behind the angle it can be considered angular, if 5° behind a succedent house it can be considered succedent, and if 3° behind a cadent cusp it can be considered cadent. The reference he gives is Guido Bonatti: *Liber Astronimae* Part II but all this yields is a reference in the Third Part of the Second Tractate Chapter L - "On the Division of the Circle by House" where Bonatti quotes Ptolemy's division of the circle, saying that if a sign is 5° behind any cusp, it can be considered part of the following house. Obviously he is here referring to Whole Sign Houses but it also appears to be the precursor to the above. At Astro Logos we therefore take the following stance: if a planet is close to the cusp of a house, say at 3° Sagittarius in the 2nd house and is in the same sign as the cusp of the 3rd house which is, say, 6° of Sagittarius, then by whole sign houses, the planet will expresses itself through the 3rd house rather than the 2nd house. So we tend to use Whole Sign houses but let Placidus, which is a time-based system, sit on top of that, as we live in a time-based society. In Edward's case, since the Sun is in Pisces and Pisces forms the cusp of the 9th house by both Whole Sign Houses and Placidus and the Sun is less than 5° from the cusp, it will express itself more through the 9th house than the 8th house.

16. Davies, Russel T. (creator/writer/co-producer) (1999) *Queer As Folk*. Producer: Nicola Shindler. © Red Production Company and Channel 4, London, UK. *Queer As Folk* is a drama serial set in Manchester's gay village which chronicles the lives of Stuart, his best friend, Vince, and fifteen-year old Nathan who is in love with Stuart.

17. *Cat's In The Cradle* by Harry Chapin (lyrics by Sandra Chapin) was originally recorded on Chapin's album 'Verities & Balderdash', Elektra records, 1974.

7
New Wine In Old Bottles: The Centaurs and Grief

Cleopatra: The odds is gone
                              And there is nothing left remarkable
                              Beneath the visiting moon.
                              Shakespeare, *Antony and Cleopatra*, (4.16.68-70)

For thousands of years the astrological arbiter of Time was Saturn. Visible and conscious, Saturn represented the Edge, the Keeper at the Gate, the Guardian of the Threshold. In the mythology of Saturn, or Cronos, Cronos eats Time. His children represent his own mortality, so he consumes them in order to control or stop Time. He does this because, according to a prophecy, Cronus was to be dethroned by a son destined to be greater than he. In action and emotion the family history was being repeated. One infant after another disappeared, devoured by "Time", which creates only to destroy. We know from the unfoldment of the myth, and from the universe in which we live, that Time will not be stopped, yet Time brings in its wake the notion of change and change is a function of Time. Hence we can define grief as a Möbius Strip of Time and Change. [1]

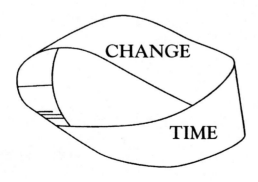

Time has also brought us the discovery of the outer planets and as much as we like to think that our entire chart is ours, the outer planets unquestionably are not. If we lived a simple village life in pre-Renaissance times, our lives would not be affected by the Collective but at this moment in time we live lives that are highly exposed to, and influenced by, the Collective. How many of us own television sets and mobile phones? How many of us are connected to the Internet? Could the war in Iraq in March 2003 with its embedded journalists, video phones and night vision cameras have involved us any more closely or intimately without us actually being there? We take these tools for granted but they have made the world smaller and other people's lives, whether we want them to be or not, almost as intimate as our own. The other side to this is Reality TV which encourages us to be voyeurs rather than witnesses, detached "viewers" rather than people fully participating in and responding authentically to the joys and sadnesses of another's life. So we are, in the same experience, both more connected to the global village and more isolated when it comes to expressing genuine and real emotions to each other.

The outer planets also connect us globally. Invisible to our naked eyes, they represent encounters with that which is beyond our control, only making personal statements in a chart if they are aspecting a luminary or personal planet. Hence the discovery of the Centaurs brings in their wake a particularly interesting phenomenon and, like many new discoveries, the steps forward are small at first and then gain in momentum.[2]

Background

The Centaurs, in the form of Chiron, first appeared on photographic plates in 1895. It was not called this at the time and several important astronomical steps had to be taken before it could be identified as such. In 1950, Jan Oort (1900-1992), a Dutch astronomer who made major contributions to the knowledge of the structure and rotation of our galaxy, put forward a theory, now widely accepted, that our Sun and its solar system are surrounded by a vast and distant cloud of comet material and that segments of this cloud, now referred to as the Oort cloud, are occasionally hurled into the solar system as long-period comets. [3] American astronomer Gerard Kuiper (1905-1973), considered to be the father of modern planetary science, suggested that there may be a belt of comet-like debris at the edge of our solar system, a large population of small bodies orbiting the Sun beyond Neptune. It was not until 1992, twenty years after Kuiper's death, that this theory was proven true when David Jewitt and Jane Luu of the University of Hawaii discovered 1992 QB1.[4] Known as "trans-Neptunians", there are at least 70,000 of them with diameters larger than a hundred kilometres. Astronomers have come to understand that these bodies are on the ecliptic which in turn gave rise to the realisation that they form a ring or belt around the Sun beyond Neptune but stop just past Pluto's orbit. [5] This belt, now known as the Kuiper (pronounced "Coy-per") Belt, is much closer in than the Oort Cloud and the source of short-period comets. The Kuiper Belt is generally thought to be made of extremely primitive remnants from the time when the solar system was being formed. Gathering inside Pluto's orbit, they were then slung out beyond it through an encounter with Neptune. The major planets accreted from more dense material tens of millions of years ago. These less dense Kuiper Belt Objects remained orbiting in freezing conditions beyond the orbit of Neptune. When they were recaptured by Neptune and flung into orbit within our known solar system, they became known as the Centaurs.

The Coming of the Centaurs
On 18th October, 1977 an astronomer named Charles Kowal located an object he called 1977 UB but which later came to be known as Chiron.[6] He presumed it was a maverick asteroid, for it was the same size as an asteroid, though it ranged far beyond the orbits of other asteroids which travel in a belt between Mars and Jupiter. A decade later there was evidence of a coma around Chiron similar to that of a comet, yet Chiron was more than fifty thousand times the volume of a typical comet. So the controversy began - was Chiron a Comet or an Asteroid? It was too large to be a comet and too ice-like for usual asteroids. To add to the mystery of the situation, astronomers noted that its 51-year orbit moved between Saturn and Uranus. Here was the first instance of a link between The Edge as we knew it and the planets of the Collective. Kowal proposed a name which typified this "half/half" nature of comet/asteroid form and its Saturn-Uranus orbit by choosing the mythological figure that was half man-half horse: the Centaur. Thus was it called Chiron. Fifteen years later, on 9th January, 1992, astronomer David L. Rabinowitz discovered another body, with a comet-like orbit of 92.26 years but without a tail, orbiting between Saturn and Neptune. It was officially called 1992 AD and classified as a "minor planet" but it got the nickname "Son of Chiron" and eventually it was officially named Pholus. Finally on 25th April 1993, Rabinowitz discovered a third body named 1993 HA2, later named Nessus, also classified as a minor planet, with an orbit of 123.2 years, orbiting between Saturn and Pluto. These three have now been officially classified as The Centaurs. Within months, other bodies like them were found and, as of August 2002, there are forty-one known Centaurs. [7] However, as with the myriad of asteroids, if we as astrologers are to use them effectively in our work, it is necessary for us to sort out which Centaurs are of major importance, and why.

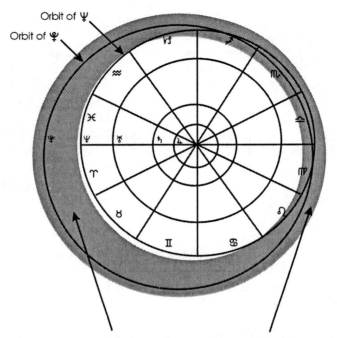

Orbit of ♅

Orbit of ♇

Location of Kuiper Belt of Comets

Source: Drawn by author

LOCATION OF THE KUIPER BELT OF COMETS

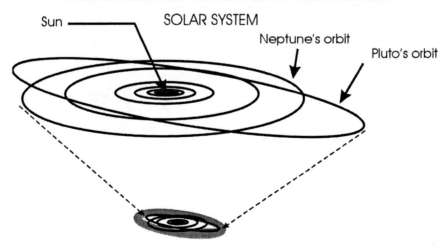

SOLAR SYSTEM

Sun

Neptune's orbit

Pluto's orbit

Source: Drawn by author.
After Alan Stern.

What is a Centaur?

The astronomical definition of a Centaur is any minor body whose heliocentric orbit lies between Jupiter and Neptune and crosses the orbits of Saturn, Uranus or Neptune. Hence they are known as "outer planet crossers". Made of the ancient source material from which the solar system was formed, by the nature of their orbits they bring two opposing forces into conflict with one another:

- **Chiron** with its 51 year orbit links **Saturn with Uranus.**
- **Pholus** with its 92.26 year orbit links **Saturn with Neptune.**
- **Nessus** with its 123.2 year orbit links **Saturn with Pluto.**

Yet something else is happening here. When two opposing forces come into conflict with each other, a unique space called a mandorla - the space between two opposing elements - is created. "Mandorla" is the Italian word for almond. This ancient symbol appears in the images and myths of cultures around the world, from the Igbo people of West Africa to the old Celtic tribes of Europe. These earliest shapes symbolically represented the mysterious Feminine aspect of life as a sacred womb, a portal between the realm of spirit and the realm of matter, through which all life passes into this world. Also known as the "Vesica Piscis", symbolizing the interactions and interdependence of opposing worlds and forces, the Mandorla demonstrates that opposites overlap and are finally the same.[8] The space within the overlap is the place in which we are asked to stay whilst change occurs. This is a threshold or liminal space, a space that occupies both sides of a boundary, the place at which you arrive after you leave one room and have not yet entered another. Living on such thresholds requires faith, for all change takes place in liminal space.

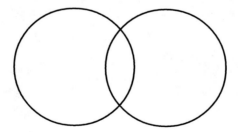

Robert Johnson speaks of this in *Owning Your Own Shadow*:

> Whenever you have a clash of opposites in your being and neither will give way to the other… you can be certain that God is present. We dislike this experience intensely and avoid it at any cost. But if we can endure it, the conflict-without-resolution is a direct experience of God…. the space between these two opposing elements is a place of healing.[9]

The idea, says Johnson, is that gradually the two spaces overlap to become one so that there is no longer the separation between me and my shadow self or that which is projected outwards and unowned.

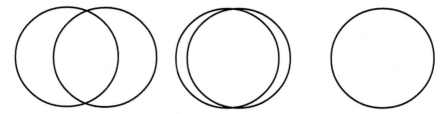

The cover of the Chalice Well at Glastonbury in southwest England depicts a mandorla.

The Centaurs are themselves a mandorla, a meeting of human and horse: the animal, chthonic, wild and instinctive aspect of humanity and the conscious, civilised facet. As such they represent the more unrefined and feral desires, appetites and purposes struggling to express themselves through the human dimension.

Chalice Well, Glastonbury.
Photo taken by author.

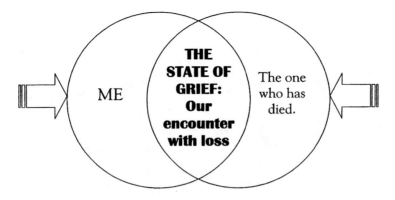

Grief as a Mandorla

Grief also expresses itself as a mandorla. If one of the circles is us and the other our encounter with the death of a beloved, then the mandorla is the space of grief. With consciousness, gradually the two spaces overlap to become one, so that finally the separation no longer exists between me and "the other", the one who is dead. Instead there is the realisation of a newer level of awareness where the memory of "the other" is contained within us in a different way.

In considering their relevance to grief, Chiron, Pholus and Nessus form a particular group in linking Saturn with each one of the outer planets:

1. They bring unconscious issues (Uranus, Neptune and Pluto) into concrete manifestation in our lives (Saturn).

2. By the nature of their orbits they bring two opposing forces into conflict with one another and form a mandorla.

3. In linking Saturn with the outer planets, they make a statement about Time, for the orbits of the Centaurs are erratic, moving quickly through some signs and slower through others, reflecting how people in grief experience time. Grief is also erratic. The common responses felt in grief do not respond to linear time but wash across the fragmented life, unpredictably overwhelming. Slowly, as we piece our lives together, the two circles become one. Wholeness has occurred.

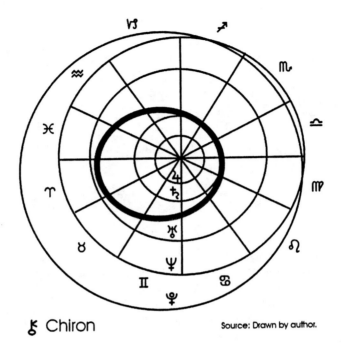

ϟ Chiron

Source: Drawn by author.

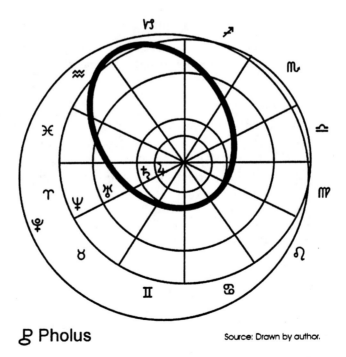

⚷ Pholus

Source: Drawn by author.

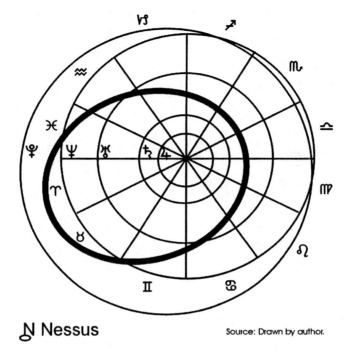

♇ Nessus   Source: Drawn by author.

When the three centaurs, Chiron, Pholus and Nessus, are strongly placed in a person's chart - conjunct an angle, conjunct or square the nodal axis, conjunct or square the luminaries, or part of a stellium or a grand aspect pattern - such people are what I call "Centaur people," and they will carry their centaur myths into their lives through the process of grief.

A brief deconstruction of the Centaurs in history

The Centaurs, or Kentauroi, were depicted as men from the head down to their human loins but with the four feet and the body of a horse. Sometimes they contained the facial features of normal men. At other times they had the snub noses and pointed ears of Satyroi. How they came to be part of the mythos is unclear. What is clear is that the cauldron of time had to simmer with the domestication of the horse, the invention of the bow and arrow and the leap from horse drawn chariots to cavalry before the myth could take root.

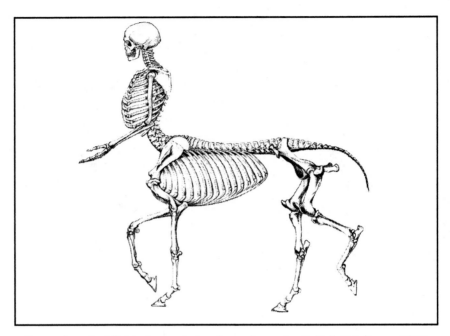

Reproduced with kind permission from the artist © C.A.Stigliano, 1982

Horse, chariot, archer

The first undisputed evidence for the domestication of the horse dates to circa 2,000 BCE, when horses were found buried with chariots at Sintashta, on the south Ural steppe. [10] A short time after this, the domestic horse erupted across Europe. By the middle of the second millennium BCE, horses were being used to pull chariots in places as far apart as Greece, Egypt, Mesopotamia, Anatolia, the Eurasian steppe and in China by the 14th century BCE. Chariots were the new technology of the day. They were fast, mobile platforms for composite bow archers and were prominent in the accounts and pictorial representations of battles from 1700 BCE to 1200 BCE.

In all the settled kingdoms and palaces of the late Bronze Age, from Egypt to Babylon to Assyria to Anatolia (the Hittites) to Knossos (Crete) and Mycenean Greece, chariots dominated battles. Chariots were designed to contain two men, driver and archer. The constellation Auriga, The Charioteer, the harnesser of the horse, located close to the North Pole, indicates how pivotally important was this fighting machine to these cultures at this time. [11] The archer was the killing machine on the moving chariot. The archer in ancient times was a feared and powerful warrior. Essential to his work were his sharp, piercing eyesight and steady stance. Indeed keen eyesight was the archer's most valued possession. Facies, the nebula in the face of the constellation Sagittarius, The Archer, represents the piercing stare of a lethal weapon which penetrates without regard. [12]

"The Catastrophe"

It is in the period 1225-1175 BCE that chariots finally lost their battlefield dominance In a period of roughly fifty years, they toppled into obscurity, coinciding with the collapse of most of the great kingdoms and palaces of the Eastern Mediterranean and Near East. City after city, including Troy of *The Iliad*, were combusted, destroyed beyond repair and the cuneiform clay tablets they left behind became silent. Three major ingredients are necessary to warfare: force or firepower, security and mobility. Changes in any one of them, such as an improved bow, better armour, the invention of chariots or changes to how horses are used will, in the short-term, throw the status quo out of kilter. Around 1200 BCE the barbarians on the fringes of the civilized world made too many changes too rapidly to these fundamental units of warfare. Before new tactics could be learnt and equilibrium re-established, most of the civilized world was lost. This widespread destruction of cities, termed by historians "The Catastrophe", swept across the entire region, affecting Mycenaean Greece, Crete, Anatolia and the Hittite empire, Cyprus, Syria, the Southern Levant and, to a lesser extent, Egypt and it signifies the beginning of the transition from Bronze Age to Early Iron Age societies in the eastern Mediterranean.[13]   The regimes in the region were, until this time, secure, palace-centred, prosperous and relatively peaceful. Only Egypt and Assyria escaped immediate destruction and the region entered a five-hundred year Dark Age.

The emergence of horseback archers

The defining element in steppe warfare was now the massed attack by mounted archers. By the middle of the ninth century cavalries were well established and mounted archers using saddle, stirrups and better bridles emerged between 900-700 BCE. Ninth-century BCE Assyrian bas-reliefs [14] show that the Assyrians were the first military power to deploy both mounted archers and war chariots in battle. The Assyrian army was the largest standing army ever seen in the Middle East or Mediterranean, for the demands of war stimulated technological innovations which made the Assyrians almost unbeatable: iron swords, lances, metal armour and battering rams. The success of war was a prerequisite to the social and political changes that followed, for with the Iron Age came the development of alphabetic writing, the growth of nationalism, republican forms of government, monotheism and, eventually, rationalism.

Scholars explain the long interval between chariot and archer as the result of needing to breed larger and stronger horses to carry an armoured man. This may be so. Certainly placing the archer on the back of a horse was an idea of powerful luminosity. Freed of the bulky chariot, the combination of man, horse, bow and arrow fused into armies of horsemen, welded as a weapon of war, trained to attack and retreat as one, firing clouds of arrows in unison, must have been an awesome and fearful sight. The word "cavalry" comes from the Italian cavallo "horse" and the Latin caballus and from this period on until late into the nineteenth century, cavalry has remained one of the essential parts of "civilized" warfare.

And what of the Greeks at this time?

The Greeks travelled by walking or riding in chariots; if they were wealthy, they were carried in a sedan chair. The roads between the cities were not in good condition and could be difficult in bad weather, although messengers commonly moved between the cities by running. Goods were carried on two-wheeled carts hauled by oxen, horses, mules, donkeys or dogs and people who needed to travel long distances lived near a port and travelled by ship. Most trips were made within sight of land and in the Aegean Sea. Venturing into the Mediterranean was rare. [15]

No saddles are found among the ancient Greek works of art, apart from a mosaic of Alexander the Great (336 - 323 BCE). By the time of *The Iliad*, the story of the conflict between the early Greeks and the people of Troy in western Anatolia, dated by historians to Late Bronze Age (circa 1190 BCE), heroes rode to the battlefield in horse-drawn chariots, drove them up and down the field in display, dismounted them to fight or charged into the thick of the battle, fighting from their chariots. [16]

These epic poems of the late Bronze Age washed down through the Dark Ages, rich in the language and customs of the oral community, to meet the new technology of seventh and sixth centuries BCE: the phonetic alphabet of the Phoenician traders which permitted the Greeks to write down these stories of heroes for a warrior society no longer fighting on the battlefields of Troy but basing themselves in cities. It is easy to see how the Greeks, who knew only of chariots, hearing of a barbarian, ferocious and militaristic society that used new techniques of warfare, could only make sense of these men seated on a horse with easy mobility and the accuracy of the archer by calling them "uncivilised Centaurs". They were incorporated into Greek mythology as lustful, feral and barbaric and the many fights between humans and centaurs, known as the centauromachy, became a popular feature of Greek art, as witnessed from pottery shards dated 700 - 300 BCE [17] and by the marble friezes on the south side of The Parthenon,[18] built between 447 - 432BCE which depicts in frozen action, the roar of battle, the sweat of bodies and the drumming of hooves as Greeks and Centaurs do battle.[19]

The Greek sky

As these are Greek myths, it is appropriate to ask about the sky, the canvas on which the constellations were painted, at the time these myths were being written down. That The Centaur and Sagittarius, The Archer, were of profound importance in the minds of early Iron Age Greek civilisation is reflected in the fact that they both rose together and stood with each other fully visible

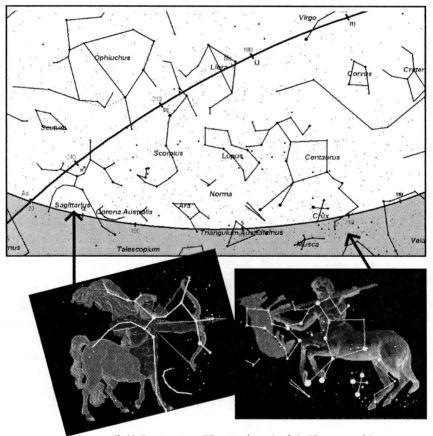

(*left*) Sagittarius, The Archer, (*right*) Chiron and Lupus
900 BCE, Athens, Greece. Source: Starlight Astrological Software [20]

on the horizon as night constellations during the summer and early dawn constellations in the winter in Athens, Greece, in 900 BCE. Today in Athens, when Sagittarius stands on the horizon, only the top half of the Centaur and Lupus the Wolf are visible:

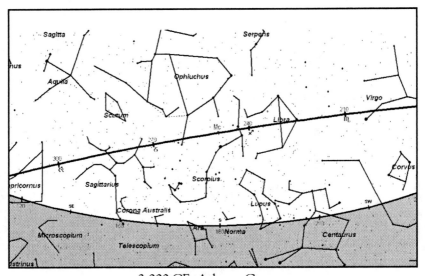

2,000 CE, Athens, Greece.
Source: Starlight Astrological Software

The Centaurs in Greek Mythology

There are two variations on the origins of the centaurs. One version concerns a man named Ixion, king of the Lapithae in Thessaly, on the eastern mainland of Greece, who murders his father-in-law and wanders the earth in search of purification. Zeus agrees to perform the ceremony and invites him up to Olympus but Ixion falls in lust with Hera and tries to seduce her. Outraged, Zeus fashions a cloud in her shape and leaves it in her bed and that night when Ixion makes love to the cloud, Zeus catches him and binds him to a fiery wheel, set revolving eternally in the heavens. However, the joke is on Zeus, for the cloud conceives and gives birth to Centaurus and it is from him that all the Centaurs are born. The other version is that the cloud gives birth to all the Centaurs directly, apart from Chiron. Diodorus Siculus, writing in the 1st century BCE, tells us that the cloud-born centaurs "were gods on their mother's side, who possessed the swiftness of horses, who had the strength of two bodies, and enjoyed in addition the experience and wisdom of men." [21] However, they are primitive, as if struggling to overcome the animalistic parts of themselves as the next episode of the myth tells, for it came to pass that King Pirithoüs of the Lapithae, the son of Ixion, inherits part of Thessaly from his father which provokes the Centaurs, as sons/grandsons of Ixion, to claim they are entitled to part of the land. Fighting breaks out and when they have made up their differences, they are invited to a wedding. Unfortunately when the centaur Eurytus catches sight of the bride, "drunkenness twinned with lust" rules his heart and he grabs the bride by the hair and drags her off by force. Theseus springs to her defence, heaves an ancient mixing-bowl at Eurytus' face and kills him. With a single voice the Centaurs shout: "To arms! To arms!" The marriage cave is a scene of carnage. At the end of a gruelling fight, the Centaurs are defeated and driven from the area and eventually they settle at the base of Mount Pholoë in Arcadia.

Chiron

Chiron was different to the other Centaurs, being born in truly ancient times. Some say he was conceived earlier than the other Centaurs at the time when Zeus was hiding in Crete from his father, Cronos, who sought to devour him. In searching for Zeus, Cronos laid eyes on the nymph, Philyra, daughter of Oceanus and Tethys, and his passion was aroused. In her attempts to escape, Philyra turned herself into a mare but Cronos assumed the form of a steed and mounted her and she conceived. However, when she saw Chiron, the strange alloy of human and creature to whom she had given birth, she felt disgusted and begged Cronos "to change her into another form, and she was transformed into the tree which is called the linden." [22] So Chiron was Chronos-sired, not Ixion-sired. His ancestry was that of a god and a nymph, in contrast to the other Centaurs, born of a human and an illusion. Chiron was given to Apollo, who became his foster father and who taught him archery, hunting, divination and, among other things, healing. In turn Chiron founded a school at Mount Pelion in Thessaly and became mentor to such Greek heroes as Jason, Achilles, Hercules and Asklepios. When the Lapiths drove him from Mount Pelion, he settled on Malea with his wife, Khariklo. Chiron was said to have surpassed men in justice, conscientiousness and diligence and so powerful was his healing influence, that the core of his name has found its way into common language with such words as chiropractor, chiropodist and the French word for surgeon, "chirurgien".

How does such a wise and gentle Centaur as Chiron come to exist amongst the ferocious, tough, barbaric Centaurs? Any battlefield has its healers. In modern warfare they are the MASH units, performing meatball surgery under demanding conditions but the rise of the imperium meant ancient fighting forces had men in the field for months, sometimes years, at a time. In the Assyrian culture the dramatic growth in science and mathematics, as well as a sophisticated medical discipline, developed somewhat paradoxically alongside war and the Assyrians greatly influenced medicine as far away as Greece. We can draw the conclusion that healers at the field of battle would have been part and parcel of the Assyrian war machine, riding into the combat zone on horseback, looking for the wounded and carrying them safely away to be given medical care and attention.

A modern-day counterpart suggests how this might have happened. Private J.S. Kirkpatrick was born on 6 July 1892, at Tyneside, Durham, in the North East of England. He moved to Australia and enlisted in the Australian Imperial Force in August 1914. He was accepted into the Australian Army Medical Corps as Private John Simpson, allocated as a stretcher-bearer with "C" section of the 3rd Field Ambulance, with the 1st Division of the AIF and served at Gallipoli the following year. When Simpson arrived at Gallipoli, he found that the stretchers used to carry wounded soldiers from the firing lines to the dressing station at ANZAC Cove were not being returned. Trained to work as part of a team of six, the unit now found themselves working in pairs or singly. On Day Two, having carried several wounded on his own back, Simpson noticed an abandoned donkey nearby. He created a makeshift halter from bandages, put the wounded man on the donkey's back and worked eighteen-hour days as a one-man band over the next four days, taking water from the beach to the men in the trenches and returning with the wounded. Anxious about lack of proper food for the donkey, Simpson teamed up with the 21st Kohat Indian Mountain Artillery Battery. They called him "Bahadur", the "Bravest of the Brave". With the Indian Battery he was able to rest his donkey and use other donkeys, brought by the unit to move the cannons, in rotation. The Indians made him a saddle and bridle and he worked twenty-hour days. He gained a reputation for being undaunted by enemy fire and carried more than three hundred wounded men from no man's land back to the ship's hospital between 25 April, when he landed, and his death in action on 19 May, 1915. Simpson was shot by a Turkish sniper but his donkey continued on to the beach with a critically wounded soldier on his back, before leading other concerned stretcher-bearers back to where Simpson's body lay. Simpson achieved legendary status and has been depicted on Australian stamps, coins and banknotes.[23] Known as "The Man With the Donkey", here is the modern-day healer, the noble soul amongst the ruffians, compassionate and courageous, joining forces with a member of the equine genus. Perhaps in the ancient world, amongst the ferocious, tough and warlike Assyrians, there was such a healer on the Assyrian battlefields, foraging amongst the blood and gore for life still tenuously holding on, carrying these wounded carefully on the back of a horse to safety and healing hands - and the myth of Chiron was born.

The myths of Chiron and Pholus begin together but diverge at their ending. Chiron and Pholus are said to be the only two learned and level-headed Centaurs. Unlike the rest of the tribe, wise-hearted Chiron was usually depicted with the forelegs of a man instead of those of a horse and clothed in a chiton. Hyginus tells us that Pholus "was more skilled in augury than the rest". Both are friends of Hercules. Indeed Hercules is central to the myths of the Centaurs.

Hercules

One could argue that stories of wild, feral warriors, part-man-part-horse, became part of the mythos at a time when The Centaur and Sagittarius, The Archer, rose on their hind legs in the sky and stood on the earth together in the summer evenings. One can see how this gave rise to the necessity for a Greek hero, half human-half god who, with his own bow and arrow, overcame and suppressed this undomesticated madness, cementing once and for all the supremacy of the Greek culture. A man for his time, Hercules plays a central role in the myths of the Centaurs.

Hercules was the son of immortal Zeus and a mortal woman called Alamena, although his Greek name, "Herakles", means glorious gift of Hera. One version of the story has it that Hera suckled this abandoned baby whom Zeus had fathered and from Hera's milk Hercules gained his final piece of immortality. When he sucked too hard, Hera threw him from her breast and the milk that sprayed from her breast created The Milky Way. [24] Unable to punish Zeus for his infidelity, Hera's wrath fell on Hercules. She attempted to kill him by placing snakes in his crib but he simply strangled them with his chubby hands. At one stage she sent him mad and caused him to murder his wife, Megara, and his children. He was too strong for anyone to enforce punishment upon him but he willingly undertook the Twelve Labours, so he might purify himself for the spilling of his family's blood, indicating a fundamental sense of justice. [25] That he persevered through the terrible things that Hera visited upon him as a result of her hatred born of Zeus' infidelity to her demonstrates a moral fortitude beyond mere strength. Best known as the strongest of all mortals, he was the deciding factor in the battle where the Olympian gods defeated the Giants. He was the only man in Greek mythology born of mortal woman to become a god upon his death. However, Hercules' behaviour shows he was reckless, easily offended and held onto grudges. His strength was outweighed by his ignorance and lack of wisdom, epitomized by his chosen weapon: a massive club. Once, feeling too hot, he pulled out a bow and arrow and threatened to shoot the Sun. His appetites for food, wine and women were as massive as his strength. This combination of strength and stupidity frequently got him into trouble and many of his great deeds occurred whilst he was doing penance for brainless acts born of anger or carelessness. He had a more positive side to him in that he would do anything to help a friend and once his anger had passed, he was a severe critic of his own actions. Time changed the view of Hercules, from a bad manager of his obvious gifts and the Greek playwrights' portrayal of him as a muscle-bound buffoon, to one which focused on his virtues. It was the Romans who valued him as their "best fit" for a hero and in the fullness of time he had a cult following that honoured him as a god.

The story
On his way to the Erymanthian Mountains, where he has been sent to catch the notorious wild boar, Hercules guests with Pholus, chief of the Centaurs, on Mount Pholoë and Pholus cooks him a meal befitting a friend. The story diverges slightly here depending on which writer of antiquity we follow. Apollodorus,[26] writing in the second century BCE, tells us that Hercules asks for wine but Pholus demurs, for he is the guardian of the large pithos, or cask, of sacred wine which had been given to him by Dionysius, god of wine and ecstasy and a friend of his father, Seilenos, and this pithos belongs to all the Centaurs. When Hercules insists that he open it, Pholus does so against his better judgement. Diodorus Siculus tells us that this jar of sacred wine had been given to a Centaur by Dionysius four generations previously with orders only to open it when Hercules is present.

However the story transpires, the smell of the intoxicating drink, now sweet with age and strength, immediately attracts the Centaurs living nearby and drives them mad with desire. They storm towards Pholus' cave, brandishing rocks and uprooted trees, and set about plundering the wine in a way both awe-inspiring and terrifying. Pholos hides in fear but to his great surprise, Hercules faces the Centaurs, returns a volley of fire-brands, then pulls out his bow and lets loose with his arrows, killing some Centaurs and driving the rest off the mountain. Still others he pursues and these take refuge with Chiron. In a white-hot lather, irrational and overcharged, blindly Hercules shoots. An arrow sings through the air, penetrates the arm of the Centaur Elatos and embeds itself in Chiron's thigh. Hercules freezes, for these are no ordinary arrows. They have been dipped in the deadly gall of the Lernaean Hydra and they are fatal. Realising too late what he has done, in horror and remorse Hercules rushes to Chiron and pulls out the arrow. Chiron "blends picked herbs from the Pagasean hills, and soothes the wound with different treatments",[27] yet despite all efforts, the poison of the Hydra leaves a festering wound beyond cure. In agony, Chiron retreats to his cave and yearns for death but Chiron is immortal and cannot die. All he can do is to live with the torment and trauma of the wound, suffering in agony and often in silence, unable to gain help from anyone. After years of affliction, a chink of light penetrates the grey haze in the shape of a renegade with the temerity to light his torch at the eternal lamp of the sun and give lumps of clay fashioned into creatures resembling the gods the divine spark of knowledge, art, commerce and civilisation. This is Prometheus, a Titan and an immortal, now pinioned to a craggy peak of Mount Caucasus in adamantine chains for siding with these creatures against Zeus. His punishment binds him to an eagle (some say a vulture) whose "long quill-feathers of each wing rose and fell like a bank of polished oars" [28] and who gnaws out his liver by day only to have it grow back by night, a fate designed to repeat ad infinitum for thirty years (some say a thousand or even thirty thousand years). Prometheus' anguish and lamentations ripple through the pantheon of Olympus. The gods plead with Zeus for mercy but his amnesty to Prometheus is conditional upon one of two things: firstly, since Prometheus has the power of foresight, that he reveal the name of the mother who is to bear the son who will eventually overthrow Zeus and to such a condition Prometheus never yields; secondly, that Prometheus finds a mortal willing to kill the eagle and unchain him and an immortal god willing to change places with him and die for him. Hercules kills the eagle with an arrow and Chiron agrees to die for him. So it is that Prometheus is unbound and lives and Chiron is released and dies.

The symbolism
In the myths, Hercules represents the changing focus from the matriarchy to the patriarchy. The sky is full of stories depicting this. For example, the story of Hercules and his destruction of the Nemean Lion is the story of the crushing of the worship of the goddess or non-Zeus-centred religions, for the Nemean Lion is no domesticated zoo animal but a grandchild of Gaia, Mother Earth, and the child of a destroying Moon goddess, a giant, magical lion whose coat remained impenetrable to the masculine weapons of sword and spear. Hercules' final option was to wrap his arms around its back and squeeze it to death.[29] The Centaurs, with their wild nature and associated with the earth, represent a similar illogical fear, for they epitomize processes which are taboo, hidden or unrecognised by the patriarchy and which must be killed or suppressed by it. So Hercules, the three Centaurs and his poisoned arrows form a tripartite coalition fated to meet through time.

So what does this mean for someone encountering grief if they have Chiron strongly placed in his or her chart? Chiron finds it hard to die. He is faced with incurable suffering and rather than blame the Centaurs or Hercules, his solution is to withdraw to his cave and let it fester for years. Chiron is active in grief when we are looking into a vale of sorrow and pain that is destined to be with us for a long time. This may be grief which takes a long time to reconcile or it may be an old grief bound up with a family pattern trying to resolve itself. The solution for Chiron comes after many years of suffering when he uses his intellect to deal with the situation. Thus the myth offers a two-pronged solution: the problem requires the clear light of the intellect and wisdom to solve the pain - the recognition that immortality which contains severe pain without end is a life not worth living; and the problem can only move forward to completion after many years with the help of another (Prometheus) - the recognition that we cannot live isolated lives and our pain may be the solution to someone else's healing. For his selflessness, and self-sacrifice, Zeus puts Chiron into the starry sky as the constellation Centaurus, The Centaur.

Case Study

Michael J. Fox

Data source: A. The birth data comes from the Clifford2000 data set - birth time given from Fox to J. Berlow. The information on his life comes from his autobiography, *Lucky Man*, published by Ebury Press, UK, 2002.

Michael J. Fox is best known for his comic role as Alex. P. Keaton in *Family Ties* which began in September 1982. He launched into feature films with the smash hit of 1985, *Back to the Future*, released in July of that year. Two sequels followed but it seemed his career had peaked by 1987.

Natal Placement
Michael J. Fox has Chiron conjunct his South Node in Pisces. When still young he rushes towards intimate relationships and business partnerships (North Node in the 7th house) and achieves early success: intense, profound and passionate and involving great sums of money (North Node conjunct Pluto) underpinned by travel and the world of film-making, a modern form of publishing (Pluto rules the 9th house). The North Node initially offers triumph and victory but it sits on hollow ground. Issues of boundaries (North Node in Virgo) around partnerships (North Node in the 7th house) and money (Pluto

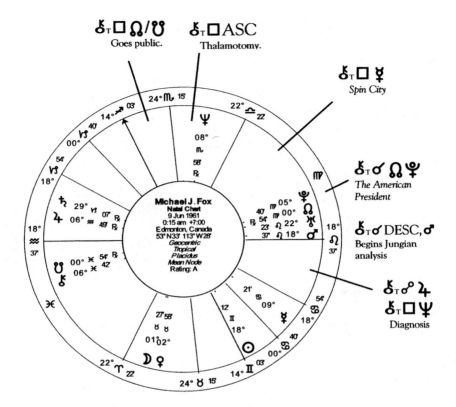

⚷ₜ□☊/☋
Goes public.

⚷ₜ□ASC
Thalamotomy.

⚷ₜ□☿
Spin City

⚷ₜ☌☊♅
The American
President

⚷ₜ☌DESC,♂
Begins Jungian
analysis

⚷ₜ☌♃
⚷ₜ□♆
Diagnosis

Michael J. Fox
Natal Chart
9 Jun 1961
0:15 am +7:00
Edmonton, Canada
53°N33' 113°W28'
Geocentric
Tropical
Placidus
Mean Node
Rating: A

conjunct the North Node) lack life experience and he is forced to return to his South Node to learn the truth of illusion and fantasy (the film industry) through ignored talents. These express themselves either as loss, confusion or illness (South Node in Pisces) or through metaphysics, spirituality, art and music. This pathway also contains a wound (South Node conjunct Chiron) which sits there waiting, like a time bomb, offering him an issue from his past or ai issue regarding his health, which takes a Chironic expression. Remember, Chiron finds it hard to die; he is immersed in incurable suffering which becomes immobilised in some way when he hides in his cave and he is trying to deal with this in an ethical, noble way, from the intellect.

Chiron in Action
In November 1990 Michael wakes to find the little finger of his left hand trembling. Tests show nothing wrong with him and because he is not yet thirty and it's his Saturn Return (one hit only in late January 1991) and natal Saturn in his chart is in rulership, he ignores it.

Twelve months later, however, in **October 1991**, as **transiting Chiron opposes his natal Jupiter** (also in the 12th house and in Saturn's sign) and **squares natal Neptune**, he is diagnosed with Young Onset Parkinson's Disease.[31] Parkinson's Disease is a chronic, progressively degenerative brain disease whose symptoms include muscular rigidity, slowness and poverty of movements and tremors. Michael was placed on medication: "The bad news was obvious: here was yet another confirmation I had Parkinson's disease. The good news was, now I could hide it." [31] He was promised "another ten good years of work ahead of you" and he hid it with medication and alcohol (natal Chiron in Pisces/transiting Chiron square natal Neptune).

By October 1992, as transiting Chiron conjuncts his Descendant and Mars for the first time, he admits to his wife, Tracey Pollan, that he has a drinking problem (Pisces South Node) which he has used to cover feelings of inadequacy his whole life. As Chiron rises above the horizon, so it allows the issue to be made visible. Fox gives up drinking and this is the beginning of his slow journey towards clarity.

In **September 1993, transiting Chiron conjuncts Michael's North Node once and then moves on to his natal Pluto in October 1993.** In December 1993, embroiled in a mundane court case over property sale, the effort of hiding the fact that he had Parkinson's disease and the growing estrangement from his wife and three-year old son, he feels he has reached rock bottom. The day after Christmas 1993 he begins his first session with a Jungian analyst to work on his denial.

In **1994**, as Chiron retrogrades back across his natal Pluto, his life starts to turn around. It has been the rush towards his North Node-Pluto which propelled him towards early business success. Now, with better understanding of and insight into his actions, he decides to work only in New York where he lives and where he can spend valuable time with his family and, rather than working on films that simply generate money, only to work on films he loves and of which he can be proud. To this end he accepts the part of Lewis Rothschild, the American President's Chief Domestic Policy Advisor, in the feature film *The American President* and produces one of his finest roles in film to date.

In **November 1995 transiting Chiron squares his natal Mercury, the dispositor of his North Node, for the first time.** Gary Goldberg and Bill Lawrence pitch Fox an idea for a new television series with a part for him that is similar to "Lewis" only a little shadier and more openly comic. The transit completes in July 1996 and in September Fox returns to series television as actor in and executive producer of *Spin City*. [32] He wins critical praise, a Golden Globe Award, an Emmy nomination and a People's Choice Award for his portrayal of Michael Flaherty, the Deputy Mayor of New York City, "a man who knows how to expertly spin the most difficult situations at City Hall, but usually spins out of control when it comes to his personal life" [33] - an ironic reflection of Michael's own past.

In **1998, as transiting Chiron squares his Ascendant-Descendant axis and natal Mars,** Fox decides to undergo a thalamotomy, a cauterising of a number of brain cells to ease the symptoms of PD. The surgery is successful. Buoyed by this success and in a much stronger position emotionally, in late November, 1998, he decides to go public with his disease **(transiting Chiron squares his nodal axis for the first time in mid-January 1999).** Initially holding off doing so through fear of rejection from the public and his fans, instead he finds only respect and acceptance. He also encounters a new role to play in his life, using his fame as a driving force for the dissemination of information about Parkinson's Disease and setting up a foundation for research. Finally, after many years of hiding in his cave, Fox builds up the courage to admit to his vulnerability; in so doing he finds Prometheus, assistance which comes from an external source. Through allowing the irrevocable change of Parkinson's Disease to deepen his intimate relationships and business partnerships **(natal Pluto conjunct natal North Node),** now he truly is able to heal others through his visibility in the public arena.

Conclusion

I give you this example to show you how having a strongly-place Chiron in a chart means the person often takes a long time to own and deal with the grief-causing situation. In Michael J. Fox's case his loss was a loss of health, life expectancy and life experience. However, when Chiron is involved in loss and grief from death, the process takes on a similar quality: an extended period of pain and anguish which turns into insight of great value. Such people are those who lose children to abduction and murder and make their grief a cause through disseminating information about child safety, or people who lose spouses to major illness without cure, such as cancer, leukaemia, or AIDS and turn that tragedy into a motif for their life's work.

An example...

Marjorie Jackson was born at Coffs Harbour, NSW, Australia, (30S18, 153E08) on 13th September, 1931, and moved to Lithgow with her family when she was still a child. Her birth time is unknown but her chart has two interlocking T-squares, one between Mars in detriment in Libra opposite Uranus with Pluto at the apex, expressed as a talent for athletics; the other a T-square of Saturn in rulership in Capricorn opposition Pluto with Uranus at the apex, expressed as the slow, grinding, hard work of training. Chiron is natally at 23° Taurus, trining a Sun-Venus-Moon conjunction in Virgo and Saturn in Capricorn.

Between 1950 and 1954 Marjorie Jackson won every State and Australian athletics title for the 100 yards, 100 metres, 220 yards and 200 metres. At the 1950 Commonwealth Games in Auckland, New Zealand, she won four gold medals. In the 1952 Olympic Games in Helsinki, Finland, she won two gold medals and became the first Australian woman to win an Olympic gold medal for track and field and the first Australian (male or female) to win an Olympic gold medal on the running track since 1896. Her win in the 100 metres equalled the world record and in the 200 metres she set a new world-record which lasted seventeen years. Known as "The Lithgow Flash", she was the fastest woman in the world; she broke world sprint records on ten occasions and her record margin win, greater than ever in history, still stands.[34] In 1952 when she was named Australia's "Sportsman of the Year", the Helms Foundation in the United States awarded her the prestigious title of "Outstanding Athlete 1952" and she was presented with an MBE for her service to athletics in the 1952 Coronation Honours.

Marjorie Jackson retired from athletics in 1953 at the age of twenty-two and married her boyfriend, Peter Nelson, an Olympic cyclist. The Nelson family joke was that "it took a man on a bicycle to catch her". In 1975, when transiting Chiron opposed her natal Mars in detriment (the transit began in June 1975 and completed in April 1976), Peter was diagnosed with leukaemia and he died in 1977. Marjorie Jackson-Nelson came out of retirement and launched the Peter Nelson Leukaemia Research Fellowship. She has raised in excess of three million dollars, used to sponsor a Leukaemia Laboratory in Adelaide, to appoint a second researcher of Leukaemia at the Flinders Medical Centre and to establish a full time research fellowship with the Department of Microbiology and Immunology at the University of Adelaide.[35] Marjorie Jackson-Nelson served as a member of SOCOG (Sydney Organising Committee of the 2000 Olympic Games) and was bearer of the Olympic flag at the opening ceremony. In 2001, Charles Sturt University in Bathurst, NSW, conferred the degree of Doctor of the University on her; she was appointed a Companion of the Order of Australia; and, on 3 November 2001, she became the governor of South Australia. In February 2002, as Governor, she was appointed a Commander of the Royal Victorian Order by Her Majesty The Queen, when the Queen visited Adelaide. Marjorie Jackson-Nelson continues to promote the cause of leukaemia research.

Pholus

Pholus' story carries on from the battle of the Centaurs with Hercules. Pholus' father is Seilenos, an elderly satyr god of drunkenness, a companion of Dionysus and the grandfather of the tribe of Satyroi; his mother is a nymph, one of the Meliai. Pholus has not been involved in the battle but simply witnessed it and so he moves amongst the fallen Centaurs and sets about burying them, for they are his kin. Curiosity gets the better of him and he pulls out an arrow from one of the Centaurs and marvels at how such tiny arrows can kill such huge Centaurs so fast. However, it slips from his fingers and strikes his foot "and since the wound could not be healed, he came to his death." [36] Recognising he is the inadvertent cause of his friend's demise, Hercules is distraught and mortified and gives him a magnificent funeral, burying him at the foot of the mountain Pholus so dearly loved and naming the mountain after him. Three aspects of the myth stand out for examination:

1. **Pholus is an augur.** An augur is the one in the tribe who observes the natural signs and interprets these as an indication of divine approval or disapproval. An augur also interprets omens by reading the entrails of sacrificed animals, yet Pholus is blind to his own fate. In mythology seers are often physically blind, for it is much easier to see the future when the present doesn't cloud the issues.

2. **Pholus is the guardian of sacred wine given to him by Dionysus.**
    If we follow Apollodorus' version of events, then ordained with responsibility (Saturn) by the Centaurs, Pholus is unable to maintain clear boundaries or ethics (Neptune) and bows to the pressure of Hercules to open the wine, much as Pandora bows to her nemesis and opens the box she is warned not to open. The release of the intoxicating substance causes a chain of non-negotiable events of which Hercules is the catalyst. If we follow Diodorus Siculus' version of events, then the wine waits, gaining potency for four generations, allowing time to bring Hercules to Pholus' cave and place all players into position on the chessboard.

3. **Pholus is naïve.**
    He picks up the arrow without thinking that it could harm him and then pays for the consequences with his life.

All of these facets of Pholus – his blindness to the future, his confusion of boundaries, his naivety – are aspects of Neptune struggling with the material world of Saturn, trying to bring spirit or spirituality into some form of manifestation and hence productivity. Wine, as an intoxicating substance, can either be harmful when it is misused or a door to greater insight when used in ceremony. The word "toxic" comes from medieval Latin "toxicus" poisoned, from the Latin "toxicum" poison and from the Greek "toxikon pharmakon" poison for smearing arrows, from "toxon" bow.

Someone with Pholus strongly placed in their chart will encounter grief from a naïve space. There may be boundaries which are confused or crossed without thought or the person may be forced to deal with old issues which have fermented over time. From a position of blind faith, Pholus in grief leads one to understand the weight of innocence, how dearly we can sometimes pay for lack of clarity. In the end there are two options: blindness or visionary power; naivety and deception, or access to sacred, creative knowledge.

Case Study

Vanessa Gorman

Natal Placement
Vanessa has Pholus conjunct her Ascendant at 12° 22' Aquarius conjunct Mercury and the Sun. The questions that immediately arise are:

- What is Vanessa naïve about?
- What issues involving her father (Pholus conjunct the Sun) is she unable to hear or talk about(Pholus conjunct Mercury)?

Background
Vanessa's father died on 3rd March, 1973, when Pholus was at 5° Pisces. She had just turned twelve. It would take another year before it was exactly conjunct the South Node. She says: "At the time it wasn't safe to grieve, so I went back to boarding school and buried it all." Vanessa had been desperate to have a baby since she was a little girl. A seven-year relationship ended at her Saturn Return (transiting Pholus swept over her natal Mars in Cancer in the 5th house in Fall) and so - she thought - did her dreams of becoming a mother.

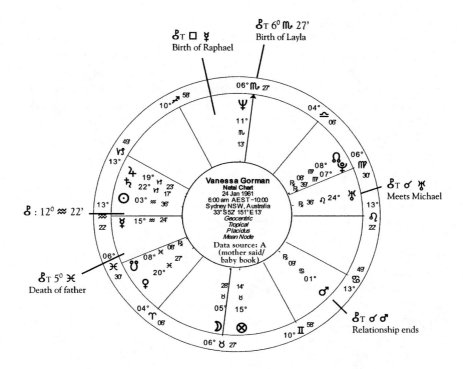

♂T 6° ♏ 27'
Birth of Layla

♂T □ ☿
Birth of Raphael

♂ : 12° ≈ 22'

♂T σ ⛢
Meets Michael

♂T 5° ♓
Death of father

♂T σ ♂
Relationship ends

Vanessa Gorman
Natal Chart
24 Jan 1961
6:00 am AEST –10:00
Sydney NSW, Australia
33° S 52 151° E 13'
Geocentric
Tropical
Placidus
Mean Node

Data source: A
(mother said/
baby book)

The Present

In 1993, at the age of thirty-two, (transiting Pholus conjunct her natal Uranus in the 7th house), she met Michael, a gentle, sensitive, committed man, and she dared to hope again. Michael was ambivalent about having children. As Vanessa neared thirty-seven, she became desperate to conceive. Vanessa, who is a television producer by profession, began making a video diary of her conversations with Michael, chronicling that journey of trying to get pregnant. Knowing he was still uncertain, she took matters into her own hands and became pregnant by him without telling him. When he heard the news, Michael was still unreconciled to the situation. Vanessa kept filming throughout the pregnancy, turning it into a documentary about how a modern couple deals with the arrival of a child in a period in history when women have the right to have a career and a baby, and men have the right to be doubtful - "two lovers navigating their way through the territory of the heart".[37]

Vanessa was ecstatic at the imminent birth and impending motherhood. The cameras continued to roll during the birth but the baby was in distress. In a semi-conscious state Vanessa was wheeled into theatre for an emergency caesarean where her daughter, Layla, was pulled from her belly at 3:25 pm on

16th February, 2000, at Lismore hospital (transiting Pholus was exactly conjunct Vanessa's MC). Layla suffered from Meconium aspiration syndrome (MAS), a common cause of illness in newborns. MAS occurs when a newborn inhales (aspirates) a mixture of meconium (baby's first faeces, ordinarily passed after birth) and amniotic fluid during labour and delivery. The inhaled meconium can cause a partial or complete blockage of the baby's airways. Air flows past the meconium trapped in the baby's airways as she breathes in but becomes trapped in her airways when she exhales. The inhaled meconium also irritates the baby's airways and makes it difficult for her to breathe.[38] Layla inhaled it and began to suffocate. She was airlifted to the nearest main city, Brisbane, and died at 11:40 that night, just over eight hours after she had been born.

In the myth Pholus naïvely reaches for the arrow without consideration of the consequences and dies quickly. Pholis in Greek means "squama," or skin and the process of Pholic grief metaphorically strips away the skin of a situation as one enters a journey of despair and misery. The results bring either naivety and deception or access to sacred, creative knowledge. At Layla's birth and subsequent death Pholus was conjunct Vanessa's MC, the point of public interface, so she kept filming, talking to the camera through the shock and the tears, utilising her natal conjunction of Pholus with Mercury and finally expressing her unresolved pain and grief. She took the dead body of little Layla home with her so she could grieve in a way that was once forbidden to women whose dead babies were usually whisked away by over-zealous hospital staff.

Six weeks after Layla died, Vanessa began making a new documentary. Instead of her original idea of how a baby impacts on a person's life and relationship, this time it was about the death of Layla. "Scratch any woman and you'll find pain around reproduction," she says. "Babies who've died, babies intended but never had, terminations, miscarriages. These feelings need to be aired." The documentary went to air on 1st March, 2001 (transiting Pholus conjunct Vanessa's natal Neptune in the 10th house). The response was powerful: the film won the ATOM (Australian Teachers of Media) Award for Best Documentary 2001, received an AFI (Australian Film Institute) nomination and was sold to a number of countries, including HBO in the USA who bought a 45-minute version. On winning the ATOM Award she wrote:

> Thanks so much for your email and the congrats. It's a very weird feeling... and you could have knocked me over with a feather. Same with the AFI nomination. It feels such a small personal film that I feel shocked to be up against some of the big documentary

makers and their big expensive documentaries. I have had such extraordinary feedback from many viewers and that has made the whole experience a wonderful one. I feel very grateful that Layla will not be forgotten and has been able to affect so many lives.

Vanessa had to deal not only with her initial deception of her partner, Michael, but also with issues around the death of her father at age twelve when it wasn't safe to grieve. As she approached forty, Vanessa could build a more mature understanding of how suppressing that grief had affected her, for unresolved grief is cumulative and influences every other experience of loss in our lives. **In August 2000,** Vanessa gained those insights for herself:

> It was such a journey for me, of happy expectation that turned into such an enormous journey of grief but in some ways healing also. As you know, I lost my father when I was twelve and that grief experience was totally underground and extremely painful because of my age and the time. I had no skills. Now I do - so I have just been letting myself go deeply into the centre of grief, as I know the consequences of suppressing it in my life.

From the excruciating loss of Layla, Vanessa has now given a huge number of people access to images and feelings, thoughts and ideas which were once taboo, for film is our modern dreaming, the modern visionary's raw material.

Michael stayed with Vanessa for eight months after the death of Layla but their relationship was unable to contain the immense loss. However, this story has a happy ending. **In October 2001,** shortly before transiting Pholus squared her natal Mercury, Vanessa again fell pregnant but not to Michael:

> **May 2002:** Not sure if I told you I am having another baby end of June. A little boy. Couldn't wait a few more years as I felt too desperate and "outside" of life. He has been such a healing pregnancy. Fingers crossed everything will be OK. So far so good. So that's my adventure! Michael isn't the father, although we maintain a very close and loving friendship and only want the best for one another. After Michael left, I got to the point where I decided I would maybe just have a baby by myself. James was a guy I started to see but he didn't seem the settling down type. But he offered to have a baby with me and I said OK! and not long after that I was pregnant. So here we all are!! James looking forward to it in between little bouts of trepidation, me trying to stay calm and believe that it won't happen again and this baby will live.

Raphael was born on the retrograde hit of transiting Pholus square Vanessa's natal Mercury:

I called him Raphael after the archangel who comes to earth to heal as that has certainly been his gift to me. All my anxiety during the pregnancy was released in a great woosh when he was pulled from the womb, outraged at being disturbed and let out an enormous yell. He came in to the world at 1:32 pm on 20th June, 2002. His Apgar scores were nine and nine.[39] Top of the class. I cried with joy and relief that he was out and safe and well. My partner, James, followed him around the theatre as he was weighed and measured and bathed. The caesarean was a bit traumatic due to an epidural that didn't want to work properly but the recovery has been so different from last time. I felt active and well within days.

For Vanessa, Pholus brought her sudden loss. She had to make lightning shifts and adjustments but it also brought her clarity. She did not replace the loss, she did not isolate from people and deny her feelings. She became a visionary, using the raw material of her experience to help others on their journey of grief. Most importantly she entered this next pregnancy wiser, less complicated, clear with James about her intentions and with no ambiguous boundaries. The memory of her first child will always be with her and whilst she still "aches for Layla", rather than continue a relationship to the pain of loss, she has a relationship with Layla's memory that is rounded and full, warm without gaps.

Nessus

Nessus is the third Centaur in this trinity. During the battle with the Lapithae, Absolus, the augur, tries to dissuade the Centaurs from fighting without success. Nessus distinguishes himself in combat but just as he turns to run away, fearful of being wounded, Absolus shouts: "Do not flee! You are fated to be preserved for Hercules' bow." Nessus heeds his words, turns back and is successful in killing several heroes. The Centaurs are, however, eventually defeated and driven from Thessaly, so Nessus establishes himself as a ferryman on the river Evenus, carrying people across the river for a fee. He claims this post as a godly appointment due to his good character or "moral rectitude", as Apollodorus tells us. In reality he is a self-appointed ferryman, operating in the mundane world as a bridge between two river banks. In India, where the whole subcontinent is land sacred to the goddess, such places are called *tirthas*, "crossings over", nodal points between the worlds which are said to have the power to change us. Tirthas are believed to possess sacred powers, for they are places where one can connect with the divine.[40] Is this place on the river

Evenus a tirtha? We don't know. Valerius Flaccus calls him "the black Centaur" [41]; Ovid terms him "savage Nessus" and "mighty in muscle".[42] Yet Nessus' actions suggest he is trying to reach beyond his bestial nature, since every time he carries someone across the river, he in effect bathes in the river, the appropriate rite of pilgrims in such sacred places; and by setting the foundations of his new life here and taking on this role, his deeds suggest a desire to utilise the sanctity of the place as a way of reforming or transforming the undomesticated parts of himself.

In this way years pass. Hercules marries a woman called Deianeira and in their travels they come to this same river Evenus, now swollen by the winter's rains and impassable. Fearless for himself but anxious for his wife, Hercules observes the tumultuous waters. Nessus is enchanted with Deianeira's beauty and begs Hercules to let him ferry her across the river without paying a fee. Hercules agrees and so "to Nessus then the Theban hero gave his bride of Calydon, pale and afraid, dreading the river, dreading the Centaur too." [43] Nessus plunges into the river with Deianeira but now inflamed with passion, he accosts her and tries to rape her. Angry beyond belief, Deianeira cries out and beats her fists against Nessus' body. Hercules grabs his bow and with an arrow still contaminated with the poisonous venom of the Hydra, shoots it directly into Nessus' heart. The dying Nessus falls to his knees. He grasps Deianeira by the arm and begs her forgiveness. He tells her that if she wants to stop Hercules from straying, all she has to do is to mix the semen spilled on the ground with the blood flowing from his wound. "Take this potion," he wheezes, "and if at any time you feel your husband's love straying, anoint his shirt with it. You will never again have cause to complain of his unfaithfulness" - and he dies.

Now Hercules being who he is, it is inevitable that his lust should rise sooner or later. Victorious in conquest, he captures a maiden and sends his attendant for the garment he wears to celebrate a sacrifice. Lichas of the loose tongue tells Deianeira of the love affair and thus is the end game announced: Deianeira, the garment, the blood and time, waiting only for her deeds to complete the pattern. As jealousy writes itself into Deianeira's heart, so her hands reach for Nessus' elixir of love, intending to bind her husband with her love. However, this is a story of posthumous revenge, a story where the dead dictate from the grave. The shirt warms Hercules' body so much that the Hydra's venom cooks his flesh. Deianeira is horrified and immediately hangs herself. On the advice of the oracle of Delphi, Hercules goes to Mount Oeta and builds a funeral pyre. He throws himself on it and begs his friends to set it alight. They baulk at his request, for this is the son of Zeus but finally Philoctetes complies, and for this he is given Hercules' bow and arrow, a later lever of victory in the Trojan War. In compassion for his son, Zeus allows the mortal part of Hercules to perish and he takes the immortal part and places him amongst the stars.

So what does this mean if someone has Nessus strongly placed in their charts?

In mythology, when someone crosses a river they have reached a turning point in their lives, confronted by an emotional force that either engulfs and overwhelms them or allows them to make the transition. Hercules chooses to swim across the river. He plunges into the stream of life but he does not recognise the raw and unformed energy of Nessus which reflects the raw and unformed energy inside himself. He acts without thinking and kills with the same poison that eventually kills him. Nessus in a chart brings up old issues of grief and loss thought long ago to be buried which erupt in a monstrous or poisonous way. They may be issues which stem from hatred, humiliation or rage and which cause us to burn or smoulder. They may involve bitterness or acrimony or seem like an attack from the outside (Hercules' shirt) but soon it becomes clear that the issue is not just skin deep but one that spreads to the very core of our being. It is the blow to the heart which kills but which has repercussions further down the track for the one who initiates it. The valley of grief is crossed by passing through intensity, violence and suffering. The key is to recognise and take responsibility for old quarrels from the past, fouled with toxins, which come back to haunt us, for this is a tale of passion and bitterness, caused by a situation which burns and infuriates so much that one wants only to take revenge. It is the pitch-black face of Pluto-made-manifest-through-Saturn, for these are still waters that run deep, black and toxic. The final outcome is gaining immortality which, in mythic terms, means freedom from the issue but its pathway is through dark venom. Nessus suffers a violent death and it has repercussions. In Shakespeare's *Antony and Cleopatra*, (4.13.43; *The Norton Shakespeare*, p.2688) realising that he has been betrayed by Cleopatra, Antony exclaims: "The shirt of Nessus is upon me." "Bad blood" is defined medically as any blood that is physically contaminated or "tainted," thus causing obvious changes in a person's health and lifestyle but it also exists metaphorically in families when an act by one family member causes revenge from another. This is so prevalent wherever death and money via wills and inheritance are concerned that it is almost commonplace. Nessus knows that Time has run out for him as he encounters Death but he also knows that Death awaits Hercules in Time.

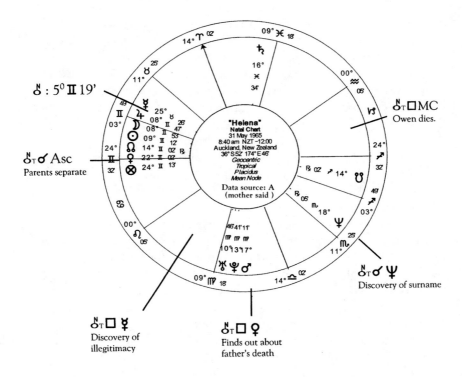

Case Study

Helena

Natal Placement

Helena has Nessus at 5° Gemini conjunct a partile Jupiter-Moon conjunction conjunct the Sun-North Node in the 12th house, although they are in the same sign as the Ascendant, square to the Uranus-Pluto-Mars conjunction in the 3rd house. This is part of mutable T-square in cadent houses. Jupiter is in detriment.

Helena's chart shows issues about the lost or weakened father-figure (Sun in the 12th house) and a close relationship to the mother (Moon in the 12th house). Helena also perceives either her mother or grandfather as the great benevolent force in her life, yet this is a relationship which never quite yields its full potential (Jupiter in detriment).

Background

Helena's father, Roger, was born in Hobart, Tasmania, the illegitimate child of an American soldier (Jupiter, the grandfather, in detriment in the 12th house). His family dispersed shortly afterwards and he was raised by his grandmother. Sometime after serving in New Guinea in WWII, he moved to New Zealand. Roger was forty-five and already had a family of his own although he was separated, when he met Helena's mother, Joan, aged eighteen. Helena's family moved to Australia when she was three. In 1972, when Helena was seven, (transiting Nessus conjunct her Ascendant) her parents separated but rather than tell Roger directly, Joan waited until he had left for work, called a taxi truck, took all her goods and the children and left him a goodbye note. Three years before Helena consulted me, she found out indirectly that her father's retribution for being abandoned like this was to arrange for someone to rape her mother on his behalf. The poisoned shirt had taken hold.

In 1983, when Helena was eighteen, she found out that Roger had sexually assaulted her younger sister. This in turn revealed the long-term sexual abuse of Helena's older sister and a police record of sexual assault with his first family in New Zealand. Helena's family was devastated. None of them knew how to deal with it, so they buried their heads in the sand and to date have never discussed it. In her own words, she felt extremely betrayed. Here is Nessus bringing up old issues of humiliation and rage which burn and smoulder. Helena says Roger never touched her directly but there were a number of occasions when she had felt extremely uncomfortable in his presence and thought to herself, "Fathers don't do this." She writes:

> In recent times it has become clear to me that neither of my sisters has ever dealt with their abuse. It was brushed under the carpet as quickly as it was revealed, thus not allowing them the opportunity to grieve their own loss of innocence. My older sister completely blocked all memory of it until 2002 when the issue was raised in the family again by my younger sister. My sisters turned to me to give them answers I simply didn't have. I said to my mother that she should give a copy of the police report to my sisters. She said she no longer had it and then retreated back into silence. It is because of this silence that I felt it important that this story be told, one way or another.

In 1986 when Helena turned twenty-one and applied for United Kingdom ancestry entry through her grandfather, she found out that Roger and Joan had never married (transiting Nessus square natal Mercury). In this day and age such an issue seems benign but for Helena it underlined the hidden issue of illegitimacy perpetuating itself from generation to generation through the grandfather's line (Jupiter in detriment and combust the Sun). Helena saw her father for the last time in September 1986. It was his seventieth birthday and the first time she had seen him since her sister's assault but her strategy for avoiding confrontation was to get herself so drunk the night before that there was no way she could ask him about anything to do with the family. It was also the last time she saw him alive as she left Australia in August 1987, (transiting Nessus conjuncted natal Uranus in October) and he died in July 1989 (transiting Nessus square natal Venus):

> I first found out about his death a few weeks later. I had been travelling in Europe. The news was buried somewhere in the third or fourth paragraph of a letter from my mother. I was never allowed the opportunity to grieve. I started to cry and my boyfriend told me to stop and curtly said that surely it could wait to we got home - he never was comfortable with emotions. I never cried again for my father but in a way his death brought relief from having to deal with how I felt about him.

In 1994 when Helena wanted to move back to Australia from the UK (transiting Nessus was conjunct her natal Neptune), she had to reapply for Australian citizenship. To her shock she found out that Roger's surname (which her mother had taken, even though they were never legally married) was not his given name and no-one knew its origin. Information about Helena's past was slowly emerging: the rape of her mother, the sexual assault on her sisters, her illegitimacy and now the false surname. But there was still another factor in this already-complicated saga. Helena had a step-father, Owen, who first came into her life when she was ten years of age. Whilst Helena calls him "step-father", her mother never married him, for Owen had another family. Late one Friday afternoon in May, 2002, Helena received a phone call: her step-father had just had a serious stroke. He had left instructions with a friend that Helena was to be called if anything should anything ever happen. The next morning Helena rang the hospital. I'm his daughter, she said. When can I visit? The family, she was told, were coming in that afternoon. The "other" family. Helena realised that if she didn't go to the hospital immediately, she would never get to see him. She had forty minutes with Owen that day and again on Sunday, each time strategically planned before the "other family" arrived. On the Tuesday Owen was moved to another ward. "The family" had left strict instructions as to who was able to see him and neither Helena's nor her mother's names were on the list. Helena was devastated. Owen was the firm but kind father-figure, the one who discussed her potential careers with her school teacher, the one who discussed finance and management with her and helped her purchase property. Now, in the last days of his life, she was being blocked from seeing the only clear paternal role model in her life. A few weeks later Owen's friend rang again to tell her that Owen was going into kidney failure and on 27th May, 2002, (transiting Nessus square Helena's MC) Owen died from a stroke. Helena did not go to the funeral. She is still dealing with the complex, terrible mess of poisonous family jealousies.

Here we see the unmistakable signature of Nessus: a biological father with a first family in New Zealand who sexually abuses both families and contrives to have Helena's mother raped when that marriage ends and a stepfather with a first family which emotionally shuts Helena out when the stepfather is on his deathbed. This is a tale of passion and bitterness, a situation which burns and infuriates. This is a tale of "bad blood" which has taught the women of this family to fear men. As Helena says:

> I often feel that my family, and sometimes others, see me as the holder of secrets, the one who has the answers to what is hidden, but I don't. I often know incredibly little. I was taught not to enquire, not to ask questions, not to delve too deep as there was always an unspoken threat that there was something murky lying buried which shouldn't be uncovered.

Now in her late thirties, Helena is seriously questioning whether it is possible for her to get past all these skewed views, irrational fears and emotional blockages in order to have balanced and healthy relationships, let alone a committed one. This is Nessus at work. Helena emailed me in January, 2003:

> The grief of Owen's death opened the door to grieve many things in my life. The death of my father. The relationship I never got to have with Owen. The personal relationships I have never allowed myself to have and the relationships I have had which suffered because of the emotional barriers I have built up. I could not accept that another person loved me, because I was not 'allowed' to love another person - I'm supposed to get a dog. Well actually, these days I have a cat. After my year of what I call 'initiation by fire' I continue to sift through the rubble and examine the pieces which are me and my life, my beliefs, my attitudes and most significantly, my emotions and my part in relationships.
>
> I have had many dreams this year but one in particular comes to mind. I open the front door to a party of people. They are all formally dressed - the guys are all in black tuxedoes and bow ties, the women in black evening gowns. It is my friend's engagement and they have brought gifts. I haven't seen my friend since I was nineteen and I have no idea why they are bringing the gifts to my house. I know nothing of the engagement and have no idea where he is. I let them in and figure I need to find somewhere

to store the gifts. I open the hall closest, thinking that would be a good place and inside the closet there are already many beautifully wrapped boxes I didn't know were there. I take the gifts from the guests and carefully place them with the others for safe keeping. I guess it's time to start opening the boxes!

On 6th May, 2003, I received this email from Helena:

I recently had skin cancer diagnosed on my face. The appointment for the surgery was for 22 April, 2003 - one year since I had seen my stepfather before he died. I cancelled this appointment because I needed time to digest what was going on and consider my options. I rang this morning to remake the appointment and it's for 27th May, 2003 at 9:15 am - the first year anniversary of his death. The irony of the situation struck me of how I would now be wearing a visible scar created on the anniversary of Owen's death, etching that day on my face forever more.

The wash and ebb of Nessus can have different repercussions, as this next story shows.

Case study

Carly - A way through the woods

Natal Placement
Nessus in Carly's chart is in the 1st house making a partile square to Pluto combust the Sun in the 4th house. Mercury is also conjunct the Sun-Pluto.

Background
Carly was a practising acupuncturist for many years and is now an author. Her early life was difficult, as one would expect with a Sun-Pluto conjunction in the 4th house, compounded by Pluto ruling the 8th house of irrevocable change. The life force, the developing sense of self, the unfolding ego encounters the raw energy of change and intensity at a deep level. Pluto in the 4th house is a deeply uncomfortable placement, signifying violence encountered in the home environment or an intense childhood filled with passionate adult emotions, such as sexual abuse, lust, grief, incest or death. This did indeed occur in Carly's childhood. She was sexually abused by her step-father. This early betrayal by the masculine or yang model for how to take action and have power in the world taught Carly to become wary and apprehensive about trusting anyone. Nessus squaring the aspect laced it with

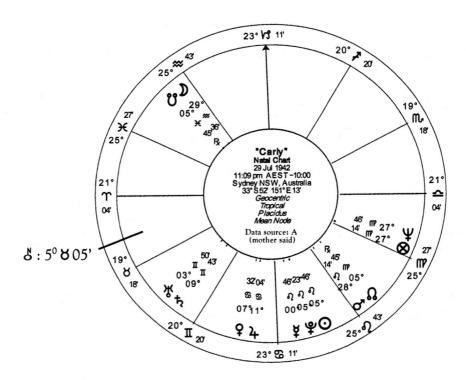

a toxic family pattern of retaliation and retribution, bad blood which cascaded back through the generations.

The Mercury-Pluto part of the equation gave Carly the option of what attitude she would take to these events, how she developed her mind. In its worst case scenario she could have become mentally stubborn and obsessive, an intractable fanatic who ends up with digestive problems and ulcers from worrying about small things and not letting them go. Nessus squaring the Mercury could have exacerbated the revenge factor by intensifying any obsessive thoughts. The other side of the coin was to hone her mind into an incisive intellect with precise, focused thinking, someone who was intense and passionate about expressing her ideas. In this case Nessus could offer her insights about the family pattern. In 1943, when Carly was one year old, her father, Enzo, was interned in a camp for un-naturalized Italians in Sydney, Australia. Her mother was given the option join him there for the duration of the war and chose to do so. Carly's mother told her this was a good thing, as they were extremely poor. This way they did not have to worry about food or housing. In the camp Carly was protected by her mother. She was a pretty child with her Italian good looks and the apple of her mother's eye. In 1947

Carly's mother felt that Enzo wasn't providing well enough for her and Carly and when she met a travelling picture showman, she took up with him. When she realised this was the wrong move and that her dreams for a better life weren't going to happen, she become bitter and began to drink too much. Carly remembers her yelling and screaming and using violence. The family was constantly on the move from country town to country town as Carly's mother made it impossible to stay there. She had now become what Carly terms "an insufficient mother". With both parents jammed in an impossible situation, Carly became the pressure tap. She was sexually abused by her step-father from age eleven until she was seventeen, when she left home to begin University. Carly's mother never knew this was happening, for by now she had become a serious alcoholic, so it was a secret between Carly and her step-father. In later years Carly was able to grasp what had allowed her mother to degenerate into this condition. She describes it this way:

> My mother was one of a pair of twins, the fourteenth child of a Glaswegian coalminer. It was a poor working-class Scottish family who had been exploited by mine bosses since the Industrial Revolution. Such families are riddled with vengeance patterns going back generations, for there is no way out of their social condition. Vengeance is part of tribal thinking but in a city these tribes are called families. Families get a grudge and they hold onto it and project it onto other people or onto each other as a way of gaining an illusion of power. This can effectively start family vendettas. My mother was the inheritor of such a family paranoia that basically ate her up completely. Her family dynamic was based on this sense of grudge. Grudge is something that prevents you from thinking. Family pride requires you to get revenge, requires you to win, to 'never let the bastards have the satisfaction'. I think my mother lived in utter misery as long as she did because she didn't want the bastards to win. By the end of her life 'the bastards' were the ghostly race who lived in the cracks of the doors. She told me she thought the Mafia owned the hospital she was in. They had a new way of spying on her which was to hide tiny microphones in the surrounding crevices. If she'd lived long enough she would have had video cameras hidden in the new electricity-conducting wall paint!
>
> As for me, I am aware that this has conditioned me in ways I still don't fully understand. I only know I have not succeeded in making what I feel is a comfortable living, although in other people's eyes I seem to be doing alright, for I have helped a lot of people and published a book. I think I've been behind the eight-ball [44] in social terms because my family background has made me

aware that you can't actually get rich without exploiting people, so I haven't got rich. I am also aware that I don't want to be exploited, so I do not like working for other people. Exploitation, either as perpetrator or victim is, it seems to me, at least one of the sources of these patterns of grudge and mutual destruction which is the pattern of my mother's family. I had insights in my early twenties about all of this but didn't have the experience or the maturity to put it into usable form until I was in my early forties.

When Carly was forty-three she went to China for three months and studied advanced acupuncture at a hospital in Nanjing. Once she returned to Sydney her practice flourished and she and her partner were successful in gaining a UK publisher for their book on traditional Chinese medical diagnostic techniques. Then in treating her patients over the next fifteen years, Carly began to formulate a model of family patterns which helped to resolve grudge and vengeance. Her model achieved extremely favourable outcomes with her patients and her current book incorporates that breadth of vision.

The Centaurs are either killers or healers. In taking hold of the myth, in finding a new resolution to the problem, Carly found they were both. She emerged from a long process of "killing"/transforming parts of herself to become someone who could use this Nessic history creatively, rather than allowing it to destroy her, as it had her mother. As Hercules cremates himself in the pyre at Mount Oeta in order to transcend himself, so it was necessary for Carly to recast, phoenix-like, the part of herself that had grown from her mother's gore. This was Nessus at work in her life.

Some twenty years older than Helena, Carly found it was not until her early forties that she could gain the necessary life experience and knowledge that would enable her to find a model to stop the flood of vitriol from her mother's life. By understanding the vendetta compulsion in her mother she has been able to resolve this motif in herself and then contribute to its resolution in others. Carly's story shows that the negative outcome of the Nessus myth is not inevitable. Helena is still in her late thirties and the resolution to her story is yet to unfold.

A word about post-modernism
The mythology of the Centaurs give us an emotional lens to guide our thoughts about how we make transitions, how we let go of things and how we gain new insights as a result and in my research I have applied this thesis to grief. The questions I proposed were: If a person has Chiron placed strongly in their chart, do they necessarily live a Chironic life? If someone has Pholus placed

strongly in their chart, do they live a Pholic life? Can the same be said of Nessus? I could have looked at where all three Centaurs sat within any one chart but that would have defeated the purpose by blurring the boundaries and cluttering the issues with "white noise". Too much information in a chart means less clear predictive work and the purpose of looking at these case studies is to make discoveries that can be useful to a client with a Centaur prominent in their chart. I have arrived at the conclusion that, whilst these are early days of exploring the Centaurs and their relationship to the natal chart and their role in predictive astrology, they seem to be alive and flourishing in the charts of certain people.

This is new wine in old bottles but new discoveries tell us new things. The Centaurs, as consciously considered components in astrology, have been with us for only a short period of time, thus the theories that we can apply to them and their interpretation in the natal chart and in predictive work are, at best, speculative. Nevertheless they come at a time when Post Modernist philosophy is re-humanising the rational, modern, utilitarian and almost uniformly undistinguished clamour of the recent past.

Traced back to the Renaissance, the theory of Modernity reached its peak in 1950s and 1960s architecture, encapsulated in le Corbusier's famous remark that "a house is a machine for living in". This was epitomised in his design for the unités d'habitation, or what we now call tower blocks, on the outskirts of Marseilles. Stripped of any symbolic significance and desensitised to anything but industrial purpose, this functional, homogeneous, reductionist thinking was unwaveringly reinforced by modern politicians and modern planners and became the basis for the economic rationalism that rose to power in the 1980s. In its extreme form, the social expression of Modernity was compacted into communism.

The leading theorist of post-modern architecture, Charles Jenks, dates the end of the modern era from 1972 when the city of St Louis, Illinois, USA, demolished the apartment blocks for which it had received architectural prizes only seventeen years before. The recognition that houses are homes and parts of communities which function in complex social ways and which require respect for basic aesthetics was crucial in this move and reflective of changes in the way we see the space around us. As the Berlin Wall fell in 1979 and heralded the collapse of communism in the Soviet bloc, so post-modern thinking began to cut a swathe in the form of pluralism (the voices of the many) and diversity. In architecture this was expressed through colour, reflective surfaces and more playful environments. An example of how this is being put into practice today is the town of Poundbury in Dorchester, England, built under the auspices of HRH the Prince of Wales in the Duchy of Cornwall.

Poundbury began its development in the 1980s and took a radical new approach to residential development and highway design. Its essence lies in the way land is integrated into the urban fabric so that employment, recreation, education and shopping are all interwoven with housing. In allowing these many aspects to be part of the tapestry, Poundbury recognises that an entity is more than the sum of its parts. This is the heart of Post-Modernism.

Modernism gave us the "whole" story. It put full stops on the multifarious and reduced all things to one, allowing only the spartan and ascetic. Post-modernism is concerned with re-codifying the past with the means and technology of the present. It allows us to hear alternative, contrasting voices and to reflect on who we are through those expressions. In this way the Centaurs are a phenomenon of post-modernism. Discovered with its rise, they are the voice of The Traveller captured inside our solar system, bridging and mixing energies in the same way that ancient and medieval astrologers spoke of the Moon. Thus they allow us to look at grief in a chart from another perspective, not overriding the natal chart but underpinning those statements with a voice more raw, more unformed than their natal counterparts.

The Centaurs have an ancient mythology and, since we have now sighted and named the three which link Saturn with each of the outer planets - the planets of the collective world in which we live today - we can no longer ignore them and what they are saying. By thoughtfully considering their mythology, they give us much more information about what is going on, helping us to better understand why some people live more tragically flawed lives than others, and why grief affects some people in such a monumental way. These are early days but the wine seems to be in solid casks and a good vintage is expected.

❋   ❋   ❋

Endnotes

1. August Möbius (1790-1868) was a mathematician, astronomer and physicist. He devised a two-dimensional surface with only one side which can be constructed in three dimensions by taking a rectangular strip of paper and joining the two ends of the strip together so that it has a one hundred and eighty degree twist. It is now possible to start at a point A on the surface and trace out a path that passes through the point which is apparently on the other side of the surface from A, and then, continuing on, to arrive again at

point A. http://www-history.mcs.st-and.ac.uk/history/Mathematicians/
Mobius.html - accessed 3rd October, 2002.

2. There has already been a great deal written about the Centaurs in the
astrological community (see Melanie Reinhart, Robert von Heeren, Dieter
Koch, Al H. Morrison and Zane Stein). Now, thanks to Karen Hamaker-
Zondag and her publishing company, Symbolon, we also have a Centaur
Ephemeris: von Heeren, Robert. (2001) *7 Centaur Ephemeris*, Amstelveen:
Symbolon. But it was Bernadette Brady who first set me on the path of linking
the centaurs with grief. Bernadette and I initially heard of the Centaurs at a
lecture given by Melanie Reinhart at the 1997 AA Conference in Cirencester,
England. A few years later we started including the Centaurs as part of one of
the modules of the Astro Logos Diploma Course, mainly because our students
kept asking us about Chiron which, prior to the discovery of the Centaurs,
was seen as the answer to all the ills of the chart, a view to which we did not
subscribe. As we embarked on this endeavour, I began to understand their
link with grief.

3. http://www.seds.org/nineplanets/nineplanets/oort - accessed 3rd October,
2002.

4. http://www.ifa.hawaii.edu/faculty/jewitt/kb.html - accessed 12th March,
2002 - and corroborated by email to the author from David Jewitt, 28th
October, 2002.

5. This information comes from email correspondence between the author
and Alan Stern, Director, Department of Space Studies, Southwest Research
Institute, Boulder, Colorado, USA, 6th April, 2003. The diagrams showing
the location of the Kuiper Belt of comets were drawn based on this information.

6. The date of the discovery photo of Chiron, (at first provisional designation
1977 UB, Slow Moving Object Kowal) was shot by Kowal on 18th October,
1977, at 9h08m30s UT 33N21/116W52. The date of "the discovery of
Chiron" (in the sense of awareness by Kowal) is 1st November, 1977 - http:/
/www.centaurresearchproject.de/menu/ - accessed 14th March, 2002. The
discovery was made using the 1.2 meter Schmidt telescope of the Mount
Palomar observatory (California, USA) - http://www.vub.ac.be/STER/
www.astro/chibio.htm - accessed 14th March, 2002. In email correspondence
with the author dated 6th April, 2004, Robert von Heeren wrote:

> Both dates are important. The official discovery data in astronomy
> are always the dates and times when the discovery photo was shot.
> Anything else ("awareness of the discoverer that he found
> something") is rarely protocoled and published, so except for
> Chiron and Kowal's "discovery" two weeks after he shot the photo,
> there are no official databases or protocols (only for Pluto such

information exists). To astronomy it is, by the way, not relevant, only the date of the photo which led to the discovery is important. We astrologers are, of course, very interested when the discoverer found it finally but that is a rare information we normally don't get because most astronomers do not remember or write down this detail.

7. http://astrologic.ru/english/element.htm - accessed 29th March, 2003.

8. Jensen, Brian. (1997) "Mandorla: Ancient Symbol of Wholeness," in *Sandplay: The Sacred Journey*, Spring. Sonoma State University, Rohnert Park, California - http://www.sandplayusa.org/mandorla.html - accessed October 18, 2002.

9. Johnson, Robert A. (1992) *Owning Your Own Shadow, Understanding the Dark Side of the Psyche*. New York: Harper Collins, pp. 107, 111.

10. Levine, Marsha A. *Domestication, Breed Diversification and Early History of the Horse*, McDonald Institute for Archaeological Research, Cambridge, UK, at: http://www2.vet.upenn.edu/labs/equinebehavior/hvnwkshp/hv02/levine.htm - accessed 14th May, 2003. Indeed several sites associated with the Sintashta-Petrovka culture in the southern Urals and northern Kazakhstan contain graves of warriors who are accompanied in death by burials of vehicles with two spoked wheels (defined either as chariots or light carts) and teams of horses. http://www.metmuseum.org/ - accessed 17th May, 2003.

11. Brady, Bernadette. (1999) *Brady's Book of Fixed Stars*, York Beach: Samuel Weiser, p. 69.

12. ibid, p. 294.

13. Drews, Robert. (1993) *The End of the Bronze Age: Changes in Warfare and the Catastrophe ca. 1200 BC*, Princeton: Princeton University Press.

14. Dossenbach, Monique and Hans D. (1985) *The Noble Horse*, Exeter: Webb & Bower, Figure 3, page 92.

15. Casson, Lionel. (1994) *Travel in the Ancient World*, Baltimore: The Johns Hopkins University Press.

16. For examples of chariot fighting in *The Iliad*, see, 5.9ff, 5.38-47, 5.159f, 5.608f, 7.13ff, 8.78ff, 8.256ff, 8.309ff, 11.91ff, 11.122ff, 11.179ff, from: Gallucci, Ralph. *The Horse in Early Greek Myth*, University of California, Santa Barbara, at: http://cla.calpoly.edu/~jlynch/Gallucci.html - accessed 18th September, 2001.

17. Filpus, John W. *A Catalogue of Centaurs on Greek and Related Painted Pottery*, at: http://members.aol.com/JWFvases/page2/index.htm - accessed 3rd June, 2002.

18. The Parthenon Marbles are currently on display in the British Museum, London, UK.

19. In the Medieval period, depictions of Centaurs varied from a symbol of evil to a helpful guide, yet retained popular status through the common art of the period, the Books of Hours, the main prayer book used in medieval Europe and often the first and only book an individual owned in his or her lifetime, where illuminators inserted Centaurs into the marginalia and illustrations. Mythical creatures with their origins in antiquity had value in the medieval period in illustrating the Christian religious, dogmatic, allegorical meaning that was considered steeped in nature. See for example, the *Physiologus*, a collection of moralized beast tales and one of the most popular books of the Middle Ages. At the same time, as Western Europe was expanding its trading routes into the Far East, its view of the animal kingdom expanded as merchants brought back tales of equally bizarre animals such as the giraffe, the hippopotamus and the ostrich. (see: http://www.geocities.com/Paris/3963/bestiary.html and http://gateway.uvic.ca/spcoll/physiologum/commentary/txt_physiologus.htm - accessed 9th April, 2003).The Centaur was also used by some writers to symbolize the duality of humanity, combining intellect (the human half) with primal drives (the horse half), another version being the Minotaur with the head of a beast and the body of a man. In the late twentieth and early twenty-first century the Centaur has reappeared in popular art, literature and on television in the genres of fantasy and science fiction. Such works include C.S. Lewis' *The Narnian Chronicles*, Piers Anthony's *Xanth* series, John Varley's *The Gaean Trilogy* (*Titan, Wizard, Demon* series), Jack Chalker's *Wellworld* series, Walter Jon Williams' *Knight Moves*, J.K. Rowling's *Harry Potter* series where the Centaur has regained its original mythical character of magic and nobility, and through the television series *Hercules* and *Xena, Warrior Princess*.

20. Image from Starlight astrological software, reproduced with kind permission from Zyntara Publications: http://www.zyntara.com.

21. Diodorus Siculus. *Library of History*, ed. and trans. C.H. Oldfather. (1954) Cambridge: Harvard University Press. 4.12.3.

22. Hyginus, Caius Julius. 'Fabulae' in *The Myths of Hyginus*, trans. and ed. Mary Grant. (1960) Lawrence: University of Kansas Publications, p.138.

23. http://www.diggerhistory.info/pages-heroes/simpson.htm and http://www.awm.gov.au/encyclopedia/simpson.htm - accessed 3rd May, 2003.

24.http://www.fact-index.com/h/he/ heracles.html#Birth%20and%20Childhood - accessed November 19, 2003.

25. http://www.perseus.tufts.edu/Herakles/bio.html - accessed November 19, 2003.

26. Apollodorus of Athens. *The Library of Greek Mythology*, trans. Keith Aldrich (1975), Lawrence: Coronado Press.

27. Ovid. *Fasti*, trans. A. J. Boyle and R. D. Woodard. (2000) London: Penguin Books, 5.379 at: http://www.theoi.com - accessed 17th August, 2003.

28. Apollonius Rhodius. *Argonautica*. trans. E.V. Rieu, London: Penguin Books, 2.1238 at: http://www.theoi.com - accessed 17th August, 2003.

29. op. cit. Brady (1999) p. 260.

30. It is called "Young Onset" as symptoms appear in people under forty.

31. Fox, Michael J. *Lucky Man*, (2002) London: Ebury Press, p.150.

32. *Spin City* is produced by UBU Productions in association with DreamWorks Television. The series was filmed before a studio audience and premiered September 17, 1996. Fox stayed in the series until 2000. The series ended production in 2002.

33. http://www.wchstv.com/abc/spincity - accessed 3rd September, 2002.

34. At the Sydney Olympics it was announced that Marion Jones' winning margin was the greatest, with the exception of Marjorie Jackson's winning margin in 1952.

35. http://wwwdb.csu.edu.au/division/marketing/ne/grad01/grad01wsm28.htm and http://www.governor.sa.gov.au/html/governor.html#bio - both accessed 14th April 2003.

36. op. cit. Diodorus Siculus 4.12.3.

37. http://abc.net.au/layla/ - accessed 2nd March, 2001.

38. http://kidshealth.org/parent/medical/lungs/meconium.html - accessed 4th August. 2003. Although meconium is passed in up to twenty percent of births, not all infants who pass meconium develop MAS. Of the babies who pass meconium, twenty-to-thirty either inhale the meconium in utero or with the first breath.

39. An Apgar score is a score given for each sign: A = Activity (Muscle Tone); P = Pulse; G = Grimace (Reflex Irritability); A = Appearance (Skin Colour); R = Respiration, at one minute and five minutes after the birth. If there are problems with the baby, an additional score is given at ten minutes. A score of 7-10 is considered normal, while 4-7 might require some resuscitative measures. A baby with apgars of 3 and below requires immediate resuscitation. http://www.childbirth.org/articles/apgar.html - accessed 23rd April, 2003.

40. Gadon, Elinor W. 'Sacred Places in India: The Body of the Goddess' in *The Power of Place: Sacred Ground in Natural and Human Environments*, Bath: Gateway, 1993, p.82.

41. Valerius Flaccus, Gaius. *The Argonautica*, trans. J. Mozley. (1978) Cambridge, Massachusetts: Harvard University Press.

42. Ovid. *Metamorphoses*, trans. A.D. Melville, Oxford: Oxford University Press.

43. ibid. 9.102-158.

44. Eight-Ball is a call shot game played with a cue ball and fifteen object balls, numbered one through fifteen. One player must pocket balls of the group numbered one through to seven (solid colours), while the other player has nine through to fifteen (stripes). The player pocketing either group first, and then legally pocketing the eight-ball wins the game. The term "behind the eight-ball" means to be put into a difficult position.

8
Afterword - Sedna

Space isn't remote at all. It's only an hour's drive away if your car
could go straight upwards.
Fred Hoyle, astronomer, mathematician, writer (1915-)

On 15 March, 2004, the NASA-funded astronomical team of Michael
Brown (Caltech), Chad Trujillo (Gemini Observatory, Hawaii) and
David Rabinowitz (Yale), using the 48-inch Samuel Oschin Telescope at the
Caltech's Palomar Observatory, east of San Diego, USA, announced the
discovery of the coldest, most distant object known to orbit the Sun.[1]
(Discovery data: 14th November, 2003, at 6h 32m 57s UT, Palomar Mountain,
San Diego 116W51'50"/ 33N10'46". Zodiacal longitude approximately 18°
Taurus. [2]) The discovery was confirmed with other observatories and the
object's size was pinned down using NASA's new Spitzer Space Telescope.
The object was found at a distance ninety times greater than the distance
between the Sun and the earth, three times farther from the Sun than Pluto
or Neptune. Standing on its surface, a person holding the head of a pin at
arm's length could block out the Sun. It takes 10,500 years to orbit the Sun in
an extreme ellipse. Estimated at no more than 1,100 miles (1,770 kilometres)
in diameter, it is an anomaly of our solar system: it may be the largest object
after Pluto, it sits in an area some astronomers had previously thought empty,
opening up years of research regarding the nature of space beyond Neptune, it
is redder and brighter than anything astronomers have seen in the outer solar
system with no plausible explanation and it may even have its own little
moon. "There's absolutely nothing else like it known in the solar system,"
said Brown. Other researchers say they're not even sure how to classify the
object. Brown believes it may be the most primordial object ever detected,
having undergone very little heating by the Sun and having had few collisions
in the sparse region of space where it resides. According to the latest thinking,
other objects in the solar system have typically been transformed significantly
since their formation. Officially known to astronomers as 2003 VB12, based
on the day of its discovery, of more interest is the fact that, due to its frigid
temperatures - its surface temperature is about minus 400 degrees Fahrenheit
(-240 Celsius), the coldest known place in the solar system - the team has

proposed that the object be named Sedna, in honour of the Inuit goddess of the sea from whom all sea creatures were created.

Here is a brief retelling of the myth of Sedna [3]
Sedna was a young woman who lived with her widowed father by the Arctic sea. Conditions were extreme and hunting and fishing were dangerous. As a result, food was sparse but Sedna always made sure her father had the larger portion. The lovely Sedna was courted by many suitors but she would not leave her father. Then came a handsome man wearing fine grey and white clothing. He talked of soft bearskins in a warm tent and scented oil for her lamp and he promised that, if Sedna would marry him, her father would never go hungry. At her father's urging she accepted his offer, and left with her husband for a better life across the sea.

However, the stranger had spoken falsely, for soft bearskins were in fact hard walrus hide, fish skins with holes replaced the warm tent, the lamp was a dream through the long dark nights and all her meals were raw fish. To add insult to injury, not a skerrick of food was sent back to her father. For Sedna had been tricked into marrying a fulmar, a sea bird who had taken the form of a man in order to court her, and all around them her husband's relatives filled the night skies with constant shrieks.

When the ice broke that season, her father visited - and was shocked by what he saw. Beside himself, he killed Sedna's fulmar husband with his knife and gathered his daughter into his kayak. The relatives returned and found the dead body. Enraged they flew off to look for the pair, invoking the sea spirits as they flew. A great storm arose with waves that threatened their lives and in the terror of the moment, her father pushed Sedna out of the kayak. Valiantly she clutched onto the side. "Let go", her father, pleaded, "or I'll die with you." In desperation he took out his knife and cut off the tips of her fingers. They fell into the water and immediately became seals but still Sedna clung to the kayak. Her father cut off the middle joints of her fingers, and they fell into the sea and became fishes but still she clung to the hope of life. Finally her father cut off her finger joints and they fell into the water and became whales. With no other means of gripping the kayak, Sedna slipped into the ocean. Satisfied she would now drown, the fulmars flew away across a calm and mirror-like sea.

Slowly Sedna sank to the bottom of the sea where she lives to this day in a rock house. Her hair is filled with crabs and anemone which no comb can remove. And it is said that all the broken taboos and sins against nature, all the foul matter of those who live in the above world collects on Sedna's body and when the weight is too heavy, Sedna sobs in sorrow and grief. The sea creatures gather by her door to comfort her and in the above world there is hunger and sickness. The people know they must gather in a circle with their Shaman and publicly confess their broken taboos and crimes against nature. They send Sedna their prayers and the men, remembering the name of Sedna's father, do a slow dance of contrition, singing a song of remorse for all the sins done by man to women, to earth, and to her children.

Then the Shaman purifies herself and travels down to Sedna and, with fine sand and seaweed, lovingly she cleans the filth from Sedna's body and gently removes the crabs from her hair, softly singing the confessions of those above. She repeats their prayers of respect, their promises to change their personal stories, to be kind and loving to each other, to the earth and to all other creatures and Sedna listens carefully and her heart opens. Then Sedna sends a prayer to Creator, asking Creator to forgive them for all of the ways they have become out of balance. The sounds of her sobbing are no longer heard in the waves or on the wind and the sea animals end their vigil and swim away to offer themselves again as food.

Despite her suffering, Sedna's compassion and generosity are abundant and from her great forgiveness comes the wealth of the sea. In this way, the Inuit are inspired to make their life stories better by treating their relations with love and respect.

I present this myth to you not so much with the aim of interpretation but with the observation that there is much which resonates with the myth of Proteus, the seals not being the least. However, in Sedna's myth we are being taken deep into the sea, deep into the emotions and the unconscious where Sedna is so weighed down by taboos and foul matter, so heavy with grief, that in the end all she can do is sob her heart out until the Shaman comes to free her.

Does Sedna's discovery suggest that perhaps we are entering a time when grief will be acknowledged more consciously and respectfully in the community?

Endnotes

1. http://www.gps.caltech.edu/~mbrown/sedna/ - accessed 15th March 2004; and http://www.space.com/scienceastronomy/new_object_040315.html - accessed 7th April, 2004.

2. A Sedna ephemeris can be generated using Juan Revilla's free software Riyal at: http://www.expreso.co.cr/centaurs/whatsnew.html - from email correspondence with the author dated 16th March, 2004.

3. After Grey Eagle to whom the story was given in Alaska by the Inuit: http://www.rainewalker.com/sedna.htm - accessed 15th March, 2004.

9
Terminus

In the midst of winter, I finally learned that there was in me an
invincible summer.
                    Albert Camus, playwright/novelist (1913-1960)

A man walking down a road sees a ferocious lion. The lion sees the man,
emits a great roar and bounds towards him. Fearful for his life, the man
turns on his heels and flees. The lion races after him, growling all the way,
finally overtaking the man who drops to the ground quivering and waits to be
eaten. The lion says to him: "Why are you running away? I have a message for
you."

The world of common day is crammed with messages about how to let
go but like the man running from the lion, we fear they will destroy us. Minor
losses and disappointments, expectations that never come to fruition or
different endings to situations force us to reassess our situation and to replace
these expectations with other goals. Rather than listening to these messages
and using them as small ceremonies for reassessment, we tend to suppress
them with food, medication, alcohol, drugs, material goods and fantasy.

Everyone remembers and laughs at Otto, the character in *A Fish Called
Wanda* [1] who opens a safe expecting to find twenty million dollars worth of
jewellery and instead finds nothing. We laugh at his reaction ("Disappointed!")
because there is a gulf of unspoken material between what he says (a mild
word) and how he says it (spoken in fury). Playwright Harold Pinter describes
this lacuna of speech as "a necessary avoidance, a violent, sly, and anguished
or mocking smoke screen which keeps the other in its place." [2] It is this
avoidance of what is really going on inside us and the fact that we are socialised
to show a brave face to the world that causes emotional blockages that can
have such devastating consequences when faced with major loss.

Grief is not a process that happens alone. It is a team effort, a dialogue
with those we love. Later in *A Fish Called Wanda*, screenwriters Cleese and
Crichton sum up what they see as the detrimental aspect of being English in
a speech lawyer Archie Leach makes to American Wanda Gershwitz when
they meet in a secret rendezvous:

"Wanda, do you have any idea what it's like being English? Being so correct all the time, being so stifled by this dread of doing the wrong thing, of saying to someone 'Are you married?' and hearing 'My wife left me this morning', or saying 'Do you have children?' and being told 'They all burned to death on Wednesday.' You see, Wanda, we're all terrified of embarrassment. That's why we're so… dead. Most of my friends are dead, you know. We have these piles of corpses to dinner. But you're alive, God bless you. And I want to be. I'm so fed up with all this." [3]

Cleese and Crichton are writing about a particular trait of the English in dealing with emotion, yet it also sums up most of modern western society's attitude to loss and grief, the fear of saying the wrong thing, the fear of responding to another's acute pain and discomfort. Pinter calls this "the weight of the unsaid and the unutterable".

Author Diane Ackerman wrote, "I don't want to get to the end of my life and find that I lived just the length of it. I want to have lived the width of it as well." My friend, Pietro Ballinari, added, "I want to have lived the height, the weight, the light, the dark, the colours, the circumference, the content, the complexity, the simplicity, the allness, the nothingness and much more of it as well." To have lived well means we will experience loss and undergo grief, yet none of us are prepared for its impact on our lives. Instead we pretend that death does not exist and that grief will never touch us. Furthermore, since western society is unaccustomed to seeing the expression of grief in the community, preferring instead to placate it and hide it away, we are generally not aware of the intensity or duration of the pain involved unless we've experienced it ourselves.

Grief is marked by sacrifice - not the act of slaughtering or surrendering a possession in order to appease a god, nor the act of submission and becoming a martyr. The sacrifice of grief is the process of becoming sacred - sacrum facere - in the transitional space of the mandorla where the only obligation is to harness the natural review that occurs with the loss, sieve the spectrum of emotions created by that relationship and bring the unique and lacerating pain of grief to a conclusion in ways that are satisfying. As Sean Kane notes, "a death with no story is no death at all. A death that cannot be told is an unfinished life". [4]

Grief isn't an event. It is an ever-changing process that takes place over time. It is Lying Down with the Seals; it is encountering Proteus in order to deal with the slippage between reality as we have known it and what it has now become as a result of the loss of a loved one. The responsibility of the consulting astrologer is to be present in this sacred space and by utilising a client's context and the tools of natal and predictive astrology, to tell the truth about the nature of what lies ahead of them. Knowing the shape of grief and its consequences over time means that we can throw light onto this pathway for a client and give edges and boundaries to this most relevant of rituals. Helping a client connect with their unique journey in this way means they can encounter a changed future with focus, determination and understanding when grief comes to call.

✳   ✳   ✳

Endnotes

1. Cleese, John and Crichton, Charles. (1988) *A Fish Called Wanda*. London: Methuen, 1988, p.15.
2. Pinter, Harold. (1998) *Various Voices*. London: Faber and Faber, p.19.
3. op.cit. Cleese and Crichton, p.58.
4. op.cit. Kane. (1998) p.208.

God bless this tiny little boat

And me who travels in it.

It stays afloat for years and years

And sinks within a minute.

And so the soul in which we sail,

Unknown by years of thinking,

Is deeply felt and understood

The minute that it's sinking.

Appendix 1

Firdaria - The Disposed Years

Planetary periods form a vital part of Ancient and Medieval astrology. The Firdaria or "the years of the alfirdar", as ibn Ezra refers to them [1], are a Persian concept and alludes to a system of planetary periods where the life is divided into irregular periods of years with each period being ruled by a planet, luminary or nodal axis. The quality of that period of time and the style of events was thus dictated by the condition of the planet in the chart.

Abu Ma'shar (787-886 CE) writes:

Know that the planets have certain numbers; some of these are called fardarat, others are called "years". The fardar of the Sun is 10 years, the fardar of Venus is 8 years, the fardar of Mercury is 13 years, the fardar of the Moon is 9 years, the fardar of Saturn 11 years, the fardar of Jupiter 12 years, the fardar of Mars 7 years, the fardar of the Head 3 years, and the Tail, 2 years: that is 75 years. [2]

Al-Biruni, writing in 1029 CE, states:

Ma firdarat al-kawakib. The years of a man's life according to the Persian idea are divided into certain periods (firdar) governed by the lords of these known as Chronocrators. When one period is finished another begins. The first period always begins with the Sun in a diurnal nativity and with the Moon in a nocturnal one; the second with Venus in the one case, in other with Saturn; the remaining periods with the other planets in descending order. The years of each period are distributed equally between the seven planets, the first seventh belonging exclusively to the chronocrator of the period, the second to it in partnership with the planet next below it, and so on.[3]

Bonatti, in his *Liber Astronomae*, written sometime after 1282 CE, states:

The Ancient wise men considered certain years in nativities which are not called major nor middle not even minor but they called them the years of the Firdaria, that is, disposed years. For each planet disposes its own part of the life of the native according to its part of the years of the Firdaria in this method. Whatever kind of nativity it is, the disposition of the years of the Firdaria begins from the luminary whose authority it is and that luminary disposes the life of the native according to the quantity of its years of the Firdaria, however not without the participation of the other planets. [4]

So the orders of the planets and the number of years of each are as follows:

Diurnal	Nocturnal
Sun = 10 years	Moon = 9 years
Venus = 8 years	Saturn = 11 years
Mercury = 13 years	Jupiter = 12 years
Moon = 9 years	Mars = 7 years
Saturn = 11 years	Sun = 10 years
Jupiter = 12 years	Venus = 8 years
Mars = 7 years	Mercury = 30 years
North Node = 3 years	North Node = 3 years
South Node = 2 years	South Node = 2 years

The sum of one series of years of Firdaria is seventy-five and if one lives longer than seventy-five, then the disposition begins again.

This sequence follows the Chaldean order of the planets, based on how fast the planets move: Moon, Mercury, Venus, Sun, Mars, Jupiter, Saturn. From that fundamental rhythm we gain the order of the Firdaria. Linking the Chaldean order of the planets into the days of the week - Moon (Monday), Mars (Tuesday), Mercury (Wednesday), Jupiter (Thursday), Venus (Friday), Saturn (Saturday), Sun (Sunday) - produces a seven pointed star.

The Nodes

All ancient written sources say that the Nodes should always be placed at the end of the sequence, whether the chart is diurnal or nocturnal and for all diurnal charts there is no debate that the Nodes fit into this arrangement. All ancient written sources also state that the Nodes come at the end of the sequence for a nocturnal birth and when the Firdaria are set up as a table, this seems logical. In spite of this, Robert Zoller posits that this is in error and goes on to emphasise that if the planets are placed in the circle, then the Nodes rightfully come between Mars and the Sun.

The deciding factor to this argument is whether one works with the circle (Zoller's method) and recognises the inherent measure and cadence of life or follows the more linear, table-based method of Al-Biruni. Acknowledging Zoller's work as an empirical medieval astrologer and recognising the nature of the circle as reflecting the days of the week and the inherent cadence and measure of the Moon, then one would be drawn towards Zoller's method. Indeed, in working with clients, I have had better results using Zoller's method than the other.

Once the order has been established, then each period is divided into seven subdivisions, each one-seventh of the number of years the ruler rules, with the nodes giving the number of years without any subdivision:

Diurnal	Nocturnal
Sun	Moon
Sun-Venus	Moon-Saturn
Sun-Mercury	Moon-Jupiter
Sun-Moon	Moon-Mars
Sun-Saturn	Moon-Sun
Sun-Jupiter	Moon-Venus
Sun-Mars	Moon-Mercury
Venus	Saturn
Venus-Mercury	Saturn-Jupiter
Venus-Moon	Saturn-Mars
Venus-Saturn	Saturn-Sun
Venus-Jupiter	Saturn-Venus
Venus-Mars	Saturn-Mercury
Venus-Sun	Saturn-Moon
Mercury	Jupiter
Mercury-Moon... and so on	Jupiter-Mars... and so on

FIRDARIA (Nodal Variation)								
☽	23 Nov 1957	0.0	☉ / ☿	1 Oct 2004	46.9	♄ / ☽	28 Apr 2051	93.4
☽ / ♄	7 Mar 1959	1.3	☉ / ☽	6 Mar 2006	48.3	♃	22 Nov 2052	95.0
☽ / ♃	19 Jun 1960	2.6	☉ / ♄	10 Aug 2007	49.7	♃ / ♂	10 Aug 2054	96.7
☽ / ♂	1 Oct 1961	3.9	☉ / ♃	13 Jan 2009	51.1	♃ / ☉	27 Apr 2056	98.4
☽ / ☉	14 Jan 1963	5.1	☉ / ♂	19 Jun 2010	52.6	♃ / ♀	13 Jan 2058	100.1
☽ / ♀	27 Apr 1964	6.4	♀	23 Nov 2011	54.0	♃ / ☿	1 Oct 2059	101.9
☽ / ☿	10 Aug 1965	7.7	♀ / ☿	13 Jan 2013	55.1	♃ / ☽	18 Jun 2061	103.6
♄	23 Nov 1966	9.0	♀ / ☽	6 Mar 2014	56.3	♃ / ♄	6 Mar 2063	105.3
♄ / ♃	19 Jun 1968	10.6	♀ / ♄	28 Apr 2015	57.4	♂	21 Nov 2064	107.0
♄ / ♂	14 Jan 1970	12.1	♀ / ♃	18 Jun 2016	58.6	♂ / ☉	22 Nov 2065	108.0
♄ / ☉	11 Aug 1971	13.7	♀ / ♂	10 Aug 2017	59.7	♂ / ♀	22 Nov 2066	109.0
♄ / ♀	7 Mar 1973	15.3	♀ / ☉	1 Oct 2018	60.9	♂ / ☿	22 Nov 2067	110.0
♄ / ☿	1 Oct 1974	16.9	☿	23 Nov 2019	62.0	♂ / ☽	21 Nov 2068	111.0
♄ / ☽	27 Apr 1976	18.4	☿ / ☽	1 Oct 2021	63.9	♂ / ♄	22 Nov 2069	112.0
♃	22 Nov 1977	20.0	☿ / ♄	10 Aug 2023	65.7	♂ / ♃	22 Nov 2070	113.0
♃ / ♂	10 Aug 1979	21.7	☿ / ♃	18 Jun 2025	67.6	☊	22 Nov 2071	114.0
♃ / ☉	28 Apr 1981	23.4	☿ / ♂	28 Apr 2027	69.4	☋	22 Nov 2074	117.0
♃ / ♀	14 Jan 1983	25.1	☿ / ☉	6 Mar 2029	71.3	☉	21 Nov 2076	119.0
♃ / ☿	1 Oct 1984	26.9	☿ / ♀	13 Jan 2031	73.1	☉ / ♀	27 Apr 2078	120.4
♃ / ☽	19 Jun 1986	28.6	☽	22 Nov 2032	75.0	☉ / ☿	1 Oct 2079	121.9
♃ / ♄	6 Mar 1988	30.3	☽ / ♄	6 Mar 2034	76.3	☉ / ☽	6 Mar 2081	123.3
♂	22 Nov 1989	32.0	☽ / ♃	19 Jun 2035	77.6	☉ / ♄	9 Aug 2082	124.7
♂ / ☉	23 Nov 1990	33.0	☽ / ♂	30 Sep 2036	78.9	☉ / ♃	13 Jan 2084	126.1
♂ / ♀	23 Nov 1991	34.0	☽ / ☉	13 Jan 2038	80.1	☉ / ♂	18 Jun 2085	127.6
♂ / ☿	22 Nov 1992	35.0	☽ / ♀	28 Apr 2039	81.4	♀	22 Nov 2086	129.0
♂ / ☽	22 Nov 1993	36.0	☽ / ☿	9 Aug 2040	82.7	♀ / ☿	13 Jan 2088	130.1
♂ / ♄	22 Nov 1994	37.0	♄	22 Nov 2041	84.0	♀ / ☽	6 Mar 2089	131.3
♂ / ♃	23 Nov 1995	38.0	♄ / ♃	19 Jun 2043	85.6	♀ / ♄	27 Apr 2090	132.4
☊	22 Nov 1996	39.0	♄ / ♂	13 Jan 2045	87.1	♀ / ♃	18 Jun 2091	133.6
☋	23 Nov 1999	42.0	♄ / ☉	10 Aug 2046	88.7	♀ / ♂	9 Aug 2092	134.7
☉	22 Nov 2001	44.0	♄ / ♀	6 Mar 2048	90.3			
☉ / ♀	28 Apr 2003	45.4	♄ / ☿	1 Oct 2049	91.9			

The Firdaria table shown above has been generated for "Xena" (see Chapter 4) using Solar Fire v.5.

Meaning

The great joy of the Firdaria is, as Zoller says, "they represent a kind of astrological method of forecasting in which an underlying pattern common to all those with their diurnal or nocturnal natal figures is made individual through the condition and determination of the several planets in their natal figure." [5] So whilst all diurnal charts will begin with the Sun period, the condition of the Sun in the natal chart by house, sign, rulership and aspects will tell you how the individual will experience that period of their life. It will also govern the transits a person is having in that period of time. So for example, if a person has a major Jupiter transit and they are in their Saturn Firdaria and the Saturn is in detriment in a cadent house and ruling a cadent house, then Jupiter is not going to be as benefic as one would normally expect it to be. However, if they are having a major Saturn transit and they are not in their Saturn Firdaria or any Saturn sub-period, then the Saturn will not necessarily be as forceful or as strong. The quality of the nodal period depends on the dispositor of the particular node and whether there are planets conjunct it or at the Bends.

A change of Firdaria makes as big an impact on the person's life as their progressed Sun changing signs. It represents a new world view for the individual and this impacts upon and colours the years in which they are in that Firdaria. This does not apply to changes of the sub-periods within the Firdaria which act more as gear shifts within the major theme, expressing the motif through the planet or luminary. The long period ruler will always have dominion.

Robert Hand in his workshop on Planetary Periods at the Australis '97 Conference (Adelaide, Australia, January 1997) discussed Firdaria in terms of Form and Matter, that great foundation stone upon which ancient Greek philosophy is based. He suggested that the long period ruler is the Matter from which the short period ruler takes Form. As milk (the matter) can be made into butter, cheese or yoghurt (the form), so then the matter of Saturn in a Saturn-Jupiter sub-period will take on a Jupiterian form. The person may see benefit and growth (Jupiter, the form) through their labour and toil (Saturn, the matter), a job promotion with a great deal of responsibility or an overseas trip with a focus on business. In a Saturn-Mercury sub-period, the person may be exerting hard work and industry (Saturn, the matter) in writing a book (Mercury, the form). They may also as easily be fighting a court case, depending on the natal placement of the planets involved, the condition of the planets in the chart and the given history of the client.

However, I prefer to think of it the way Australian aboriginal teacher Bobby McLeod put it to Robert Lawlor in Sean Kane's *The Wisdom of the Mythtellers*.[6] While walking through downtown Sydney, McLeod noted to Lawlor how white people's mentality believed that the tall buildings were the results of the dreams and plans of architects, engineers and builders. Some would say that the matter of the stones and brick had taken form as buildings. However, from the Aboriginal perspective, the stones and bricks themselves contain an inner potential, "a dreaming to become a structure". In a Saturn-Mercury sub-period then, for example, hard work and words have the dreaming to become a published work. Kane sums this up in the story of the Haida Raven epic which includes a description of the creation of a world for the gods. The Raven flies up to the boundary of the sky and pushing through it, finds himself amongst the world of the Sky People. He does this by dreaming into it:

> And then he flew right up against it.
> He pushed his mind through
> And pulled his body after. [7]

Knowing one's Firdaria means one can become conscious of what the dreaming anticipates.

*   *   *

Endnotes

1. ibn Ezra, Abraham. *The Beginning of Wisdom*, trans. Raphael Levy (1939), Baltimore.
2. Abu Ma'shar. *The Abbreviation of the Introduction to Astrology*, ed. and trans. Charles Burnett). ARHAT, 1994, p.50.
3. Al-Biruni. *The Book of Instruction in the Elements of the Art of Astrology*, trans. R. Ramsay Wright. (1934) London: British Museum, p.239.
4. Zoller, Robert. (1981) *Tools and Techniques of the Medieval Astrologer*. Robert Zoller, p.73.
5. ibid. p. 76.
6. Kane, Sean. (1998) *The Wisdom of the Mythtellers*. Ontario: Broadview Press, p 252.
7. ibid. p.105.

Appendix 2

Secondary Progressed Lunation Cycle

One of the most important predictive tools that an astrologer can have in their tool kit is an understanding of the Secondary Progressed Lunation Cycle, first brought to the attention of astrologers through the work of Dane Rudhyar, one of the key figures in restoring cycles to late twentieth century astrology. In the same way that the synodic cycle of the Sun and the Moon will cause lunar phasing to occur over a 29.5 day period, so the same lunar phasing will occur when the Secondary Progressed Sun makes a synodic relationship with the Secondary Progressed Moon but now covering a 29.5 year period. (Secondary Progressions are based on the day-for-a-year formula where the movement of the planets over the course of a day represents the movement of the Progressed planets over the course of a year. With a day of movement in the ephemeris equal to a year of life, it easy to see that the most commonly used bodies are the luminaries and the faster moving planets, Mercury, Venus and Mars, for the movement of the planets from Jupiter outwards over the course of ninety days or so is only going to represent, in some instances, a few degrees of movement from the natal position.) On an average, a person can expect to experience two or three complete Secondary Progressed Lunation cycles in their life, with each Secondary Progressed New Moon occurring in consecutive signs and houses. The Secondary Progressed Lunation Cycle predicts not so much particular events but the seasons of one's life, the ebb and flow of energy, and indicates times when it is appropriate for a client to push forward with their dreams and make them a reality and times when it is appropriate to withdraw. The meanings of the Secondary Progressed Lunation Phase are as follows:

New Moon
This is the first flicker, the thin sliver of the emergent New Moon, the beginning of the cycle when the full potential, range and possibility of what is being offered and developed over the next twenty-nine or so years lies ahead of the person. The New Moon phase (the Secondary Progressed Sun conjunct the Secondary Progressed Moon) will begin at a particular degree of the zodiac,

thus its unfoldment can be described by the house and sign in which it is placed, as well as whether this degree is conjunct, square or opposition to a natal luminary, planet or Node (within an orb of up to 8°). This is a time when new ideas are being planted and watered. If this occurs when the person is young, or even later in life when they may still refuse to take responsibility for their actions, then they usually have no idea of what they are establishing and may not like what comes to fruition some fifteen or so years later. As the person matures and gains in awareness, the more conscious they can be of what it is they are setting in motion and how they want that to unfold in time, the better the results will be as the years pass. It is in the New Moon phase that the person can lay down fresh ideas and plans and, whilst they are often accompanied by a large degree of vulnerability, for all is possible and nothing is yet substantial, the thrust and drive of life at this time is to begin new projects.

Crescent Moon

This is the classic crescent shape of the Moon that occurs in the evening sky and represents emergence. In this time period the new direction of life starts to become visible and apparent to other people, taking a greater importance on the stage of a person's life. The person wants to make themselves heard and felt in the world, yet needs a steady guiding hand and constant feedback on their endeavours, for this is the waxing, growing phase of the cycle and the focus of the energy is towards learning and new information.

First Quarter Moon

This is the classic half-moon shape that occurs in the evening sky and represents a period of active growth. The person is putting down roots and starting to gain strength in the area in which they want to achieve. They will be invigorated by the challenges of life and ready to press forward with their ideas, eager for people to see what they are doing and to take notice of them. This is a time to take risks for even though it is the waxing phase of the cycle when the energy is young and vulnerable, it embraces the dynamics of the square and so the person is willing to take appropriate action to make this happen.

Gibbous Moon

This is the illuminated convex shape that is greater than a semicircle and less than a circle that occurs in the evening sky and represents expression. In this period of time the person is working with the energy, appreciating its possibilities and integrating it into their life. Now confident of where they are headed, they are required to have faith that they have all the resources they need to convey their ideas to others, even if faced with obstacles and setbacks. This is a time of articulation, of fine-tuning and focusing the energy with which they have been working for the last several years and giving it a voice.

Full Moon
This is the classic full-moon shape that occurs in the evening sky and represents the fullness, the climax of the cycle. Now it becomes clear exactly what has been planted at the New Moon phase, anything from a rich harvest to a field of weeds. At this time the person is required to work diligently in order to harvest what has been produced. Hanging on until the situation gets better is illogical, for no amount of waiting or further input will make the situation better. The fruit is ripe on the tree and needs to be picked. In many respects this phase is the mirror image of the Balsamic phase containing the same process of letting go of data, goods, people and sometimes places which are no longer useful in one's life. However, unlike the Balsamic phase, these extraneous items are removed so they can be replaced with better resources. The Full Moon phase is an active, assertive time, full of hard work and industry. It clearly and precisely shows a person where they have placed a glass ceiling in their lives and at the same time offers them the opportunity to change that ceiling into a floor so it can be used as a springboard into the waning, productive part of the cycle.

Disseminating Moon
This is the hump shape that occurs in the late evening and/or the small hours of the morning sky and represents a synthesis and dissemination of one's resources. In this waning part of the cycle, the climax has been reached, the reaping is now complete and the season has changed. In the same way that gathered fruit must be bottled or stored or harvested wheat must be threshed and turned into flour, so this is the time to amalgamate the person's entire expertise which has now reached its peak and transform it in some way. This is done through the dissemination of information, either to a group of people or to the community at large, scattering seeds as widely as possible so that the greatest growth may take place. People will often change jobs in this phase, realising that the challenges they sought are no longer contained in their work, for this is the waning part of the cycle when growth has stopped and change from one form into another occurs.

Third Quarter Moon

This is the classic half-moon shape that occurs in the small hours of the morning sky and represents productivity. The bottled fruit is now ready to be opened; the results of one's toil are ready to be savoured. Like the First Quarter Moon, this is a time of hard work and activity. However, as this is the waning square, wisdom learned from earlier parts of the cycle can be used to organize old skills differently. If original ideas enter the system, they will reshape earlier issues, rather than open up new paths of exploration.

Balsamic Moon

This is the last arc of reflected sun, the thin sliver of the dying moon in the pre-dawn light, and represents release. This the old cycle passing, the tree hibernating, the wave pulling back from the shore. Now the person enters astrological winter and as the light that is reflected onto the Moon by the Sun seems to disappear under this geometrical relationship, so their rules of how to engage with the world that have functioned for the last twenty-seven or so years fade, also. This is the period of shedding and releasing, letting go of that which is no longer useful. Now the cosmic sieve goes through the person's life, paring it back to the essence, not the skills and abilities developed as resources, nor their understanding of their own failings which hopefully have become strengths but the focused participation with the material world. For this phase is about clearing the way for new incoming energy in several year's time which builds on the understandings of this last cycle. For most people the cycle closes in the same house and sign as that which in which it began. This can be the most difficult lunar phase of all, since we are taught Replacement Theory. However, learning to let go, learning to allow things to leave one's life without substitute, can be the most rewarding of lessons to learn, for if we are not willing to learn this lesson and release with grace, the cosmos has a way of doing it for us.

SUMMARY:

New Moon	Moon is 0° - 45° ahead of the Sun
Crescent Moon	Moon is 45° - 90° ahead of the Sun
First Quarter Moon	Moon is 90° - 135° ahead of the Sun
Gibbous Moon	Moon is 135° - 180° ahead of the Sun
Full Moon	Moon is 180° - 225° ahead of the Sun
Disseminating Moon	Moon is 225° - 270° ahead of the Sun
Third Quarter Moon	Moon is 270° - 315° ahead of the Sun
Balsamic Moon	Moon is 315° - 360° ahead of the Sun

Secondary Progressed Lunation Cycle
The visuals of the Moon shown here are for the northern hemisphere.

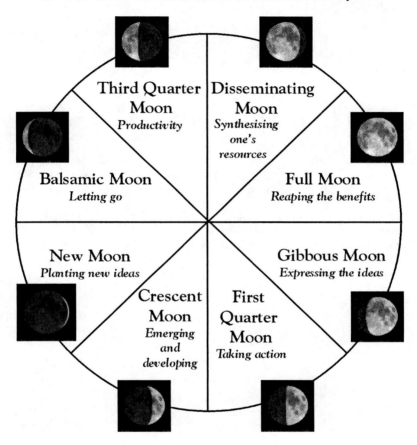

http://tycho.usno.navy.mil/vphase.html - accessed 11th November, 2002.

Appendix 3
Ephemeris 1900-2050 for Chiron, Pholus and Nessus

Positions given are for the beginning of the month at 0 hours Universal time (UT, previously GMT). Please be aware of the possibility of interpolation errors due to the wide steps of the ephemeris, especially for sign changes.

	⚷	⯛	⯜
January 1900	18 Sagittarius 53	5 Cancer 03 ℞	10 Pisces 18
March	24 Sagittarius 06	2 Cancer 08	12 Pisces 12
May	24 Sagittarius 27 ℞	5 Cancer 23	14 Pisces 08
July	20 Sagittarius 31 ℞	13 Cancer 34	14 Pisces 34 ℞
September	19 Sagittarius 00	21 Cancer 21	13 Pisces 13 ℞
November	22 Sagittarius 27	25 cancer 22	11 Pisces 46 ℞
January 1901	28 Sagittarius 43	23 Cancer 07 ℞	11 Pisces 59
March	4 Capricorn 05	19 Cancer 08 ℞	13 Pisces 49
May	5 Capricorn 15 ℞	20 Cancer 37	15 Pisces 45
July	1 Capricorn 48 ℞	27 Cancer 56	16 Pisces 13 ℞
September	29 Sagittarius 31 ℞	6 Leo 02	14 Pisces 56 ℞
November	1 Capricorn 52	11 Leo 27	13 Pisces 29 ℞
January 1902	7 Capricorn 28	10 Leo 52 ℞	13 Pisces 37
March	12 Capricorn 50	6 Leo 30 ℞	15 Pisces 23
May	14 Capricorn 37 ℞	6 Leo 07	17 Pisces 18
July	11 Capricorn 43 ℞	12 Leo 05	17 Pisces 50 ℞
September	8 Capricorn 58 ℞	20 Leo 02	16 Pisces 53 ℞
November	10 Capricorn 22	26 Leo 24	15 Pisces 08 ℞
January 1903	15 Capricorn 20	27 Leo 27 ℞	15 Pisces 12
March	20 Capricorn 36	23 Leo 35 ℞	16 Pisces 54
May	22 Capricorn 49 ℞	21 Leo 25	18 Pisces 49
July	20 Capricorn 28 ℞	25 Leo 45	19 Pisces 24 ℞
September	17 Capricorn 28 ℞	3 Virgo 08	18 Pisces 12 ℞
November	18 Capricorn 06	9 Virgo 56	16 Pisces 44 ℞
January 1904	22 Capricorn 26	12 Virgo 21 ℞	16 Pisces 45
March	27 Capricorn 32	9 Virgo 08 ℞	18 Pisces 23
May	0 Aquarius 07	5 Virgo 59 ℞	20 Pisces 24
July	28 Capricorn 16 ℞	8 Virgo 39	20 Pisces 54 ℞
September	25 Capricorn 09 ℞	15 Virg0 10	19 Pisces 46 ℞
November	28 Capricorn 08	22 Virgo 01	8 Pisces 18 ℞
January 1905	28 Capricorn 59	25 Virgo 23	18 Pisces 16
March	3 Aquarius 53	23 Virgo 06 ℞	19 Pisces 52
May	6 Aquarius 37	19 Virgo 27 ℞	21 Pisces 45
July	5 Aquarius 13 ℞	20 Virgo 36	22 Pisces 22 ℞
September	2 Aquarius 06 ℞	26 Virgo 10	21 Pisces 16 ℞
November	1 Aquarius 38	2 Libra 45	19 Pisces 48 ℞
January 1906	4 Aquarius 55	6 Libra 39	19 Pisces 43

March	9 Aquarius 36	5 Libra 18 ℞	21 Pisces 16
May	12 Aquarius 32	1 Libra 30 ℞	23 Pisces 08
July	11 Aquarius 33 ℞	1 Libra 22	23 Pisces 48 ℞
September	8 Aquarius 30 ℞	5 Libra 54	22 Pisces 44 ℞
November	7 Aquarius 36	12 Libra 04	21 Pisces 16 ℞
January 1907	10 Aquarius 24	16 Libra 18	21 Pisces 08
March	14 Aquarius 53	15 Libra 46 ℞	22 Pisces 38
May	17 Aquarius 57	12 Libra 06 ℞	24 Pisces 29
July	17 Aquarius 21 ℞	11 Libra 00	25 Pisces 12 ℞
September	14 Aquarius 23 ℞	14 Libra 34	24 Pisces 11 ℞
November	13 Aquarius 09	20 Libra 13	22 Pisces 43 ℞
January 1908	15 Aquarius 31	24 Libra 34	22 Pisces 32
March	19 Aquarius 48	24 Libra 41 ℞	23 Pisces 58
May	23 Aquarius 06	21 Libra 02 ℞	25 Pisces 56
July	22 Aquarius 42 ℞	19 Libra 31	26 Pisces 34 ℞
September	19 Aquarius 52 ℞	22 Libra 14	25 Pisces 35 ℞
November	18 Aquarius 20	27 Libra 22	24 Pisces 07 ℞
January 1909	20 Aquarius 23	1 Scorpio 46	23 Pisces 54
March	24 Aquarius 28	2 Scorpio 17 ℞	25 Pisces 19
May	27 Aquarius 56	28 Libra 41 ℞	27 Pisces 22
July	27 Aquarius 39 ℞	27 Libra 04	27 Pisces 53 ℞
September	24 Aquarius 56 ℞	29 Libra 07	26 Pisces 56 ℞
November	23 Aquarius 14 ℞	3 Scorpio 45	25 Pisces 28 ℞
January 1910	24 Aquarius 55	7 Scorpio 59	25 Pisces 13
March	28 Aquarius 48	8 Scorpio 53 ℞	26 Pisces 35
May	2 Pisces 04	6 Scorpio 12 ℞	28 Pisces 24
July	2 Pisces 20 ℞	3 Scorpio 44 ℞	29 Pisces 11 ℞
September	29 Aquarius 46 ℞	5 Scorpio 10	28 Pisces 16 ℞
November	27 Aquarius 52 ℞	9 Scorpio 20	26 Pisces 49 ℞
January 1911	29 Aquarius 14	13 Scorpio 27	26 Pisces 32
March	2 Pisces 55	14 Scorpio 37 ℞	27 Pisces 51
May	6 Pisces 14	12 Scorpio 16 ℞	29 Pisces 39
July	6 Pisces 45 ℞	9 Scorpio 38 ℞	00 Aries 28 ℞
September	4 Pisces 21 ℞	10 Scorpio 34	29 Pisces 35 ℞
November	2 Pisces 18 ℞	14 Scorpio 18	28 Pisces 08 ℞
January 1912	3 Pisces 21	18 Scorpio 17	27 Pisces 48
March	6 Pisces 52	19 Scorpio 39 ℞	29 Pisces 05
May	10 Pisces 24	17 Scorpio 21 ℞	1 Aries 00
July	10 Pisces 58 ℞	14 Scorpio 55 ℞	1 Aries 43 ℞
September	8 Pisces 43 ℞	15 Scorpio 26	0 Aries 53 ℞
November	6 Pisces 33 ℞	18 Scorpio 46	29 Pisces 26 ℞
January 1913	7 Pisces 22	22 Scorpio 39	29 Pisces 04
March	10 Pisces 43	24 Scorpio 07 ℞	0 Aries 19
May	14 Pisces 04	22 Scorpio 19 ℞	2 Aries 06
July	14 Pisces 59 ℞	19 Scorpio 37 ℞	2 Aries 57 ℞
September	12 Pisces 53 ℞	19 Scorpio 51	2 Aries 08 ℞
November	10 Pisces 38 ℞	22 Scorpio 53	0 Aries 42 ℞
January 1914	11 Pisces 12	26 Scorpio 32	0 Aries 19

March	14 Pisces 23	28 Scorpio 07 ℞	1 Aries 31
May	17 Pisces 45	26 Scorpio 33 ℞	3 Aries 17
July	18 Pisces 53 ℞	23 Scorpio 52 ℞	4 Aries 10 ℞
September	16 Pisces 56 ℞	23 Scorpio 49	3 Aries 24 ℞
November	14 Pisces 36 ℞	26 Scorpio 33	1 Aries 58 ℞
January **1915**	14 Pisces 56	0 Sagittarius 03	1 Aries 32
March	17 Pisces 57	1 Sagittarius 44	2 Aries 42
May	21 Pisces 20	0 Sagittarius 23 ℞	4 Aries 27
July	22 Pisces 39 ℞	27 Scorpio 44 ℞	5 Aries 22 ℞
September	20 Pisces 53 ℞	27 Scorpio 28	4 Aries 38 ℞
November	18 Pisces 28 ℞	29 Scorpio 54	3 Aries 12 ℞
January **1916**	18 Pisces 34	3 Sagittarius 16	2 Aries 44
March	21 Pisces 26	5 Sagittarius 01	3 Aries 52
May	25 Pisces 03	3 Sagittarius 39 ℞	5 Aries 44
July	26 Pisces 20 ℞	1 Sagittarius 16 ℞	6 Aries 33
September	24 Pisces 43 ℞	0 Sagittarius 48	5 Aries 51 ℞
November	22 Pisces 16 ℞	3 Sagittarius 00	4 Aries 26 ℞
January **1917**	22 Pisces 10	6 Sagittarius 17	3 Aries 56
March	24 Pisces 54	8 Sagittarius 02	5 Aries 02
May	28 Pisces 18	7 Sagittarius 00 ℞	6 Aries 46
July	29 Pisces 56 ℞	4 Sagittarius 28 ℞	7 Aries 43
September	28 Pisces 26 ℞	3 Sagittarius 54	7 Aries 02 ℞
November	25 Pisces 57 ℞	5 Sagittarius 55	5 Aries 37 ℞
January **1918**	25 Pisces 41	9 Sagittarius 01	5 Aries 06
March	28 Pisces 16	10 Sagittarius 48	6 Aries 10
May	1 Aries 40	9 Sagittarius 55 ℞	7 Aries 54
July	3 Aries 28	7 Sagittarius 28 ℞	8 Aries 52
September	2 Aries 09 ℞	6 Sagittarius 45	8 Aries 13 ℞
November	29 Pisces 38 ℞	8 Sagittarius 35	6 Aries 48 ℞
January **1919**	29 Pisces 09	11 Sagittarius 33	6 Aries 16
March	1 Aries 35	13 Sagittarius 23	7 Aries 17
May	5 Aries 00	12 Sagittarius 38 ℞	9 Aries 00
July	6 Aries 58	10 Sagittarius 15 ℞	10 Aries 00
September	5 Aries 49 ℞	9 Sagittarius 25	9 Aries 23 ℞
November	3 Aries 16 ℞	11 Sagittarius 04	7 Aries 59 ℞
January **1920**	2 Aries 36	13 Sagittarius 56	7 Aries 24
March	4 Aries 53	15 Sagittarius 47	8 Aries 24
May	8 Aries33	15 Sagittarius 01 ℞	10 Aries 13
July	10 Aries 26	12 Sagittarius 51 ℞	11 Aries s08
September	9 Aries 27 ℞	11 Sagittarius 56	10 Aries 32 ℞
November	6 Aries 54 ℞	13 Sagittarius 25	9 Aries 08 ℞
January **1921**	6 Aries 03	16 Sagittarius 14	8 Aries 32
March	8 Aries 13	18 Sagittarius 04	9 Aries 30
May	11 Aries 38	17 Sagittarius 31 ℞	11 Aries 12
July	13 Aries 54	15 Sagittarius 15 ℞	12 Aries 14
September	13 Aries 03 ℞	14 Sagittarius 18	11 Aries 39 ℞
November	10 Aries 30	15 Sagittarius 40	10 Aries 16 ℞
January **1922**	9 Aries 30	18 Sagittarius 21	9 Aries 39

March	11 Aries 31	20 Sagittarius 12	10 Aries 35
May	14 Aries 57	19 Sagittarius 45 ℞	12 Aries 16
July	17 Aries 22	17 Sagittarius 34 ℞	13 Aries 20
September	16 Aries 42 ℞	16 Sagittarius 32	12 Aries 47 ℞
November	14 Aries 09 ℞	17 Sagittarius 46	11 Aries 24 ℞
January 1923	12 Aries 59	20 Sagittarius 21	10 Aries 45
March	14 Aries 51	22 Sagittarius 13	11 Aries 39
May	18 Aries 16	21 Sagittarius 52 ℞	13 Aries 20
July	20 Aries 52	19 Sagittarius 44 ℞	14 Aries 25
September	20 Aries 24 ℞	18 Sagittarius 39	13 Aries 55 ℞
November	17 Aries 52 ℞	19 Sagittarius 46	12 Aries 32 ℞
January 1924	16 Aries 30	22 Sagittarius 16	11 Aries 51
March	18 Aries 12	24 Sagittarius 08	12 Aries 43
May	21 Aries 55	23 Sagittarius 45 ℞	14 Aries 31
July	24 Aries 24	21 Sagittarius 49 ℞	15 Aries 30
September	24 Aries 08 ℞	20 Sagittarius 40 ℞	15 Aries 02 ℞
November	21 Aries 38 ℞	21 Sagittarius 41	13 Aries 39 ℞
January 1925	20 Aries 06	24 Sagittarius 08	12 Aries 57
March	21 Aries 41	25 Sagittarius 59	13 Aries 48
May	25 Aries 07	25 Sagittarius 46 ℞	15 Aries 28
July	28 Aries 01	23 Sagittarius 46 ℞	16 Aries 35
September	27 Aries 46 ℞	22 Sagittarius 36	16 Aries 01 ℞
November	25 Aries 26 ℞	23 Sagittarius 32	14 Aries 45 ℞
January 1926	23 Aries 46 ℞	25 Sagittarius 53	14 Aries 02
March	25 Aries 11	27 Sagittarius 45	14 Aries 52
May	28 Aries 37	27 Sagittarius 36 ℞	16 Aries 31
July	1 Taurus 42	25 Sagittarius 39 ℞	17 Aries 40
September	1 Taurus 49 ℞	24 Sagittarius 27 ℞	17 Aries 14 ℞
November	29 Aries 24 ℞	25 Sagittarius 17 ℞	15 Aries 52 ℞
January 1927	27 Aries 33 ℞	27 Sagittarius 34	15 Aries 07
March	28 Aries 47	29 Sagittarius 26	15 Aries 55
May	2 Taurus 12	29 Sagittarius 21 ℞	17 Aries34
July	5 Taurus 29	27 Sagittarius 28 ℞	18 Aries 44
September	5 Taurus 51 ℞	26 Sagittarius 13 ℞	18 Aries 20 ℞
November	3 Taurus 29 ℞	26 Sagittarius 58	16 Aries 58 ℞
January 1928	1 Taurus 27 ℞	29 Sagittarius 11	16 Aries 12 ℞
March	2 Taurus 30	1 Capricorn 03	16 Aries 58
May	6 Taurus 14	0 Capricorn 56 ℞	18 Aries 44
July	9 Taurus 24	29 Sagittarius 12 ℞	19 Aries 48
September	10 Taurus 00 ℞	27 Sagittarius 56 ℞	19 Aries 26 ℞
November	7 Taurus 45 ℞	28 Sagittarius 36	18 Aries 05 ℞
January 1929	5 Taurus 31 ℞	0 Capricorn 47	17 Aries 17 ℞
March	6 Taurus 25	2 Capricorn 38	18 Aries 02
May	9 Taurus 50	2 Capricorn 38 ℞	19 Aries 41
July	13 Taurus 29	0 Capricorn 51 ℞	20 Aries 53
September	14 Taurus 19 ℞	29 Sagittarius 34 ℞	20 Aries 31 ℞
November	12 Taurus 09 ℞	0 Capricorn 12	19 Aries 10 ℞
January 1930	9 Taurus 46 ℞	2 Capricorn 18	18 Aries 22 ℞

March	10 Taurus 27	4 Capricorn 09	19 Aries 05
May	13 Taurus 51	4 Capricorn 13 Rx	20 Aries 43
July	17 Taurus 43	2 Capricorn 28 Rx	21 Aries 56
September	18 Taurus 51 Rx	1 Capricorn 10 Rx	21 Aries37 Rx
November	16 Taurus 49 Rx	1 Capricorn 43	20 Aries 17 Rx
January 1931	14 Taurus 16 Rx	3 Capricorn 45	19 Aries 27 Rx
March	14 Taurus 42	5 Capricorn 37	20 Aries 08
May	18 Taurus 03	5 Capricorn 44 Rx	21 Aries 45
July	22 Taurus 09	4 Capricorn 03 Rx	23 Aries 00
September	23 Taurus 37 Rx	2 Capricorn 43 Rx	22 Aries 43 Rx
November	21 Taurus 46 Rx	3 Capricorn 11	21 Aries 23 Rx
January 1932	19 Taurus 02 Rx	5 Capricorn 11	20 Aries 31 Rx
March	19 Taurus 12	7 Capricorn 02	21 Aries 10
May	22 Taurus 51	7 Capricorn 08 Rx	22 Aries 55
July	26 Taurus 50	5 Capricorn 34 Rx	24 Aries 04
September	28 Taurus 40	4 Capricorn 13 Rx	23 Aries 48 Rx
November	28 Taurus 02 Rx	4 Capricorn 38	22 Aries 29 Rx
January 1933	24 Taurus 05 Rx	6 Capricorn 37	21 Aries 35 Rx
March	24 Taurus 01	8 Capricorn 27	22 Aries 14
May	27 Taurus 18	8 Capricorn 39 Rx	23 Aries 51
July	1 Gemini 51	7 Capricorn 02 Rx	25 Aries 08
September	4 Gemini 03	5 Capricorn 41 Rx	24 Aries 53 Rx
November	2 Gemini 39 Rx	6 Capricorn 04	23 Aries 33 Rx
January 1934	29 Taurus 35 Rx	7 Capricorn 58	22 Aries 40 Rx
March	29 Taurus 10	9 Capricorn 49	23 Aries 17
May	2 Gemini 21	10 Capricorn 04 Rx	24 Aries 53
July	7 Gemini 10	8 Capricorn 30 Rx	26 Aries 12
September	9 Gemini 49	7 Capricorn 07 Rx	25 Aries 59 Rx
November	8 Gemini 46 Rx	7 Capricorn 26	24 Aries 40 Rx
January 1935	5 Gemini 34 Rx	9 Capricorn 18	23 Aries 44 Rx
March	4 Gemini 46	11 Capricorn 09	24 Aries 19
May	7 Gemini 50	11 Capricorn 27 Rx	25 Aries 55
July	12 Gemini 54	9 Capricorn 55 Rx	27 Aries 15
September	16 Gemini 03	8 Capricorn 32 Rx	27 Aries04 Rx
November	15 Gemini 26 Rx	8 Capricorn 48	25 Aries 46 Rx
January 1936	12 Gemini 09 Rx	10 Capricorn 37	29 Aries 49 Rx
March	10 Gemini 55	12 Capricorn 28	25 Aries 22
May	14 Gemini 10	12 Capricorn 45 Rx	27 Aries 06
July	19 Gemini 07	11 Capricorn 19 Rx	28 Aries 19
September	22 Gemini 50	9 Capricorn 55 Rx	28 Aries 10 Rx
November	22 Gemini 47 Rx	10 Capricorn 07	26 Aries 53 Rx
January 1937	19 Gemini 24 Rx	11 Capricorn 56	25 Aries 54 Rx
March	17 Gemini 45	13 Capricorn 47	26 Aries 26
May	20 Gemini 26	14 Capricorn 08 Rx	28 Aries 02
July	26 Gemini 01	12 Capricorn 40 Rx	29 Aries 24
September	0 Cancer 18	11 Capricorn 16 Rx	29 Aries 16 Rx
November	0 Cancer 52 Rx	11 Capricorn 27	27 Aries 58 Rx
January 1938	27 Gemini 37 Rx	13 Capricorn 12	26 Aries 59 Rx

March	25 Gemini 24	15 Capricorn 03	27 Aries 30
May	27 Gemini 44	15 Capricorn 27 ℞	29 Aries 05
July	3 Cancer 32	14 Capricorn 02 ℞	0 Taurus 29
September	8 Cancer 31	12 Capricorn 36 ℞	0 Taurus 23 ℞
November	9 Cancer 56 ℞	12 Capricorn 44	29 Aries05 ℞
January 1939	6 Cancer 55 ℞	14 Capricorn 26	28 Aries 05 ℞
March	4 Cancer 08 ℞	16 Capricorn 18	28 Aries 34
May	5 Cancer 58	16 Capricorn 44 ℞	0 Taurus 09
July	11 Cancer 55	15 Capricorn 22 ℞	1 Taurus 34
September	17 Cancer 36	13 Capricorn 55 ℞	1 Taurus 30 ℞
November	20 Cancer 03 ℞	14 Capricorn 00	0 Taurus 13 ℞
January 1940	17 Cancer 34 ℞	15 Capricorn 40	29 Aries 11 ℞
March	14 Cancer 10 ℞	17 Capricorn 32	29 Aries 38
May	15 Cancer 40	17 Capricorn 58 ℞	1 Taurus 21
July	21 Cancer 18	16 Capricorn 40 ℞	2 Taurus 40
September	27 Cancer 43	15 Capricorn 13 ℞	2 Taurus 38 ℞
November	1 Leo 23	15 Capricorn 15	1 Taurus 22 ℞
January 1941	29 Cancer 41 ℞	16 Capricorn 55	0 Taurus 18 ℞
March	25 Cancer 48 ℞	18 Capricorn 46	0 Taurus 44
May	26 Cancer 10	19 Capricorn 16 ℞	2 Taurus 19
July	2 Leo 00	17 Capricorn 57 ℞	3 Taurus 47
September	9 Leo 04	16 Capricorn 29 ℞	3 Taurus 46 ℞
November	14 Leo 00	16 Capricorn 30	2 Taurus 29 ℞
January 1942	13 Leo 34 ℞	18 Capricorn 07	1 Taurus 25 ℞
March	9 Leo 24 ℞	19 Capricorn 59	1 Taurus 49
May	8 Leo 37	20 Capricorn 31 ℞	3 Taurus 24
July	13 Leo 57	19 Capricorn 14 ℞	4 Taurus 54
September	21 Leo 31	17 Capricorn 45 ℞	4 Taurus 54 ℞
November	27 Leo 48	17 Capricorn 43	3 Taurus 39 ℞
January 1943	29 Leo 04 ℞	19 Capricorn 18	2 Taurus 33 ℞
March	25 Leo 08 ℞	21 Capricorn 10	2 Taurus 55
May	23 Leo 00	21 Capricorn 45 ℞	4 Taurus 29
July	27 Leo 22	20 Capricorn 30 ℞	6 Taurus 01
September	5 Virgo 07	19 Capricorn 01 ℞	6 Taurus 04 ℞
November	12 Virgo 37	18 Capricorn 56	4 Taurus 49 ℞
January 1944	15 Virgo 48 ℞	20 Capricorn 29	3 Taurus 41 ℞
March	12 Virgo 50 ℞	22 Capricorn 22	4 Taurus 01
May	9 Virgo 22 ℞	22 Capricorn 57 ℞	5 Taurus 44
July	12 Virgo 16	21 Capricorn 46 ℞	7 Taurus 08
September	19 Virgo 43	20 Capricorn 16 ℞	7 Taurus 14 ℞
November	28 Virgo 01	20 Capricorn 08	6 Taurus 00 ℞
January 1945	3 Libra 08	21 Capricorn 41	4 Taurus 50 ℞
March	1 Libra 41 ℞	23 Capricorn 34	5 Taurus 09
May	27 Virgo 29 ℞	24 Capricorn 12 ℞	6 Taurus 43
July	28 Virgo 28	23 Capricorn 00 ℞	8 Taurus 18
September	5 Libra 05	21 Capricorn 30 ℞	8 Taurus 24 ℞
November	13 Libra 41	21 Capricorn 21	7 Taurus 10 ℞
January 1946	20 Libra 10	22 Capricorn 52	5 Taurus 59 ℞

March	20 Libra 42 ℞	24 Capricorn 45	6 Taurus 17
May	16 Libra 29 ℞	25 Capricorn 26 ℞	7 Taurus 51
July	15 Libra 21	24 Capricorn 16 ℞	9 Taurus 27
September	20 Libra 32	22 Capricorn 45 ℞	9 Taurus 36 ℞
November	28 Libra 49	22 Capricorn 34	8 Taurus 22 ℞
January 1947	6 Scorpio 13	24 Capricorn 03	7 Taurus 10 ℞
March	8 Scorpio 36 ℞	25 Capricorn 57	7 Taurus 25
May	5 Scorpio 10 ℞	26 Capricorn 40 ℞	8 Taurus 59
July	2 Scorpio 18	25 Capricorn 32 ℞	10 Taurus 37
September	5 Scorpio 41	24 Capricorn 00 ℞	10 Taurus 48 ℞
November	13 Scorpio 09	23 Capricorn 46	9 Taurus 36 ℞
January 1948	20 Scorpio 52	25 Capricorn 13	8 Taurus 22 ℞
March	24 Scorpio 41	27 Capricorn 08	8 Taurus 35
May	22 Scorpio 07 ℞	27 Capricorn 53 ℞	10 Taurus 17
July	18 Scorpio 35 ℞	26 Capricorn 49 ℞	11 Taurus 48
September	20 Scorpio 07	25 Capricorn 16 ℞	12 Taurus 02 ℞
November	26 Scorpio 26	24 Capricorn 59	10 Taurus 50 ℞
January 1949	4 Sagittarius 07	26 Capricorn 26	9 Taurus 34 ℞
March	8 Sagittarius 46	28 Capricorn 21	9 Taurus 46
May	7 Sagittarius 46 ℞	29 Capricorn 08 ℞	11 Taurus 20
July	3 Sagittarius 33 ℞	28 Capricorn 03 ℞	13 Taurus 02
September	3 Sagittarius 35	26 Capricorn 30 ℞	13 Taurus 16 ℞
November	8 Sagittarius 39	26 Capricorn 13	12 Taurus 05 ℞
January 1950	15 Sagittarius 46	26 Capricorn 37	10 Taurus 48 ℞
March	20 Sagittarius 57	29 Capricorn 33	10 Taurus 58
May	21 Sagittarius 05 ℞	0 Aquarius 23 ℞	12 Taurus 31
July	13 Sagittarius 01 ℞	29 Capricorn 20 ℞	14 Taurus 15
September	15 Sagittarius 47	27 Capricorn 46 ℞	14 Taurus 33 ℞
November	19 Sagittarius 35	27 Capricorn 26	13 Taurus 22 ℞
January 1951	26 Sagittarius 06	28 Capricorn 49	12 Taurus 03 ℞
March	1 Capricorn 31	0 Aquarius 46	12 Taurus 11
May	2 Capricorn 31 ℞	1 Aquarius 38 ℞	13 Taurus 44
July	28 Sagittarius 55 ℞	0 Aquarius 38 ℞	15 Taurus 30
September	26 Sagittarius 47	29 Capricorn 03 ℞	15 Taurus 51 ℞
November	29 Sagittarius 26	28 Capricorn 39	14 Taurus 41 ℞
January 1952	5 Capricorn 17	0 Aquarius 01	13 Taurus 21 ℞
March	10 Capricorn 44	1 Aquarius 59	13 Taurus 26
May	12 Capricorn 20 ℞	2 Aquarius 53 ℞	15 Taurus 08
July	9 Capricorn 22 ℞	1 Aquarius 55 ℞	16 Taurus 47
September	6 Capricorn 41 ℞	0 Aquarius 19 ℞	17 Taurus 10 ℞
November	8 Capricorn 20	29 Capricorn 53	16 Taurus 01 ℞
January 1953	13 Capricorn 36	1 Aquarius 15	14 Taurus 38 ℞
March	18 Capricorn 56	3 Aquarius 13	14 Taurus 43
May	21 Capricorn 02 ℞	4 Aquarius 10	16 Taurus 16
July	18 Capricorn 30 ℞	3 Aquarius 12 ℞	18 Taurus 06
September	15 Capricorn 33 ℞	1 Aquarius 36 ℞	18 Taurus 30 ℞
November	16 Capricorn 25	1 Aquarius 08	17 Taurus 22 ℞
January 1954	20 Capricorn 59	2 Aquarius 28	15 Taurus 59 ℞

March	26 Capricorn 10	4 Aquarius 27	16 Taurus 01
May	28 Capricorn 38	4 Aquarius 26	17 Taurus 33
July	26 Capricorn 39 ℞	4 Aquarius 31 ℞	19 Taurus 25
September	23 Capricorn 33 ℞	2 Aquarius 54 ℞	19 Taurus 53 ℞
November	23 Capricorn 44	2 Aquarius 24	18 Taurus 46 ℞
January **1955**	27 Capricorn 42	3 Aquarius 42	17 Taurus 20 ℞
March	2 Aquarius 41	5 Aquarius 42	17 Taurus 20
May	5 Aquarius 26	6 Aquarius 44	18 Taurus 52
July	3 Aquarius 56 ℞	5 Aquarius 51 ℞	20 Taurus 46
September	0 Aquarius 48 ℞	4 Aquarius 13 ℞	4 Taurus 18 ℞
November	0 Aquarius 25	3 Aquarius 40	20 Taurus 11 ℞
January **1956**	3 Aquarius 50	4 Aquarius 56	18 Taurus 44 ℞
March	8 Aquarius 37	6 Aquarius 58	18 Taurus 41
May	11 Aquarius 39	8 Aquarius 03	20 Taurus 22
July	10 Aquarius 31 ℞	7 Aquarius 13 ℞	22 Taurus 09
September	7 Aquarius 25 ℞	5 Aquarius 33 ℞	22 Taurus 44 ℞
November	6 Aquarius 35	4 Aquarius 57	21 Taurus 39 ℞
January **1957**	9 Aquarius 34	6 Aquarius 14	20 Taurus 09 ℞
March	14 Aquarius 08	8 Aquarius 16	20 Taurus 04
May	17 Aquarius 11	9 Aquarius 23	21 Taurus 36
July	16 Aquarius 28 ℞	8 Aquarius 34 ℞	23 Taurus 35
September	13 Aquarius 28 ℞	6 Aquarius 53 ℞	24 Taurus 12 ℞
November	12 Aquarius 19	6 Aquarius 16	23 Taurus 07 ℞
January **1958**	14 Aquarius 50	7 Aquarius 30	21 Taurus 36 ℞
March	19 Aquarius 11	9 Aquarius 35	21 Taurus 29
May	22 Aquarius 20	10 Aquarius 45	23 Taurus 00
July	21 Aquarius 59 ℞	9 Aquarius 58 ℞	25 Taurus 02
September	19 Aquarius 06 ℞	8 Aquarius 16 ℞	25 Taurus 42 ℞
November	17 Aquarius 39	7 Aquarius 36	24 Taurus 40 ℞
January **1959**	19 Aquarius 46	8 Aquarius 49	23 Taurus 07 ℞
March	23 Aquarius 54	10 Aquarius 54	22 Taurus 56
May	27 Aquarius 08	12 Aquarius 08	24 Taurus 26
July	27 Aquarius 06 ℞	11 Aquarius 24 ℞	26 Taurus 31
September	24 Aquarius 22 ℞	9 Aquarius 42 ℞	27 Taurus 16 ℞
November	22 Aquarius 40 ℞	8 Aquarius 58	26 Taurus 15 ℞
January **1960**	24 Aquarius 24	10 Aquarius 09	24 Taurus 39 ℞
March	28 Aquarius 21	12 Aquarius 16	24 Taurus 25
May	1 Pisces 48	13 Aquarius 35	26 Taurus 06
July	1 Pisces 54 ℞	12 Aquarius 52 ℞	28 Taurus 03
September	29 Aquarius 19 ℞	11 Aquarius 09 ℞	28 Taurus 51 ℞
November	27 Aquarius 25 ℞	10 Aquarius 22	28 Taurus 53 ℞
January **1961**	28 Aquarius 52	11 Aquarius 33	26 Taurus 14 ℞
March	2 Pisces 37	13 Aquarius 42	25 Taurus 59
May	5 Pisces 56	15 Aquarius 01	27 Taurus 29
July	6 Pisces 23 ℞	14 Aquarius 22 ℞	29 Taurus 39
September	3 Pisces 57 ℞	12 Aquarius 37 ℞	0 Gemini 30 ℞
November	1 Pisces 56 ℞	11 Aquarius 48	29 Taurus 32 ℞
January **1962**	3 Pisces 04	12 Aquarius 57	27 Taurus 53 ℞

March	6 Pisces 38	15 Aquarius 08	27 Taurus 34
May	9 Pisces 59	16 Aquarius 31	29 Taurus 04
July	10 Pisces 41 ℞	15 Aquarius 55 ℞	1 Gemini 17
September	8 Pisces 24 ℞	15 Aquarius 09 ℞	2 Gemini 13 ℞
November	6 Pisces 15 ℞	13 Aquarius 17	1 Gemini 17 ℞
January **1963**	7 Pisces 06	14 Aquarius 24	29 Taurus 36 ℞
March	10 Pisces 29	16 Aquarius 36	29 Taurus 13
May	13 Pisces 52	18 Aquarius 04	0 Gemini 42
July	14 Pisces 47 ℞	17 Aquarius 31 ℞	2 Gemini 59
September	12 Pisces 40 ℞	15 Aquarius 44 ℞	3 Gemini 59
November	10 Pisces 24 ℞	14 Aquarius 48	3 Gemini 07 ℞
January **1964**	10 Pisces 59	15 Aquarius 53	1 Gemini 23 ℞
March	14 Pisces 12	18 Aquarius 07	0 Gemini 56
May	17 Pisces 48	19 Aquarius 42	2 Gemini 34
July	18 Pisces 43 ℞	19 Aquarius 10 ℞	4 Gemini 44
September	16 Pisces 46 ℞	17 Aquarius 22 ℞	5 Gemini 50
November	14 Pisces 25 ℞	16 Aquarius 22	5 Gemini 00 ℞
January **1965**	14 Pisces 48	17 Aquarius 26	3 Gemini 13 ℞
March	17 Pisces 51	19 Aquarius 43	2 Gemini 44
May	21 Pisces 15	21 Aquarius 18	4 Gemini 12
July	22 Pisces 31 ℞	20 Aquarius 51 ℞	6 Gemini 35
September	20 Pisces 41 ℞	19 Aquarius 01 ℞	7 Gemini 45
November	18 Pisces 18 ℞	17 Aquarius 59	6 Gemini 57 ℞
January **1966**	18 Pisces 27	19 Aquarius 01	5 Gemini 09 ℞
March	21 Pisces 22	21 Aquarius 20	5 Gemini 35
May	24 Pisces 45	23 Aquarius 00	6 Gemini 02
July	26 Pisces 13 ℞	22 Aquarius 37 ℞	8 Gemini 29
September	24 Pisces 33 ℞	20 Aquarius 46 ℞	9 Gemini 45
November	22 Pisces 06 ℞	19 Aquarius 39 ℞	9 Gemini 00 ℞
January **1967**	22 Pisces 03	20 Aquarius 39	7 Gemini 10 ℞
March	24 Pisces 47	23 Aquarius 00	6 Gemini 31
May	28 Pisces 11	24 Aquarius 46	7 Gemini 57
July	29 Pisces 49 ℞	24 Aquarius 28 ℞	10 Gemini 28
September	28 Pisces 20 ℞	22 Aquarius 36 ℞	11 Gemini 50
November	25 Pisces 50 ℞	21 Aquarius 24 ℞	11 Gemini 09 ℞
January **1968**	25 Pisces 34	22 Aquarius 22	9 Gemini 17 ℞
March	28 Pisces 09	24 Aquarius 45	8 Gemini 33
May	1 Aries 48	26 Aquarius 41	10 Gemini 08
July	3 Aries 22	26 Aquarius 23 ℞	12 Gemini 32
September	2 Aries 02 ℞	24 Aquarius 30 ℞	14 Gemini 00
November	29 Pisces 31 ℞	23 Aquarius 14 ℞	13 Gemini 24 ℞
January **1969**	29 Pisces 04	24 Aquarius 10	11 Gemini 28 ℞
March	1 Aries 32	26 Aquarius 36	10 Gemini 41
May	4 Aries 56	28 Aquarius 33	12 Gemini 04
July	6 Aries 52	28 Aquarius 23 ℞	14 Gemini 43
September	5 Aries 40 ℞	26 Aquarius 29 ℞	16 Gemini 17
November	3 Aries 08 ℞	25 Aquarius 08 ℞	15 Gemini 44 ℞
January **1970**	2 Aries 31	26 Aquarius 02	13 Gemini 48 ℞

March	2 Aries 50	28 Aquarius 31	12 Gemini 54
May	8 Aries 14	0 Pisces 34	14 Gemini 15
July	10 Aries 20	0 Pisces 30 ℞	16 Gemini 59
September	9 Aries 18 ℞	28 Aquarius 35 ℞	18 Gemini 41
November	6 Aries 45 ℞	27 Aquarius 09 ℞	18 Gemini 14 ℞
January 1971	5 Aries 57	28 Aquarius 00	16 Gemini 15 ℞
March	8 Aries 07	0 Pisces 31	15 Gemini 15
May	11 Aries 32	2 Pisces 42	16 Gemini 34
July	13 Aries 47	2 Pisces 45 ℞	19 Gemini 22
September	12 Aries 56 ℞	0 Pisces 49 ℞	21 Gemini 12
November	10 Aries 23 ℞	29 Aquarius 17 ℞	20 Gemini 51 ℞
January 1972	9 Aries 24	0 Pisces 04	18 Gemini 51 ℞
March	11 Aries 24	2 Pisces 38	17 Gemini 44
May	15 Aries 05	5 Pisces 04	19 Gemini 11
July	17 Aries 14	5 Pisces 08 ℞	21 Gemini 52
September	16 Aries 35 ℞	3 Pisces 12 ℞	21 Gemini 51
November	14 Aries 02 ℞	1 Pisces 33 ℞	23 Gemini 38 ℞
January 1973	12 Aries 52	2 Pisces 18	21 Gemini 35 ℞
March	14 Aries 46	4 Pisces 56	20 Gemini 23
May	18 Aries 11	7 Pisces 22	21 Gemini 37
July	20 Aries 44	7 Pisces 39 ℞	24 Gemini 34
September	20 Aries 13 ℞	5 Pisces 42 ℞	26 Gemini 41
November	17 Aries 41 ℞	3 Pisces 58 ℞	26 Gemini 34 ℞
January 1974	16 Aries 23	4 Pisces 38	29 Gemini 31 ℞
March	18 Aries 07	7 Pisces 20	23 Gemini 11 ℞
May	21 Aries 32	9 Pisces 55	24 Gemini 21
July	24 Aries 15	10 Pisces 22 ℞	27 Gemini 23
September	23 Aries 56 ℞	8 Pisces 26 ℞	29 Gemini 40
November	21 Aries 25 ℞	6 Pisces 34 ℞	29 Gemini 43 ℞
January 1975	19 Aries 57	7 Pisces 09	29 Gemini 40 ℞
March	21 Aries 31	9 Pisces 54	26 Gemini 12 ℞
May	24 Aries 56	12 Pisces 39	27 Gemini 16
July	27 Aries 49	13 Pisces 18 ℞	0 Cancer 23
September	27 Aries 42 ℞	11 Pisces 23 ℞	2 Cancer 52
November	25 Aries 14 ℞	9 Pisces 22 ℞	3 Cancer 05 ℞
January 1976	27 Aries 35 ℞	9 Pisces 51	1 Cancer 03 ℞
March	25 Aries 00	12 Pisces 39	29 Gemini 26 ℞
May	28 Aries 42	15 Pisces 47	0 Cancer 36
July	1 Taurus 28	16 Pisces 28 ℞	3 Cancer 36
September	1 Taurus 34 ℞	14 Pisces 35 ℞	6 Cancer 16
November	29 Aries 09 ℞	12 Pisces 25 ℞	6 Cancer 42 ℞
January 1977	27 Aries 18 ℞	12 Pisces 48	4 Cancer 39 ℞
March	28 Aries 35	15 Pisces 41	2 Cancer 54 ℞
May	2 Taurus 00	18 Pisces 49	3 Cancer 49
July	5 Taurus 13	19 Pisces 53 ℞	7 Cancer 05
September	5 Taurus 30 ℞	18 Pisces 02 ℞	9 Cancer 58
November	3 Taurus 08 ℞	15 Pisces 43 ℞	10 Cancer 35 ℞
January 1978	1 Taurus 09 ℞	15 Pisces 59	8 Cancer 36 ℞

March	2 Taurus 15	18 Pisces 55	6 Cancer 41 Rx
May	5 Taurus 39	22 Pisces 17	7 Cancer 27
July	9 Taurus 03	23 Pisces 39 Rx	10 Cancer 47
September	9 Taurus 35 Rx	21 Pisces 52 Rx	13 Cancer 54
November	7 Taurus 17 Rx	19 Pisces 23 Rx	14 Cancer 48 Rx
January 1979	5 Taurus 08 Rx	19 Pisces 28	12 Cancer 54 Rx
March	6 Taurus 02	22 Pisces 27	10 Cancer 47 Rx
May	9 Taurus 25	26 Pisces 05	11 Cancer 23
July	13 Taurus 01	27 Pisces 47 Rx	14 Cancer 47
September	13 Taurus 48 Rx	26 Pisces 08 Rx	18 Cancer 08
November	11 Taurus 38 Rx	23 Pisces 28 Rx	19 Cancer 21 Rx
January 1980	9 Taurus 17 Rx	23 Pisces 20	17 Cancer 34 Rx
March	9 Taurus 58	26 Pisces 22	15 Cancer 16 Rx
May	13 Taurus 39	0 Aries 33	15 Cancer 51
July	17 Taurus 08	2 Aries 23	19 Cancer 06
September	18 Taurus 13 Rx	0 Aries 55 Rx	22 Cancer 43
November	16 Taurus 10 Rx	28 Pisces 04 Rx	24 Cancer 17 Rx
January 1981	13 Taurus 38 Rx	27 Pisces 42	22 Cancer 38 Rx
March	14 Taurus 08	0 Aries 47	20 Cancer 10 Rx
May	17 Taurus 29	4 Aries 49	20 Cancer 23
July	21 Taurus 29	7 Aries 32	23 Cancer 51
September	22 Taurus 50 Rx	6 Aries 16 Rx	27 Cancer 44
November	20 Taurus 55 Rx	3 Aries 14 Rx	29 Cancer 39
January 1982	18 Taurus 15 Rx	2 Aries 36	28 Cancer 13 Rx
March	18 Taurus 30	5 Aries 40	25 Cancer 35 Rx
May	21 Taurus 48	10 Aries 13	25 Cancer 32
July	26 Taurus 01	13 Aries 19	28 Cancer 58
September	27 Taurus 43 Rx	12 Aries 25 Rx	3 Leo 07
November	26 Taurus 00 Rx	9 Aries 12 Rx	5 Leo 30
January 1983	23 Taurus 10 Rx	8 Aries 11	4 Leo 22 Rx
March	23 Taurus 07	11 Aries 12	1 Leo 34 Rx
May	26 Taurus 22	16 Aries 06	1 Leo 11
July	0 Gemini 49	19 Aries 53	4 Leo 33
September	2 Gemini 55	19 Aries 28 Rx	8 Leo 58
November	1 Gemini 27 Rx	16 Aries 09 Rx	11 Leo 51
January 1984	28 Taurus 27 Rx	14 Aries 40	11 Leo 07 Rx
March	28 Taurus 05	17 Aries 32	8 Leo 11 Rx
May	1 Gemini 36	23 Aries 13	7 Leo 32
July	5 Gemini 57	27 Aries 20	10 Leo 39
September	8 Gemini 28	27 Aries 37 Rx	15 Leo 20
November	7 Gemini 20 Rx	24 Aries 17 Rx	18 Leo 44
January 1985	4 Gemini 08 Rx	22 Aries 14	18 Leo 28 Rx
March	3 Gemini 29	24 Aries 55	15 Leo 29 Rx
May	6 Gemini 34	0 Taurus 31	14 Leo 21
July	11 Gemini 31	5 Taurus 54	17 Leo 24
September	14 Gemini 28	6 Taurus 59 Rx	22 Leo 18
November	13 Gemini 40 Rx	3 Taurus 48 Rx	26 Leo 14
January 1986	10 Gemini 25 Rx	1 Taurus 09 Rx	26 Leo 33 Rx

March	9 Gemini 22	3 Taurus 25	23 Leo 37 ℞
May	12 Gemini 17	9 Taurus 15	21 Leo 59
July	17 Gemini 29	15 Taurus 34	24 Leo 43
September	20 Gemini 58	17 Taurus 48 ℞	29 Leo 46
November	20 Gemini 40 ℞	15 Taurus 06 ℞	4 Virgo 16
January 1987	17 Gemini 22 ℞	11 Taurus 45 ℞	5 Virgo 17 ℞
March	15 Gemini 51	13 Taurus 20	2 Virgo 33 ℞
May	18 Gemini 33	19 Taurus 15	0 Virgo 25 ℞
July	24 Gemini 00	26 Taurus 28	2 Virgo 41
September	28 Gemini 04	0 Gemini 03	7 Virgo 48
November	28 Gemini 24 ℞	28 Taurus 16 ℞	12 Virgo 50
January 1988	25 Gemini 08 ℞	24 Taurus 18 ℞	14 Virgo 39 ℞
March	23 Gemini 06	24 Taurus 52	12 Virgo 16 ℞
May	25 Gemini 52	1 Gemini 12	9 Virgo 36 ℞
July	1 Cancer 10	8 Gemini 34	11 Virgo 20
September	5 Cancer 52	13 Gemini 36	16 Virgo 22
November	6 Cancer 59 ℞	13 Gemini 11 ℞	21 Virgo 52
January 1989	3 Cancer 51 ℞	8 Gemini 52 ℞	24 Virgo 33
March	1 Cancer 18 ℞	8 Gemini 14	22 Virgo 39 ℞
May	3 Cancer 21	13 Gemini 24	19 Virgo 41 ℞
July	9 Cancer 12	21 Gemini 50	20 Virgo 41
September	14 Cancer 34	28 Gemini 09	25 Virgo 33
November	16 Cancer 34 ℞	29 Gemini 22 ℞	1 Libra 23
January 1990	13 Cancer 50 ℞	25 Gemini 22 ℞	2 Libra 49
March	10 Cancer 42 ℞	23 Gemini 15	3 Libra 39 ℞
May	12 Cancer 09	27 Gemini 19	0 Libra 25 ℞
July	18 Cancer 06	5 Cancer 44	0 Libra 34
September	24 Cancer 11	13 Cancer 06	5 Libra 02
November	27 Cancer 18	16 Cancer 10 ℞	11 Libra 03
January 1991	25 Cancer 16 ℞	13 Cancer 08 ℞	15 Libra 16
March	21 Cancer 34 ℞	9 Cancer 41 ℞	14 Libra 56 ℞
May	22 Cancer 13	12 Cancer 10	11 Libra 39 ℞
July	28 Cancer 05	20 Cancer 02	10 Libra 55
September	4 Leo 52	28 Cancer 02	14 Libra 47
November	9 Leo 15	2 Leo 44	20 Libra 50
January 1992	8 Leo 19 ℞	1 Leo 13 ℞	25 Libra 40
March	4 Leo 14 ℞	26 Cancer 58 ℞	26 Libra 15 ℞
May	4 Leo 05	27 Cancer 57	22 Libra 52 ℞
July	9 Leo 21	4 Leo 24	21 Libra 33
September	16 Leo 43	12 Leo 30	24 Libra 42
November	22 Leo 28	18 Leo 26	0 Scorpio 34
January 1993	23 Leo 00 ℞	18 Leo 34 ℞	5 Scorpio 55
March	18 Leo 54 ℞	14 Leo 16 ℞	7 Scorpio 18 ℞
May	17 Leo 21	13 Leo 13	4 Scorpio 32 ℞
July	22 Leo 11	18 Leo 35	2 Scorpio 17
September	29 Leo 54	26 Leo 21	4 Scorpio 39
November	6 Virgo 53	2 Virgo 57	10 Scorpio 12
January 1994	9 Virgo 13 ℞	4 Virgo 36 ℞	15 Scorpio 44

March	5 Virgo 44 ℞	0 Virgo 51 ℞	17 Scorpio 54 ℞
May	2 Virgo 51 ℞	28 Leo 21	15 Scorpio 40 ℞
July	6 Virgo 25	2 Virgo 01	12 Scorpio 52 ℞
September	14 Virgo 03	9 Virgo 06	14 Scorpio 22
November	22 Virgo 04	15 Virgo 59	19 Scorpio 24
January 1995	26 Virgo 21	18 Virgo 50 ℞	25 Scorpio 02
March	24 Virgo 14 ℞	16 Virgo 01 ℞	27 Scorpio 51
May	20 Virgo 16 ℞	12 Virgo 36 ℞	26 Scorpio 14 ℞
July	22 Virgo 02	14 Virgo 36	23 Scorpio 06 ℞
September	29 Virgo 03	20 Virgo 44	23 Scorpio 45
November	7 Libra 36	27 Virgo 31	28 Scorpio 12
January 1996	13 Libra 35	1 Libra 11	3 Sagittarius 47
March	13 Libra 22 ℞	29 Virgo 23 ℞	7 Sagittarius 05
May	8 Libra 45 ℞	25 Virgo 24 ℞	5 Sagittarius 52 ℞
July	8 Libra 42	26 Virgo 06	2 Sagittarius 51 ℞
September	14 Libra 30	1 Libra 12	2 Sagittarius 43
November	22 Libra 59	7 Libra 39	6 Sagittarius 31
January 1997	0 Scorpio 12	11 Libra 49	12 Sagittarius 00
March	1 Scorpio 50 ℞	10 Libra 50 ℞	15 Sagittarius 36
May	27 Libra 59 ℞	7 Libra 03 ℞	15 Sagittarius 09 ℞
July	25 Libra 47	6 Libra 29	11 Sagittarius 56 ℞
September	29 Libra 59	10 Libra 38	11 Sagittarius 13
November	7 Scorpio 52	16 Libra 36	14 Sagittarius 24
January 1998	15 Scorpio 30	20 Libra 55	19 Sagittarius 32
March	18 Scorpio 46 ℞	20 Libra 40 ℞	23 Sagittarius 22
May	16 Scorpio 00 ℞	17 Libra 06 ℞	23 Sagittarius 26 ℞
July	12 Scorpio 27 ℞	15 Libra 41	20 Sagittarius 22 ℞
September	14 Scorpio 46	18 Libra 53	19 Sagittarius 07
November	21 Scorpio 37	24 Libra 21	21 Sagittarius 40
January 1999	29 Scorpio 18	27 Libra 43	26 Sagittarius 29
March	3 Sagittarius 41	29 Libra 03 ℞	0 Capricorn 26
May	2 Sagittarius 14 ℞	25 Libra 49 ℞	0 Capricorn 58 ℞
J1uly	28 Scorpio 04 ℞	23 Libra 48	28 Sagittarius 07 ℞
September	28 Scorpio 38	26 Libra 12	26 Sagittarius 28
November	4 Sagittarius 13	1 Scorpio 08	28 Sagittarius 25
January 2000	11 Sagittarius 33	5 Scorpio 28	7 Capricorn 52
March	16 Sagittarius 37	6 Scorpio 13 ℞	6 Capricorn 52
May	16 Sagittarius 07 ℞	3 Scorpio 04 ℞	7 Capricorn 40 ℞
July	12 Sagittarius 12 ℞	0 Scorpio 59 ℞	5 Capricorn 12 ℞
September	11 Sagittarius 22	2 Scorpio 42	3 Capricorn 15 ℞
November	15 Sagittarius 38	7 Scorpio 07	4 Capricorn 40
January 2001	22 Sagittarius 31	11 Scorpio 24	8 Capricorn 49
March	27 Sagittarius 52	12 Scorpio 25 ℞	12 Capricorn 46
May	28 Sagittarius 30 ℞	9 Scorpio 52 ℞	13 Capricorn 55 ℞
July	24 Sagittarius 40 ℞	7 Scorpio 19 ℞	11 Capricorn 36 ℞
September	22 Sagittarius 53	8 Scorpio 31	9 Capricorn 29 ℞
November	26 Sagittarius 01	12 Scorpio 31	10 Capricorn 29
January 2002	2 Capricorn 09	16 Scorpio 34	14 Capricorn 14

March	7 Capricorn 36	17 Scorpio 50 ℞	18 Capricorn 08
May	9 Capricorn 00 ℞	15 Scorpio 37 ℞	19 Capricorn 31 ℞
July	5 Capricorn 42 ℞	12 Scorpio 57 ℞	17 Capricorn 29 ℞
September	3 Sagittarius 14 ℞	13 Scorpio 42	15 Capricorn 14 ℞
November	5 Capricorn 17	17 Scorpio 16	15 Capricorn 49
January 2003	10 Capricorn 45	21 Scorpio 10	19 Capricorn 13
March	16 Capricorn 09	22 Scorpio 37 ℞	23 Capricorn 02
May	18 Capricorn 07 ℞	20 Scorpio 42 ℞	24 Capricorn 36 ℞
July	15 Capricorn 23 ℞	17 Scorpio 59 ℞	22 Capricorn 52 ℞
September	12 Capricorn 31 ℞	18 Scorpio 21	20 Capricorn 32 ℞
November	13 Capricorn 40	21 Scorpio 33	20 Capricorn 46
January 2004	18 Capricorn 28	25 Scorpio 18	23 Capricorn 50
March	23 Capricorn 44	26 Scorpio 53 ℞	27 Capricorn 32
May	26 Capricorn 08 ℞	24 Scorpio 59 ℞	29 Capricorn 16 ℞
July	23 Capricorn 57 ℞	22 Scorpio 30 ℞	27 Capricorn 46 ℞
September	20 Capricorn 52 ℞	22 Scorpio 34	25 Capricorn 26 ℞
November	26 Capricorn 17	25 Scorpio 26	25 Capricorn 21
January 2005	25 Capricorn 32	29 Scorpio 05	28 Capricorn 10
March	0 Aquarius 37	0 Sagittarius 43 ℞	1 Aquarius 44
May	3 Aquarius 15	29 Scorpio 14 ℞	3 Aquarius 32
July	1 Aquarius 32 ℞	26 Scorpio 34 ℞	2 Aquarius 15 ℞
September	28 Capricorn 24 ℞	26 Scorpio 26	29 Capricorn 55 ℞
November	38 Capricorn 16	29 Scorpio 02	29 Capricorn 38
January 2006	1 Aquarius 55	2 Sagittarius 29	2 Aquarius 08
March	6 Aquarius 47	4 Sagittarius 11	5 Aquarius 35
May	9 Aquarius 38	2 Sagittarius 55 ℞	7 Aquarius 29
July	8 Aquarius 24 ℞	0 Sagittarius 18 ℞	6 Aquarius 24 ℞
September	5 Aquarius 17 ℞	29 Scorpio 57	4 Aquarius 06 ℞
November	4 Aquarius 39	2 Sagittarius 17	3 Aquarius 36
January 2007	7 Aquarius 46	5 Sagittarius 35	5 Aquarius 50
March	12 Aquarius 26	7 Sagittarius 22	9 Aquarius 09
May	15 Aquarius 27	6 Sagittarius 16 ℞	11 Aquarius 08
July	14 Aquarius 38 ℞	3 Sagittarius 43 ℞	10 Aquarius 15 ℞
September	11 Aquarius 36 ℞	3 Sagittarius 11	8 Aquarius 00 ℞
November	10 Aquarius 33	5 Sagittarius 17	7 Aquarius 18
January 2008	13 Aquarius 12	8 Sagittarius 28	9 Aquarius 18
March	17 Aquarius 39	10 Sagittarius 16	12 Aquarius 30
May	20 Aquarius 55	9 Sagittarius 10 ℞	14 Aquarius 34
July	20 Aquarius 21 ℞	6 Sagittarius 51 ℞	13 Aquarius 48 ℞
September	17 Aquarius 25 ℞	6 Sagittarius 11	11 Aquarius 37 ℞
November	16 Aquarius 03	8 Sagittarius 05	10 Aquarius 46
January 2009	18 Aquarius 21	11 Sagittarius 10	12 Aquarius 35
March	22 Aquarius 34	12 Sagittarius 59	15 Aquarius 40
May	25 Aquarius 46	12 Sagittarius 09 ℞	17 Aquarius 41
July	23 Aquarius 36 ℞	9 Sagittarius 44 ℞	17 Aquarius 06 ℞
September	22 Aquarius 48 ℞	8 Sagittarius 58	14 Aquarius 58 ℞
November	21 Aquarius 13	10 Sagittarius 43	14 Aquarius 02
January 2010	23 Aquarius 06	13 Sagittarius 39	15 Aquarius 38

March	27 Aquarius 08	15 Sagittarius 29	18 Aquarius 35
May	0 Pisces 24	14 Sagittarius 47 ℞	20 Aquarius 38
July	0 Pisces 32 ℞	12 Sagittarius 26 ℞	20 Aquarius 12 ℞
September	27 Aquarius 52 ℞	11 Sagittarius 34	18 Aquarius 08 ℞
November	26 Aquarius 04 ℞	13 Sagittarius 09	17 Aquarius 05
January 2011	27 Aquarius 37	15 Sagittarius 58	18 Aquarius 30
March	1 Pisces 26	17 Sagittarius 49	21 Aquarius 20
May	4 Pisces 45	17 Sagittarius 15 ℞	23 Aquarius 25
July	5 Pisces 09 ℞	14 Sagittarius 58 ℞	23 Aquarius 06 ℞
September	2 Pisces 39 ℞	14 Sagittarius 01	21 Aquarius 06 ℞
November	0 Pisces 40 ℞	15 Sagittarius 26	19 Aquarius 58
January 2012	1 Pisces 54	18 Sagittarius 09	21 Aquarius 13
March	5 Pisces 31	20 Sagittarius 01	23 Aquarius 56
May	9 Pisces 04	19 Sagittarius 24 ℞	26 Aquarius 06
July	9 Pisces 31 ℞	17 Sagittarius 20 ℞	25 Aquarius 50 ℞
September	7 Pisces 12 ℞	16 Sagittarius 18	23 Aquarius 54 ℞
November	5 Pisces 04 ℞	17 Sagittarius 35	22 Aquarius 41 ℞
January 2013	6 Pisces 02	20 Sagittarius 15	23 Aquarius 49
March	9 Pisces 30	22 Sagittarius 06	26 Aquarius 26
May	12 Pisces 51	21 Sagittarius 41 ℞	28 Aquarius 30
July	13 Pisces 40 ℞	19 Sagittarius 32 ℞	28 Aquarius 22 ℞
September	11 Pisces 28 ℞	18 Sagittarius 29	26 Aquarius 31 ℞
November	9 Pisces 16 ℞	19 Sagittarius 40	25 Aquarius 16 ℞
January 2014	9 Pisces 58	22 Sagittarius 12	26 Aquarius 15
March	13 Pisces 15	24 Sagittarius 03	28 Aquarius 46
May	16 Pisces 38	23 Sagittarius 44 ℞	0 Pisces 49
July	17 Pisces 39 ℞	21 Sagittarius 39 ℞	0 Pisces 48 ℞
September	15 Pisces 37 ℞	20 Sagittarius 32 ℞	29 Aquarius 01 ℞
November	13 Pisces 19 ℞	21 Sagittarius 36	27 Aquarius 42 ℞
January 2015	13 Pisces 46	24 Sagittarius 04	28 Aquarius 33
March	16 Pisces 53	25 Sagittarius 55	0 Pisces 58
May	20 Pisces 16	25 Sagittarius 41 ℞	3 Pisces 02
July	21 Pisces 30	23 Sagittarius 40 ℞	3 Pisces 06 ℞
September	19 Pisces 38 ℞	22 Sagittarius 30 ℞	1 Pisces 23 ℞
November	17 Pisces 15 ℞	23 Sagittarius 28	0 Pisces 02 ℞
January 2016	17 Pisces 28	25 Sagittarius 50	0 Pisces 46
March	20 Pisces 24	27 Sagittarius 43	3 Pisces 05
May	24 Pisces 02	25 Sagittarius 26 ℞	5 Pisces 15
July	25 Pisces 13 ℞	25 Sagittarius 35 ℞	5 Pisces 18 ℞
September	23 Pisces 31 ℞	24 Sagittarius 23 ℞	3 Pisces 39 ℞
November	21 Pisces 05 ℞	25 Sagittarius 15	2 Pisces 15 ℞
January 2017	21 Pisces 06	27 Sagittarius 35	2 Pisces 54
March	23 Pisces 55	29 Sagittarius 26	5 Pisces 09
May	27 Pisces 18	29 Sagittarius 19 ℞	7 Pisces 11
July	28 Pisces 51 ℞	27 Sagittarius 24 ℞	7 Pisces 22 ℞
September	27 Pisces 17 ℞	26 Sagittarius 11 ℞	5 Pisces 46 ℞
November	24 Pisces 48 ℞	26 Sagittarius 59	4 Pisces 22 ℞
January 2018	24 Pisces 38	29 Sagittarius 14	4 Pisces 55

March	27 Pisces 17	1 Capricorn 05	7 Pisces 05
May	0 Aries 42	1 Capricorn 02 ℞	9 Pisces 06
July	2 Aries 25 ℞	29 Sagittarius 10 ℞	9 Pisces 22 ℞
September	1 Aries 01 ℞	27 Sagittarius 56 ℞	7 Pisces 50 ℞
November	28 Pisces 30 ℞	28 Sagittarius 38	6 Pisces 25 ℞
January 2019	28 Pisces 08	0 Capricorn 49	6 Pisces 52
March	0 Aries 38	2 Capricorn 40	8 Pisces 57
May	4 Aries 02	2 Capricorn 41 ℞	10 Pisces 58
July	5 Aries 56	0 Capricorn 53 ℞	11 Pisces 18 ℞
September	4 Aries 42 ℞	29 Sagittarius 36 ℞	9 Pisces 49 ℞
November	2 Aries 10 ℞	0 Capricorn 14	8 Pisces 23 ℞
January 2020	1 Aries 35	2 Capricorn 21	8 Pisces 44
March	3 Aries 56	4 Capricorn 13	10 Pisces 44
May	7 Aries 36	4 Capricorn 12 ℞	12 Pisces 51
July	9 Aries 24	2 Capricorn 32 ℞	13 Pisces 09 ℞
September	8 Aries 21 ℞	1 Capricorn 14 ℞	1 Pisces 44 ℞
November	5 Aries 48 ℞	1 Capricorn 47	10 Pisces 16 ℞
January 2021	5 Aries 03	5 Capricorn 53	10 Pisces 34
March	7 Aries 17	5 Capricorn 43	12 Pisces 31
May	10 Aries 42	5 Capricorn 49 ℞	14 Pisces 29
July	12 Aries 52	4 Capricorn 06 ℞	14 Pisces 55 ℞
September	11 Aries 57 ℞	2 Capricorn 47 ℞	13 Pisces 33 ℞
November	9 Aries 24 ℞	3 Capricorn 18	12 Pisces 05 ℞
January 2022	8 Aries 30	5 Capricorn 19	19 Pisces 19
March	10 Aries 35	7 Capricorn 10	14 Pisces 11
May	14 Aries 00	7 Capricorn 19 ℞	16 Pisces 09
July	16 Aries 20	5 Capricorn 39 ℞	16 Pisces 38 ℞
September	15 Aries 35 ℞	4 Capricorn 19 ℞	15 Pisces 19 ℞
November	13 Aries 02 ℞	4 Capricorn 46	13 Pisces 51 ℞
January 2023	11 Aries 58	6 Capricorn 44	14 Pisces 00
March	13 Aries 53	8 Capricorn 34	15 Pisces 49
May	17 Aries 18	8 Capricorn 46 ℞	17 Pisces 46
July	19 Aries 48	7 Capricorn 09 ℞	18 Pisces 18 ℞
September	19 Aries 15 ℞	5 Capricorn 48 ℞	17 Pisces 02 ℞
November	16 Aries 43 ℞	6 Capricorn 11	15 Pisces 34 ℞
January 2024	15 Aries 27	8 Capricorn 06	15 Pisces 39
March	17 Aries 14	9 Capricorn 56	17 Pisces 23
May	20 Aries 55	10 Capricorn 07 ℞	19 Pisces 26
July	23 Aries 18	8 Capricorn 37 ℞	19 Pisces 54 ℞
September	22 Aries 56 ℞	7 Capricorn 14 ℞	18 Pisces 42 ℞
November	20 Aries 26 ℞	7 Capricorn 34	17 Pisces 13 ℞
January 2025	19 Aries 00	9 Capricorn 28	17 Pisces 15
March	20 Aries 39	11 Capricorn 18	18 Pisces 57
May	24 Aries 04	11 Capricorn 33 ℞	20 Pisces 52
July	26 Aries 52	10 Capricorn 01 ℞	21 Pisces 27 ℞
September	26 Aries 39 ℞	3 Capricorn 38 ℞	20 Pisces 16 ℞
November	24 Aries 10 ℞	8 Capricorn 56	18 Pisces 48 ℞
January 2026	22 Aries 36 ℞	10 Capricorn 46	18 Pisces 47

March	24 Aries 05	12 Capricorn 36	20 Pisces 25
May	27 Aries 29	12 Capricorn 55 ℞	22 Pisces 19
July	0 Taurus 28	11 Capricorn 24 ℞	22 Pisces 58 ℞
September	0 Taurus 28 ℞	10 Capricorn 01 ℞	21 Pisces 50 ℞
November	28 Aries 01 ℞	10 Capricorn 15	20 Pisces 21 ℞
January 2027	26 Aries 16 ℞	12 Capricorn 03	20 Pisces 17
March	27 Aries 35	13 Capricorn 53	21 Pisces 52
May	0 Taurus 59	14 Capricorn 14 ℞	23 Pisces 45
July	4 Taurus 09	12 Capricorn 47 ℞	24 Pisces 26 ℞
September	4 Taurus 22 ℞	11 Capricorn 22 ℞	27 Pisces 21 ℞
November	1 Taurus 59 ℞	11 Capricorn 33	21 Pisces 52 ℞
January 2028	0 Taurus 03 ℞	13 Capricorn 18	21 Pisces 44
March	1 Taurus 11	15 Capricorn 09	23 Pisces 16
May	4 Taurus 53	15 Capricorn 29 ℞	25 Pisces 16
July	7 Taurus 55	14 Capricorn 07 ℞	25 Pisces 51 ℞
September	8 Taurus 22 ℞	12 Capricorn 42 ℞	24 Pisces 49 ℞
November	6 Taurus 04 ℞	12 Capricorn 50	23 Pisces 20 ℞
January 2029	3 Taurus 57 ℞	14 Capricorn 35	23 Pisces 10
March	4 Taurus 57	16 Capricorn 25	24 Pisces 40
May	8 Taurus 20	16 Capricorn 49 ℞	26 Pisces 31
July	11 Taurus 50	15 Capricorn 25 ℞	27 Pisces 15 ℞
September	12 Taurus 30 ℞	14 Capricorn 00 ℞	26 Pisces 14 ℞
November	10 Taurus 16 ℞	14 Capricorn 07	24 Pisces 46 ℞
January 2030	8 Taurus 01 ℞	15 Capricorn 48	24 Pisces 34
March	8 Taurus 48	17 Capricorn 39	26 Pisces 00
May	12 Taurus 11	18 Capricorn 06 ℞	27 Pisces 50
July	15 Taurus 53	16 Capricorn 44 ℞	28 Pisces 36 ℞
September	16 Taurus 49 ℞	15 Capricorn 18 ℞	27 Pisces 38 ℞
November	14 Taurus 42 ℞	15 Capricorn 22	26 Pisces 10 ℞
January 2031	20 Taurus 17 ℞	17 Capricorn 01	25 Pisces 55
March	12 Taurus 50	18 Capricorn 52	27 Pisces 18
May	16 Taurus 11	19 Capricorn 21 ℞	29 Pisces 08
July	20 Taurus 06	18 Capricorn 02 ℞	29 Pisces 56 ℞
September	21 Taurus 20 ℞	16 Capricorn 35 ℞	29 Pisces 01 ℞
November	19 Taurus 23 ℞	16 Capricorn 36	27 Pisces 33 ℞
January 2032	16 Taurus 46 ℞	18 Capricorn 12	27 Pisces 15
March	17 Taurus 05	20 Capricorn 04	28 Pisces 35
May	20 Taurus 44	20 Capricorn 33 ℞	0 Aries 32
July	24 Taurus 31	19 Capricorn 19 ℞	1 Aries 14 ℞
September	26 Taurus 06 ℞	17 Capricorn 51 ℞	0 Aries 22 ℞
November	24 Taurus 20 ℞	17 Capricorn 49	28 Pisces 54 ℞
January 2033	21 Taurus 31 ℞	19 Capricorn 26	28 Pisces 34
March	21 Taurus 38	21 Capricorn 17	29 Pisces 53
May	24 Taurus 54	21 Capricorn 49 ℞	1 Aries 41
July	29 Taurus 15	20 Capricorn 33 ℞	2 Aries 31 ℞
September	1 Gemini 90	19 Capricorn 05 ℞	1 Aries 39 ℞
November	29 Taurus 34 ℞	19 Capricorn 02	0 Aries 12 ℞
January 2034	26 Taurus 38 ℞	20 Capricorn 36	29 Pisces 51

March	26 Taurus 26	22 Capricorn 28	1 Aries 07
May	29 Taurus 39	23 Capricorn 03 ℞	2 Aries 54
July	4 Gemini 14	21 Capricorn 49 ℞	3 Aries 47 ℞
September	6 Gemini 32	20 Capricorn 20 ℞	2 Aries 57 ℞
November	5 Gemini 15 ℞	20 Capricorn 14	1 Aries 30 ℞
January 2035	2 Gemini 10 ℞	21 Capricorn 46	1 Aries 07
March	1 Gemini 38	23 Capricorn 38	2 Aries 20
May	4 Gemini 44	24 Capricorn 16 ℞	4 Aries 07
July	9 Gemini 34	23 Capricorn 04 ℞	5 Aries 01 ℞
September	12 Gemini 19	21 Capricorn 34 ℞	4 Aries 14 ℞
November	11 Gemini 24 ℞	21 Capricorn 26	2 Aries 47 ℞
January 2036	8 Gemini 12 ℞	22 Capricorn 56	2 Aries 21
March	7 Gemini 17	24 Capricorn 48	3 Aries 32
May	10 Gemini 36	25 Capricorn 27	5 Aries 26
July	15 Gemini 19	24 Capricorn 19 ℞	6 Aries 14
August	18 Gemini 35	22 Capricorn 48 ℞	5 Aries 29 ℞
November	18 Gemini 07 ℞	22 Capricorn 37	4 Aries 03 ℞
January 2037	14 Gemini 47 ℞	24 Capricorn 07	3 Aries 35
March	13 Gemini 30	26 Capricorn 00	4 Aries 44
May	16 Gemini 19	26 Capricorn 40 ℞	6 Aries 30
July	21 Gemini 39	25 Capricorn 31 ℞	7 Aries 26
September	25 Gemini 26	24 Capricorn 01 ℞	6 Aries 42 ℞
November	25 Gemini 28 ℞	23 Capricorn 49	5 Aries 16 ℞
January 2038	22 Gemini 10 ℞	25 Capricorn 16	4 Aries 47
March	20 Gemini 23	27 Capricorn 09	5 Aries 54
May	22 Gemini 56	27 Capricorn 53 ℞	7 Aries 38
July	28 Gemini 30	26 Capricorn 46 ℞	8 Aries 36
September	2 Cancer 54	25 Capricorn 14 ℞	7 Aries 55 ℞
November	3 Cancer 39 ℞	25 Capricorn 00	6 Aries 29 ℞
January 2039	0 Cancer 28 ℞	26 Capricorn 25	5 Aries 58
March	28 Gemini 08 ℞	28 Capricorn 19	7 Aries 02
May	0 Cancer 19	29 Capricorn 05 ℞	8 Aries 46
July	6 Cancer 05	28 Capricorn 00 ℞	9 Aries 46
September	11 Cancer 09	26 Capricorn 28 ℞	9 Aries 07 ℞
November	12 Cancer 46 ℞	26 Capricorn 11	7 Aries 41 ℞
January 2040	9 Cancer 53 ℞	27 Capricorn 35	7 Aries 08
March	6 Cancer 57 ℞	29 Capricorn 29	8 Aries 10
May	8 Cancer 58	0 Aquarius 17 ℞	10 Aries 01
July	14 Cancer 31	29 Capricorn 15 ℞	10 Aries 55
September	20 Cancer 17	27 Capricorn 42 ℞	10 Aries 17 ℞
November	22 Cancer 56	27 Capricorn 22	8 Aries 52 ℞
January 2041	20 Cancer 33 ℞	28 Capricorn 46	8 Aries 18
March	17 Cancer 05 ℞	0 Aquarius 41	9 Aries 19
May	18 Cancer 09	1 Aquarius 31 ℞	11 Aries 02
July	24 Cancer 04	0 Aquarius 29 ℞	12 Aries 03
September	0 Leo 32	28 Capricorn 55 ℞	11 Aries 26 ℞
November	4 Leo 19	28 Capricorn 34	10 Aries 02 ℞
January 2042	2 Leo 49 ℞	29 Capricorn 56	9 Aries 26

March	28 Cancer 53 ℞	1 Aquarius 52	10 Aries 25
May	29 Cancer 01	2 Aquarius 44 ℞	12 Aries 07
July	4 Leo 43	1 Aquarius 45 ℞	13 Aries 10
September	11 Leo 50	0 Aquarius 10 ℞	12 Aries 36 ℞
November	16 Leo 57	29 Capricorn 47	11 Aries 12 ℞
January 2043	16 Leo 46 ℞	1 Aquarius 07	10 Aries 34
March	12 Leo 37 ℞	3 Aquarius 04	11 Aries 31
May	11 Leo 35	3 Aquarius 58	13 Aries 13
July	16 Leo 44	3 Aquarius 01 ℞	14 Aries 17
September	24 Leo 18	1 Aquarius 26 ℞	13 Aries 45 ℞
November	0 Virgo 46	1 Aquarius 00	12 Aries 21 ℞
January 2044	2 Virgo 18 ℞	2 Aquarius 19	11 Aries 42
March	28 Leo 28 ℞	4 Aquarius 16	12 Aries 36
May	26 Leo 11	5 Aquarius 14 ℞	14 Aries 25
July	0 Virgo 14	4 Aquarius 18 ℞	15 Aries 24
September	7 Virgo 56	2 Aquarius 42 ℞	14 Aries 53 ℞
November	15 Virgo 33	2 Aquarius 14	13 Aries 30 ℞
January 2045	19 Virgo 01	3 Aquarius 33	12 Aries 49
March	16 Virgo 10 ℞	5 Aquarius 31	13 Aries 43
May	12 Virgo 38 ℞	6 Aquarius 30	15 Aries 24
July	15 Virgo 18	5 Aquarius 35 ℞	16 Aries 30
September	22 Virgo 41	3 Aquarius 58 ℞	16 Aries 00 ℞
November	1 Libra 02	3 Aquarius 29	14 Aries 37 ℞
January 2046	6 Libra 15	4 Aquarius 45	13 Aries 56
March	5 Libra 56 ℞	6 Aquarius 45	14 Aries 47
May	0 Libra 50 ℞	7 Aquarius 46	16 Aries 28
July	1 Libra 29	6 Aquarius 54 ℞	17 Aries 36
September	7 Libra 55	5 Aquarius 17 ℞	17 Aries 08 ℞
November	16 Libra 30	4 Aquarius 44	15 Aries 45 ℞
January 2047	23 Libra 09	5 Aquarius 59	15 Aries 02
March	23 Libra 59 ℞	5 Aquarius 59	15 Aries 52
May	19 Libra 49 ℞	9 Aquarius 04	17 Aries 31
July	18 Libra 24	8 Aquarius 14 ℞	18 Aries 41
September	23 Libra 21	6 Aquarius 36 ℞	18 Aries 15 ℞
November	1 Scorpio 33	6 Aquarius 00	16 Aries 53 ℞
January 2048	9 Scorpio 02	7 Aquarius 13	16 Aries 08
March	11 Scorpio 41 ℞	9 Aquarius 15	16 Aries 56
May	8 Scorpio 01 ℞	10 Aquarius 24	18 Aries 43
July	5 Scorpio 20	9 Aquarius 36 ℞	19 Aries 46
September	8 Scorpio 27	7 Aquarius 56 ℞	19 Aries 22 ℞
November	15 Scorpio 46	7 Aquarius 17	18 Aries 01 ℞
January 2049	23 Scorpio 37	8 Aquarius 31	17 Aries 14
March	27 Scorpio 32	10 Aquarius 34	18 Aries 01
May	25 Scorpio 26 ℞	11 Aquarius 43	19 Aries 40
July	21 Scorpio 29 ℞	10 Aquarius 57 ℞	20 Aries 51
September	22 Scorpio 52	9 Aquarius 16 ℞	20 Aries 28 ℞
November	29 Scorpio 03	8 Aquarius 36	19 Aries 06 ℞
January 2050	6 Sagittarius 35	9 Aquarius 48	18 Aries 19 ℞

March	11 Sagittarius 22	11 Aquarius 52	19 Aries 04
May	10 Sagittarius 34 ℞	13 Aquarius 04	20 Aries 42
July	6 Sagittarius 20 ℞	12 Aquarius 21 ℞	21 Aries 55
September	6 Sagittarius 08	10 Aquarius 39 ℞	21 Aries 34 ℞
November	11 Sagittarius 01	9 Aquarius 56	20 Aries 13 ℞

Bibliography

Abu Ma'shar. *The Abbreviation of the Introduction to Astrology*, ed. and trans. Charles Burnett). ARHAT, 1994, p.50.

Al-Biruni. *The Book of Instruction in the Elements of the Art of Astrology*, trans. R. Ramsay Wright. (1934) London: British Museum.

Allende, Isabel. (1994) *Paula*, trans. Margaret Sayers Peden, London: HarperCollins.

Apollodorus of Athens. *The Library of Greek Mythology*, trans. Keith Aldrich (1975), Lawrence: Coronado Press.

Apollonius Rhodius. *Argonautica.* trans. E.V. Rieu, London: Penguin Books, 2.1238 at: http://www.theoi.com - accessed 17th August, 2003.

Axline, Virginia. (1964) *Dibs: In Search of Self*, Harmondsworth: Penguin Books.

Bandler, Richard. (1985) *Using Your Brain For A Change*, Moab: Real People Press.

Barrett, Deirdre (ed.) (1996) *Trauma and Dreams*, Cambridge: Harvard University Press.

Berger, John. (1972) *Ways of Seeing*, London: BBC and Penguin.

Beston, Henry. (1928) *The Outermost House: A Year of Life On The Great Beach of Cape Cod*, New York: Doubleday.

Birren, J.E., and Deutchman, D.E. (1991) *Guiding Autobiography*, Baltimore: Johns Hopkins Press.

Bolen, Jean Shinoda. (1994) *Crossing To Avalon*, New York: Harper Collins.

Bonatti, Guido. *Liber Astronomiae*, trans. Robert Zoller (1998) Brisbane: Spica Publications.

Boss, Pauline. (1999) *Ambiguous Loss: Learning to Live with Unresolved Grief.* Cambridge, Massachusetts: Harvard University Press.

Brady, Bernadette. (1992) *The Eagle and The Lark: A Textbook of Predictive Astrology.* York Beach: Samuel Weiser.

_____. (1997) 'Life, Death and the Whole Damn Thing!' in *Astrology: An Ancient Art in the Modern World*, ed. Mari Garcia, Adelaide: Australis '97 The Congress Papers.

_____. (1999) *Brady's Book of Fixed Stars*, York Beach: Samuel Weiser.

_____. (1999) *Study Guide for Medieval and Ancient Astrology*, Adelaide: Astro Logos.

Brockett, Oscar G. (1969) *The Theatre, An Introduction*, New York: Holt, Rinehart and Winston Inc.

Campbell, Joseph. (1988) *The Hero With The Thousand Faces*, London: Palladin.

Casson, Lionel. (1994) *Travel in the Ancient World*, Baltimore: The Johns Hopkins University Press.

Charles, Prince of Wales. (1989) *A Vision of Britain: A Personal View of Architecture*, London: Doubleday.

Chinen, Allan B. (1989) *In The Ever After*, Wilmette: Chiron Publications.

Cleese, John and Crichton, Charles. (1988) *A Fish Called Wanda*, London: Methuen.

Coehlo, Paulo. (1998) *Veronika Decides To Die*, trans. Margaret Jull Costa, London: Harper Collins.

Cooper, J.C. (1983) *Fairy Tales; Allegories of the Inner Self*, Wellingborough: The Aquarian Press.

Cousse, Raymond. *Kids' Stuff*, trans. Katharine Sturak (1984) Melbourne: Australian Nouveau Theatre Publications.

_____. (1979) *Enfantillages*, Flammarion: Paris.

Curtis, Richard. (screenplay dated 18/1/1993). *Four Weddings and a Funeral*, © Working Title Films, London, UK.

Dickens, Charles. (1907) *Oliver Twist*. London: Chapman & Hall Ltd.

Diodorus Siculus. *Library of History*, ed. and trans. C.H. Oldfather. (1954) Cambridge: Harvard University Press.

Dossenbach, Monique and Hans D. (1985) *The Noble Horse*, Exeter: Webb & Bower.

Drews, Robert. (1993) *The End of the Bronze Age: Changes in Warfare and the Catastrophe ca. 1200 BC*, Princeton: Princeton University Press.

Eisler, Riane. (1987) *The Chalice and The Blade*, London: Unwin Hyman Limited.

Firmicus Maternus. *Ancient Astrology Theory and Practice*, trans. Jean Rhys-Bram. (1975) Park Ridge: Noyes Press.

Frey II, William H. with Muriel Langseth. (1985) *Crying, The Mystery of Tears,* Minneapolis: Winston Press.

Furth, Gregg M. (1989) *The Secret World of Drawings: A Jungian Approach to Healing through Art,* Inner City Books: New York.

Gallucci, Ralph. *The Horse in Early Greek Myth,* University of California, Santa Barbara, at: http://cla.calpoly.edu/~jlynch/Gallucci.html - accessed 18th September, 2001.

Garcia, Joseph. (1999) *Sign with Your Baby,* Seattle: Northlight Communications.

Garcia, Mari (ed.) (1997) *Astrology: An Ancient Art in the Modern World,* Adelaide: Australis '97 The Congress Papers.

Garfield, Patricia. (1997) *The Dream Messenger: How Dreams of the Departed Bring Healing Gifts,* New York: Simon & Schuster.

Garraty, John A. and Carnes, Mark C. (general eds) (1999) *American National Biography,* Oxford: Oxford University Press.

Gibson, Faith. (1998) *Reminiscence and Recall,* London: Age Concern Books.

_____. (2000) *The Reminiscence Trainer's Pack,* London: Age Concern Books.

Greenblatt, S., Cohen, W., Howard, J.E. and Maus, K.E. (eds) (1997) *The Norton Shakespeare,* New York and London: W.W. Norton.

Greene, Liz. (1976) *Saturn: A New Look at an Old Devil,* York Beach: Samuel Weiser.

_____. (1978) *Relating: An Astrological Guide to Living With Others on a Small Planet,* York Beach: Samuel Weiser.

_____. (1983) *The Outer Planets and Their Cycles,* Reno: CRCS Publications.

_____. (1984) *The Astrology of Fate,* London: George Allen and Unwin.

_____. (1996) *The Astrological Neptune and the Quest for Redemption,* York Beach: Samuel Weiser.

_____. (2003) *The Dark of the Soul: Psychopathology in the Horoscope,* London: CPA Press.

Greene, Liz and Arroyo, Stephen. (1984) *The Jupiter/Saturn Conference Lectures,* Reno: CRCS Publications.

Greene, Liz and Sasportas, Howard. (1987) *The Development of the Personality,* York Beach: Samuel Weiser.

_____. (1988) *Dynamics of the Unconscious,* York Beach: Samuel Weiser.

Grof, Stanislov and Christina. (1980) *Beyond Death, The Gates of Consciousness*, London: Thames and Hudson.

Gunzburg, Darrelyn (ed.) (1989) *Under Capricorn: An Australian Anthology of Astrology*, Adelaide: The FAA's Board of Publications.

Haight, B.K. and Webster, J.D. (eds.) (1995) *The Art and Science of Reminiscing: Theory, Research, Methods and Applications*, Washington, DC: Taylor and Francis.

Hamaker-Zondag, Karen. (2000) *Yods and Unaspected Planets*, York Beach: Samuel Weiser.

Hartnoll, Phyllis. (1968) *A Concise History of the Theatre*, London: Thames and Hudson.

Hermes Trismegistus. *Liber Hermetis*, trans. Robert Zoller. (1998) Brisbane: Spica Publications.

Hesiod, *The Homeric Hymns and Homerica*, at http://sunsite.berkeley.edu/OMACL/Hesiod/hymns.html - accessed 14th July, 2002.

Hippocrates. *Works*. eds. and trans. W.H.S. Jones, E.T. Withington and Paul Potter (1923-88), London: Loeb Classical Library/Heinemann.

Hodgins, Philip. (1986) *Blood and Bone*, Sydney: Angus and Robertson.

Homer. *The Iliad*, trans. E.V.Rieu. (1966) Harmondsworth: Penguin Books.

_____. *The Odyssey*, trans. E.V.Rieu (1946) Harmondsworth: Penguin Books.

Houck, Richard. (1994) *The Astrology of Death*, Gaithersburg: Groundswell Press.

Hubler, Edwin. (ed.) (1963) *The Tragedy of Hamlet, Prince of Denmark*, New York: Signet.

Hunt, Jan. (2001) *The Natural Child: Parenting from the Heart*, Gabriola Island: New Society Publishers.

Hyginus, Caius Julius. *The Myths of Hyginus*, trans. and ed. Mary Grant. (1960) Lawrence: University of Kansas Publications.

ibn Ezra, Abraham. *The Beginning of Wisdom*, trans. Raphael Levy (1939), Baltimore.

James, John W. and Friedman, Russell. (1998) *The Grief Recovery Handbook* (Revised Edition), New York: Harper Collins.

James, J. and Friedman, R. with Dr Leslie Landon Matthews. (2001) *When Children Grieve*. New York: Harper Collins.

Johnson, Robert A. (1993) *Owning Your Own Shadow, Understanding the Dark Side of the Psyche*, New York: Harper Collins.

Kane, Sean. (1998) *The Wisdom of the Mythtellers*, Ontario: Broadview Press.

Kennedy, Alexandra. (1991) *Losing a Parent: Passage to a New Way of Living*, Harper SanFrancisco.

_____. (2001)*The Infinite Thread: Healing Relationships Beyond Loss*, Hillsboro: Beyond Words.

Kottler, Jeffrey A. (1996) *The Language of Tears*, San Francisco: Jossey-Bass.

Kramer, Samuel Noah. (1981) *History begins at Sumer*, Philadelphia: University of Pennsylvania Press.

Kubler-Ross, Elisabeth. (1969) *On Death and Dying*, New York: Macmillan Publishing Company.

_____. (1975) *Death, The Final Stage of Growth*, Englewood Cliffs: Prentice-Hall Inc.

_____. (1983) *On Children and Death*, New York: Macmillan Publishing Company.

_____. (1997) *The Wheel of Life: A Memoir of Living and Dying*, London: Bantam Books.

Kubler-Ross, Elisabeth and Warshaw. Mal. (1978) *To Live Until We Say Goodbye*, Englewood Cliffs: Prentice-Hall Inc.

_____. (1982) *Working It Through*, New York: Macmillan Publishing Company.

Lamm, Maurice. (1969) *The Jewish Way in Death and Mourning*, New York: Jonathon David Publications.

Leonard, Linda Schierse. (1982) *The Wounded Woman; Healing the Father-Daughter Relationship*, Boston: Shambhala.

Lerner, Harriet. (1985) *The Dance of Anger*, New York: Harper Collins.

_____. (1989) *The Dance of Intimacy*, New York: Harper and Rowe.

_____. (1993) *The Dance of Deception*, New York: Harper Collins/Pandora.

Leunig, Michael. (1990) *A Common Prayer*, Melbourne: CollinsDove.

_____. (1991) *The Prayer Tree*, Melbourne: CollinsDove.

_____. (1998) *Introspective*, Sydney: New Holland Publishers Pty Ltd.

Levine, Stephen. (1982) *Who Dies?* New York: Anchor Books.

Lewis, C.S. (1963) *A Grief Observed*, New York: Bantam Books.

Levine, M., Renfrew, C. and Boyle, K. (eds) (2004) *Prehistoric Steppe Adaptation and the Horse*, Cambridge: McDonald Institute for Archaeological Research.
Littauer, M.A. and Crouwel, J.H. (1996) 'The origin of the true chariot', in *Antiquity*, pp. 934-939.

Lutz, Tom. (2001) *Crying: A Natural and Cultural History of Tears*, New York: W.W. Norton & Company.

Lynn, Joanne and Harold, Joan. (1999) *Handbook for Mortals: Guidance for People Facing Serious Illness*, Oxford: Oxford University Press.

Malchiodi. Cathy A. (1998) *Understanding Children's Drawings*, The Guildford Press: New York.

McKissock, Mal. (1985) *Coping With Grief*, Sydney: ABC Enterprises.

Nieman, Henry and Cooper, Judith. (1986) *Astrology Conjunct Psychology: The Reference Book For Counsellors*, Tempe: The American Federation of Astrologers Inc.

Omar of Tiberius. *The Three Books of the Nativities*, trans. Robert Hand, ed. Robert Schmidt. (1997) Berkeley Springs: The Golden Hind Press.

Orona, Celia J. (1997) 'Temporality and Identity Loss Due to Alzheimer's Disease' in *Grounded Theory In Practice*, eds. Anslem Strauss and Juliet Corbin, Thousand Oaks: Sage Publications, Inc.

Oschman, J.L. (2000) *Energy Medicine: The Scientific Basis*, Edinburgh: Churchill Livingstone.

Ovid. *Fasti*, ed. and trans. A. J. Boyle and R. D. Woodard. (2000) London: Penguin Books.

Ovid, *The Metamorphoses*, Book XII, at: http://www.tkline.freeserve.co.uk/Webworks/Website/Metamorph12.htm#_Toc486225990 - accessed 12th April, 2003.

Pennebaker, James. (1997) *Opening Up: The Healing Power of Expressing Emotion*, New York: Guilford Press.

Piaget, Jean and Inhelder, Barbel. *The Psychology of the Child*, trans. Helen Weaver. (1973) London: Routledge and Kegan Paul.

Piggott, S. (1992) *Wagon, Chariot and Carriage*, London: Thames and Hudson.

Pinter, Harold. (1998) *Various Voices*. London: Faber and Faber.

Proust, Marcel. *Du Côté de chez Swann*, Book One of *Remembrance of Things Past*, trans. C.K. Scott Moncrieff and Terence Kilmartin. (1984) Harmondsworth: Penguin.

Ptolemy, Claudius. *Tetrabiblos*, trans. J.M. Ashmand. (1969) Mokelumne Hill: Health Research.

Raphael, Beverley. (1984) *The Anatomy of Bereavement*, London: Routledge.

Reinhart, Melanie. (2002) *Saturn, Chiron and The Centaurs: To the Edge and Beyond*, London: CPA Press.

Rudhyar, Dane. (1967) *The Lunation Cycle*. Santa Fe: Aurora Press.

Sasportas, Howard (1989). *The Gods of Change*, London: Arkana.

Shaw, I. (2001) 'Egyptians, Hyksos and military technology: Causes, effects or catalysts?' in *The Social Context of Technological Change, Egypt and the Near East, 1650-1550 BC*, ed. A.J. Shortland, Oxford: Oxbow.

Schwab, Dr Reiko, (1998) 'A Child's Death and Divorce: Dispelling the Myth' in *Death Studies*, Vol. 22, No. 5, pp. 445-468.

Skynner, Robyn and Cleese, John. (1983) *Families and How to Survive Them*, London: Methuen.

Sorkin, Aaron (1995) *The American President*. © Castle Rock Entertainment and Universal City Studios, Inc. at: http://plaza26.mbn.or.jp/%7Ehappywel/script/apresident.htm - screenplay downloaded 9th November, 1999.

Spielberger, Charles D. (1979) *Understanding Stress and Anxiety*, London:Harper & Row.

Spretnak, Charlene. (1997) *The Resurgence of the Real: Body, Nature, and Place in a Hypermodern World*, Reading: Addison-Wesley.

Stone, Thomas A. (1997) *Cure By Crying*, Des Moines: Cure By Crying Inc..

Sweet, Jeffrey. (1993) *The Dramatist's Toolkit: The Craft of the Working Playwright*, Portsmouth; Heinemann.

Symes, Mary. (1987) *Grief and Dreams*, Melbourne: René Gordon Pty. Ltd.

Thorpe, Thomas. (1609). *The Sonnets of William Shakespeare*. The Royal Shakespeare Theatre Edition, 1974. Ninth impression 1999. Calligraphy: Frederick Marns, London: Shepheard-Walwyn (Publishers) Ltd.

Turner, Ann Warren. (1976) *Houses For The Dead*, New York: David McKay Company, Inc.

Valcarenghi, Marina. (1997) *Relationships*. York Beach: Nicolas-Hays.

Valerius Flaccus, Gaius. *The Argonautica*, trans. J. Mozley. (1978) Cambridge, Massachusetts: Harvard University Press.

Van Gennep, Arnold. *The Rites of Passage*, trans. Monika B. Vizedom and Gabrielle L. Caffee. (1977) London: Routledge and Kegan Paul.

Von Franz, Marie-Louise. (1986) *On Dreams and Death*. Boston: Shambhala.

von Heeren, Robert. (1995) Pholus - *Wandler zwischen Saturn und Neptun* (Wanderer between Saturn and Neptune, German), Tübingen: Chiron Verlag,.

_____. (1997) *Chiron ephemeris 2000-2050 (German/English)*, Tübingen: Chiron Verlag.

_____. (2001) *7 Centaur Ephemeris*, Amstelveen: Symbolon.

_____. 'New Discoveries Beyond the Orbits of Neptune and Pluto' in *The Mountain Astrologer*, January, 1995.

von Heeren, Robert & Koch, Dieter, 'The New Planet Pholus', *The Mountain Astrologer*, July 1996.

Waldrop, Mitchell M. (1993) *Complexity: The Emerging Science at the Edge of Order and Chaos*, New York: Simon & Schuster.

Walker, Barbara G. (1985) *The Crone: Woman of Age, Wisdom and Power*, San Francisco: Harper Collins.

Wilcox, Ella Wheeler. (1883) *Poems of Passion*, Belford, Chicago: Clarke & Co.

Woodward, Joan. (1998) *The Lone Twin: Understanding Twin Bereavement and Loss*, London: Free Association Books Ltd.

Young, J.Z. (1975) *The Life Of Mammals: Their Anatomy and Physiology*, Oxford: Clarendon Press.

Zoller, Robert. (1981) *Tools and Techniques of the Medieval Astrologers*, Robert Zoller.

_____. 'Medieval Delineation of Character', in *Astrology: An Ancient Art in the Modern World*, ed. Mari Garcia (1998) Adelaide: Australis '97 The Congress Papers.

Zoja, Luigi. (1989) *Drugs, Addiction and Initiation: The Modern Search for Ritual*, Boston: Sigo Press.

INDEX

A

C

Printed in the United Kingdom
by Lightning Source UK Ltd.
101625UKS00002B/46-255